The Independent Filmmaker's Law and Business Guide

Financing, Shooting, and Distributing Independent and Digital Films

SECOND EDITION

Jon M. Garon

CHICAGO REVIEW PRESS

Library of Congress Cataloging-in-Publication Data
Garon, Jon M.
  The independent filmmaker's law and business guide : financing, shooting, and
distributing independent and digital films / Jon M. Garon. — 2nd ed.
    p. cm.
  Includes bibliographical references.
  ISBN 978-1-55652-833-0
  1. Motion picture industry—United States—Finance. 2. Motion pictures—
United States—Distribution. 3. Motion picture industry—Finance—Law and
legislation—United States. 4. Motion pictures—Distribution—Law and legisla-
tion—United States. 5. Motion picture industry—Law and legislation—United
States. 6. Independent filmmakers. I. Title.

  PN1993.5.U6G34 2009
  384'.830973—dc22   2009006434

Cover and interior design: Monica Baziuk
Cover photograph: © Peter vd Rol, via Shutterstock
Typesetting: Jonathan Hahn

Published by Chicago Review Press, Incorporated
814 North Franklin Street
Chicago, Illinois 60610
ISBN 978-1-55652-833-0
Printed in the United States of America
5 4 3 2 1

Contents

PART ① MAKING A FILM COMPANY TO MAKE A MOVIE

PART ④ Appendixes

Preface

WITH A VIDEO camera and an Internet connection, anyone can shoot a movie. Advancements in film and digital video camera technology have made it easier than ever to access quality equipment. But as independent film companies have proliferated, competing for funding and audiences has become more challenging than ever before. Professional filmmaking requires much more than just access to equipment; it also requires a deep understanding of the laws, contracts, and business practices that shape the production and distribution of motion pictures. Whether a filmmaker is interested in creating documentaries, fictional films, or docudramas, he must understand the rules to bring a story to life on film, the techniques to sell that film, and the strategies to promote the film to audiences.

The Independent Filmmaker's Law and Business Guide provides a distillation of the best practical advice available for independent filmmakers today. It answers the legal, financial, and organizational questions that an independent or guerrilla filmmaker must face, problems that will doom a project if left unanswered. In chronological order, it demystifies issues such as developing a concept, founding a film company, obtaining financing, casting, securing locations, shooting, granting screen credits, distributing, exhibiting, and marketing a film. It even anticipates the "problems" generated by a blockbuster hit: soundtrack albums, merchandizing, and licensing.

This second edition includes new chapters that deal with the unique concerns of documentary filmmaking and "no-budget" productions. Other chapters have been expanded to provide guidance on the use of film clips, soundtracks, background artwork, and commercial products. The new edition also provides comprehensive coverage of domestic and international distribution, and addresses new possibilities for digital distribution through Internet retailers and online digital media outlets. Expanded appendixes offer sample contracts, copyright circulars, a guide to writing credits, studio contact information, and a host of other resources that provide the filmmaker with all the tools necessary to make a successful film.

Acknowledgments

↓

In the acknowledgments for this second edition of *The Independent Filmmaker's Law and Business Guide,* I add to the already long list of friends and professionals who assisted me with the book's production. Since writing the first edition, I have had the pleasure to serve as the chairperson of the New Hampshire Film Commission and to represent some tremendously talented independent filmmakers. The New Hampshire Film Office is now under the stewardship of the New Hampshire commissioner of cultural resources, Van McLeod. Many filmmakers throughout New England owe Van a debt of gratitude for believing in their work and supporting the arts.

Every project teaches me a great deal, but particular recognition goes to the creators behind two of those projects: Buzz McLaughlin and Aaron Wiederspahn for *The Sensation of Sight,* and Derrick Comedy, the brilliant collaboration behind *Mystery Team.* In both these projects and in many others, I have been fortunate to work with an excellent legal team from the law firm of Gallagher, Callahan & Gartrell, including Denis Maloney, Esq., and Dodd Griffith, Esq., sophisticated securities and tax attorneys who have had the fortune—good and bad—to learn independent filmmaking as our needs have grown.

As I explained in the acknowledgments to the first edition, the two people whom I most wish to recognize for the completion of this book were unaware that I had written it, yet they were central to both the need for the book and many of its underlying themes. As a young attorney in Southern California, I had the opportunity to work with two separate clients,

Jonny Solomon and Peter Henry Schroeder, on a number of projects. Jonny is a brilliant comic and talented producer. Peter Henry is a gifted writer and electrifying director. Neither is famous, but both are extremely talented and resourceful. Through working with Jonny, Peter Henry, and many other clients early in my legal practice, the most central theme of this book was developed. That theme—*you cannot find opportunities; you must create them*—is central to many of the guiding principles for independent filmmakers. The experience I had working on independent film projects with these two individuals was the primary impetus for writing this book and for teaching hundreds of lawyers the art of trying to serve creative, driven individuals.

There are also a great many people I need to thank for the development and completion of this book, beginning with my mother, Lorraine Garon, who instilled in me a passion for theater and film, and my longtime editor, critic, and wife, Stacy Blumberg Garon, Esq. Stacy has become an expert on most of the subjects about which I teach or write, simply because my urge to discuss these issues greatly exceeds her ability to discourage me from doing so.

I wish to thank many colleagues at both Hamline University School of Law and Franklin Pierce Law Center. At Hamline, Susan Stephan, Esq., Carol Swanson, Esq., Anne Johnson, Esq., and Barb Gritzmacher helped me in so many ways, reviewing drafts of the book or simply undertaking other projects so that I could focus on this challenge. Many of my colleagues at Franklin Pierce, including Susan Richey, Esq., Sophie Sparrow, Esq., Mary Sheffer, Esq., Bill Hennessey, Esq., and Donna Jakusik, provided helpful advice and ongoing encouragement. Many other friends and colleagues also shared their experience and provided helpful suggestions. Dan Satorius, Esq., motion picture expert at Lommen, Abdo, Cole, King & Stageberg, P.A.; Jeremy Williams, Esq., deputy general counsel for Warner Bros.; Greg Hartmann, Esq.; Wendy Baldinger and Doug Baldinger; Shimona Pratap Singh; and Deepak Nambier each contributed material that helped shape the text and encouraged my completion of it.

Finally, I thank my sons, who seldom complained on those nights I rushed through a goodnight song and who knew when to entice me away from the computer and back to the more important things. Their enthusiasm for art and science provides me the motivation I need when my own focus blurs. As this book is written for new filmmakers and artists, I dedicate it to the artists to come, my sons Avery and Noah, and to their brother, Alec "Sasha" (*z"l*).

Introduction

↓

TECHNOLOGY IS CHANGING the way the entertainment industry does business. For film distributors, new technologies are transforming the system of print distribution that has existed since the end of the 19th century. Internet video sites such as YouTube, MySpace, and Atom are introducing new distribution opportunities for short films that will only increase as delivery continues to improve. Peer-to-peer services like Morpheus have advanced beyond Napster.com, allowing for the file sharing of feature length films.

Technology is also changing the medium itself. Film, the standard medium of the feature motion picture since its inception, is starting to be replaced with digital recording devices. Proponents of digital production like *Star Wars* creator George Lucas focus on the greater flexibility and reduced costs associated with state-of-the-art digital image recording. Since today's special effects rely heavily on digital manipulation of the image, capturing that image directly in the digital medium eliminates one step of the process, adding greater speed and flexibility. And with digital equipment, feature length and short films can be made for thousands rather than hundreds of thousands or millions of dollars. The Internet and lower-cost DVD production create new distribution methods for these low-budget projects that expand the potential audience well beyond the traditional college campus and film festival circuit. At a minimum, they are creating new opportunities for rookie filmmakers to showcase their skills to the traditional industry.

Despite the increased opportunities to make and distribute a movie, many artistic, business, and legal barriers continue to frustrate filmmakers and stop movies from being completed or distributed. This book and the associated Web site at www.lawbizbooks.com are designed to provide guidance through the rocky waters of independent motion picture production.

Making a movie, even a small-budget, backyard production, is a long process of negotiating and signing contracts; complying with labor, health, safety, and revenue codes; recognizing and protecting the rights of artists, writers, musicians, performers, bystanders, and others; and becoming a specialist in dozens of areas of business and law in a matter of weeks. This book will serve as your guide.

About This Book

This book is a guide, not a blueprint. At some point in the process, the filmmaker must build a team that includes not only a cast and crew but also a lawyer and an accountant. But the book should save the filmmaker legal fees, eliminating hours an attorney would have to spend explaining the items discussed in the book.

The book does not constitute the practice of law or provide legal advice that can be relied upon as authoritative. This information is general in nature, and should only be used in conjunction with a licensed attorney, properly familiar with the issues presented in the specific legal matter in question.

This book identifies particular individuals, firms, and companies. Nothing herein constitutes an endorsement of these entities or of their services, and the book cannot be relied upon as the legal basis for engaging such services.

Although many of the companies listed are the largest or most visible in the respective fields, the names are used either for illustrative purposes or to provide a starting point for the reader's own research. Conversely, the failure to appear in the book should not be deemed a negative assessment of any particular product, service, or organization.

The book uses some terms that might not seem appropriate. The most striking is to call the digital creation of a motion picture "filmmaking" and the creators "filmmakers." The choice reflects the history of the craft rather than the current state of the medium. Historically-based terms evolve new meanings. Americans still use the term "album" for a collection of songs recorded and sold together as a compilation, although the cardboard album that held a collection of 78 RPM records has been long abandoned as the distribution mechanism for music. Motion pictures that run longer than an hour will be known as "feature films" long after the celluloid and optical processes that originally characterized them have faded into distant memory like cardboard albums.

A Chronology: From Idea to Academy Awards

Independent filmmaking generally begins with a single idea, an original concept that will serve as the core of the film project. The owner of that idea may be a writer who can shape the idea into a written script, a director who can visualize how to tell that story, a performer who knows how to portray a character central to the story, or a producer who knows where to find the elements for telling the story. The originator of the idea starts from her strength and shares the idea with the other creative people necessary to translate the idea into a story, and the story into a screenplay. Even at this early stage, many legal and business choices must be made. One individual becomes the "owner" and others become employees of that owner—or the parties agree to work as partners, or choose a more complex legal relationship. The idea is translated from something not protected by copyright into an expressive work that cannot be copied without the owner's consent (although the ideas and general plot concept will not be protected by copyright). Rights to the story must be acquired, the production entity formed, budgets penciled in, and some employment commitments initiated.

Once the organizational approach has been selected and the script developed, the creative process moves into high gear. A script can be shared with potential investors, shown to actors, entered into contests, and used to introduce the project to the public. Fundraising can range from simple loans from the filmmaker's family to very sophisticated financial transactions. Financial decisions must be made carefully to protect the growth and success of the project.

A successful script will gain momentum for the project. If the filmmaker is not the director, then a director will be selected. With a working script, the director and producer can agree on a budget for the film that can range from the cost of buying (or even borrowing) the cheapest of cameras to a budget in excess of $250 million for an effects-laden film with well-known stars. The budget—not the screenplay—may also dictate where filming will take place. Locations are selected or rejected based on availability, the cost of filming in those locations, and the locations' ability to further the story.

The director, having accepted a working script and projected budget, can begin to make casting choices. Actors are auditioned or interviewed for parts. Since casting is often about chemistry and the interaction of actors with each other, it becomes a logistical puzzle: the director must make offers so the right combination of people will accept. At the same time, the director needs to assemble the creative crew behind the camera. A cinematographer and set, lighting, and costume designers are hired to refine the decisions tentatively made by the producer and director.

Throughout the preproduction process, money is needed. The director, writer, and producer may require payments. Expenses begin to mount for the budgeting, casting, and design work. As the money is found, so are the additional people necessary to build the project. Additional writers, producers, directors, designers, and cameramen are hired and added to the team. The script will undergo changes to accommodate the locations available, the cast assembled, and the suggestions of the growing production team. With efforts underway to finalize script revisions, select locations, rent equipment, secure financing, and finish casting, production can begin.

Preproduction ends and principal photography begins with the first day of filming. Each day, a few more minutes of film footage are captured. Filming is often done out of sequence, based on weather, availability of locations, sets, or cast, or other script requirements. Typically, the day's work is reviewed that night in the form of videotapes called *dailies* or *rushes* to be sure the production is ready to move on to the next scene. As the footage accumulates, rough editing of the film may be taking place. Finally, after weeks or months of filming, principal photography ends.

With the filming completed, the filmmaker is halfway home. The next stage of the process is postproduction. The footage is edited into a cohesive, linear film that hopefully translates the filmmaker's original idea into a visual narrative form. A composer creates a musical score to highlight the story and enhance the effectiveness of the film. Sound effects, songs, and special effects are added. The finished film, complete with sound, is finally ready for marketing and distribution.

If the film is an independent production, then often no prior arrangements exist for the marketing and distribution of the film. Since the filmmaker usually does not do her own marketing and distribution, the filmmaker shows the film to potential distributors and negotiates for payments based on an advance and a portion of the royalties. Distributors are often exposed to independent films through film festivals or business events called *film markets,* but independent filmmakers can also send videotape or DVD copies of their film to potential distributors without waiting for entry into competitions.

Once a distributor buys the rights to a motion picture, it takes over, creating or changing the marketing of the film. If the film runs in movie theaters in the United States, it becomes eligible for a number of award competitions. If the film remains as potent on the screen as it was in the original concept, the filmmaker's peers in the industry may vote to nominate the film for an Oscar from the Academy of Motion Picture Arts and Sciences. Following exhibition in U.S. movie theaters, the film may be distributed in movie theaters throughout the rest of the world. After theatrical distribution comes distribution on DVD and through pay-per-view cable television. Approximately a year after theatrical distribution come showings on premium cable (e.g., HBO or Showtime), then broadcast television, then finally basic cable. If successful, the movie could be shown for decades, or even centuries, to come.

At each stage in this process, the filmmaker and her team must make hundreds of artistic, business, and legal decisions. Some of those choices are truly unique to the particular film. Other choices, however, have been faced by many filmmakers before.

Most important, filmmaking is a long, complicated, and complex process, involving thousands of choices, strong personalities, and emotional decisions. Given the pressures of too little time and money, even small mistakes can be exacerbated by poor communication or haphazard planning and escalate into disaster. To reduce that risk, the filmmaker must be proactive; he must anticipate and plan for future crises and fully understand the consequences of every choice made. That's where *The Independent Filmmaker's Law and Business Guide* comes in. It analyzes each stage in the process in detail, outlines the common choices available to the filmmaker, and provides information for making the most appropriate decision under the circumstances.

Please remember this book when you thank the Academy for your Oscar.

Making a Film Company to Make a Movie

Preparing to Make a Film

ONLY ONE THING separates great films from the thousands of finished films that go undistributed each year: great storytelling. A powerful story featuring engaging characters, dramatic tension, and a well-crafted plot helps make a successful movie. What went on behind the camera or in the cutting room rarely influences the audience's experience watching the film. Most viewers will never know whether the filmmaker was delighted with the completed film or devastated that his first choice of cast rejected the script. The audience pays the same price for the theater seat and popcorn whether the film's budget was $100,000 or $100 million.

But at each stage in the filmmaking process, business and financial decisions will affect the story being told. Without the business structure, casts will not be paid, locations will not be available, and the film cannot be exhibited. The filmmaker's job is to manage the tremendous amount of time, funds, talent, and energy expended off screen to assure the best possible result onscreen. During the feverish pace of principal photography, he has little opportunity for reflection. Effective preparation and thoughtful contingency planning made in advance of the filming can save a movie from ruin. The more thoroughly he has prepared every step in the filmmaking process, the better chance he has of creating a finished film that captures his vision.

A. Who Is the Filmmaker?

Filmmaking is a communal process. The filmmaker becomes parent, artistic mentor, instructor, boss, and police officer to the small army that join together to bring the filmmaker's vision to the screen. Although each project requires a strong writer, producer, and director to shape the process, each one has a very different set of responsibilities and priorities, so there is a constant tension among the three. Ultimately, the filmmaker will dictate how those tensions are resolved, and bring together the creative and business aspects of the film. He stands at the center of every production, serving as its spine and brain.

It is important that the filmmaker on the team be recognized early. Productions vary, but generally the filmmaker will be the producer or director, or occasionally the writer. Typically a single individual holds the role, but a collaborative team may share the duties.

1. Independent vs. Guerrilla Filmmaking

Guerrilla filmmaking is a special subspecies of independent filmmaking. The guerrilla filmmaker is generally a storyteller with a vision. Sources for guerrilla films come from the stage, from life experience, or from literature that transfixes the filmmaker and makes the production his reason for being. Spike Lee, producer/director/writer/actor of *Bamboozled* and *Do the Right Thing*, Jim Jarmusch, producer/director/writer of *Night on Earth*, and John Sayles, writer/director of *Eight Men Out* and *Matewan*, are a few of the more prominent guerrilla artists, but many established filmmakers, including Michael Apted, Joel and Ethan Coen, Keenan Ivory Wayans, David Zucker, and Jerry Abrams, created their first films as guerrilla filmmakers.

The essence of the guerrilla filmmaker is twofold. First, the filmmaker must need, desire, and crave to bring his movie—not any movie, *his* movie—to the screen. Second, the filmmaker must have this craving despite the fact that no money, social network, business connections, studio interest, or external support exists to make this possible.

Another way to describe the guerrilla filmmaker is to characterize him like any other filmmaker—only more so. The guerrilla filmmaker is an entrepreneur with the desire to make a film rather than start a business. Like the typical entrepreneur, the guerrilla filmmaker is an extreme risk taker. By contrast, the traditional independent filmmaker described in this book is a more cautious businessperson, typically more willing to make reasonable compromises to make a film. Both the traditional independent filmmaker and the guerrilla filmmaker will use loans to make their films, but only the guerrilla would be willing to mortgage his house—or the houses of friends and family. This book will outline the path for the independent filmmaker, but wherever possible it will also note those few guideposts available for the guerrilla filmmaker as he cuts his own trail.

2. Independent vs. Studio Filmmaking

Independent filmmaking, whether traditional or guerrilla, is different from a studio production because, unlike with many commercial films, an independent film dictates the package. Producers of studio films often describe their preproduction development as "creating a package." They create line-ups of stars, bestsellers, merchandizing tie-ins, audience demographics, locations, directors, and writers that, if executed properly, will inevitably result in blockbusters.

Independent and guerrilla filmmakers, on the other hand, focus on a personal vision instead of working to accommodate stars, investors, prior contractual commitments, or audience response cards. Unlike carefully packaged studio films, movies by smart independent filmmakers tend to be highly opportunistic, using available locations, actors, situations, or other organic elements that can enhance or even redirect the story. As a result, many of the steps in the independent filmmaking process are different than with studio productions. Still, when everything works, the resulting films are the best the industry can create.

Given the tremendous consolidation in the entertainment industry, independent moviemaking has become increasingly difficult to define. Technically, an independent feature is any film not made at one of the major studios—Sony (home to Columbia Pictures, MGM, and United Artists), Warner Bros., Universal, Disney, Paramount, or Fox. This would include such films as *Rambo* (produced and distributed by Lionsgate), *Trumbo* (distributed by Samuel Goldwyn Films), *Juno* (produced by Mandate Pictures), and many others.

For a 10-year period beginning in 1996, independent films were considered a very profitable market. All the major studios acquired independent production companies or developed their own indie houses, creating a group of production entities that were small and somewhat autonomous, but still within the influence of the studio system. Recently, the market has turned quite bearish for independent films, and a number of these companies have been closed.

For the first-time filmmaker, the largest practical difference between studio and independent filmmaking is the amount of authority and control she retains over the artistic and budgetary decisions that make up the film. With an independent film, the filmmaker possesses substantial autonomy in these decisions—usually accompanied by significant financial risk. If the film has studio distribution, each major decision is usually subject to approval by the studio, and such approvals generally transform the project from an independent film into studio product.

3. The Filmmaker's Team

Filmmaking is an intensely collaborative, communal process. While there are exceptional guerrilla filmmakers who can successfully walk around with a handheld camera, capture content, edit it themselves, and compose their own score to accompany their film, most films require a large company of specialists to successfully complete. Composed initially of a director, writer, and producer, the production team should quickly grow to include members of the business and artistic teams. In the beginning, the prospective team members may simply be consulted for their availability and interest in the project. But once a decision to go forward with a film is made, there is often limited opportunity to deal with logistical concerns before principal photography must begin. If the filmmaker lines up his team in advance, he can ensure that the launch of the film company will go much more smoothly and that the team behind the film will have had the time needed to build a common vision.

The artistic team includes the location manager, the director of photography, and designers for sets, costumes, and lighting. Collaboration between the director and this group of professionals will help clarify the vision of the film and establish the look and feel of the project. The artistic team should also include the principal actors. The leading actors will champion their characters, and the filmmaker will need them to display their enthusiasm for the script during the struggles for financing and distribution. An independent film with committed actors is far more likely to succeed than one with a cast that treats it like just another job.

The business team should include the line producer, the law firm, accountants, and key investors. Inexperienced filmmakers often wait too long to seek the assistance of lawyers and accountants. Since many of the critical decisions regarding financing, production, and distribution are made quite early in development, filmmakers should not try to avoid the costs of experienced legal and financial counsel. Mistakes in structuring the financing can close down a production or lead to criminal violations of securities laws.

Filmmakers should also consider their lead investors to be part of the filmmaking process. For projects that require more funding than is available from a family member or a credit card, the investors' opinions on the business structure and financing strategy will be critical to success. Moreover, few investors are willing to tie up their funds unless they know the funding will be completed, so first investors are harder to lure into a project than later investors. But film investors are generally willing to invest because of their interest in the project. Allowing them to contribute to the business strategy can help solidify their support and encourage them to help raise the necessary additional funds.

B. Selecting the Scale

By choosing to make an independent film, the filmmaker has already begun to make the first critical decision regarding the film: determining the scale of the production. The scale determines the size of the cast and crew and how much they are paid, the cost of the locations, the nature of the equipment to be used, the extent of any special effects, and the length of the shoot. These aspects of a production need not be proportional to each other, but they usually are.

It is commonly assumed that the subject matter dictates scale, but this is a misconception. A two-person love story can be told in exotic locales with expensive panoramic shots, requiring a budget of well over $150 million. A story about Alexander the Great or Napoleon can distill the conflict into a personal tragedy that can be shot for less than $1 million.

The scale of the production will dictate every subsequent choice. It shapes the vision of the filmmaker. For example, Francis Ford Coppola recalls his original concept for *Apocalypse Now:* he hoped to sneak his independent production company into Vietnam to shoot the film surreptitiously against the backdrop of the actual "police action." Instead, the movie was shot in the Philippines after Coppola had become a Hollywood success. The production became a bloated Hollywood extravaganza that required well over a year of principal photography. The scale of the movie had changed in the filmmaker's mind, reshaping every decision regarding the production.

Independent filmmakers often back into the scale of their projects based on the financial resources available. If they choose to avoid unions, they will have a lower budget but may face unanticipated costs caused by a relatively inexperienced talent and crew. If they choose to acquire the film rights to a particular novel, short story, or comic book, the rights holders may require them to adopt a higher budget and a higher-profile cast as a condition of selling the rights. In each case, the key decision sets the scale against which all other budgetary decisions will be made.

Another choice that can set the scale of an independent film is the decision to shoot on 35mm stock. Not long ago, the choice to shoot on 16mm stock or use a digital camera guaranteed a lower-quality print and potentially limited distribution options but saved money on film stock, equipment rentals, and lighting costs. Today a range of digital camera systems is available that equals the range of quality available with 35mm film cameras. The prices of these systems keep dropping while the quality continues to improve, making the format much less of a defining choice than it once was.

Setting the overall scale of the film production may not be a conscious choice, but the individual decisions that determine scale are usually carefully considered. Most filmmakers have definite opinions about budget, film stock, and Screen Actors Guild member actors. Together, these preferences set the scale of the production. Being aware of them and the scale they imply will help the filmmaker prepare for the many choices that will flow from this first step in the filmmaking process.

C. Planning

A filmmaker may be compared to a military general, commanding armies of cast and crew. If the plan of engagement has not been carefully developed, if contingencies have not been incorporated into the plan, the campaign will falter in the field. Once in the heat of battle, the opportunity for careful planning has been lost. Effective generals and artistic filmmakers are great at improvising because both have planned ahead and are able to incorporate any necessary changes into their overall strategy.

Well before principal photography begins, the filmmaker should have reviewed all the delivery obligations for the project to assure that the script meets all artistic and legal needs, the right shots are taken, the correct releases are signed, the funds will be disbursed, locations are available despite any vagaries of the weather, materials for marketing are created, the postproduction process is ready, and the strategy to distribute or sell to a distributor is fully thought out.

1. Planning for Distribution

Good planning dictates that the filmmaker consider the realities he will eventually face when the time comes to exhibit and distribute his film. At a minimum, distribution requirements dictate the running length of the film and the level of adult content. Very few theatrical distributors will accept a film that is too long or cannot receive an MPAA rating of R or lower. Some countries impose censorship standards on films, requiring the filmmaker to edit the film accordingly for that country. The filmmaker should plan to shoot alternate versions of potentially problematic scenes, so the story can be edited easily to address issues of alcohol, nudity, profanity, or other subjects likely to trigger censorial cutting.

The economics of independent film are highly volatile. The independent and documentary boom of recent years has now given way to a glut of films and a dearth of financing. U.S. theatrical distribution reflects an ever-shrinking portion of motion picture revenue, but remains critical to the potential success in other media. DVD/Blu-ray sales and rentals, cable, broadcast, and Internet distribution, and international distribution have all become larger segments of the revenue stream. More importantly, the Internet has made access to entertainment nearly limitless and the ability of a particular film to reach the audience much more difficult. So from the start of the planning process, the filmmaker should be formulating a strategy to engage the audience with his film.

The audience engagement strategy should build upon the filmmaker's existing audience base, if any. It should include Web sites, e-mail lists, RSS feeds, and social networks based on the film's content, cast, location, or other significant attributes. Budget and staffing decisions should take these elements into account.

2. Planning for the Filmmaker's Future

Good planning requires the filmmaker to be vigilant regarding the goal of the production. For some filmmakers, the goal may be to launch a film company. For others, the goal is simply to gain experience and increase their employability in the entertainment industry. An actor-turned-filmmaker may want to prove that she has the artistic range to play a role, the vision to shape her own content, and the clout to have the film distributed nationally. Another filmmaker may have a passion to tell his own story, and once that film or documentary is distributed, he may not make another film. Still another may make films as artistic expressions with little regard for the audience. Each of these examples reflects a very different reason to make an independent film. Each will require different choices during the process.

For the filmmaker hoping to launch a business, the development of ongoing relations with investors and vendors becomes a significant part of the planning. Such a filmmaker may wish to convince investors to prepare for investing in a few movies before making money, with protections that all investments will be repaid if the money ever does pour in. Such a filmmaker should plan a whole slate of projects and learn to always have one project in preproduction, one in production, and a third in distribution. Such a professional filmmaker will approach the business with a bit more distance than the filmmaker who has only one film.

The actor-turned-filmmaker, in contrast, will be using the film as a calling card to reshape her professional profile. Relations with the media and Hollywood will be as important as the film itself. The goal of the film is to change the nature of the scripts being offered, so the actor should be looking to accept additional film roles even before this film is theatrically distributed—protecting against career-ending unfavorable reviews.

Often the true reasons for making a movie are closely guarded personal secrets. Even if the filmmaker is not forthcoming with others, he must be sufficiently honest with himself to achieve the goals of the project. The filmmaker must acknowledge his true reasons for making the film and organize the business and filmmaking strategy to maximize this opportunity.

3. Planning Beyond the Film

Even an independent film has the potential to become a *tent pole* production, a literary phenomenon that creates multiple franchise opportunities: sequels, books, toys, television productions, video games, and other merchandise. George Lucas's *Star Wars* represents the ultimate tent pole franchise: it has generated seven movies (so far), books, animated series, and a vast merchandizing empire. The brand's power even propelled the development of Industrial Light & Magic, Lucas's premier visual effects company. Industrial Light & Magic had been the special effects team on the original *Star Wars,* and as the franchise grew, Lucas developed the company into a separate enterprise that has gone on to set the professional standard for the industry.

While filmmakers should not expect to achieve the success of *Star Wars,* they should still plan ahead to take advantage of the opportunities created by a successful film. At a minimum, every film should have an Internet strategy, which begins while the film is still in development and continues throughout its commercial release. If the film has strong graphical elements, its financial strategy should include the development of video games, graphic novels, merchandise, or other ancillary products. More than just financial opportunities, ancillary products create a relationship between the production and the audience. Independent filmmakers should seek to foster this relationship rather than allowing it to be controlled by the film's eventual distributor.

Particularly for films that might spin off video games and other graphical projects, the filmmaker must plan early to acquire the correct rights and develop the appropriate content to maximize this opportunity for the film.

D. Choosing to Make a Film

While it may seem strange that a book on independent filmmaking asks whether the project should even be made into a film, this should be the threshold question for any production today. By tradition, making a motion picture—whether it's shot on film stock or captured digitally—means shooting and editing a feature length project of 73 to 200 minutes (preferably 93 to 130 minutes) for distribution initially in movie theaters and later via DVD/Blu-ray, cable, broadcast television, and the Internet.

Financially, this remains an extremely challenging business. Though there are notable successes in selling feature films and documentaries, the vast majority of films are never theatrically distributed—or picked up for any distribution at all.

In contrast, the ability to make one's content publicly available has never been easier. Anyone can shoot a two- to five-minute scene and post it on Web sites and social networks. These shorts, sometimes labeled *memes,* can be used to capture the essence of a feature or its characters. In some cases, they consist of scenes from the larger project, while others are original expressions of the ideas of the feature project. The popularity of these shorts can be used to build enthusiasm and financial support to launch a full-length film.

Although shorts are easy to distribute, that does not mean that high-quality shorts are easy to produce. Tight writing and powerful acting are just as important to a short as to a feature film. In fact, it can be much more difficult to communicate all one's ideas in three minutes instead of an hour and a half. Still, a good scene will communicate to investors much more effectively than a screenplay, and a popular video clip will help assure investors and distributors of audience interest in the project.

The Film Company

THE SCOPE OF an independent film project can range dramatically from a single filmmaker walking the countryside with a digital camera to a massive business involving hundreds of employees and millions of dollars in expenses and revenue. But even the smallest film is big business. A typical low-budget feature film project must include a payroll for salaried employees, payments to independent contractors, and agreements with trade unions, property owners, lenders, suppliers, and a multitude of support services. The filmmaker may be obligated to become licensed within one or more states, pay federal and state taxes, meet employer documentation requirements and withholding obligations, execute contracts to rent property, license copyrighted works, sell securities, and obtain credit. Inevitably, the project will take on the trappings of a "real" business, so the filmmaker should organize a film company to anticipate the legal and business issues.

The structure of the business will determine the relationship between the filmmaker and the investors, cast, and crew, so thoughtful consideration of the structure should be given early in the filmmaking process. The filmmaker should select the business structure best suited to the project and the filmmaker's short-term and long-term goals. The purpose of business planning is to address four primary concerns: control, financing, liability, and tax obligations.

Control reflects who within the film company has legal authority over decision making. The movie's director may have artistic control over the look of the film and the selection of shots, but only the film company can grant that authority. If the director wants to shoot a scene in Hawaii and the film company decision maker says that a trip to Hawaii is not in the budget, the artistic control of the director will take second place to the financial control of the film company. Artistic control may even be revoked if the film company judges the director's decisions to be highly unreasonable. Therefore, if the filmmaker wishes to retain absolute control of the film, then she must also retain control of the film company.

Financing refers to the practical problems of funding the filmmaking process. If the filmmaker hopes to use other people's money to finance the film, then the nature of the film company must be designed to accommodate that financial participation. Financial participation is closely tied to the issue of control as well. Even in the arts, investors will want some say in the manner in which their money is spent and will insist on measures to protect their investments and returns.

Exposure to financial *liability* can also be reduced through careful business planning. The film company is legally liable for the contractual obligations and any tort liability that may arise while making the film. Contractual obligations include the duty to pay bills, return rental equipment, withhold and pay taxes, and generally deliver on the promises made by the filmmaker. Tort liability generally reflects the duty to pay for any damages or cover costs associated with accidents (or intentional misconduct) that may arise during the making of the film. If a pedestrian is hit by a car while the filmmaker shoots a car chase scene, then the film company is responsible for paying the injured person. Financial exposure from tort liability should be managed through the purchase of insurance, but the responsibility still rests with the film company.

Tax obligations are a specific type of liability that the film company must undertake. They need to be planned for separately from other financial obligations, early in the development process, because the choice of business structure will determine the amount of taxes owed and shift the tax obligations between the company and its owners—which, in turn, will affect both the cost of raising capital and the benefit of profits earned each year. The goals in tax planning are to minimize the total amount of tax due and to ensure that any tax obligations that do arise can be covered with cash payments. Since every dollar saved can be applied directly to the film, and the profits will go to the film's creators and investors, thoughtful early tax planning sets the stage for good management throughout the project.

Professional tax planning is beyond the scope of this book, but it is important for the filmmaker to work with an experienced accountant or attorney. Preliminary discussions in the planning stage may save the filmmaker thousands of dollars in taxes later in the process.

The best choice of business structure will depend on the objectives of the filmmaker in balancing each of these four considerations. Often control, financing, liability, and tax obligations are in conflict. The filmmaker must determine the nature of the project early in its existence, because the planning choices may dictate some of the subsequent choices available to the filmmaker. Still, as with everything else in filmmaking, business organizations can change as the situation evolves. If a filmmaker starts out making a small film, but the project suddenly doubles in budget and scope, the filmmaker can revise the business plan to reflect the new situation.

The following sections describe five different structures for organizing a film business, listing each one's advantages and disadvantages. Section F (p. 25) discusses which structures work best for which purposes and section G (p. 27) describes a particular variation on one of these structures that is used by many independent filmmakers.

A. Sole Proprietorship

A sole proprietor is a single person who is personally responsible for all aspects of a business. Unless the filmmaker works with a partner or adopts a more formal legal structure for his film company, he is considered a sole proprietor by default. A sole proprietorship is never separate from its owner, and all control stays with the sole proprietor. All liability, including all debts, promises, and obligations, remains the personal responsibility of the business owner.

1. Benefits of the Sole Proprietorship

The primary benefit of working as a sole proprietor is that of simplicity. Without any separate legal entity to manage, there are few if any formalities needed to conduct the filmmaking business. A second potential benefit is that an individual has a credit history and assets that a new business entity may not have. Of the independent films financed on credit cards—

like Spike Lee's *She's Gotta Have It*—most relied on the personal credit of the filmmaker (as well as the once-liberal card issuance policies of the credit card companies). If the income and expenses of the film project are relatively small, the choice to remain a sole proprietor may be a very reasonable one.

The legitimate business expenses of a sole proprietorship may be tax-deductible business expenses. The filmmaker must use Schedule C on the 1040 annual tax form and report the expenses and income that he has carefully itemized during the filmmaking process. Additional rules apply to ensure that the sole proprietorship is truly a business rather than a hobby. The filmmaker must show positive income in three of every five years or the IRS can treat the filmmaking costs as nondeductible hobby expenses.

2. Risks of the Sole Proprietorship

The single biggest drawback to operating as a sole proprietor is the personal liability that the filmmaker undertakes. By comparison, corporations and limited liability companies provide *limited liability,* a corporate shield that protects the filmmaker from personal obligation for any contractual obligations and for any tort liabilities if the filmmaker is sued as an officer or director of the film company.

This distinction may sometimes be more theoretical than real. When a corporation or limited liability company enters into a contractual obligation, it is not uncommon for the creditor to demand a personal guarantee from the filmmaker. This is a legally enforceable promise that the individual will cover the contractual obligations in the event that the film company cannot. The effect of the personal guarantee is to render the corporate protection meaningless.

More seriously, tort creditors may also be able to circumvent corporate protection. The filmmaker is often the individual conducting or supervising the activity that leads to a tort claim. In the earlier example, the filmmaker shooting the car chase would be personally responsible for the car accident if he negligently allowed the car to be driven in an unsafe manner or the pedestrian to be too close to it. If the filmmaker is found negligent, then he will be personally liable regardless of the limited liability afforded by the corporation. No legal entity will protect a filmmaker from responsibility for his own actions.

Because there are many instances in which personal liability is not shielded by the legal entity, control and fundraising become the more pressing reasons to select a particular business form. The sole proprietorship provides the filmmaker with the maximum level of control, but does not accommodate fundraising. The filmmaker can raise money by taking out personal loans (debt financing), but the sole proprietorship is not suitable for raising capital from third parties. Since the third party cannot receive ownership in the film company and can only receive contractual rights to the film's revenue, most investors will balk at the arrangement. In addition, if an investor does contribute funds to the sole proprietor, the investment may transform the sole proprietorship into a general partnership, because the investor has joined with the filmmaker in the business enterprise. This undermines the control sought by the filmmaker without offering any benefits to the investor.

3. Using a DBA with a Sole Proprietorship

A sole proprietorship is not restricted to the name of the filmmaker. The filmmaker can still use a production company name if he wishes by filing a Fictitious Business Name Statement—often known as a "DBA" or "doing business as" form—with the state in which the filmmaker resides. The DBA gives the filmmaker only the right to use a fictional name in a particular state. It confers no limits on liability, nor does it give the filmmaker trademark rights to the name. In the early stages of planning a film project, the filmmaker may elect to file a Fictitious Business Name Statement as the first preliminary step toward creating the film company. It may give the filmmaker some priority for use of the name in that state if he later wishes to create a formal business entity, and in the meantime it gives him the legal right to conduct business under that name.

B. General Partnerships

A general partnership is any business conducted by two or more people for profit. Like a sole proprietorship, no formalities need be followed for a general partnership to be formed. Also, like the sole proprietorship, the partners are each fully and completely responsible for all contractual and tort liabilities of every kind. The general partnership differs from the sole proprietorship in that two or more people share control.

1. Legal Presumption of Forming General Partnerships

State law creates a presumption that when two or more people come together to run a business, they have created a general partnership and share all aspects of control and liability. Unless additional steps are taken to assign authority or limit the control of the partners, each partner shares equally in everything. This means that if any general partner agrees that the business will do something, that contract will be binding on the partnership, even without the other partners being aware of it. On the other hand, decision making is conducted by majority vote. Neither of these situations is healthy for a filmmaking exercise.

The nature of the filmmaking process leads to too many situations in which last-minute decisions and ill-informed promises can be made. Granting contractual power to everyone involved may undermine the management of the film company. For example, it may be that the director—in order to get one last shot at 2 A.M.—promises an actor improved billing if only he will do the scene one additional time. That promise will be binding on the film company only if the director has the authority to make such a bargain. If the director is the sole proprietor, then she has only herself to blame if the offer was imprudent. If the director is one of three general partners—along with the producer and the screenwriter—then the other partners will be bound by a hasty bargain over which they had no say.

2. Formalizing and Structuring General Partnerships

The rules that govern a general partnership can usually be changed by agreement among the partners. The general partners can create an *operating agreement* to assign duties, give primary authority to one partner, and restrict the authority of each partner to particular matters.

For projects of limited scope, such as Web shorts, with few contracts to sign and very small budgets, a general partnership may be appropriate. The filmmaker should insist on a written operating agreement signed by the partners that sets out the responsibilities of each general partner. As a safety precaution, the operating agreement should specify that any obligation to spend more than an agreed-upon dollar amount requires the approval of all partners. Similarly, the authority to make major decisions should either be assigned to particular parties or require the approval of all parties.

3. Risks of General Partnerships

General partnerships are commonly used in very informal situations, so despite the advice in this book, formal partnership agreements are often never drafted or signed. In the absence of an agreement to the contrary, the partners in a general partnership all share equally in the profits and losses. They also share in the responsibility for the partnership's debts and obligations. The obligation to share in the debts does not limit the liability of any individual partner. If only one of three partners has any assets, then that partner will be responsible for all obligations of the film company. That partner can look to the other partners for repayment, but the other partners' duty to her will not reduce her obligation to creditors.

Because of the total responsibility each partner has for the debts of the partnership, general partnerships should only be used for projects of limited scope, and the filmmaker should insist on a written operating agreement before undertaking a general partnership.

4. Tax Status of General Partnerships

General partnerships are not taxed. Instead, the profits and losses are allocated proportionately to the partners, who then pay personal income tax on the profits or deduct the business losses. The tax rules that allow the partnership not to be taxed are probably the best feature of the general partnership. The only difficulty is that the partners are obligated to pay their share of the taxes regardless of whether the partnership has actually distributed the profits.

Tax benefits aside, it should be clear from the description that a general partnership is not a good business form for operating a film company. A general partnership maximizes risk and minimizes the filmmaker's control. Nonetheless, general partnerships are often formed inadvertently when two people start working together in a profit-making activity, such as a writer and director who plan to split the profits from an independent film. To avoid accidentally entering into a general partnership, the filmmaker should formalize her working arrangements early in the planning process.

C. Limited Partnerships

Limited partnerships differ dramatically from general partnerships. These are formal, documented, legal entities that protect the investors from personal liability for debts while treating the partnership's managers as general partners. A limited partnership is formed by filing the necessary papers with the state in which it will be based.

1. Participants in Limited Partnerships

Limited partnerships have two categories of participants—general partners and limited partners. *General partners* are those who actually manage the business on behalf of the partnership. A general partner may be a corporation or other business entity.

Limited partners are investors who contribute money or property as capital in exchange for ownership in the company and participation in its profits and losses. To remain limited partners, they must have very little to do with the control and operation of the business. They vote only on selected issues that affect the survival of the business or to appoint a new general partner if a current general partner has died or become unavailable or unable to act.

Limited partnerships are primarily fundraising vehicles, particularly well suited to sole proprietors who need to raise capital. The limited partners participate by contributing the necessary capital for the business, but they do not interfere with its operations. As the general partner of a limited partnership, the filmmaker retains most of the operational control over the film company. The filmmaker must account to the limited partners regarding how money was spent, collected, and disbursed, but such fiduciary obligations are often set at the lowest level allowed by law.

2. Risks of Limited Partnerships

The long, successful history of limited partnerships may make that structure an attractive form for the filmmaker seeking to raise funds. It combines some of the better features of the sole proprietorship and the corporation. The partnership itself has primary responsibility for all contractual and tort liability. Only if the company is unable to meet these obligations do the general partners become responsible.

The investments made by the limited partners are used to pay any liabilities of the partnership. The limited partners are not personally responsible to pay any additional money or cover debts of the partnership. In contrast, the general partners of a limited partnership are personally responsible for any debts that cannot be covered by the assets of the limited partnership.

One note of caution: the sale of limited partnership interests, like corporate stock, is the sale of a "security" that is highly regulated under both state and federal law. Many filmmakers violate these laws, as well as federal Securities and Exchange Commission regulations, by arranging for financing without consulting a qualified attorney. A filmmaker who does so may be compelled to return all the funds to the investors, incur significant fines, and even face criminal penalties. Please see chapter 8 (p. 141) for an introduction to securities law and an explanation of how to safely raise funds.

3. Tax Status of Limited Partnerships

Limited partnerships may provide tax benefits as well. Limited partnerships are taxed like general partnerships—or rather, like general partnerships, they are not taxed. The profits and losses are allocated to the partners, who pay the taxes or deduct the losses on their individual returns. If the filmmaker has little income to offset the losses, the partnership agreement may make the investment more attractive to the investor by allocating a greater portion of the loss deductions to the limited partners. Unfortunately for the filmmaker, tax rules have changed over the years, so that the benefits of investing in money-losing limited partnerships have been significantly reduced, but there may still be some tax benefits for investors.

D. Corporations

Corporations are the legal entities that operate the largest companies in the world—and many of the smallest companies as well. They can range in size from an entity owned by millions of investors to one owned by a single person. A corporation is managed by a board of directors, operated by its officers, and owned by its shareholders. The corporation provides the shareholders with limited liability for all acts conducted on behalf of the corporation and protects the officers, directors, and employees from many forms of personal liability.

1. Participants in Corporations

One of the key features of corporations is the separation of management from control. The shareholders—the investors who have contributed cash or property in exchange for ownership—control the corporation. The shareholders operate by electing a board of directors. The board of directors is made up of professionals who manage the business and hire the employees of the company. The board of directors is bound by operating rules established in the corporation's bylaws. For a digital filmmaker, such complexity may seem extreme. Nonetheless, most states allow a corporation to have a single person serve as the board of directors. Unanimous written agreements among the shareholders can bind the shareholders to elect the same person as officer and director of the corporation. Using these techniques, the same corporate form that works for General Motors can be adapted to My Film Company, Inc.

There are no significant downsides to operating as a corporation. Forming one requires a certain amount of formality, but the steps are relatively simple, and thousands of books and software programs are available to guide one through them.

2. Risks of Operating as a Corporation

Perhaps the greatest danger of structuring the film company as a corporation is that the filmmaker will oversimplify the task. Many publishers, lawyers, and Internet resources provide standard documents for corporations, but these one-size-fits-all materials often create problems for their users. Filmmakers should avoid adopting "corporate form book" documents uncritically.

For example, most independent filmmakers intend to return the profits from a film to the investors, rather than using those returns to fund future films. The business is most often formed to create and market a single motion picture, but most corporations are designed to "engage in any lawful business." So form documents often fail to include the necessary restrictions against holding onto the profits. This could lead to significant disputes between the filmmaker and investors, which can easily be avoided if the corporate documents are drafted to take the specifics of the film project into account.

The second risk of operating as a corporation may come from relying too heavily on the corporate form to shield the filmmaker from personal liability. As a general matter, both contractual and tort creditors must look first to the corporation for payment of any debt. But if the corporation never had sufficient assets to operate as a business, a court may disregard the corporation and compel the owners to pay the debt. In addition, the corporation would not provide immunity for a person's own negligent or criminal actions. For example, if a production assistant were to injure a pedestrian while running errands for the film company, the corporation would be responsible to pay for the accident. But if the corporation was unable to pay, then the production assistant would remain personally responsible for the accident he caused. The corporate form minimizes financial and legal liability, but it does not eliminate it. Acquisition of sufficient funds to pay debts and purchase of insurance to cover the risks associated with filmmaking are both necessary steps regardless of the business structure selected.

3. Tax Status of Corporations

Corporations typically fall into two separate tax categories. Most corporations are *subchapter C corporations,* which pay their own taxes on the net profits they earn. When the shareholders receive dividends or payments from the corporation, those shareholders also pay taxes on those distributions. Known as *double taxation,* this may significantly increase the amount of taxes paid each year. In addition, any corporate losses are attributed to the business rather than its shareholders, so losses do not provide investors with any potential tax benefits.

To avoid double taxation, the company can instead be organized as a *subchapter S corporation,* which is treated as a partnership for tax purposes—and therefore not taxed as a separate entity. To elect to be taxed as a partnership, the company must limit the number of shareholders to 100 and limit the types of stock sold: an S corporation can issue only a single class of stock, although the stockholders' voting rights may vary. For the small film company, these and the other restrictions often do not pose significant burdens.

E. Limited Liability Companies

The limited liability company, or LLC, is a relatively new form of business entity, but it has grown to become a very popular choice for small business. It is extremely well suited to the independent film company. As defined by most state statutes, the LLC is owned by its *members* and operated through its *managers*. Like shareholders in a corporation, members have limited liability. Some states require that an LLC have two or more members, but other states do not impose this requirement, so the filmmaker should review the information on the secretary of state's Web site for the state where the business will be formed.

1. Forming the LLC

The required filings—the Articles of Organization—are often one-page fill-in-the-blank forms that must be submitted, along with a tax payment, to the secretary of state in the state in which the film company will be located. While simple to fill out, the Articles of Organization provide no information about how the business should be run. So in addition to this certificate, a film company LLC should have a written, signed *operating agreement* that serves as the articles and bylaws of the organization.

The operating agreement establishes the rules for managing and operating the business. Many of its provisions are common to every LLC, and these provisions will be found in virtually every form book. They establish the name and place of business of the LLC, regulate the admission and removal of participants, and provide for maintenance of capital accounts, terminations, and transfers of interest. Nonetheless, there are a few additional issues of particular concern for the filmmaker.

In many states, the operating agreement may simply indicate that the manager—the filmmaker—has sole management authority, that there will be no meetings, and that the profits and losses will be shared in a specified manner between the manager and the other members of the LLC. Investors in the film company, however, may not wish to give such unbridled discretion to the filmmaker, particularly over the raising of capital or other financial decisions. One of the primary benefits of the LLC is the opportunity to shape the business entity to reflect the nature of the investors' interests and the filmmaker's needs. Because the filmmaker needs to encourage investment in the film—a very risky investment—the filmmaker should provide operational protections for the investor as a way of encouraging investment and demonstrating responsibility regarding the enterprise.

2. Risks of the LLC

The greatest drawback to the limited liability company is that the business and investment community has had limited experience with this organizational structure. Investors may be more willing to purchase shares of a corporation than to invest in an LLC, because they are used to financing businesses that use the more traditional form.

A second risk flows from the need to draft an operating agreement for each LLC. As with a corporation, standardized LLC operating agreements found in form books may not be appropriate for independent filmmakers. Each company will have its own investment strategies, distribution plans, and expectations regarding sequels and other projects, and these specifics should be reflected in the operating agreement. Some productions, for example, will restrict the movement of additional capital into the LLC to protect the original investors. (More often, however, film investors are not concerned about the size of other parties' investments, as long as all the funds raised are used exclusively to make the film.)

3. Tax Status of the LLC

The LLC has become a favorite vehicle for small business planners because it gives the owners maximum flexibility regarding the structuring of control and financing while reducing not only liability but also tax obligations. The owners of the LLC have the option to be treated as a partnership for tax purposes.[1] In 1997, the Internal Revenue Service adopted rules that allow the LLC to elect whether to be taxed as a C corporation or as a partnership. By default, LLC entities are taxed as partnerships.

F. Choosing the Best Structure

For many independent filmmakers, the LLC is the best choice for forming a film production company. It can be taxed as either a corporation or a partnership, and its operating agreement is more flexible than corporate bylaws for structuring the film company's operations, but it limits personal liability as effectively as a corporation. Another advantage of the LLC and partnership forms is the ability to allocate gain, loss, deductions, and credits to participants in a way that maximizes their value to investors.

Nonetheless, a different structure may be preferred, depending on the particular makeup of filmmakers and investors. For films heavily financed by outside investors, the traditional corporate form may be best. Some investors may be reluctant to participate in an LLC, a relatively new business form, and may prefer the more traditional corporate structure. An S corporation combines this familiarity with the tax benefits of a partnership.

C corporations may serve the interests of the investors most effectively. The filmmaker can issue multiple classes of stock and draft different shareholders' agreements to achieve the same results as with an LLC's operating agreement. The company will lose the tax advantages of a partnership, but for some investors they will have little value, particularly if the investors are more interested in the long-term growth of their investments than in deducting short-term losses. Corporations are strongly favored for investments such as technology firms that have the possibility of expanding into the public markets. While going public is not a significant possibility for most film companies, the structure may further encourage investors.

Limited partnerships are well suited to individual filmmakers who need to raise capital but want to retain sole operational control over most aspects of the film company. The limited partners participate by contributing the necessary capital for the business, but they do not interfere with its operations. The filmmaker is not protected by limited liability, but since it only shields the filmmaker from liability as an officer or director of the business, and most risk of tort liability will arise from activities in which the filmmaker is personally involved, that protection would be of little value.

If an individual filmmaker is not seeking investment financing, there may not be any benefit to forming a corporation, an LLC, or a limited partnership. Not only is the value of limited liability negligible, but most debt will come from personal loans or unsecured personal credit cards, and the financial risk associated with these obligations will not be changed by using a formal business structure. If the filmmaker is a guerrilla artist, or if she is shooting a short project with a small cast and crew, then she may be best advised to remain a sole proprietor.

On the other hand, if the size of the project increases or if investors are brought in, it is very important that the filmmaker switch to a formal business entity. The worst choice is to ignore the problem and have the law treat the project as a general partnership. The decision to switch need not be made immediately. Tax laws allow the sole proprietor to exchange the business for the assets of a new entity without paying a tax penalty.[2] But from the outset of the film project, the filmmaker should have the business management in mind, and she should work with a lawyer and accountant as early as possible so that the necessary business entity can be created when the filmmaker is ready.

G. The Nested-LLC Model for Continuity and Protection

Many filmmakers hope to launch an ongoing film company with the creation of their first film. At the same time, they need to keep the investments of each film project separate in order to ensure that the profits from each film are distributed to the investors of the particular project. To accomplish both goals, a popular structure calls for the creation of two limited liability companies, one to serve as the ongoing film business and the other to serve as the fundraising vehicle for the particular project.

1. The Umbrella Company Organized for Multiple Projects

The umbrella company is formed as an LLC owned and operated by the production team. The team may be organized in many different ways: it may consist of a group of producers; a team of writer, director, and producer; a director and actors; or any other possible combination. This company generally has only limited financial needs, and any investors are investing in the overall success of the business, not a particular project. The structure provides for limited liability for all participants and the taxation benefits of a partnership.

The umbrella LLC then serves as the sole manager of a second LLC formed to finance, develop, and distribute a particular motion picture. The investors in the movie are members of the second LLC. This maximizes the control that the filmmakers have over the project while allowing the relationship among the filmmaking team to be carefully crafted to reflect the rights and interests of each of its members.

In the operating agreement of the umbrella LLC, each member of the filmmaking team will negotiate the appropriate arrangement for compensation, responsibility, and control. If the team is composed solely of producers, the arrangements may be very similar for each member of the team. If the team is organized more like a rock band, with a writer, director, actor, and producer each contributing different talents and financial resources, the operating agreement can be drafted to reflect those differences. In addition, these terms may be modified without having to be ratified by the film's investors, since they are members of the other LLC, not this one.

The umbrella company is only necessary when a team of people are working together to create the movie, but given the highly collaborative nature of filmmaking, these projects have a much greater chance of success than projects attempted by a single filmmaker.

2. The Subsidiary Company Organized as an Investment Vehicle for the Film

The terms of the film project LLC should establish that the company's activities are limited to the particular motion picture. The company is managed by the umbrella LLC, so the operating agreement should be very clear regarding the authority of the manager—the managing company must have sufficient latitude to make the movie and clear direction regarding its authority to operate, and the role of the investor-members should generally be limited. This does not mean that the filmmakers are not obliged to update investors regarding finances, production, or distribution plans.

Most film investment companies are organized to make a single motion picture. But if the filmmakers know they are making a tent pole project—involving, for instance, a film, sequels, and video game tie-ins—the operating agreement can indicate that the manager has authority to retain earnings to invest in these additional projects. Such authority should be very clearly specified.

It is also important that the investment LLC's operating agreement grant the filmmakers latitude to be involved in other projects while making the film. In the film industry, filmmakers typically work on multiple projects simultaneously, but this creates a situation in which these projects may be competing for investor dollars, time, and attention, or even film festival admission. To ensure that the investors are fully aware of this reality, the operating agreement should specify that the services of the umbrella LLC and its members are provided on a nonexclusive basis.

Finally, the operating agreement should set forth all the structures for recoupment of investments and profit participation, as well as the fees paid to the umbrella LLC for the management of the film project. While the operating agreement does not take the place of financial disclosure documentation, the two documents will closely resemble each other in many regards. This should allow the attorney to draft the two documents together, saving time and money. And since the operating agreement works as a blueprint for the operations of the company, it should also make it easier for the filmmakers to meet their obligations to their investors.

Technically, the managers of the umbrella LLC have no direct relation to the investors in the film project LLC, but the parties should not rely on this legal fiction; each filmmaker should treat his duties to the investors as if he were a personal manager of the film project LLC. The two-LLC structure is not likely to immunize the filmmakers from their ethical and fiduciary obligations, described in chapter 3, and should not be used for that purpose.

Duties of the Film Company

As MENTIONED IN chapter 2, a typical film company of even modest size quickly undertakes all the attributes of a well-established business. If at all possible, these operational duties—engaging employees, renting equipment, paying taxes, raising working capital, etc.—should be separated from the creative duties of filmmaking. While many filmmakers serve as chief cook and bottle washer, more regimented efforts tend to be more successful. That way, a filmmaker who works with an actor regarding character does not have to discuss her payroll or tax forms at the same time. Separating business obligations from artistic functions improves both professionalism and focus.

The most important business obligations are the duties of the film company to its investors and employees. Unless the film company fulfills these obligations successfully, the film cannot be successfully made and distributed—and the company risks violating state and federal law. The filmmaker must, therefore, pay close attention to the following duties.

A. Financial Accounting and Responsibility

The financial accounting of a motion picture is extremely detailed, complex, and vital. It is not a coincidence that Michael Eisner became the CEO of Disney by learning the business in the accounting department. Many other studio heads were lawyers earlier in their careers. A film company should plan to assign accounting and internal auditing functions to someone early in the development of the film company. While not a glamorous role, a good production accountant can help ensure that the film company will have the funds necessary to pay salaries, rent equipment when needed, and still edit the film.

1. Planning

Often, participants in an independent filmmaking project agree to be paid from the film's profits. For this arrangement to work, profit participants must have confidence that there will be profits to share in if the film becomes a success. This requires that the film's costs be carefully itemized and reported.

The most critical phase in filmmaking accounting is the first step: budgeting. Chapter 7 (p. 129) provides a detailed description of the budgeting process and an analysis of the items that go into a budget. The production budget provides a blueprint for the structure of the film company and the film project. It allows the filmmaker to identify the scope of the project, calculate the magnitude of the financial resources needed, schedule receipts and payments, and prepare for the long-term obligations that might arise if the film is not a financial success. For unions such as the Screen Actors Guild (SAG) and the Directors Guild of America (DGA), the film's budget also determines the film company's eligibility to utilize the unions' reduced-pay-scale contracts. The filmmakers must submit a budget to the unions, and each union will scrutinize its assumptions before agreeing to allow union members to work for the film company under the terms of a low-budget contract.

Often, filmmakers will also create a business plan that anticipates each phase of the film project from financing to distribution, and assesses factors such as the market conditions for the film and the likelihood of profitability. That business plan will help map out the road ahead for the benefit of potential investors and more cautious creative participants who demand a realistic chance of success before they commit to a project. It is much more important to filmmakers who hope to develop further projects rather than those who are shooting and distributing a single film. If the filmmaker elects to create a business plan, it must be accurate and realistic.

2. Record Keeping

Just as important as preparing a budget is keeping careful records of financial transactions. Record keeping serves two distinct goals. First, it provides the documentary proof of the production's expenses, which is essential to calculating tax liability and compliance with contractual obligations to the unions and to determining the film company's profits. Since many participants' payments are based on the profit of the film company, failure to document expenses will lower the break-even point at which the profit participants must be paid. In addition, some financing options may require documentation to prove that the specific expenses were actually incurred.

Second, record keeping allows the filmmaker to monitor the costs of ongoing expenses like set construction. If 14 days into a 21-day shoot the film company has already spent 90 percent of its set construction budget, the filmmaker will have to make some choices. Perhaps most of the money was spent on a single set that has been used throughout filming. Then the remaining 10 percent of the budget should be satisfactory. If, however, the set construction costs are generally the same for each day of filming, then the filmmaker can expect to run as much as 40 percent over budget on set construction. Knowing this, the filmmaker can choose to scale back on set construction, increase the set construction budget by reducing other costs, or plan to increase the production expense. Without the advance knowledge, the filmmaker could find himself without funds in a checking account, suddenly shut down in the middle of production. A good accountant may not improve the film, but she certainly will improve the chances of completing the film.

3. Accountability

The budget is the road map for which the accountant must serve as vigilant navigator. When money begins to flow, the danger always exists that it may be misspent. *Misspent funds* refers to money stolen, personal purchases improperly attributed to the production company, and expenses attributed to the wrong budget line. In the heat of principal photography, dozens of individuals may be authorized to start purchasing supplies. It is wasteful for three different production assistants to each buy bottles of glue. It is criminal for one of those production assistants to buy an extra bottle of glue for his own supplies and charge it to the production. The film company must be attentive and efficient so that a culture of lax accounting does not encourage the volunteers and independent contractors to take advantage of the film's limited resources.

For accounting purposes, misspent funds do not include failed creative choices, such as purchasing a wedding dress for a scene that is later rewritten to take place in a dance club. While that may be a regrettable expenditure, the money purchased the intended costume and the balance sheet reflects the value of the dress even if the finished film does not. Filmmakers must be conscientious, but accountability should be a tool in support of the artistic goal rather than an obstacle.

Whenever someone other than a sole proprietor is handling the film company's payments, a specific system of accountability must be established. The nature of the system depends on the size of the project and the number of individuals authorized to spend company money. A film company can authorize its scene designer to buy materials as necessary, as long as the expense remains within the agreed budget. The key is that for each expenditure a receipt is obtained, and each receipt is attributed to a particular budget line. As payments are made, the receipts are tabulated. This helps to guarantee that the designer has actually spent the money on set materials and allows the business manager to compare the expenditures to the approved budget.

The ability to maintain careful accounting becomes most difficult near the end of principal photography. As the tension mounts to finish filming on schedule, the frenetic pace often encourages frenzied choices. Late hours result in crumpled receipts piling up in ashtrays. After the frenzy, the receipts are flattened and submitted for reimbursement. The delay in submission allows the expenses to balloon, possibly eliminating the funds left for postproduction. Particularly on low-budget films, money is tight. Even a few bad choices at the end of principal photography can derail the project.

4. Reporting

The final aspect of accounting relates to the obligations to report income and pay taxes. Unless the filmmaker operates a sole proprietorship, the film company must report income or losses. That information is used to pay taxes, either directly by the corporation or indirectly by the participants in a partnership or LLC. Movies are unique assets subject to illogical and highly manipulable accounting rules. It is generally accepted that a film company will either speed up the depreciation of the film to generate business losses and reduce tax liability, or slow the depreciation down by predicting long-lasting revenue from the movie, which increases the value of film as an asset on the books of the company.

Although the guerrilla filmmaker may pay little heed to the accounting possibilities, investors and financiers will. The successful film company should engage the services of a qualified accountant who can help the company establish a strategy to deal with the tax and reporting obligations for the project.

One additional note of caution: the tax reporting for a marginally successful film may continue for years, and in some cases, the tax forms will outlast the prints of the film itself. When creating the film company, the filmmaker must be prepared to accept this obligation to continue to collect fees and provide tax reports.

B. Fiduciary Obligations

The record keeping and financial reporting obligations are duties owed to investors, unions, and the IRS. In addition, the filmmaker's role as business operator creates specific duties of care and loyalty to the investors. Because the filmmaker is also an employee of the company and a primary beneficiary of the film project, the filmmaker must take great care to respect these fiduciary obligations and to carefully disclose the various conflicts of interest to the investors before they agree to invest in the project.

1. Duty of Loyalty

Whether serving as a general partner, managing member, or corporate officer and director, the filmmaker has a primary duty to act in the best interests of the business rather than out of personal self-interest. As a general matter, this duty limits self-dealing transactions. A manager should never give herself a loan from the business, pay herself a bonus, divert business opportunities, or otherwise take for herself any benefit that should go to the company.

For example, if the film company owns the sequel rights to the movie, the manager should not buy those rights from the company for the purpose of reselling them at a substantially higher price. Similarly, the manager cannot agree to sell the sequel rights cheaply on behalf of the company in exchange for a highly lucrative contract to direct the sequel. Although a rights transaction might be perfectly appropriate between the manager and an unrelated party, the manager has a duty to maximize the profits off the sale for the business; she cannot take that benefit for herself.

To honor the duty of loyalty, the filmmaker should plan ahead. First, certain situations will create clear conflicts of interest between the filmmaker and the business. As much as possible, the filmmaker should disclose the terms of any material conflicts to prospective investors. The disclosure should be in a private placement memorandum or other offering document as well as in the language of the operating agreement, bylaws, or subscription agreement:

- All contracts among officers, directors, managers, and partners must be disclosed to potential investors before they agree to invest. These contracts may include the writer's agreement, director's agreement, or actor's agreement, or other agreements between the filmmakers and the company.
- If the officers, directors, managers, and partners want to work on projects other than this film, they must disclose their nonexclusive status.
- If the officers, directors, managers, and partners are fundraising for multiple projects, this creates a direct conflict of interest, which must be disclosed.
- The ownership interests held by the officers, directors, managers, and partners must be clearly distinguished from the rights owned by the business. For example, if one of the managers is the original author of the screenplay who sold the business the right to film the script but retained the copyright—including rights to sequels, characters, and similar projects—then that arrangement must be made clear.

When individuals choose to invest in the business after having received full disclosure of these preexisting conflicts of interest, they cannot effectively complain that the transaction unfairly benefits the managers rather than the business. On the other hand, if the information was not made available in advance of the investment, the investors may have grounds to charge that the manager misrepresented the transaction. Once the investment is made, the filmmaker is of course restricted from making further arrangements that benefit the managers to the detriment of the business or its investors.

2. Disclosure and Approval for Conflicts of Interest

In independent filmmaking, even when a manager is scrupulous about adhering to the duty of loyalty, conflicts of interest will arise throughout the filmmaking process. To be of concern to investors, the conflict must be material. Contracts to acquire rights, to distribute the film, and to compete with the film company by working for another company are among the types of transactions that are clearly material. Eating the catering on the set is not. The manager must use common sense in determining whether a reasonable investor would consider the conflict important, erring on the side of overdisclosure.

To resolve conflicts of interest, the operating agreement, partnership agreement, or bylaws should provide clear provisions. For example, the policy might mandate that when officers, directors, managers, or partners have a conflict of interest, such a transaction can only be completed after the following steps have been taken:

1. The conflict of interest is fully disclosed.
2. A disinterested group meets for discussion and approval of the transaction without the participation of the interested person. This may mean the disinterested directors on the board of directors, disinterested managers among the managing members, or a committee formed specifically for this purpose.
3. If the conflict includes a bid to provide services, a competitive bid or comparable valuation is solicited, if possible.
4. The body approving the transaction determines that the transaction is in the best interest of the organization.
5. The decision to approve the conflict of interest is summarized in writing, to be kept in the minutes of the corporation or the records of the business.

In many situations, no disinterested board of directors or managers will be available. In such a case, the operating agreement or bylaws should specify that substantially similar steps are taken by the members of the LLC, partners of the partnership, or shareholders of the corporation. In that situation, the best approach is to seek unanimous written consent of all investors by providing the information in writing and seeking signatures of approval.

3. Duty of Care

The duty of care requires that the officers, directors, managers, or partners act in good faith and exercise prudent decision making in the undertaking of the business for the benefit of the business and its investors. Whereas the duty of loyalty provides a very demanding standard, the duty of care sets a low threshold to meet. Independent filmmaking is a highly risky enterprise, so wide latitude is given to the filmmakers to act reasonably in an uncertain business.

The duty of care essentially requires that the filmmakers avoid being grossly negligent in the operation of the business. The filmmakers must be fully informed of their obligations and make every reasonable effort to meet those obligations. The duty of care would make the filmmakers liable to the company and its shareholders for failing to keep records, failing to acquire the rights necessary to make the film, or materially violating tax or professional obligations.

Other potential breaches of the duty of care are more ambiguous. Perhaps the most interesting and difficult situation would arise if the filmmakers determined that a film project would cost $100,000 to shoot under their business plan but they chose to begin principal photography when only $50,000 was raised. Is it unreasonable and grossly negligent to hope that an angel investor will appear before the money runs out? Certainly it would have been more prudent to adjust the shooting schedule or other expectations to make a $50,000 film or to wait until full financing was in place. It might have been more prudent to spend $10,000 to create a trailer to help raise the additional funds. Nevertheless, the filmmakers may not have been grossly negligent in going forward with the shoot, depending on how reasonable it was to expect that the additional funds would be raised. If the filmmaker's expectations were low, then such a strategy may very well have been grossly negligent, in which case the filmmakers would be personally obligated to repay their investors. Fortunately, independent film investors know how risky the industry can be, so they are generally reluctant to seek personal reimbursement.

The duty of care should serve as a check on the risks that independent filmmakers are willing to take. If there is no reasonable likelihood of a return, then the investors' money should not be spent. If the filmmaker goes into a project knowing the risks are very high, then she should disclose the high-risk strategy to the investors, or seek to fund the movie with gifts from friends and family.

C. Employer Obligations

Employment and labor obligations are perhaps the most detailed and the least followed aspect of independent filmmaking. The myriad federal and state laws are poorly suited to addressing the realities of the filmmaking industry. Luckily for independent filmmakers, production typically ends and the employees are dismissed before regulators have an opportunity to object to offending business practices, and the employees themselves are often young and indifferent to their legal rights.

Nonetheless, employer obligations can create significant headaches for the successful filmmaker. If a crew member is paid only a small stipend, she may successfully claim that she was supposed to be protected by minimum wage laws, and that she is due overtime pay for working in excess of a 40-hour week—or even an eight-hour day in California. Filmmakers are not permitted to characterize every employee as an independent contractor if the individuals are working under the direction and control of the film company for an extended period of time. Employers must pay particular attention not only to wage and hour laws but also to hiring practices and antidiscrimination policies when managing the significant labor force involved with even the most modest of film projects.

1. Hiring

For a motion picture, hiring includes both very subjective choices regarding casting and much more routine decisions regarding support staff and technical personnel. Although casting is a form of hiring, the subjective nature of casting requires that employers have more discretion to be arbitrary in their hiring choices than employment laws might otherwise allow.

To fill the remaining positions, the filmmaker must adhere to a broad range of legal rules and limitations designed to ensure that job applicants are treated fairly. An employer may not discriminate on the basis of categories such as race, national origin, gender, sexual orientation, age, or disability. In particular, the Americans with Disabilities Act requires that the employer make reasonable accommodations for an employee's disability unless that disability affects an essential job function. So, for example, the filmmaker would not have to consider a deaf candidate for the job of sound engineer, because hearing and judging sound quality is an essential function of the position, but that same candidate, if otherwise qualified, should be considered for the job of stunt person.

To deny a job on the basis of a disability, that disability must affect an essential job requirement. A deaf stunt person could not properly be passed over for a less-qualified applicant who is not hearing impaired merely because the person might be given a few lines of dialogue later in the production process. Similarly, an employer must make reasonable accommodations for an employee's disability, so the film company would be required to find a method to provide visual rather than auditory cues to begin and end action during filming.

Because discrimination is illegal, the company must take steps to avoid asking interview questions that could give rise to discriminatory practices. According to the Equal Employment Opportunity Commission, on both written questionnaires and in oral interviews, the interviewer should focus on issues related to the applicant's experience and skills, availability, and ability to fulfill the job requirements, and avoid questions unrelated to those issues. Often interviewers make small talk to break the ice during an interview, but questions regarding marital status, religion, or other personal issues that might be used to discriminate are inappropriate and impermissible. The rules apply whether the person being hired is the film's director or the assistant script supervisor.

The hiring process also involves a significant amount of salesmanship by the film company. Often with independent film production, the company must convince the applicant to work for a deferred salary or minimum wage in exchange for a chance to participate in the potential windfall if the movie hits it big. While such optimistic projections are part of the vision of the independent filmmaker, the company must take care not to misrepresent the financial status of the project or the professional expertise of the participants. Filmmakers commonly lie about such matters, but doing so constitutes unfair trade practices under the Federal Trade Commission Act, and it may be grounds for lawsuits if the project fails to meet employees' expectations.

Once the applicant has been hired, the film company must also verify the person's eligibility to work in the United States. This must be done by following the instructions on Form I-9 from U.S. Citizenship and Immigration Services. Employees must complete this form within three days of beginning work and provide documentation within three weeks. The I-9 form is not submitted to any government agency, but must be retained by the company and presented in case of government inspection. The company must retain the I-9 for one year following the termination of the employee or three years from the date of hire, whichever is later. In addition, all employment applications and resumes must be retained for one year, even if the person was not hired.

2. Employment Status: Independent Contractors and Employees

One of the common techniques to avoid dealing with employment laws in the independent film community is to treat everyone as an independent contractor instead of an employee. This approach is only occasionally appropriate, and the overuse of the independent contractor designation can lead to significant tax and insurance liability for the film company.

An independent contractor is a person who is self-employed and provides service to the hiring party by taking it on as a client. For example, the catering company would typically be an independent contractor, providing craft services for a number of clients including the film company. Unfortunately there are no precise standards, but the IRS and the courts first look to the company's ability to control the activities of the worker. If the hiring party dictates the hours, the manner of the work, and the location where the work will be done, that level of control will generally indicate that the worker is an employee. If the person engaged controls those factors, it suggests that the person is an independent contractor. Another significant characteristic of independent contractors is the ability to provide services for multiple clients. Similarly, ownership of one's own tools and equipment suggests an independent contractor.

Under these general parameters, most participants on a film project are not independent contractors. The cast, director, and designers work under the direction of the film company using equipment rented by the film company. They should be considered employees. On the other hand, caterers, costumers, sound engineers, and special effects teams tend to be on a shoot part-time, to bring their own tools, and to service multiple clients when the work is available. For these individuals, independent contractor status may be more appropriate.

The difference between the two categories is significant. The employer must pay Social Security taxes and withhold employment taxes on behalf of the employees. Independent contractors have no deductions taken from their paychecks and retain responsibility for all taxes. (Independent contractors also do not need to complete Form I-9 documentation.) However, if the IRS or a state's labor department discovers that an employer has improperly treated an employee as an independent contractor, the company will face significant consequences, including not only the payment of back taxes but also interest and penalties.

In many states, employers have another reason not to overuse the independent contractor designation: it lessens the protection of workers' compensation insurance. An employee is covered by workers' compensation insurance in the event of a work-related injury, and in exchange the injured employee may not sue the employer for negligence. An independent contractor does not have the benefit of this insurance and has no restrictions on suing the film company in the event of a personal injury on the set of a production.

Workers' compensation may also be an issue for a third class of worker common on film projects—unpaid assistants. Depending on state laws, these assistants may or may not be covered by workers' compensation insurance. Unfortunately, due to long hours, dangerous equipment, and crew inexperience, independent film productions have a high risk of accidents. A company may find it is cheaper to pay volunteers a minimum wage, qualifying them for employee status and thus workers' compensation, rather than to purchase separate liability insurance to cover them.

3. Employment Status: Exempt or Salaried Employees

Like the difference between independent contractors and employees, the distinction between exempt and salaried employees affects the employer's obligations toward workers. Minimum wage laws protect salaried employees, providing overtime pay for work in excess of 40 hours per week, or even eight hours per day in some states. Exempt employees, on the other hand, are not bound by wage and hour laws, and are instead paid for the scope of the project rather than the hours worked.

To qualify as exempt, employees must earn at least $455 per week and fall into one of the following categories: executives, administrators, professionals, and salespeople. *Professionals* include creative workers such as actors, musicians, composer, painters, and writers. They must utilize originality, creativity, or specialized knowledge in the position, generally from advanced training. If the salary minimum is met, then many of the employees working in specialized positions on a film would qualify.

Executives include employees who supervise at least two other individuals. Generally, anyone with supervisory duties on a film will be working in an executive or professional capacity. *Administrators* must exercise independent judgment in their administrative duties. This category may sound unnecessarily vague since, one hopes, every employee exercises independent judgment throughout the day. Maybe this is less true outside of the film industry.

Although stretching the definition of exempt employee does not carry the same magnitude of risk as misapplying independent contractor status, a film company should make every effort to comply with the law wherever possible.

4. Tax and Withholding Status

The film company has a number of specific obligations regarding employee tax payments. Immediately upon being hired, the employee should complete IRS Form W-4 to determine the amount of money that is to be withheld from the payroll for the purposes of paying federal, state, and local income taxes. The employer must deduct the appropriate amount of money from each employee paycheck and deposit this money in a separate account. Severe fines and even potential criminal liability can be incurred for withholding an employee's tax payments and failing to submit those payments to the government. The W-4 must be kept for four years following the termination of the employee.

The company must withhold not only income taxes but also Social Security and Medicare taxes. Presently the Social Security tax is withheld at a rate of 6.20 percent for the first $102,000 earned per year. Medicare taxes are withheld at a rate of 1.45 percent on the entire amount earned each year. The company must also pay the employer's portion of Social Security and Medicare taxes, which is equal to the amount withheld from the employee.

Following the end of each calendar year, the film company must submit a statement to the IRS reflecting the annual payment and taxes for each employee. The employee must receive Form W-2 by the first of February each year, and the IRS must receive Form W-3 by the first of March. Failure to file these forms can result in fines. More important, the former cast and crew need these forms to complete their own taxes, and the film company has an obligation to provide them with this information. The company should do whatever it can to maintain goodwill with former employees, so that frustrations do not arise and the former employees do not provoke investigations into the myriad employment and labor violations that regularly occur in independent film companies.

At some point the independent filmmaker may be required to take legal risks to continue the production. If there is no money left in the production account and there are 12 pages of script left to shoot, then the film may be completed by volunteer labor—since everyone was technically laid off when the funds gave out. The bottom line is that the filmmaker must make well-informed, pragmatic choices based on the associated risks. For example, a filmmaker should never fail to submit payroll taxes, even if the only way to afford it is to treat three salaried employees as exempt. Most accountants and attorneys would further recommend that a filmmaker forgo a scene involving an expensive wind machine and avoid both employment problems—which reflects why accountants and attorneys rarely become guerrilla filmmakers.

5. Loan-Out Employment Services

For independent filmmakers who want to sidestep many of these concerns, the best solution may be to handle employer obligations through a loan-out employment service. These companies become the employer of record for the employees. Legally obligated to handle the tax forms, they ensure proper withholding; as required, they also collect funds needed for payments to the Screen Actors Guild, other unions and guilds, and talent agents. For some production companies, the cost of such services may be prohibitive, but for a production of even modest budget, a loan-out employment service may be a very sound investment in the stability of the film project and the longevity of the film company.

A less costly alternative is a *payroll service,* which handles the administration of employee payments but does not actually serve as the employer of record. Payroll services are useful for handling the details of bimonthly check writing, but they do not relieve the film company of its primary duties as an employer, nor solve the longer-term issues of record keeping.

Increasingly, small production companies can obtain the same basic payroll services equally well using commercial software, for a fraction of the cost. A payroll program requires that someone remember to operate it and provide the checks, but it offers sufficient information and support for a small filmmaker armed with a checklist of the proper forms to submit and a schedule of submission.

6. Profit Participants

For guerrilla filmmakers, the notion that minimum wage will be paid—or even that basic employment records will be filed—stands as little more than wishful thinking. While these fundamental duties should be fulfilled, practical guidance is the art of the possible. For those companies that would not otherwise attempt to meet their hiring obligations, another approach is to include all the participants in the risks and rewards of the film.

Unlike employees, the owners of an enterprise are not generally covered by hour and wage laws, nor are they included in workers' compensation insurance. The owners—general partners, managers, officers, or corporate directors—assume the risk and participate actively in the enterprise, so these legal protections are less necessary. If the film company truly consists of the cast, the director, and the producer, it may be appropriate to organize it as an LLC, with an operating agreement that treats all the participants as managing members. Thus, the filmmaker avoids many of the state and federal employment obligations, while allowing everyone to share in the risks (minimized to the extent possible using the LLC) and rewards of the project. The portions need not be equal; the filmmaker can retain a larger share, reflecting his broader role in the film.

This technique should not be abused. As the scope and budget of a project increases, the reasonableness of this approach diminishes. Nonetheless,

for guerrilla filmmaking this structure may at least serve as practical jus-
tification for looser employment practices.

D. Decision Making

For the sake of both employees and investors, the film company also has a
responsibility to practice good decision making, by communicating effectively and creating clear lines of responsibility. If the filmmaker, business
manager, and other senior staff all work closely to explore the impact of
significant decisions, they have a common basis for decision making. If
their respective responsibilities are clearly delineated, they will be more
capable of sharing the load.

The decision-making model provides the structure for planning all
aspects of the film production, from making artistic choices about locations, cast, and story to navigating business decisions regarding equipment
rentals, film permits, and service agreements. Except in the case of a sole
proprietorship or general partnership, it is very important that that the
film company and not the filmmaker be the entity responsible for every
contract and negotiation. Planning becomes the purview of the film company as a whole, and the decision-making process must allow for some delegation of authority.

As the production grows, responsibility for more decisions is delegated,
so it becomes even more critical that information is shared among the
affected parties. If possible, production meetings of the senior management
should be held regularly. Francis Ford Coppola tells the story of a very
expensive scene from *Apocalypse Now* in which he initially ordered an
extravagant set, including perfectly authentic food, wine, and costumes.
Later, as costs spiraled out of control, he ordered the scene's budget cut.
Casting greatly reduced the expense of the cast hired for this scene, but
the other departments never got the message. Out of utter frustration, Coppola stopped filming and refused to use the scene.[1] On a smaller scale, this
type of expensive mistake happens frequently. A delay in notifying the
costume designer of a casting change may result in wasted effort and
money. Location changes may cascade through the production. Conversely,
if everyone knows of a cash shortage, then every department can look to
find the least harmful ways to cut expenses and defer payments. Together,

communication and delegation allow the production company to improve the chances of successfully completing the film and free the filmmaker to focus on the important artistic issues.

E. Business Continuity

The film company also provides the continuity for the film as it moves from theatrical exhibition to DVD, foreign distribution, television, and Internet broadcasting. A successful film might continue to offer licensing opportunities, earn revenue, and demand the fulfillment of legal and contractual obligations for decades. The film company must be organized to anticipate this long-term commitment. To this end, the company maintains consistency regarding employment and tax record keeping, the regular distribution of revenues, the distribution of payments for unions and gross income participants, and the legal ownership of the film. Again, delegation may become critical.

A successful film often propels many of the production team into increasingly larger projects. This may make it difficult for them to manage the often more modest revenue from their early independent films. Delegation to a professional involved with the project, such as the accountant or attorney, may allow the film company to continue to meet its obligations while allowing the filmmakers to grow their careers.

The Property of the Film Company: The Film Concept

ONCE THE FILM company is formed and its business obligations prepared for, it can finally turn its attention to the true purpose of any filmmaking project: telling a compelling story. As an artist, the filmmaker is concerned with discovering an engaging story concept and transforming it into the motion picture she envisions. As a business, the film company must be concerned with acquiring the legal rights to that story and respecting the legal interests of its owners or those depicted in it. By carefully crafting agreements with the rights holders, the company can maximize the filmmaker's artistic flexibility while minimizing her risk of future legal problems.

A. Sources

Comic books, plays, newspapers, novels, and the filmmaker's imagination are among the many sources that serve as the basis for new film concepts. From a classic short story to a taxicab,[1] no bad source exists. The source material should not limit the creative choices of the filmmaker. From a business and legal perspective, however, each of these sources has certain limitations and certain advantages.

1. Original Ideas

From a legal perspective, original ideas are the easiest source material to develop, since there are no preexisting legal rights to consider. As long as the idea is truly conceived by the filmmaker, then the resulting story, which uses only the filmmaker's fictional characters and plot points, can be developed without limitation.

Borrowing general ideas from other sources does not violate copyright laws, but such use may run afoul of the filmmaker's preexisting duties under agreements not to use ideas that have been developed by other people. Detailed plots are more than mere ideas, and those are protected by copyright.

The business disadvantage of basing a film on an original idea is that the film lacks a "hook," or preexisting awareness of the story, making it more difficult to market. This may increase the difficulty not only in developing the film's marketing campaign but also in raising capital for the production of the film. Despite the ultimate success of the movies, filmmakers and distributors had less difficulty promoting the film *Ali* than earlier boxing films *Rocky* or *On the Waterfront*.

2. True Events

True events are also a tremendous source of material. True stories cannot be "owned" by anyone. The First Amendment grants the filmmaker the right to retell a true story using his own expression. Whether presented in documentary form or dramatized, true stories have a natural resonance for audiences, which in turn provide excellent marketing opportunities. And many true stories need to be told to promote ideas and impact society. A movie such as *Boys Don't Cry,* which highlights rape and murder, is compelling because of the awful truth it reveals. As such, the filmmaker had a story she needed to tell. In the same way, *Charlie Wilson's War* provides a fascinating glimpse into American politics and also serves as a stark reminder of the governmental policies that led to the rise of the Taliban.

Nonetheless, adapting true stories presents important legal complications. Unless the people portrayed in the movie have given their permission, or the accuracy of their portrayal can otherwise be established, the filmmaker risks being sued for libel. In *Charlie Wilson's War,* Mike Nichols and Aaron Sorkin had former congressman Wilson's blessings to tell his story and to show him drinking constantly, admitting to drug use, and fornicating with a married woman. Most filmmakers are not so fortunate. Without such permission, the risks for the filmmaker are much higher. Despite the care taken by filmmakers, *Boys Don't Cry*, *The Perfect Storm*, and *The Insider* are just a few of the many films that resulted in lawsuits or threats of legal actions over unflattering portrayals.

While it is often not possible to gain permission from all the participants in a true story, particularly if the adaptation paints them in an unflattering manner, the filmmaker can limit risk. Careful choices made throughout the writing and filming process, as well as contractual agreements with some of the participants, will allow the filmmaker to reduce exposure to crippling lawsuits or liability that could scare away distributors from otherwise brilliant films.

3. Novels and Short Stories

Novels, novellas, and short stories are a staple of feature filmmaking. Of the various forms of existing literature, the short story is the best dramatic form to transfer to film, since time constraints and other limitations on motion pictures tend to oversimplify novels. Still, filmmakers often purchase the rights to both books and short stories to serve as the basis for their films. The business advantage of doing so is that a known story may help to attract financing and talent. The literary work can also serve as a starting point for the film's marketing campaign.

The filmmaker will need to purchase the film rights to any book or short story protected by copyright. The author of the story or the author's estate generally holds these rights. The filmmaker may choose to purchase all rights in the story by acquiring the author's copyright ownership, or instead purchase a limited license granting permission to make and distribute a single film production. If the book or short story is based on true events, then the filmmaker must acquire both the rights to the story and any additional rights necessary to fictionalize a true story.

4. Song Titles and Music

Song titles and musical lyrics can also serve as the creative element at the heart of a film. Using a recognized song in the film's title can lead to increased recognition for the movie; if the song is famous, then the movie appears famous as well. Songs may be less expensive than other source materials as a method of purchasing instant recognition, particularly if the song has not been heavily licensed for use in commercials or other film productions. Neither film titles nor song titles are protected by copyright, but oftentimes they are protected as trademarks, so permission is still required.

In addition, to include the song in the soundtrack, copyright permission must be obtained from the songwriter or the songwriter's publisher. If any popular recording of the song is to be used in the film, then the permission of the record producer or record distributor, often called the *label,* is also required. Permission is generally given in exchange for a licensing fee. Separate permission is required if the filmmaker plans to release a soundtrack album.

5. Stage Plays

Plays are another popular source of film ideas. Legally, plays are treated just like novels and short stories. And as with literary sources, audience familiarity can serve as a hook. Plays are also like film remakes in the sense that the story has been told in a dramatic medium. But because plays tend to generate drama via stylized language rather than arresting visuals, translating them to film may be much more difficult than one would expect. Some play-to-film adaptations, such as the Oscar-winning *Driving Miss Daisy,* transfer successfully, but many are financial or artistic disappointments.

In the world of guerrilla filmmaking, plays serve as a mixed blessing. The stage history can help to raise funds and draw media attention for marketing purposes, but films based on plays are often treated differently from other films, which may limit some of the financial potential and turn off distributors.

6. Movies

Increasingly, filmmakers turn to the vaults of the studios for interesting stories to retell. Remakes have instant recognition for investors and audiences. Once, such projects were generally limited to color updates of black-and-white films, but today remakes of all kinds are extremely common. *The Incredible Hulk* (2008) essentially remade *Hulk* (2003), which may set a record for the shortest time between versions. The *Batman* franchise retells the same group of stories on a regular basis. Occasionally a remake may be created as a shot-by-shot reproduction, as when Gus Van Sant remade the Alfred Hitchcock classic *Psycho*. More typically, however, a remake takes substantial liberties, updating the story and characters.

Remakes may be the most difficult projects to legally structure. Since the film that is the subject of the remake may itself have been based on another work under copyright, a whole series of permissions may have to be obtained. Further, since film companies often change hands or sell their libraries, researching the chain of title for a film may prove difficult.

The legal issues are especially tricky for films from the 1920s through the 1950s. Before the advent of television, film companies were not as aggressive about retaining every possible legal interest in a film. For example, the owners of a 1940s film might have sold the right to distribute the original film on television to another company, and that sale might have included the television rights to any remakes and sequels as well. A filmmaker who wanted to pursue a remake would have to acquire those television rights separately. Since the rise of television, and especially since the dawn of the Internet, film rights have become much less diffuse. So it is often easier to acquire all necessary rights to a newer film than an older one.

7. Comic Books

Comic books have become one of the most important sources of tent pole or blockbuster films, including *Superman, Batman, X-Men, Hellboy, Ghost Rider, The Spirit, Watchmen,* and many others. As an intensively visual medium, the comic book naturally translates well into motion picture story boards with little adaptation. The strong characters and heavy reliance of visual imagery works very well. As with other previously published sources, comic books have a powerful relationship with a preexisting audience; comic book fans are especially passionate about their favorite characters and stories. However, this does put pressure on the film producer to respect the audience's expectations.

As computer generated imagery (CGI) becomes more and more commonplace in films, the physical limitations of the real world are disappearing from filmmaking, and comic books and movies continue to move closer together in content. Low-budget independent films often do not have the luxury of heavy CGI, so more and more comic book projects are studio projects rather than independent films. (DC Comics is actually owned by Warner Bros. Entertainment, but it has been Marvel and Dark Horse Comics that have produced some of the most successful comic book films.) The audiences for comic books and independent films, however, may overlap rather significantly, so a comic book story may be a good project for an independent filmmaker to coproduce with a studio.

8. Video Games and Web Sites

The newest additions to the entertainment media are also the latest sources of motion picture content: video games and Web sites. Simple Web sites like published literary diaries, or blogs, may be treated like short stories or other literary works. In contrast, obtaining the rights to adapt a complex interactive Web site or video game is like negotiating to remake a black-and-white movie. These projects' creators may have overlooked the potential of motion picture adaptation and failed to acquire the rights, so securing them requires careful analysis and contracting. Separate owners may control the rights to the story of the game, the artwork, and potentially the game play; each element to be incorporated into the motion picture must be identified and acquired separately. Similarly, if actors contributed their likenesses to the game, their permission may also have to be obtained, depending on the needs of the filmmaker and the actors' contracts.

B. Copyright Limitations on Source Material

In a number of ways, laws affecting copyright, trademarks, privacy, libel, and contract rights determine the availability of source material, limiting the options of the filmmaker. The most important of these factors is copyright.[2] A major expansion of copyright law in recent years has turned copyright into a powerful source of protection for authors and artists in all media.

For independent filmmakers, copyright is both a blessing and a curse. It protects the filmmaker's ownership of the work that she is creating, but it also creates barriers to the source material that may be used to create that work. Filmmakers find themselves on both sides of copyright transactions: they need to acquire source material and to license their finished products.

1. Exclusive Rights Under Copyright

Copyright provides an author the rights of ownership for her original work. As owner of the copyrighted work, the copyright holder has the exclusive right to reproduce the work, publicly display the work, distribute copies of the work, publicly perform the work, and prepare *derivative works*.[3]

> A "derivative work" is a work based upon one or more preexisting works, such as a translation, musical arrangement, dramatization, fictionalization, motion picture version, sound recording, art reproduction, abridgment, condensation, or any other form in which a work may be recast, transformed, or adapted. A work consisting of editorial revisions, annotations, elaborations, or other modifications, which, as a whole, represent an original work of authorship, is a "derivative work."[4]

A film based on a preexisting copyrighted work—a novel, play, earlier film, etc.—is considered a derivative work. For example, the Hitchcock thriller *Rear Window* is a derivative work based on the short story "It Had to Be Murder" by Cornell Woolrich.[5] The filmed version of *My Fair Lady* is an adaptation of the Broadway musical of the same name by Lerner and Loewe, which was itself based on the George Bernard Shaw play *Pygmalion*.[6]

The various exclusive rights of the copyright holder may be licensed separately to others. For example, the author of the short story "The Paleontologist" licensed the first publication of the story to a science fiction magazine, but retained all other rights, including the rights to any filmed version of the story. The author could then choose to sell the movie rights to a filmmaker at a later date. The scope of the license depends on the language used in the contract, as discussed in chapter 5 (p. 80).

A license may be given free of charge, but more typically the copyright holder will require a fee in the form of an immediate payment, the right to receive some percentage of the proceeds from the film, or some combination thereof. An author could sell the movie rights to his short story for a fee such as $5,000 and 1 percent of the gross profits of the film. If the filmmaker agrees to these terms, the short story author will sign a license agreement that transfers the film rights in exchange for the agreed-upon payment.

If the author is granting exclusive rights to use the copyrighted work, the assignment must be in writing, dated, and signed.[7] By law, nonexclusive permission may be granted either orally or in writing, but the film-maker will find that exhibitors and distributors will insist on written documentation for each copyright assignment, license, or release. Every written license should include a signature and date.

The need to acquire permission for the use of source materials goes well beyond simply licensing the short story or comic book on which the film is based. Every piece of set decoration that includes copyrighted material should be used only if the filmmaker has acquired a written release. The written form of the agreement creates solid documentation of the transaction. As will be discussed in chapter 13 (p. 243), if documentary filmmakers record actual events instead of creating the situations they film, they have much more latitude in filming the copyrighted background images on T-shirts, posters, and billboards. The creators of fictional works may have far less flexibility.

On the other side of the coin, as copyright holder on the film she creates, the filmmaker possesses the exclusive rights of performance and display. This allows her to control who may exhibit the finished film. This exclusive right may be sold to a distributor, and further limited in any fashion the filmmaker and distributor agree upon. The limits may be geographical, so the distributor obtains the right to exhibit the film only in a particular country, state, or city; they may be time-based, so the contract lasts for only a short period; or they may be based on the medium, so one distributor is licensed to exhibit the film in theaters while a second is selected for DVD/Blu-ray sales and a third for the Internet distribution.

In practice, this means the filmmaker may choose to allow an Internet site a short trial exhibition, limited in writing to a stated period of time, such as one month, as a way to see if there is any interest from DVD, broadcast, or even theatrical distributors in the United States or throughout the world. The one-month trial, run without publicity, may serve as an inexpensive method of distributing advance copies of the film to possible purchasers. When the trial period ends, the filmmaker can either renew the contract or sell the rights to others, depending on the response of potential distributors and the public.

2. The Term of U.S. Copyright and the Public Domain

Copyright provides only limited rights to published works. Copyrights in works created after January 1, 1978, last for 70 years after the author's death, or for 95 years if the author is a corporation. For any work created before that date, the time period varies depending on the date the work was first published and the laws applicable. For example, all published works more than 95 years old have fallen into the *public domain,* the term used for anything that has had its copyright expire or was never copyrighted. Anything less than 95 years old must be carefully screened before it is assumed to be in the public domain.[8]

Congress has gradually extended the length of copyright over time. The last extension, known as the Sonny Bono Copyright Term Extension Act, added 20 years to the length of copyrights for works that had not already fallen into the public domain. Before this act, the length of copyrights for works created before 1978 had been extended to 75 years. After 1998, the term became 95 years. This means that works 75 years old in 1998 are in the public domain—all works published in or before 1923 are free for use in the United States without copyright protection. Any work that was published beginning in 1924 may still have been protected by copyright when the term was extended, in which case the work will retain copyright protection until at least 2019.

Because the length of copyright has only recently been increased, extra care must be taken to determine whether a work is covered by copyright. Before substantial investment is made in a public domain work, the history of the copyright should be analyzed.

In addition, copyright protection has been expanded in length and scope in many other countries. As a result, there is no absolute guarantee that a particular work is in the public domain worldwide no matter how old. While famous works such as published novels by Charles Dickens or Cervantes are clearly in the public domain and free for all filmmakers to adapt, most works published in the 20th century and unpublished materials potentially hundreds of years older may remain protected by copyright in the United States or abroad.

Plays by Shakespeare are in the public domain because they were written before copyright existed. Similarly, a play such as George Bernard Shaw's *Pygmalion* (made into a number of films and adapted for the musical *My Fair Lady*) is now in the public domain because the play's copyright expired in 1988 in both the United States and Great Britain.[9] Once a copyright has expired in the United States and abroad, the filmmaker is free to utilize that material as the source or basis for his film.

3. Copyright as a Barrier to the Film

While copyright is the primary source of protection for filmmakers, it is also a curse. Many potential sources for material also are copyrighted. For the independent filmmaker, the ability to use public domain material has tremendous advantages. The material is free. There is no need to ask permission to use the material. There are no delays waiting for a response to the request. The material can be altered without the need for any additional consent.

For some materials—particularly unpublished works or those written by foreign authors—the reliance on the public domain will always include a significant amount of risk. For example, a novel may have fallen into the public domain in the United States but may still be protected by copyright in another country, such as Canada or France. Unfortunately, there are no central registries of copyrights, so the status of a novel published in Canada, Europe, or elsewhere in the world must be researched in each country. In Europe, the situation is particularly complex, because the European Union member countries are required to extend the greatest protection to any European citizen that any other member country provides. As a result, copyrights that might otherwise have fallen into the public domain in those countries with shorter copyright terms are now automatically extended to the longer German copyright period of life of the author plus 70 years. As a general rule, therefore, a European work cannot be assumed to be in the public domain unless it has been more than 70 years since the death of the author. For any other work, expensive and time-consuming research must be conducted to determine the status of the copyright. To limit this expense somewhat, the filmmaker may wish to limit the research to the most important major foreign film markets, such as Canada, England, France, Spain, Italy, Japan, and Mexico.

Despite their limitations, public domain plays in particular serve as a valuable source for independent filmmaking because the story, dramatic structure, characters, and many other literary elements are provided for the filmmaker. Translating public domain plays into film may serve as an excellent method of learning filmmaking, creating a solid self-education program for the filmmaking student.

4. Subject Matter of Copyright

Copyright ownership covers, with limited exceptions, "original works of authorship fixed in any tangible medium of expression."[10] *Fixation* is merely the requirement that the expression be recorded in some manner. It can be written, recorded, videotaped, filmed, digitized, or fixed in an entirely new way. Screenplays, novels, and all writings are fixed as soon as the words are typed into a computer's memory or written on paper. A stand-up comedian's act is not protected by copyright unless he writes it out or records his performance. (A written recording, however, can be in shorthand.) An improvisational rehearsal process is not protected unless the stage manager's notes carefully record the session, or the session is videotaped. Sheet music is sufficient to protect a new musical score, and a detailed choreographer's notation will be enough to protect a new dance. There is no requirement that the copyrighted work display a copyright symbol (©) or other notice of copyright.[11]

5. Ideas

Copyright does not protect the underlying idea or concept, however, only the expression of such an idea.[12] In practice, this means that basic plots, themes, and general subjects are not protected by copyright. No one can own "boy meets girl," since the idea is the basis for thousands of plots. But the written or filmed story of one such boy and girl, including the description of scenes, the dialogue, and the narration, is protected by copyright once it has been fixed on paper or in digital memory.

The line between the idea and the expression of an idea is often a difficult one to conceptualize. Dialogue, unless it comes from trial transcripts or other public domain sources, is invariably copyrightable expression, but copyright covers more than just a film's dialogue. Stopping a runaway bus is an idea. Add well-developed characters, a number of plot twists, and interesting locations, and it becomes the specific expression behind the movie *Speed*. A man-made monster run amok is an idea. Add a struggling scientist, his love interest, and unsolved local murders, and it remains an idea; *Frankenstein, Dr. Jekyll and Mr. Hyde, The Hulk,* and many others fit the bill. Specific characters and plot twists that are unique to the story and its characters help transform the idea into protected expression.

6. Other Matters Not Protected by Copyright

In addition to ideas, copyright does not cover facts, historical information, titles, the typeface that may appear in the film's credits, or short phrases such as "I'll be back," "I've got a bad feeling about this," or "Hasta la vista, baby." Any filmmaker is free to use them without fear of copyright violations. The Robert Wise movie *The Hindenburg,* based on the destruction of the famous German zeppelin, violated no copyright, even though the historical information it dramatized was first published as a rather speculative conspiracy theory instead of an official statement of fact.[13] The same is true of factually based movies about the sinking of the *Titanic,* the assassinations of President Kennedy and Malcolm X, and the many other historical dramas.

C. Other Legal Limitations on Source Material

In addition to the laws of copyright, there are a number of other legal concepts that limit the free use of source material. Most of these limitations can be overcome if permission is granted from the rights holder. Whether substantial payment is necessary for the permission will depend on the nature of the rights sought, the size of the film being made, and the relationship between the rights holder and the filmmaker.

1. Trademarks

Trademarks are words or symbols that identify the goods or services of a business in commerce. They range from simple product names such as Diet Coke®, to identifying marks such as the roar of the MGM lion or the pink color of Dow Corning roof insulation. Trademarked products are often licensed for use in films, providing the filmmaker free access to the product along with permission to film it. Increasingly, many product manufacturers will pay for the opportunity to have their products featured.

Unauthorized use of another's trademark is a potential problem for film-makers, but it is not automatically prohibited. Fair use and free speech doctrines require that the filmmaker be given some flexibility in projecting his message. Both state and federal law, however, protect trademarks from *disparagement,* meaning that some forms of embarrassment or criticism are prohibited, which could provide the trademark holder a basis to sue for damages or to stop the release of the film. Chapter 12 (p. 226) provides a more detailed explanation of how to obtain the necessary rights to use trademarked products or to reduce the potential for legal disputes. If an unauthorized trademark is to be featured in an independent film, it must be used carefully, in consultation with the filmmaker's attorneys.

2. Misappropriation and Idea Protection

Legal protection for ideas remains a controversial topic in intellectual property law. Fueled by high-technology fields and issues of trade secrecy, the legal limits on when someone is liable for the use of another's idea have yet to be clearly defined.[14]

Filmmakers are pitched ideas from friends, family members, and restaurant staff on a constant basis. The law provides that an idea is not protected by copyright, and unless it is the subject of an enforceable contract between the parties, a person has no obligation to pay for an idea. On the other hand, if the filmmaker has done something to suggest that "if I use your idea, I'll pay you for it," then the later use of that idea might be subject to a legitimate contractual claim.

The safest way to hear new ideas is to be sure a release is signed, clearly stating that while the filmmaker will not violate any copyright in the submission, many similar ideas are often presented, and the filmmaker cannot provide compensation for any ideas. For the writer, the safest suggestion is to refrain from sharing ideas until they have been developed sufficiently to enjoy copyright protection.

3. Defamation

A statement is defamatory if "it tends so to harm the reputation of another as to lower him in the estimation of the community or to deter third persons from associating or dealing with him."[15] At common law, a statement was defamatory if it held one out for hatred, ridicule, or contempt. Only a living person may be defamed; once he has died, his heirs may not pursue the claim. A related doctrine known as *trade libel* applies to businesses.

To be defamatory in the United States, the person alleging the defamation must prove that the statement is both false and harmful, that it pertains to the person suing, and that it has been made available to someone other than the person claiming to be defamed. Defamation requires only that the defamatory statements was shared with at least one person, so it can be done orally or through publication in a script, on a Web site, through a letter or e-mail, or via some other recorded form. Republishing a false defamatory statement will give rise to a new claim for defamation. As a result, a filmmaker is responsible for any defamatory material in the work he creates, licenses, or borrows.

Filmmakers face different legal challenges depending on the nature of the party who objects to the characterization. Public officials, such as the president or state officeholders, and public figures such as O. J. Simpson or Ralph Nader, can only win a defamation lawsuit if the filmmaker is found to have published defamatory material intentionally—with knowledge it was false—or recklessly—with reckless disregard toward the truth or falsity of the statements.[16]

A person is considered a *public official* only if he or she holds a significant public office. Merely being a public employee is not sufficient. The person must have some position of influence or importance or be subject to ongoing public scrutiny—for instance, most elected officials and others who are in the position to direct public policy. Although the U.S. Supreme Court itself has been somewhat vague as to the standard, other courts have developed a series of tests. In California, for example, a four-part test has been used:

A "public official" is someone in the government's employ who:
1.) has, or appears to the public to have, substantial responsibility for or control over the conduct of governmental affairs;
2.) usually enjoys significantly greater access to the mass media and therefore a more realistic opportunity to contradict false statements than the private individual;
3.) holds a position in government which has such apparent importance that the public has an independent interest in the person's qualifications and performance beyond the general public interest in the qualifications and performance of all government employees; and

4.) holds a position which invites public scrutiny and discussion of the person holding it entirely apart from the scrutiny and discussion occasioned by the particular controversy.[17]

The purpose of this test is to distinguish the rank-and-file employees from those government officials who are in the public eye.

The same standards have been extended to famous individuals and those who actively engage in public discourse on controversial matters. They have made themselves *public figures,* subject to the same legal standards for defamation as public officials. As one court explained, "public figures are those who command sufficient continuing public interest by their position or their purposeful activity amounting to a thrusting of their personality into the 'vortex' of an important public policy and have a realistic opportunity to counteract false statements."[18]

Many interesting films based on true events are not about public officials or public figures, however. Instead, they deal with "little people" who change the system or serve as whistleblowers. Many of the characters in films like *Norma Rae, Schindler's List,* and *Erin Brockovich* are *private figures* whose stories deeply impact us all. If the film is about a private individual involved in some matter of public interest, then the filmmaker can be liable if he is merely negligent in failing to ascertain the truth[19] or in the manner in which the truth was altered to fit the dramatic needs of the film.[20]

Finally, the person suing the filmmaker for defamation must prove that the statements or depictions represent her in a manner that is untrue and that the depiction is harmful to the person's reputation. If the jury believes the film is accurate, the filmmaker will not lose the lawsuit. If the film is inaccurate and harmful and the person suing is a private figure, the filmmaker will be held accountable for the damages if the research or depiction was made without reasonable care regarding the facts. If the person suing is an official or public figure, the research or depiction must be the result of intentional lies or reckless disregard for the truth. A filmmaker should not be held liable for honest mistakes involving public officials or public figures.

One particularly insidious form of libel is to falsely attribute quotes to a person. The Supreme Court has held that otherwise unobjectionable statements can be deemed libelous when they are transformed into quotes.[21] When a film character is based on a living person, the dialogue sometimes includes statements that were originally made by critics of that person, but are now portrayed as self-deprecating comments made by the character. This practice can increase the amount of material in the film to which objections may be made.

Fictionalization may also result in the creation of *composite characters*—fictional characters that embody attributes of a number of live individuals. Because of the requirement that the statement be of or concerning the person claiming defamation, a common practice is to create fictional characters to stand in for unsavory conduct that may have been undertaken by real people. If the fictional character or composite character is identifiable as a real person involved in the situation, then the fictionalization only adds to the potential for liability.[22] This seems to occur most frequently when the character's name bears some resemblance to the living person's name.

Fortunately for filmmakers, U.S. courts tend to disfavor defamation awards. This may be a result of their strong respect for the First Amendment—but it may also reflect their respect for the detailed investigative process that major motion picture studios and television networks follow for their docudramas and other fact-based works. Needless to say, the latter will not extend to guerrilla and other independent filmmakers shooting on-the-fly films on shoestring budgets. For this reason, it is vital that when producing a fact-based motion picture, the filmmaker document every step taken to verify the truth of the story before creating the script and shooting the film. As discussed below, if the people involved in true stories sign agreements with the filmmaker, they are less likely to sue for defamation, but unless every person depicted in a fact-based story has signed a release, the risk of a defamation claim remains.

Filmmakers should also be mindful that the United States is much more protective of the rights of free expression than other countries. The standards for defamation and libel are very different in Europe and Asia, so a project that is not libelous in the United States may still draw defamation claims abroad. Even if the filmmaker intentionally avoids distribution in libel-friendly countries, the sale of DVDs on Amazon or other international Web sites may provide a sufficient basis for a lawsuit in a foreign jurisdiction—particularly if it is the home country of the person offended.

4. False Light Privacy Invasion

The common law doctrine of false light creates liability for invasion of privacy if a published work provides a person with "unreasonable and highly objectionable publicity that attributes to him characteristics, conduct, or beliefs that are false," and thereby causes that person to be "placed before the public in a false position."[23] The depiction may be laudatory, but if it is highly objectionable and false, it may be actionable even if it is not defamatory. A good example would be a story that incorrectly attributed a heroic self-defense shooting to a particular police officer. Since shooting in self-defense is not illegal or immoral, the claim would not be defamatory, but it may still be deemed highly offensive to the officer and a reasonable person, depending on the situation. A docudrama that falsely connected a New Jersey firefighter to the World Trade Center rescue effort could result in injury to his career as he struggled to live up to the false impression caused by the suggestion. If he suffered financial or other damage as a result, he may be entitled to recover them from the film company.

False light has evolved into a close approximation of defamation for statements that are injurious but not so contemptuous as to be defamatory. But unlike alleged libelous statements made against private persons, false light claims require intent or reckless disregard of the truth rather than mere negligence.[24]

5. Matters of Private Concern and Intrusion into Seclusion

Not all statements have to be false to be actionable. The right to privacy goes further than defamation or false light to protect a private individual from having unfavorable information published or presented to the public, even if the information is true.

The right to privacy is limited in scope. It will not protect either a public figure or a private individual if the information is newsworthy, but the law does offer limited protection "to keep a man's business his own."[25] Under common law, an individual may be entitled to damages if unauthorized, highly offensive details of that person's private life are widely disseminated.[26] A filmmaker can be held liable for broadly publishing information about a subject's physical or mental health issues, identifying the individual involved—or even for creating a well-meaning public service notice, intended to promote social responsibility, that identifies a family in dire financial need.

Generally, if a person is out in public, she cannot claim to have any protections for intrusion into seclusion. But this may overstate the situation, and filmmakers should be respectful of "private" public areas, such as locker rooms or bathrooms, and be wary of using cameras to zoom in on unblinded windows. In such cases, the defense that the filmmakers themselves were in public may not withstand the growing protections of personal privacy.

6. Publicity Rights

The right of publicity is the right to control the commercial exploitation of a person's identity, name, or likeness.[27] This right has also been extended to protect a person's performance.[28] Publicity differs from privacy because it recognizes that individuals have the right to make money from their good name. New York, California, and many other states protect publicity rights very broadly. The California statute is representative:

> Any person who knowingly uses another's name, voice, signature, photograph, or likeness, in any manner, on or in products, merchandise, or goods, or for purposes of advertising or selling, or soliciting purchases of, products, merchandise, goods, or services, without such person's prior consent . . . shall be liable for any damages sustained by the person or persons injured as a result thereof.[29]

The law limits publicity rights to the selling or advertising of goods or services. These protections do not extend to the editorial content of newspapers, magazines, literature, film, television, radio, or DVDs, which is protected by the First Amendment. A newspaper could run an article about Britney Spears and illustrate it with a photo of Spears eating a famous brand of popcorn without obtaining her permission.[30] On the other hand, advertising the popcorn using the same photos is constrained by publicity rights; the newspaper could not run that picture of Spears in an ad paid for by the popcorn manufacturer without Spears's consent. Similarly, while a Web site may be analogous to a publishing venture with

First Amendment protection, courts have recognized that a site used to promote the goods or services of an organization can be subject to publicity rights protections.[31]

Further, most states do not just afford publicity protection to famous people.[32] For instance, if a photograph shows recognizable individuals from corporate events or panels, it creates the impression of association with a company's products or services. When that photograph is used to advertise or otherwise commercially benefit the product or service, permission must be obtained from each person who is identifiable in the photograph.

Publicity rights should not interfere with a filmmaker's interest in making a biography or even of introducing real persons into fictional drama. Unfortunately, publicity rights law varies greatly from state to state, so there is some ambiguity as to the risks that might arise. Because of this ambiguity, insurance companies and distributors are sometimes quite conservative about these potential risks and demand that anyone who is identifiable provide a written release. As a result, filmmakers must anticipate not only the legal limitation placed on their expression but also the additional reservations that may come from distributors or insurance carriers.

D. Literary Tools: Treatments, Storyboards, and Screenplays

Movies have been sold to distributors based solely on the posters shown at film markets, but more commonly, films are developed using treatments, storyboards, and screenplays. These are tools for the filmmaker to capture the story before it is shot on film, to communicate with the investors, buyers, cast, and crew, and to keep all parties wedded to a common vision for the project. Ultimately, however, no matter how much time and effort is placed in their development, they are merely tools, scaffolding to allow the movie to be made.

These tools may be created in any order, depending on the filmmaker's needs and the audience for whom the tool is intended. For example, investors often find a full screenplay to be difficult to read and understand; they may respond better to a short synopsis rather than a lengthy treatment. For a highly visual story, the storyboards may communicate more than any other tool.

1. Treatments and Synopses

The essence of the motion picture is usually described in a *synopsis* of 3 to 10 pages. This document simply introduces the movie's plot, characters, and theme. In contrast, a proper *treatment* of a script is typically an extensive scene-by-scene narrative summary that often runs one-third the length of the finished screenplay. Investors and others often use the term "treatment" to describe both this detailed summary and the briefer synopsis.

The synopsis serves as a teaser, drafted to pique the curiosity of the reader and create a hunger for the screenplay. It will be used to introduce the film to prospective investors, production companies, performers, and crew. Because the synopsis is the document most heavily relied upon by investors, it has more impact on the project than anything other than the completed film.

The treatment, on the other hand, serves more practical purposes. Writers will consult it while revising the screenplay, and it can help producers and department heads to visualize the budgetary implications of the project. A good exercise is to continue to update the treatment to match the screenplay as it progresses.

Tremendous care must be made not to distribute the synopsis or treatment too freely or hastily. Filmmakers seldom have a chance to present a film project twice. If an early synopsis or treatment is drafted in a rush, or if it is written by a producer or other participant who does not possess the ability to capture the essence of the script, it may end the interest of a potential investor.

2. Storyboards

Storyboards provide a scene-by-scene visual outline of the motion picture, almost like a comic book. Because of their visual impact and the increasing ease with which they can be produced via computer-based imaging, storyboards have become more and more common as a tool to communicate with both investors and the creative team being assembled for the film. At the same time, well-crafted storyboards are still time-consuming and expensive to create. They work best for science fiction or other genre films in which the imagery is exotic or expressionistic. For films that are more realistic in style—for instance, a movie set in a New York apartment—storyboards may not be worth the expense.

3. Screenplays

The screenplay is the most important tool for making the film, serving as road map, guide, and final authority. The screenplay must lay out the entire story, including all the dialogue, action, sets, scenery, and characters. A typical screenplay runs between 90 and 120 pages in length.

Screenplays follow a very stylized and specific format, to which even the independent filmmaker should adhere. Innovation should be seen on the screen, not in the page layout. Appendix A (p. 345) provides an overview of screenplay formatting, and many other guides have written on the subject. In addition, computer programs such as Final Draft or Movie Magic provide helpful tools to write in the correct style—but once a writer learns the basics of the screenplay format, any word processor can generate a properly formatted script.

A screenplay must serve many roles, depending on the reader:

Literature
First and foremost, a great screenplay will work as a piece of writing. Like a short story, it must capture the atmosphere of each scene with only a few words. The merits of the story, the characters, and the structure must be strong, powerful, and believable. This is true of even the silliest of parody films. If the script does not make for a compelling story, the film is unlikely to succeed.

Character list
The screenplay must include enough information about the characters that casting decisions and costume choices can be made. The script should also tell the actors about the characters they are portraying and provide them information and tools to develop those characters.

Visual guide
Since film is a visual medium, the screenplay should create snapshots of each scene that could translate directly into storyboards. (For a film

that actually utilizes storyboards, the artist will draw them based on the screenplay.) The screenplay creates the visual style that controls all the other visual elements of the project.

Screen stopwatch

The screenplay is often used as a guide to timing the film. As a rule of thumb, one page in the script equals one minute on the screen. While this may not work page for page, a 120-page script translates fairly consistently into a two-hour film. It's not an absolute rule, but the principle is sufficiently common that it should be kept in mind when structuring the screenplay.

Production clock

Another rule of thumb for the timing of traditional feature film scripts is that one page of script equals half a day's filming. Television scripts shoot five pages a day. While digital filmmaking does not yet have any established guides, once a pace is established, it is often followed closely. The writer can improve the accuracy of time estimates by using more text to describe longer, more difficult shots and briefer language to describe shorter, simpler setups.

Calling card

Finally, every actor, investor, production company, or other person who considers becoming involved with the film will use the script as a method of evaluating the project. The script becomes the point of introduction for many of the key participants. It becomes part of the contractual relationship, binding the filmmaker to deliver a movie that is substantially similar to the script.

Because the screenplay plays so many different parts in the filmmaking process, before any other work is done, the screenplay must be substantially completed. While stories abound of movie projects in which the script is hastily rewritten on the set, this practice wastes time and increases editing costs. The independent filmmaker does not have this luxury.

This should not suggest that the finished screenplay will exactly match what appears on the screen. A host of changes, compromises, and new ideas will force the movie to evolve from the original script, but it remains critical that the script be as strong as possible before shooting begins. Even if the choice is made to improvise the story, a script remains important to establishing the dramatic structure, the locations, the emphasis, and the relative timing of scenes. The only obvious exception would be a documentary, but even many documentaries are well structured and partially scripted before shooting begins.

E. Protecting the Filmmaker's Property

As the concept of the film is developed into a screenplay and eventually into the film, the filmmaker must protect the material from theft. For screenplays and treatments, protection will come from federal copyright law as well as from well-drafted contracts. The Writers Guild of America also provides an evidentiary role.

1. Copyright Protection for the Unpublished Screenplay

As described earlier in this chapter, federal copyright law protects a script or film as soon as it is written down or otherwise recorded. As an unpublished work, a screenplay does not have to be registered with the U.S. Copyright Office. Registration costs only $45, however, and should be filed as soon as there is a hint of difficulty with anyone involved with the project. The money spent on the copyright filing buys a strong negotiating chip.

Generally speaking, it is also a good idea to put a copyright notice on the work. The notice is only necessary for a published work to be registered, but it may serve as a good reminder to discourage theft even when used on an unpublished work. A proper notice includes the copyright symbol ©, or the word *copyright,* the year of the copyright, and the name of the copyright holder. For example, the notice on this book reads "© 2009 Jon M. Garon."

Proper registration creates a presumption of a valid copyright. The Copyright Office describes the simple process:

To register a claim in a dramatic work, submit the following to the Library of Congress, Copyright Office, 101 Independence Avenue S.E., Washington, DC 20599-6000:

1.) a completed and signed Form PA

    2.) a nonrefundable filing fee of $45 made payable to the Register of
         Copyrights

    3.) if unpublished, one copy of the work; if published, two complete
         copies of the best edition of the work

    4.) for a script, the copy may be a manuscript, printed copy, a film video
         recording, or a phonorecord

All of the elements must be submitted in the same package or envelope. Registration of the work is normally effective on the day all of the material is received in the Copyright Office in acceptable form, although your certificate of registration may not be mailed until 6 months after receipt of your submission.[33]

Similar rules apply to copyright registration of the completed film. See Appendix B, circular 45 (p. 353) for a discussion of the deposit of the finished film.

2. Writers Guild Registration

The Writers Guild of America (Writers Guild, or WGA) has a system by which a treatment or screenplay can be placed in deposit, to serve as evidence if there is a dispute over its authorship. For $20, any treatment, television script, or screenplay may be registered. The Writers Guild will also accept stage plays and other written ideas prepared for audiovisual works. Registration lasts for five years and may be renewed.

    The Writers Guild registration does not replace copyright, but it does serve to create evidentiary proof of the existence of the work as of the date of registration. When the submission is received by the Writers Guild, it is sealed in an envelope and the date and time are recorded. The Writers Guild then returns a numbered receipt to the author that serves as the official documentation of registration. The work remains in a sealed envelope that the WGA can forward to a court, unopened, as evidence. The Writers Guild also accepts electronic deposits, providing a similar process for digital submissions by authors.

    Many independent film companies that accept unsolicited submissions insist that the Writers Guild registration number be marked on the script, so that there is documentary proof of the material submitted.

3. Film Titles

Although neither copyright law nor the Writers Guild protects titles, the Motion Picture Association of America (MPAA) provides a title registry for its members and contracting film companies. Film distributors must avoid duplicating the names already taken on the MPAA registry. To consult the registry, the filmmaker must sign the Non-Member Title Registration Agreement. The fees for membership in the annual subscription agreement are $300 annually plus $200 for the cost of registering 1 to 10 titles. The proposed titles are distributed to all members and members may file objections to the use of titles. Since titles are often changed by distributors, the filmmaker may not need to check with the MPAA prior to production, but if a title is derived from a memorable piece of dialogue or significant action in the movie, then it may be wise to know of any potential conflicts before it is filmed.

Availability in the MPAA system should not be the only review. Motion picture titles are really trademarks (see p. 60), and may compete with similar trademarks in other literary works, including novels, songs, albums, and video or computer games. On the eve of the marketing campaign, the filmmaker or the distributor should enlist the service of an attorney or otherwise conduct a trademark search. One useful source for such a search is Thomson Compumark. The company will provide a comprehensive trademark search, including the use in film titles and in other media. Such a search costs between $200 and $500.

Contracts

THROUGHOUT THE FILMMAKING process, the filmmaker will negotiate and enter into a wide range of contracts, but the entire process begins with the agreement to purchase the literary rights to the story or the original screenplay. The terms of that agreement will set the stage for the financing, employment, and many other agreements that follow.

While each agreement has its own particular terms, the purchase agreement can serve as a model for negotiating and structuring the other contracts. The parties to any of the film company's agreements are likely to be engaged with each other throughout the life of the film production, and possibly for decades as the film continues to be shown. The negotiating strategy should take into account the long-term nature of the parties' relationships.

The goal of the agreement should be to provide each party with what he needs to be successful. All information should be as accurate as the filmmaker can provide. The film company should build professional and economic incentives for the other parties into each contract to encourage the success of the film. This does not mean that the filmmaker should be unduly "soft" or overly generous, but rather she should understand that there are many reasons people support independent films and incorporate those motivations into the contracts. Payments, residuals, credits, thankyous, DVDs, screening invitations, and other incentives should all be utilized by the filmmaker to help make the movie possible. When approached

from this perspective, negotiating contracts becomes much simpler and
success is much easier to achieve.

A. Purchasing a Literary Property

To obtain the right to make a movie out of an existing short story, novel,
comic book, or play, the filmmaker must license the movie rights from the
author or rights holder. Once the proper copyright holder has been identified, a license must be negotiated that awards the filmmaker the right to
produce and distribute the motion picture. The nature of the license may
vary significantly depending on the type of source material, its commercial value, and its age.

1. Identification of the Copyright Holder

The first step is one of the most important: confirming who actually owns
the interests needed by the filmmaker. This process is not always as
straightforward as it seems: the apparent rights holder may not in fact have
the authority to grant the necessary license. While it is standard practice
for the license to include warranties from the seller of the literary work
that he is the owner of the work and has full authority to sell the rights,
the filmmaker should take steps in advance to avoid any problems.

For example, if a short story author transferred the film rights to the
publisher of the book collection in which it was included, then an agreement between that short story author and the filmmaker will fail to grant
the filmmaker the rights needed for the film. The filmmaker may have a
valid legal claim against the short story author, but that will be little solace
when the film project grinds to a halt and litigation begins.

If the work is based on literary characters that appear in more than one
work, the filmmaker should research the origin of those characters and be
sure either that the characters are in the public domain or that the seller
of the works is the owner of those characters and has not sold those rights
to other parties. This may be particularly important for a comic book, since
characters may have moved from one work to another. If the comic book
publisher failed to properly purchase the characters, then it may not be
the sole copyright holder of the literary property in question.

Licensing a film based on a Broadway musical will also raise complex ownership issues. The musical may have three authors: the "book" writer who created the story and dialogue, the composer who wrote the songs, and the lyricist who wrote the lyrics for those songs. Depending on the agreement between the book writer, composer, and lyricist, the group may operate by majority vote or may require unanimous consent to transfer the film rights. In addition, the producer of the musical will have acquired some interest in the motion picture production.

The filmmaker must identify everyone with a stake in the project to ensure that the license covers all possible claimants and that he will not have to meet any surprise obligations. While it may be preferable to have an attorney experienced in copyright searches research the rights holders, this is an area where some opportunity for self-help is available. The Copyright Office provides guidance and information on copyright searches in one of its circulars—circular 22, which is included in appendix B (p. 359).

The filmmaker should first find out as much information as he can from the work itself. For example, if the work is a novel, he should look up the name of the author, publisher, location of the first publication, and first publication date. This may be more difficult for a short story, since publishers commonly place a copyright notice for the entire work rather than separate notices for each short story. Nonetheless, the more information the filmmaker can obtain from the source, the more efficient the subsequent searches will be.

A good second step is to check the Copyright Office's Catalog of Copyright Entries, which is available online in many public libraries throughout the United States. The catalog will reflect all the information that was given when a work was registered for copyright; unfortunately, it will not provide much detail beyond that. It does not include information on assignments and transfers, and since film rights are transferred by assignment, the most critical information will not appear. But, once again, the information that is available will speed up the subsequent searches.

Publishers may also serve as an excellent source of information. Because publishers of books and music collect their author's royalties, they often have an ongoing relationship with the copyright holders. In addition, the Ransom Center at the University of Texas at Austin has created the WATCH File (Writers, Artists, and Their Copyright Holders), an online database containing contact information for American and English authors at http://tyler.hrc.utexas.edu. This ongoing project should prove to be a very useful resource for independent filmmakers.

The last step in the copyright investigation is to have a professional search conducted. The Copyright Office can do the cheapest search itself. The office charges an hourly fee, so the more information the filmmaker can provide, the cheaper and quicker the search. To improve the search, the Copyright Office suggests the following information be provided:

- the title of the work, with any possible variants
- the names of the authors, including possible pseudonyms
- the name of the probable copyright owner, which may be the publisher or producer
- the approximate year the work was published or registered
- the type of work involved (book, play, musical composition, sound recording, photograph, etc.)
- for a work originally published as a part of a periodical or collection, the title of that publication and any other information, such as the volume or issue number, to help identify it
- the registration number or any other copyright data

Motion pictures are often based on other works such as books or serialized contributions to periodicals or other composite works. *If you desire a search for an underlying work or for music from a motion picture, you must specifically request such a search. You must also identify the underlying works and music and furnish the specific titles, authors, and approximate dates of these works.*[1]

If the search shows no assignments, it is time to contact the copyright holder. On the other hand, if the search shows that there has been a transfer, then a lawyer may be necessary to determine whether the rights might still be available.

2. Negotiations for the Motion Picture Rights

Once the filmmaker identifies the owner of the film rights, the next step is to enter into negotiations to acquire those rights. If possible, approach the author directly instead of communicating through an agent; the author may be more flexible on pricing and other terms. Find out if the movie rights are available and what the author wants for them.

This begins the process of negotiating the *literary property agreement,* which may be the first contract for the movie. It may mean buying the rights outright or taking out an *option* on the rights. An option agreement provides for all the terms of the purchase of the rights, but the prospective buyer makes only a small down payment in exchange for the exclusive right to complete the transaction during a specified option period. In other words, the filmmaker may pay $100 for the exclusive right to purchase the film rights at any point during the upcoming year. The filmmaker exercises the option by paying the full purchase price as specified in the agreement.

The specifics of the project will determine whether the filmmaker chooses to purchase the literary rights outright or negotiate an option agreement. A common but misguided practice is to negotiate only the option portion of an agreement, leaving the rest of the agreement to be negotiated at a future date. Invariably, any terms left to future negotiations will grow into problems that can disrupt the filmmaking process. They may even lead to disastrous outcomes at the time the option is going to be exercised. By failing to identify which rights are being acquired and the exact payment terms, the filmmaker may find that he cannot reach an agreement with the literary rights holder. The consequences of not reaching an agreement go up dramatically once the filmmaker is financially committed to the project and has begun filming. The filmmaker should not put off negotiations until a time when he is at a strategic disadvantage.

The negotiations generally focus on the following terms:

- the scope of rights
- the participation of the literary property rights holder
- the risk of noncompletion of the filmmaker's project
- the discretion of the filmmaker
- the amount of money being paid for the rights

These negotiations will proceed differently for an independent filmmaker than for a studio production company. Typically, the studio would demand all rights of every kind from the literary property rights holder and absolute discretion over how those rights are exploited. In exchange, the cost of those rights can be expected to be much higher for a studio than for an independent filmmaker. In the latter case, the negotiations can better reflect the filmmaker's ability to make the film and the rights holder's interest in protecting her work.

a. The Scope of Rights

The filmmaker must acquire the right to use the literary property, whether it is a short story or an unwritten life story, in the particular film being developed. This is the absolute minimum scope of rights being sought, but it is better for the filmmaker to acquire rights that are more broadly defined than merely the right to use the story to make the particular film. First, many independent films are produced with poor production quality. If the story is compelling, the filmmaker may have the opportunity in the future to remake the film on a grander scale. The right to make a film does not include the remake rights unless the contract includes that right. Second, the studio film industry is financed by the success of sequels and prequels. Like the potential for remakes, the ability to expand the story by making prequels and sequels will increase the opportunities to sell the completed film. Third, the media in which the movie is made may not be film. Since independent "films" are often photographed digitally, any confusion over terminology should be removed early on. Fourth, the distribution format may change the project from a full-length motion picture to a series of short webisodes (see chapter 19, p. 340) or another format.

The best scope-of-rights clause states that "the filmmaker hereby acquires the exclusive right to exploit the [literary property] in any media now known or hereafter developed, including without limitation the right to make motion pictures, sequels, prequels, remakes, live, interactive, or episodic versions." In a separate sentence, the contract should also provide that "the filmmaker may produce and distribute the work using any media now known or hereafter developed." The first sentence says that the story can be captured using any technology or media. The second sentence provides that the film, TV show, or Internet broadcast can be sold, broadcast, or packaged in any fashion.

"Literary property" should also be broadly defined so that it includes any copyrighted work, characters, story, plot, theme, or action embodied in that property. In this way, the filmmaker exclusively owns the rights even to elements of the story that are not copyrightable. While this might not stop a third party from creating a similar plot, it will stop the author of the plot from recycling it into a competing project.

As mentioned above, with an independent film project it is possible to negotiate these terms to provide more limited rights for the filmmaker. The seller of the literary property may require it if the work is already being used in other media. The broader the scope of rights, however, the better for the filmmaker, because it reduces the chances of two or more similar projects competing in the market at the same time and gives the filmmaker a bigger bundle to sell to the distributor.

b. Participation of the Literary Property Rights Holder

In the studio setting, this consideration is rarely entertained. Like an uninvited extra cook, the seller of the literary property is often considered a threat to the project and is given very little chance to participate. For the independent filmmaker, however, the owner of the literary property may be a resource rather than a burden. This is particularly true if the film is based on true events. The participation of the rights holder may also provide some marketing and press opportunities. The cost for such access is greater interaction between the filmmaker and the person whose story is being adapted.

c. The Risk of Noncompletion of the Filmmaker's Project

Very few stories that are acquired by filmmakers are actually made into feature films. This is true in both the independent and the studio film industry. But rights holders are even more concerned about selling their rights to an independent filmmaker than to an established film company, since the rights holders generally receive less compensation for their rights from independent filmmakers, and independent films tend to receive less promotion. To overcome these limitations, the independent filmmaker should include specific provisions in the contract that allow the rights holder to reclaim his rights in the event the film is not made. This right—often referred to as the right of *reversion*—allows the rights holder to either reclaim all literary rights sold to the filmmaker or to transfer those rights to a new studio.

Under the typical studio conditions regarding reversion, the rights holder must return the money the filmmaker paid to secure the rights, and the new film production company must reimburse the filmmaker for the costs incurred in preparing the abortive film. The right of reversion often does not begin for five years following the sale of the literary rights to the studio. The studio approach may meet with a good deal of opposition and may not set the proper tone for the relationship the filmmaker is trying to develop.

For that reason, the independent filmmaker may elect to vary these terms in a number of ways. The rights can be returned to the rights holder without charge, or a reimbursement payment can be tied to the completion of the film adaptation by another company. This allows the rights holder to give the independent filmmaker a chance without making a decision that becomes financially impractical to fix.

The length of the reversion term can also be varied, but as long as some progress is being made, the term should continue to run. Independent film projects often start and stop for years, so the filmmaker should not promise that the movie will be completed in six months or the project is finished. Instead, the rights holder may give the filmmaker the rights to the material for one year, but if an agreed-upon amount of money is not raised, then the rights revert. If the money is raised, then the filmmaker has three years to begin principal photography. Once principal photography has begun, the rights are generally irrevocable.

The timing of any reversion should be based on the date when the rights are actually purchased by the filmmaker; it should not count the option period. For example, the deal could specify that the filmmaker pays an option amount of $1,000 per year for a maximum of two years. When the option is exercised, the filmmaker pays a purchase amount—say, $5,000—to complete the acquisition. At this point, the filmmaker is the owner of all film and media rights in the work. Additional payments are due at various stages of production—e.g., the start of principal photography and distribution. If principal photography does not commence within a particular time period (e.g., three more years), then a reversion provision would give the author the right to return the $5,000 and reclaim the rights to the work. Typically, the option payments are not required to be returned, but the filmmaker and rights holder can make any arrangement that meets their needs. This is just one example of a structure that balances the interests of the filmmaker and the rights holder.

Reversion provisions put pressure on the filmmaker while providing the rights holder some protection. Rights holders may be more willing to enter into a transaction or accept a lower price if they know the opportunity is less likely to be squandered on a languishing project. As such, reversion provisions reflect a compromise approach to the bargain that may benefit both parties.

d. The Discretion of the Filmmaker

The biggest advantage an independent filmmaker has over the studios is the ability to earn the trust of the literary rights holder. While the filmmaker generally wants unbridled discretion in telling the story, some rights holders will only make their material available to a sympathetic filmmaker, particularly if the material is based on true events. The filmmaker must negotiate before the work has begun to determine whether he is going to limit his control or discretion in the project by allowing the rights holder to observe, participate, or veto decisions of the filmmaker. The legal power to observe, participate, or veto should be given away very carefully. The filmmaker can provide the opportunity for the rights holder to observe and participate without contractually promising access, but if the contract provides for such access, the decision cannot be undone.

The filmmaker can grant other parties the right to review choices at any of various stages in the development of the film; participation can occur in the approval of casting, script, filming, or finished film. The right of approval is a valuable commodity, but it may allow the filmmaker to acquire rights to a story for which he otherwise could not outbid a studio.

e. The Amount of Money Being Paid for the Rights

Finally, the payment provisions can be structured in a multitude of ways. The more obvious arrangements include the following:

- outright cash payment at time of purchase
- partial cash payments at each stage of financing, production, and distribution
- deferred cash payment, paid out of financing
- deferred cash payment, paid out of distribution income
- percentages of gross distribution income received by the production company
- percentages of net distribution income received by the production company

These different payment schemes may be used singly or in combination. For example, the filmmaker may offer the rights holder a payment of $100 for the literary property, with an additional payment of $4,900 when (and if) the production company secures a specified amount of financing, as well as 1 percent of the gross income from all distribution income of the film. A token up-front payment often helps to inspire trust between the filmmaker and the rights holder, while deferred compensation allows the filmmaker to reduce the cost of making the film.

If the literary property is the screenplay itself, this technique is particularly attractive. It ties the screenwriter's financial interest to the completed film, since that is when the primary payments will occur, which may create an additional incentive for the writer's participation in revisions even if the money has run low.

3. Provisions of the Purchase Agreement

The purchase agreement gives the filmmaker the right to use[2] the literary material for any of the stated purposes, including making a film, television show, videotape, or anything the contract writer can think to include. For the filmmaker, the most important provisions for the literary purchase agreement are the following:

1. the grant of rights for the broadest form of license to make movies and related types of shows using any technology
2. the *representations and warranties,* or contractually binding promises that the author owns the material being licensed, that no one else has any right to the material, and that no other party has any interest in the transaction
3. the purchase price for the literary rights
4. any royalty or percentage of net profits or gross revenues
5. screen credit

If the seller of the rights is an author, that person may want to add terms such as:

1. the right to write the first (or more) drafts of the screenplay
2. the right or option to write any sequels, prequels, or television versions
3. terms reserving the rights to live stage versions, novelizations, and other writings

4. Option Agreement Provisions

The option agreement gives the filmmaker the power to buy the film rights to a movie in the future and stops the rights holder from selling the rights to anyone else during the option period. To be enforceable and useable, it must be more than an agreement to agree. All of the material terms and conditions of the literary purchase agreement must be included. Option agreements can range in length from 2 to 17 pages.

The option agreement is essentially a literary purchase agreement with a few additional provisions:

1. the length and starting date of the option period
2. the amount to be paid if the option is exercised and the literary property is purchased
3. the price of renewing the option, the length of the renewal, and the number of times the option can be renewed

In addition, the agreement should include a recital by the author that all the rights are available and have not previously been transferred. This recital will be of some help if the filmmaker cannot afford the copyright search immediately.

In the simplest case, for example, an author has a written a short story entitled "Rosebud, the Sled of Youth." The author ("Author") published the short story once in a small magazine, retaining all other rights in the work. The contract would state that the filmmaker ("Producer") is acquiring an exclusive option to all rights in the short story entitled "Rosebud, the Sled of Youth" (the "Work"). A different section of the agreement would provide that the Author retains the literary publishing rights to the Work. The option agreement would include a payment of $500 for the exclusive right to develop the Work as a film (or in any other media) for the next year and may be renewed for up to an additional three years by additional payments of $500. The Author would represent and warrant that he has all the rights to the Work and can sell the rights to the Producer.

As mentioned above, this option agreement would also include the final sale price and the payment schedule for the film. There should be no clause that says that payments will be mutually agreed upon; all the obligations must be decided in the option agreement. Otherwise the filmmaker may find that he cannot reach an agreement with the literary rights holder when he has finally raised enough money to exercise the purchase option.

While option agreements are generally preferred over literary purchase agreements because less money must be spent initially, a tremendous amount of money may be saved by purchasing the rights in full up front. Many rights holders will accept $5,000 in hand rather than the promise of

$50,000 if and when the movie is made. Buying rights with cash remains a potent strategic choice for any filmmaker with the money to implement the strategy.

5. "Based Upon" Provisions for Synopsis and Treatment Submissions

A screenwriter will often develop the story for a film project well before the script is finished, in a brief synopsis of 3 to 10 pages or detailed 30- to 50-page treatment of the screenplay (see chapter 4, p. 68). Filmmakers often prefer to purchase the literary work at this stage in the process, because it allows the filmmaker to have control over the development of the work. Filmmakers typically acquire treatments through the same option agreement structure used for other literary works. The filmmaker pays a modest advance and agrees to pay the writer a specified amount or percentage of income if the finished film was "based upon" the treatment.

This type of arrangement was made famous when writer Art Buchwald sued Paramount Pictures over the Eddie Murphy film *Coming to America*. Paramount had entered into an agreement with Buchwald, paying him for a movie treatment and providing him with profit participation if it was used as the basis for a film. Paramount and the project's producer, John Landis, used Buchwald's work as part of the development of *Coming to America*, but the screenplay was ultimately written by Eddie Murphy, who testified that he had not read the treatment nor used it to write his script. The film was unquestionably different from Buchwald's original concept. Nonetheless, the lawsuit was decided in Buchwald's favor; he was entitled to payment.

This was the proper result of the lawsuit. The treatment had been used by Paramount and Landis to keep the production going, and it had served as a reference for the producers as Murphy developed his independent screenplay. Similarly, any contract that provides for payment if a film is "based upon" a treatment should be interpreted to mean that the treatment author will be paid unless the treatment is wholly unrelated to the subject matter of the finished film.

Because of the vague nature of the "based upon" term, the producer should try to avoid using it in contracts. Instead, the producer can offer a percentage basis to the author of the treatment if the final film is *substantially similar* to that treatment as provided under copyright law. Since "substantial similarity" is the copyright test for infringement, this contract essentially provides that if the final shooting script or the finished film uses the copyrighted work, then the writer receives the agreed-upon payment. For a simple arrangement, this provides the easiest contractual framework.

If, on the other hand, the filmmaker chooses to use the "based upon" terminology, he should expect to be obligated to pay the treatment writer even if only the basic ideas in the two works are similar.

B. Submission Agreements

The basic purpose of a submission agreement is to allow a production company to review treatments and screenplays written by writers who are not employees of the production company. Often, these are *spec scripts*—scripts written as pet projects by writers hoping to break into the motion picture industry or to move up in its ranks. Spec scripts are particularly prevalent immediately after a prolonged strike. Given recent labor unrest, there may be a tremendous number of spec scripts in the next few years.

Submission agreements are designed to protect the production company from claims by submitting writers that the company has stolen their ideas or copyrighted materials. Since themes, ideas, and characters are often based on cultural influences, and many authors may independently be developing stories along similar lines, it is important to have a contract that sets out the expectations of the submitting writer and the film company before the company receives a screenplay or treatment.

1. Significant Terms of a Submission Agreement

A submission agreement serves to limit the contractual claims of the submitting author. The production company should insist that no script be accepted unless the submitting writer first signs one. Typically, submission agreement contracts do not limit a writer's copyright claims, but focus on claims to ideas, characters, themes, and other materials that do not rise to the level of copyrightable expression. The primary provision of the agreement is that no implied contract exists that promises to compensate the submitting writer for use of her idea or an idea similar to hers.

Although, as noted in chapter 4 (p. 59), ideas are not protected by copyright, those same ideas and plots may be protected by contract.[3] The producer must be careful to avoid making promises or otherwise creating an oral contract that a submitting writer could rely on. The written contract must explicitly state that the producer will not pay for submitted ideas, explain that similar ideas may have already been submitted, and condition any submission upon the submitting writer accepting these limitations.

a. This contract represents the only understanding between the parties regarding the submission of any treatment, story, idea, screenplay, or other work (collectively "Work"). This contract supersedes any oral agreement, and it may only be modified in writing when signed by both parties.

b. The production company will accept submission of writer's Work only in exchange for entering into this agreement.

c. Because many writers submit materials, and often similar ideas are submitted or otherwise available, the production company does not pay writers for their ideas.

d. The production company is under no obligation to pay the writer for the idea submitted. The production company is under no obligation to review the Work submitted. The production company is free to use all material not protected by the laws of copyright. The production company is not obligated to keep the materials submitted.

Regardless of any submission agreement provisions, a production company should comply with copyright law. A general submission agreement should not be used to force a writer to transfer copyright ownership from the writer to the production company or to give the production company the right to make a screenplay or film from the submission. The submission agreement can explain this, in part, as a means to soften the otherwise harsh tone of the agreement.

e. In the event that the writer submits a Work protected by copyright, the writer grants permission to review the Work and make copies of the Work for its evaluation. The writer shall retain all copyright in Work unless such rights are transferred to the production company as part of a written agreement.

The submission agreement should also explain that it is the general practice to review all submissions within approximately six months, or such time as is realistic for the producer, but that because of the number of submissions, the production company will contact only those writers with whom it is interested in developing a working relationship. While it is certainly more professional to thank every author, and even to respond with comments if possible, the production company is better off simply doing so than promising to do so in a contract.

> f. The production company is not obligated to return the materials. The writer will at all times retain an original copy of the materials submitted and hereby releases the production company from any claims that may arise as a result of the production company holding the Work.

The contract might also note that materials will only be returned if the submitting author includes a self-addressed stamped envelope. Given the low price of copying and the increasing cost of postage, many authors may forgo the return of their materials.

These suggested provisions are similar to the language that a larger production company would use. They help courts dismiss frivolous lawsuits from authors who send unsolicited materials before the trial preparation becomes very expensive.

2. Solicited Ideas and the Nondisclosure Agreement

General submission provisions must be modified to fit the particular situation. If the production company wishes to solicit a plot or an idea from an author, then it must be prepared to protect that author's ideas. This arrangement takes on the form of a nondisclosure agreement. Nondisclosure agreements are frequently used in business—they have become ubiquitous in the software and other intellectual property industries—and they essentially require that both parties agree to share information in exchange for the promise that neither party will use or disclose the other party's confidential information without permission. Indeed, if the previous sentence were written on a napkin and signed by both parties, it would probably be sufficient.

In the context of solicited ideas, the nondisclosure agreement is slightly different than in the traditional business context. The essential component of the agreement is that the idea, story, plot, characters, or other elements are treated as confidential unless they were already known by the party who receives the material, or they become known in a manner that does not breach the film company's duty of confidentiality. The following contract clauses illustrate the core of the agreement.

   a. Confidentiality. Producer shall not directly or indirectly disclose, disseminate, publish, or use for its business advantage or for any other purpose, at any time during or after the term of this Agreement for a period of seven (7) years, any information received from Writer deemed confidential by the other party ("Confidential Information").

      (1.) Definitions. For purposes of this Agreement, Confidential Information shall be defined as any information not generally known in the industry about Writer's story, characters, ideas, themes, plots, writings or expressions, products, trade secrets, services, or any combination thereof, whether or not such information would be recognized as proprietary absent this Agreement.

      (2.) Limitations. Notwithstanding any other provision of this Agreement, Producer shall not be liable for disclosing, disseminating, publishing, or using information which (i) was already known prior to the receipt of the Confidential Information; (ii) is information similar to the Confidential Information of Writer so as to make such Confidential Information no longer unique to Writer; (iii) is now or becomes public information through no wrongful act of the Producer; (iv) is independently developed or acquired by Producer without any use of the Confidential Information in such development; or (v) is required to be disclosed by law. Producer shall, within 30 days of receipt of Confidential Information inform Writer of that material Producer deems not confidential pursuant to this paragraph.

   b. Documents and Materials. The documents and materials of Writer (including but not limited to all data, screenplays, treatments, records, notes, lists, specifications, and designs) are furnished in accordance with the terms of this Agreement and shall remain the sole property of Writer. This information (collectively known as "Evaluation Material") shall, upon the termination of this Agreement, be promptly returned to Writer, including all copies thereof, which are in the possession or control of Producer, its agents, and its representatives.

c. Term and Renewal. The term of this Agreement shall be one (1) year commencing as of the date hereof; provided however, that Paragraph (a) of this Agreement shall survive termination of this Agreement and shall remain in full force and effect for a period of seven (7) years.

Using these terms, the producer provides significant protection to the writer for his ideas and other materials that are not protected by copyright while still retaining the ability to avoid paying for material that has become public or that she already owns.

3. Submissions by Joint Authors

Many of the fiercest fights break out between two people who had been jointly developing a work. A simple contract that explains the duties of each party helps to eliminate these problems. The contract should have a sentence requiring that all ideas developed during the partnership may only be used by mutual consent. If the filmmaker is hiring someone to develop an idea, the contract should require that all ideas become the property of the filmmaker.

C. Contracting and the Authority of the Filmmaker

Studio films are created and financed by producers, who seek the maximum flexibility to hire and fire the artistic talent involved with a film. Similar interests are held by *producing distributors,* those companies that invest in a film so that they can acquire it for distribution. They seek to maximize their ability to change the film to suit their distribution needs. If they substantially disagree with the choices being made by the director, they may want to fire him.

More often than not, the filmmaker on an independent project is the director. So the filmmaker will want to structure the agreements to provide much less authority for the producer to replace the director. Fortunately, when an independent filmmaker raises private funds to make a movie that does not yet have distribution, he has no boss. His investors are not as well positioned as studio producers or producing distributors, and generally not as interested in asserting authority over the project. But using the wrong form agreement can substantially restructure the relationship between the parties, and it is the written agreement that will govern the relationship.

1. Identifying the Authority in the Project

For an investor-financed independent film, all the parties must agree on which of them is the filmmaker, the source of final authority on the project. Without this agreement, conflicts can never be properly resolved, and the filmmaking process is likely to end with significant frustration. (This is not an issue in studio-financed filmmaking. When studios or established production companies finance a film, they acquire final approval over every decision in the project, including the employment of writers, director, cast, editor, and crew.)

If the filmmaker is a team of writer and director, then the issues that arise must be resolved through the mutual agreement of those two parties. If, instead, the director has the ability to replace the writer, then the writer is not truly a partner of the director on the filmmaking team. Similarly, if an actor serves as filmmaker for a project, then she will retain the authority to hire the other participants, and the writer cannot insist on script changes that substantially alter or lessen her part. If an actor uses her time and energy to launch an independent film, but the contracts vest authority in the producer because the lawyers did not understand the project, the actor will be betrayed and the project will likely languish.

The contracts employing the participants, structuring the film company, and acquiring the rights must all reflect a common perspective on authority. Any party can be the filmmaker, but all the contracts and agreements must assume that the same party plays that role.

2. The Limits of Form Agreements

With the explosion of information available on the Internet, filmmakers increasingly search for sample agreements online to provide low-cost alternatives to hiring lawyers and revising agreements. Others rely on the sample contracts in books such as this. Standard or form agreements are an extremely helpful tool for verifying that the important topics of each contract are addressed. However, form agreements necessarily lack the point of view of the particular filmmaker. In some cases, the agreements between the parties are closely managed by unions through collective bargaining agreements, and the standard wording will apply without adjustment. In other situations, however, the sample language was drafted with specific other parties in mind, and it may not provide the filmmaker with the right balance of interests. As a result, sample contracts should be used as check-lists and points of comparison, but not adopted as the operating language without careful legal review.

Form agreements are particularly unsuited to an independent project's needs regarding the authority of the filmmaker. Most forms will assume a studio-based model of producer control, which is the least common approach to independent and guerrilla films. Filmmakers who seek to save a few dollars by using form agreements may find themselves giving away their movie as a result.

3. What Can Be Standard in an Agreement?

Once the source of authority in the film project has been identified, it is very helpful to standardize the key agreements. First, all key agreements should use a common language and approach, so that the defined terms of each agreement are the same. Second, each *category* of agreement should be standardized. For example, all the actors' agreements should have iden-tical language, except where unique needs arise. Similarly, all the crew agreements should use the same language, and whenever possible the same language as the cast contracts.

Also, as described in section D, below, there are many provisions that are standard in every agreement. Though labeled *boilerplate,* these provi-sions have important legal effects.

4. Assigning the Filmmaker's Story Rights

In the studio setting, writers are required to create any script as a *work for hire* so that the film studio becomes the author of the screenplay. Studios also demand that they be assigned all the rights to make the film, as well as the rights to create an unlimited number of additional works, which are often known as *sequel rights.* These sequel rights include sequels, prequels, adaptations, spin-offs involving one or more characters or settings, televi-sion versions for both episodic (weekly) television and television specials, and every other entertainment imaginable that could be based upon the film.

For the filmmaker who has created an original story, the studio approach may not be the most advantageous. If an independent film company is organized for a single production, the company may not be in a position to exploit sequel rights, and the filmmaker may be stymied in his desire to write follow-ups later in his career. Retaining these rights gives the filmmaker a measure of leverage to control future opportunities. However, such reservation of rights must be clearly spelled out so that investors are not misled about the potential for their investment. And if the film acquires studio financing, the studio will automatically insist that these rights be transferred to it.

One possible compromise is for the filmmaker to give the film company an option to exploit sequel rights, but limit the option to a particular span of time. If the rights are exploited within the first three to five years, then the film company should be in a position to participate in them. (The filmmaker should also receive some compensation as the author, even in this case.) If the rights have not been exploited in that time, then the film company has little direct financial interest, so the rights can reasonably return to the filmmaker. This compromise allows the filmmaker to return to the material later in his career without having to clear the rights with a long-defunct production company. In the event the film rights are sold to a studio or major producing distributor, however, such arrangements are likely to be renegotiated to meet the purchaser's demands for subsidiary rights.

D. Boilerplate: Understanding the Rest of the Contract

In almost every contract, the significant terms are followed by a series of provisions that control most of the rules for enforcing and operating under the contract. Regardless of the key, negotiated terms of the agreement, these provisions—often referred to as *boilerplate*—are quite similar in every contract, from manufacturing cars to selling cable service, and they apply to the thousands of different agreements into which the filmmaker will enter during the production. The following subsections provide examples of boilerplate terms and their meaning.

1. Term and Renewal

The term provision governs the length of the contract. Unless there is another provision allowing the contract to continue after that date, the contract itself ends, and the future relationships are governed by a new agreement, whether in writing or by oral understanding.

> The term of this Agreement shall commence as of the date hereof and continue for a period of one (1) year; and provided neither party shall not be then in breach of or in default under any term or provision hereof, this Agreement shall automatically renew for additional one (1) year periods thereafter, unless either party gives written notice of its election to terminate this Agreement not less than sixty (60) days prior to the expiration of the term or any renewal thereof.

This provision provides that the contract starts beginning with the date on the top of the page, which is preferable to relying on two possibly conflicting dates accompanying the signature lines of the parties. The contract has a one-year term, but that term automatically extends each year unless either party decides to terminate the contract. This automatic renewal is quite typical for ongoing relationships. For project work, an event should be specified. For example, the contract may terminate upon the completion of principal photography.

Termination provisions can also allow that some provisions of the contracts survive termination. For example, if an agreement provides for financing the film, the contract may automatically terminate if insufficient funds are pledged by a specified date. Notwithstanding the termination of the contract because that date passes, the contract may provide that the provisions relating to nondisclosure of the film idea will survive for an additional period of years.

2. Warranties and Representations of the Parties

The representations and warranties are the basic promises that serve as the basis for the agreement. They generally go to the ability of the parties to enter into the agreement, but may become very specific depending on the nature of the agreement.

Each party to this Agreement hereby represents and warrants that it has the right and authority to enter into this Agreement and that it is not subject to any contract, agreement, judgment, statute, regulation, or disability which might interfere with its full performance of all of the covenants and conditions hereunder.

It is common that the representations and warranties for the two parties to the agreement be somewhat different from each other. For instance, the representations and warranties of the author of a story will include the following additional issues:

The Seller [of the novel, screenplay, play, or other literary work] hereby represents and warrants as follows:

The Property has been written solely by and is original with Seller; neither the Property nor any element thereof infringes upon the copyright, publicity rights, trademarks, story rights, or other interests of any other literary property.

The Property is wholly fictional, no portion of the Property has been taken from any other source (other than the public domain), and the Property does not constitute defamation against any person or violate any rights in any person, including without limitation, rights of privacy, publicity, copyright (whether common law or statutory, throughout the universe), trademark, publication, or performance rights, or rights in any other property, and any rights of consultation regarding the Property or any element thereof.

The Property has not previously been exploited in any medium except the following [identify what rights have been used], and no rights have been granted to any third party to do so.

In addition, for some projects it is important that nothing interfere with the ability to market the personality involved in the project.

Neither party has committed, and throughout the term of this Agreement neither party shall commit, any act or omission which constitutes a felony or could be deemed an act of moral turpitude. Any breach of this paragraph shall be deemed a material breach.

In such a situation, the representations and warranties need to include a *morality clause,* guaranteeing good, honorable behavior both before and throughout the term of the contract. The most important aspect of this provision is that it allows the employer to revoke the contract if the misconduct of the employee makes that choice appropriate.

3. Indemnification

Indemnification is the legal obligation to pay compensation to the other party to the agreement for damage, loss, or injury suffered as a result of a breach of the contract or any duties that arise under it. For example, a screenwriter will be required to indemnify the film producer for any material copied from other sources in violation of copyright law and of the representations made by the screenwriter in his contract.

It is not sufficient that each party promises to abide by the obligations laid out in the contract. Each one runs the risk that third parties may make claims against that party as a result of what it has done. For example, the filmmaker wants to be protected from anyone claiming the screenwriter improperly copied that person's story. To provide such protection, the screenwriter must agree to defend the filmmaker, meaning the writer must provide a legal defense for the benefit of the filmmaker. The screenwriter must also indemnify the filmmaker, meaning he must agree to pay any damages if he is found to have violated some other person's or company's rights.

> Screenwriter hereby indemnifies and holds harmless [Film Company] and its employees, independent contractors, agents, and assigns against any loss or damage (including reasonable attorneys' fees) incurred by reason of any claim based upon any breach of the representations and warranties of Seller contained in this Agreement and any documents contemplated hereby. The term "person" as used herein shall mean any person, firm, corporation, or other entity.

In contrast, the filmmaker is generally in the better position to defend the screenwriter for any lawsuits that might arise as a result of the making of the film. Therefore, the filmmaker has a similar obligation to protect the screenwriter from liability.

> [Film Company] hereby indemnifies Screenwriter against any loss or damage (including reasonable attorneys' fees) incurred by reason of any claim based

upon its exploitation of the Property which does not involve the acts or omissions of the Screenwriter.

Finally, a very simple but effective provision is a general statement that each party will protect the other for any actions that it caused.

> Each party agrees to indemnify the other and to hold the other harmless from and against any and all claims, action, cause of action, liabilities, damages, judgments, decrees, losses, costs, and expenses, including reasonable attorneys' fees, arising out of any breach or alleged breach of any representations, warranties, or agreements made by it hereunder.

These sample clauses do not include the requirement that the party defend the lawsuit. Defense language is common and can readily be added to these paragraphs merely by inserting the term "and defend" after the word "indemnify" wherever applicable.

The difficult issue—which of the two actually created the situation that allowed a third party to be able to bring a lawsuit—is often highly contentious, with the result that the two parties to the contract often end up suing each other to determine which has the obligation to pay for the litigation and any damages caused by the lawsuit.

4. Resolution of Disputes

Because of the costs and delays involved in litigation, many people prefer to use some alternative, including arbitration or mediation. *Mediation* provides a person who tries to help the parties to the dispute work out the issues among themselves. *Arbitration* provides an independent person who acts much like a judge, who will listen to both sides in the dispute and make a determination. Although arbitrators in some jurisdictions may not have quite the discretion of the courts to award injunctions or punitive damages, they have substantial power to craft final remedies. In addition, if the arbitration is *binding,* then the decision of the arbitrator is as enforceable as that of a judge.

The choice to forgo the right to go to court should be considered carefully. Many protections are given up by waiving the right to use the traditional legal system. On the other hand, the independent filmmaker probably does not have a great deal of money or time to fight the dispute through trial and appeal. Also, the ability to choose the arbitrator allows the parties to use the services of a decision maker familiar with the film industry and the issues involved. As a result, arbitration may be a useful alternative for filmmakers. In fact, it is required in most agreements with union personnel (directors, actors, writers, etc.). Each union will have specific language that it requires be used.

Dispute resolution provisions vary greatly, but the following serves as an example.

> Any and all disputes hereunder shall be resolved by arbitration in accordance with the American Arbitration Association ("AAA") under the rules then obtaining. Any party hereto electing to commence an action shall give written notice to the other party hereto of such election. The location for such arbitration shall be Los Angeles, California, subject to the convenience of the parties, and any and all rights of discovery available pursuant to such arbitration shall be limited by the applicable arbitration provisions of the California Code of Civil Procedure. The award of such arbitrator may be confirmed or enforced in any court of competent jurisdiction. The costs and expenses of the arbitrator, including the attorneys' fees and costs of each of the parties, may be apportioned between the parties by such arbitrator.

5. Assignment

Most business contracts are freely assignable, or transferable. In contrast, most contracts calling for a person's individual services are not assignable. In the filmmaking scenario, both issues are occurring at once. The duties of most of the participants are personal in nature, but the filmmaker may create a film company or sell the existing company as part of the financing process. As long as the filmmaker remains involved in the project, none of these activities should trigger the assignment clause.

> The services and obligations under this Agreement are personal in nature and cannot be assigned or delegated. The services of [Film Company] may be assigned upon consent, which consent shall not be unreasonably withheld. Notwithstanding the foregoing, the transfer of this Agreement to a company owned in whole or part by [Filmmaker], a related company, or to another entity with substantially the same executive and principals of [Film Company], or to

a company that employs [Filmmaker] as [producer/director], shall not be deemed an assignment requiring approval under this paragraph.

6. Amendments

Things change. Actors may get sick, locations become unavailable, funding increases and decreases. Nonetheless, when the filmmaker goes to the trouble of creating a written agreement, it is important that any changes be put into writing, so that quick, last-minute promises do not undermine the thoughtful management of the production. As a result, every contract should include a statement that written amendments are required. The requirement is simple.

> This Agreement may be modified or amended only in a writing signed by both parties.

Even with this language, some jurisdictions will allow for oral modification of the agreement. Further, courts will often find that a party has waived its rights to require a written document as a result of statements made about or conduct relating to the transaction. Despite this risk, the provision should be included in the agreement and adhered to by the parties throughout the course of their relationship.

7. Severability

In some situations a portion of the contract cannot be enforced. The court (or arbitrator) must then decide whether to throw out the entire contract or just that provision. That choice can be provided for directly in the contract. In most situations, half a contract is better than none, as the severability provision reflects.

> If any provision of this Agreement shall be held to be invalid or unenforceable for any reason, the remaining provisions shall continue to be valid and enforceable. If a court finds that any provision of this Agreement is invalid or unenforceable, but that by limiting such provision it would become valid and enforceable, then such provision shall be deemed to be written, construed, and enforced as so limited.

8. Entire Agreement

To control the issues that may be swirling around the filmmaker, everything should be in writing. A provision that specifies that all the issues have been incorporated into the written agreement may help to overcome claims that side agreements and promises were also made. Even the most well-meaning people hear what they want to hear, so the more exact and structured the contract, the fewer the misunderstandings.

> This Agreement contains the full and complete understanding between the parties hereto with reference to the within subject matter, supersedes all prior agreements and understandings, whether written or oral, pertaining thereto, and cannot be modified except by a written instrument signed by both of the parties hereto. Each of the parties acknowledges that no representation or promise not expressly contained in this Agreement has been made by the other or its agents or representatives.

9. No Obligation

Unfortunately, many films do not get made and opportunities are often lost. A contract purchasing literary properties or services should be sure to protect the filmmaker from claims that he was required to use those properties or services.

> Notwithstanding the rights granted herein, [Film Company] is under no obligation to utilize [services/property] in any manner whatsoever, and failure to exercise any rights contained herein shall not constitute a breach of any covenant, express or implied.

This provision will not determine what payments or other obligations the filmmaker must make; the payment terms will specify under what conditions the payments are due. If the payments are due for entering the contract, then the payments are owed, even if the film is not made. However, most payment obligations are based on using the services, in which case failure to start the film results in no financial obligation.

10. No Partnership or Joint Venture

The financial and business relationship should also be specified. Courts may ignore these self-serving declarations, but at least they remind the parties how they are supposed to relate to each other, and they may have some effect on the courts if any problems do arise.

> [Screenwriter] is an independent contractor with respect to [Film Company] and not an employee. [Film Company] will not provide fringe benefits and [Screenwriter] shall be responsible for all income tax and withholding required which he may bear as a result of this Agreement. Nothing in this Agreement shall be construed as creating a partnership, joint venture, or employment relationship between the parties hereto, and each party is solely and exclusively responsible for its own debts and obligations.

11. Further Documents

Throughout the course of the filmmaking process, a wide variety of financiers, distributors, government agencies, unions, exhibitors, and others are going to request legal documentation regarding the film. Some of those documents will have been created during the production process, but others will not have been necessary or will not be in the form needed. The filmmaker must be able to compel the other participants to continue to sign documents necessary for the production and distribution of the film and the exploitation of related rights. This provision makes the willingness to sign additional papers an affirmative promise of each party.

> Each of the parties agrees to execute, acknowledge, and deliver any and all further documents which may be required to carry into effect this Agreement and its respective obligations hereunder, all of which further documents shall be in accordance with and consistent with the terms of this Agreement.

12. Notices

The contract should specify the form of delivery allowed for subsequent correspondence. E-mail is typically not included in these provisions, but increasingly it is a useful tool. If it is used, then the sender should confirm that the e-mail has been received. Many notice clauses include the address to which all notices should be sent, and often include the attorney or agent as a second address, entitled to a copy of the correspondence. Often these are left blank, however, so this paragraph provides more flexibility in selecting the applicable address.

> All notices, statements, or other documents which either party shall desire to give to the other hereunder shall be in writing and shall be deemed given as when delivered personally or by e-mail (with confirmed receipt), telecopier (with confirmed receipt), or 48 hours after deposit in the U.S. mail, postage prepaid, and addressed to the recipient party at the address set forth in the opening paragraph of this Agreement, or at such address as either party hereto may designate from time to time in accordance with this Paragraph.

13. Governing Law

The parties can also choose which state's laws govern the contract, as long as that state is related to the agreement. If one of the parties to the contract is from a particular state, or most of the work will occur in that state, then the selection will usually be respected by the court or arbitrator.

> This Agreement shall be governed by and construed in accordance with the laws of the State of California applicable to agreements entered into and wholly performed therein.

The choice of a particular state may depend on the laws of that state— for instance, a state may have particularly favorable laws regarding the contract in question. The choice varies dramatically depending on the states under consideration and the issues involved, so it should be based on the advice of a lawyer familiar with the issues.

14. Signature Line

The signature line should indicate who is signing the agreement and in what capacity. For example, if the filmmaker has formed a film company, then the filmmaker should sign only in his capacity as president of the company, manager of the LLC, etc. The contract should also identify that the film company, rather than the filmmaker himself, is the party to the agreement. This will limit the personal liability that would otherwise attach to the filmmaker if he signed in his personal capacity. Without properly drafting and properly signing the contract, the value of creating the film company will be lost.

Financing the Film Project

FILM FINANCING IS the most difficult aspect of independent filmmaking—both raising the funds and complying with the applicable state and federal laws. When raising capital, even small mistakes can result in the end of the production, fines, and criminal liability, and as the amount of money raised increases, so does the importance of working with an experienced attorney. The process requires extreme care and attention to detail.

No matter how small the project, funds are going to be required to make the motion picture. Expenses may range from a few dollars for out-of-pocket expenses to hundreds of millions of dollars for top-name stars, on-set special effects, and postproduction effects and editing. The more typical amount for guerrilla and independent filmmaking ranges from a few thousand dollars for digital cameras, computers, and software to a few million dollars for a union-cast project shot on 35mm film.

There is no "correct" way to make the film, but where it falls on this spectrum is often dictated by the cash available more than any aesthetic sensibilities. If the film company has been able to presell some of the distribution rights, then making the film directly on 35mm film enhances the production quality and the apparent professionalism of the project. If the film is being financed through a network of the filmmaker's family and friends, then shooting digitally may be more realistic and responsible. A super-low-budget digital film may still find a large audience, sell DVDs, and be distributed on cable and television; if a modestly successful digital film is produced for $25,000 and returns $75,000 in DVD and cable revenue, it will greatly exceed the rate of return from any studio film and serve as an excellent credit that helps the filmmaker and cast promote their careers. And by shooting low, the filmmaker might also have the opportunity to remake the film later in her career with the luxury of studio financing.

A. Survey of Financing Tools

There are three main categories of financing available: debt, equity, and advance sales. With *debt financing*, the filmmaker takes out loans to make cash available for the production. With *equity investment*, outsiders fund the film company in exchange for financial participation in the particular film. The third category, *advance sales financing*, is specific to the film industry—the filmmaker raises production funds by selling, prior to the film's creation, the right to distribute and exhibit the film—and will be discussed in detail in section B.

In a debt financing arrangement, a lender such as a bank gives the borrower money in exchange for a promise to repay that loan on time. The bank makes profit by charging interest on the loan. Debt financing places the risk of failure on the borrower, because the lender expects to be repaid whether the film is successful or not (and the filmmaker is generally going to be responsible for the repayments if the film's income is insufficient to cover them). On the other hand, although the borrower must pay back the principal and interest regardless of the outcome of the film, the lender receives only a fixed rate of return and is not entitled to any additional profits. As a result, the borrower stands to make significantly more profit if a successful film is debt financed rather than equity financed.

Equity financing, on the other hand, distributes the risk of the project, because the investor only receives his money back if the film shows a return. If a filmmaker sells 50 percent of the film's interest to an investor, for example, then the investor will lose his entire investment if the film is a complete failure. If the film is a tremendous success, the investor will receive 50 percent of every dollar of profit—far more than a lender would have received.

Assume that a particular digital film can be successfully shot and completed for $100,000 (including any interest payments). The filmmaker sells 50 percent of the LLC created to produce the film to an equity purchaser for $50,000, retaining 50 percent of the ownership for himself. The filmmaker takes out a loan for the remaining $50,000 (in the form of a loan to the LLC, with a personal guarantee by the filmmaker). The following reflects the return or loss to the filmmaker. First, assume the film makes a total revenue of $400,000.

	Lender	Equity Purchaser	Filmmaker's Own $$
Terms	10% Interest	50% Purchase	50% Retained Ownership
Contribution	$50,000	$50,000	——
Interest	$5,000	——	——
Gross Revenue	——	——	$400,000
Costs	——	——	• $100,000 production costs (incl. interest) • $50,000 loan
Net Income/Loss to Film Company	——	——	$250,000
Payment on Loan	$55,000	——	——
Return or Loss (Including Principal)	$5,000	$125,000	$125,000

Next, assume the film generates a total revenue of only $50,000:

	Lender	Equity Purchaser	Filmmaker's Own $$
Terms	10% Interest	50% Purchase	50% Retained Ownership
Contribution	$50,000	$50,000	——
Interest	$5,000	——	——
Gross Revenue	——	——	$50,000
Costs	——	——	• $100,000 production costs (incl. interest) • $50,000 loan
Net Income/Loss to Film Company	——	——	−$100,000
Payment on Loan	$55,000	——	——
Return or Loss (Including Principal)	$5,000	−$50,000	−$50,000

The bank must be repaid in full. Typically, this expense will come before any distribution of revenue. The bank will be repaid and the investor will lose the investment, leaving the filmmaker to repay the loan personally.

From the charts, it becomes clear that equity financing softens the losses of the film project but also reduces the profits. Debt financing maximizes the profits but places the entire cost of loss on the filmmaker—and adds the cost of interest to boot.

The most beneficial situation for the filmmaker would be to receive 100 percent of the film costs from an equity sale in exchange for substantially less than 100 percent of the income—in the range of 25 to 50 percent. In this way the filmmaker shares in a portion of the profits but undertakes no cash risk of loss. Nonetheless, many independent filmmakers, including successful directors such as Spike Lee and Francis Ford Coppola, have used their personal funds to finance all or part of their films. There are no legal limits or restrictions on this practice. Despite the adage that a filmmaker should only spend other people's money, personal funds are invariably part of the film financing mix.

B. Financing Based on Distribution Deals and Presale Arrangements

Unlike other industries, the motion picture business presents a second type of financing sale in addition to the typical model of equity financing. It involves selling the film's distribution rights. In this form of financing, the company sells its assets in exchange for a present or guaranteed payment. For example, if the film company sells its rights to European distribution in exchange for $50,000, then its future revenue will exclude any monies made in the countries identified as Europe, whether those markets generate $5,000, $50,000, or $500,000. This arrangement reduces the potential for future income, but also serves to reduce the risk of loss.

From the filmmaker's standpoint, cash for the production is the most critical requirement of any financing structure; no number of future promises will cover rental fees or payroll. Unfortunately, the business realities for presale agreements often require that the completed film be delivered prior to any payment. To actually produce the film, the filmmaker must borrow from a lender, using the presale agreement as collateral. Under this structure, the interest costs are not avoided, and the filmmaker may still shoulder the residual risk that presale fees will not materialize. Nonetheless, since a presale agreement allows the filmmaker to finance a project without risking personal funds, it remains a very attractive option.

Presale and distribution deals may vary significantly. Some of the more common structures are briefly described below.

1. Cash Deals

Only in the rarest of situations or with the lowest of budgets will a filmmaker will be able to fund the production with a cash advance on a guaranteed distribution. There was a time when companies such as Cannon Films would create *one-sheets* (theatrical advertising posters) that the company would exhibit at the international film markets. If it was successful selling enough territories based on the poster, Cannon would contact the named talent and begin the process of producing the film. If a film didn't attract enough interest, the remaining posters would be discarded and those projects never started. Today, modest cash advances may sometimes be available, but this is the exception to the rule.

2. Negative Pick-Up

Although the details can vary greatly, the term *negative pick-up* means that a film studio or distributor pays for the cost of the film to be finished to the point that a completed negative is ready to use. Generally, the filmmaker sells the film to a studio in exchange for reimbursement of production expenses and some form of profit sharing from the eventual proceeds of the film. For example, if a filmmaker had a budget of $1 million for a film project, she would "sell" the film by promising to deliver a completed motion picture substantially the same as that described in the screenplay in exchange for a payment of $1 million. Once the negative was delivered, the film studio would then have the obligation to finish the prints for the film, pay for its marketing and distribution, and split profits, if any, with the filmmaker on the agreed-upon percentage basis. The negative pick-up is the filmmaker's "field of dreams"—if she shoots it, the money will come.

The negative pick-up arrangement often operates very similarly to studio financing (see subsection 5, p. 112). Each major decision may be subject to review by the distributor. The distributor will require that the script be followed, the agreed-upon casting not be changed, the length of the film be acceptable, and the film be eligible for a particular MPAA rating, typically a PG-13 or R. Any major deviations must be approved by the financier or the filmmaker risks the company stopping payments or claiming that she has breached the agreement.

The amount paid for a negative pick-up need not be the same as the production cost of the film, although the distributor will often seek to cap the payment at this amount. If so, the filmmaker must be sure to include budget items for herself and others who have invested sweat equity as the basis for negotiations with the studio. To add these items later in the negotiations will result in little or no personal payments.

The actual payment structure can vary from arrangement to arrangement. In most cases, the purchasing studio will provide funds on a weekly basis as necessary for the film company to meets its regular obligations, but only after the filmmaker demonstrates that the project remains on budget and on schedule. In other cases the funds will be paid on delivery of the final product, so the filmmaker must use the negative pick-up agreement to obtain commercial loans to cover production expenses.

3. Distribution Guarantee

Closely related to the negative pick-up arrangement is the distribution guarantee agreement. In this case, the distributor agrees to purchase the completed film's full distribution rights in exchange for a fee and an agreed-upon royalty or gross participation amount. A distribution guarantee does not eliminate the risks to the filmmaker, because the funds are generally not made available until the filmmaker has completed the film.

Since the sale of distribution rights does not immediately result in cash to the filmmaker, she must use the sales agreement as a form of collateral against which the film company can borrow money from a bank or other lender. Under the distribution guarantee agreement, the film's distributor serves as guarantor of the loan. Since the lender is entitled to repayment regardless of the film's revenue, the distributor's guarantee may put the lender in a position of much greater security than if the filmmaker is solely responsible for the loan. If the distributor is a stable, well-established company, lenders are generally willing to finance this type of arrangement.

Invariably, the lender will require that the film company furnish a *completion bond*, which serves as insurance against the film not being completed as required by the purchasing distributor. Together, the loan interest and the premium cost of the completion bond could add 20 percent to the cost of completing the film. Short-term financing may further increase this cost substantially.

4. Foreign Distributors, Markets, and Territories

Foreign distribution has grown to become the single largest category of film distribution income, exceeding both domestic theatrical exhibition and video sales for revenue. Despite its importance, however, foreign distribution is risky territory for independent films, because the language, currency, and legal enforcement barriers often make it difficult to collect royalties or enforce contract rights. If a filmmaker seeks an advance and a royalty payment in exchange for foreign distribution rights, she must face the vagaries of currency exchange and the unfortunate but all-too-common practice by which foreign distributors refuse to distribute royalty income.

Even if royalty payments are forthcoming, the difficulties of auditing foreign receipts and dealing with clever accounting practices make this income source highly volatile. For an independent filmmaker without the leverage of an ongoing relationship, the cost of collecting small royalties from a foreign distributor in a small territory can be larger than the amount of payment being sought. Where possible, the filmmaker is best served by selling the rights to a foreign territory outright instead. More modest prepayments will result in greater cash in hand for the filmmaker and should be the preferred strategy with all but the most reputable of distributors.

Nonetheless, independent filmmakers have been increasingly successful selling the rights to foreign territories in exchange for advance payments and using these payments to finance all or most of the film's budget. These transactions can be conducted through direct cash payments or through letters of credit that are deemed sufficiently sound by the U.S. lenders.

Often the strategy in these sales follows that of Cannon Films: invest early in the poster art so that the purchaser knows what it is marketing. Few people have the skill necessary to read a screenplay (or even view a rough cut) and successfully visualize the final film. On the other hand, most people have attended at least one film solely on the basis of the poster. Perhaps this form of financing seems artistically impure, but commercial success for a film requires commercial techniques.

During the independent film boom of the 1980s, the combination of new marketing opportunities and healthy tax regulations led to an infusion of foreign capital. This financial resource, if it ever truly existed, disappeared as a result of changing economic conditions and substantially more restrictive tax regulations. When the dot-com securities market collapsed, a flurry of venture capital sought independent film opportunities, but that money has also disappeared as the next generation of investors learned the risks of independent film distribution.

But a new international market continues to expand: independent U.S. filmmakers may find opportunities to collaborate or coproduce with production companies outside of the United States. Occasionally these coproduction arrangements will provide financing to the U.S. company, but more often the foreign company enjoys subsidies for its local production and will provide services in exchange for the co-ownership of the project. While such an arrangement entails a number of unique risks, it may also afford the independent filmmaker some attractive side benefits: opportunities to travel and to benefit from the coproducers' expertise.

5. Studios

The traditional Hollywood studios *manufactured* motion pictures. They purchased the raw materials—stories and talent—and produced finished films that they exhibited in theaters throughout the world. Over time, the production activities separated from the distribution activities, so that the studios would distribute and promote films produced by other film companies, reducing the studios' risk if a film was never made.

Today, the major motion picture studios are primarily distributors rather than film production companies. Instead of directly purchasing stories or scripts, the studios work through existing relationships with established production companies. These production companies package the script, develop the budget, and manage the production. The budget will include a negotiated fee for the producer's own expenses and income. The agreement between the producer and studio will also determine the producer's participation in the film's revenue. The studio will finance the project on an incremental basis, providing the necessary funding for each step of the process. In exchange, the studio has primary control over the project and the ability to terminate it at any point in its development.

This incremental approach, known as a *production and distribution deal,* allows the studio to maximize its control while minimizing its risk. The producer will typically receive a small fee for early preproduction activities. Although the costs of script and budget preparation often exceed this payment, the producer rather than the studio covers this risk. If the studio is interested in developing the project further, it will release funds to the producer to pay for selected key aspects of preproduction. Locations will be scouted, the script rewritten or polished, and key personnel identified. Throughout this process, the producer will receive little or no additional pay.

Eventually, however, the studio may commit to the project. It "greenlights" the film and commits to principal actors, director, and designers. (For some directors and actors, the studio will be obligated to pay them whether or not the production is ever filmed.) During this phase of preproduction, the studio will typically distribute a small portion of the producer's fee. The bulk of the producer's fee will be paid during principal photography, with small payments withheld until the delivery of the first rough cut of the picture and the delivery of the final picture.[1]

For the independent filmmaker, making a picture under a studio-financed production deal is both a blessing and a curse. A well-made studio film has the potential to greatly exceed the success of any independent film. The studio's marketing budgets and promotional savvy can make a household name out of anyone, opening the door for tremendous professional control on subsequent projects.

The curse is that the independent filmmaker gives up control immediately. Rarely do studio screenplays resemble the writer's first drafts, and novice directors will be second-guessed at every turn—if the filmmaker is allowed to remain attached to the picture at all. Still, that is where the money is. For most artists it is commercial success that buys them the luxury of later artistic control.

C. Cash Management of Sales Financing

In most of the various funding scenarios, the film producer must still bear the burden of both controlling the costs and paying the bills as they accrue.

Although the filmmaker may have sold the right to distribute the film (or assigned the copyright in the completed film), these future transactions do not translate into production funds. Instead, the filmmaker must apply to a lender to provide the cash to make the movie.

1. Film Lenders

There are a few commercial banks that regularly provide this form of independent film lending. The experience and knowledge of these banks allow them to assess the credit risk of the independent production. The film company must present credible evidence that it will be able to repay the loan and that it has sufficient collateral to cover the principal amount borrowed. Just as a home purchaser must show the intended property is worth at least as much as the loan, the filmmaker must demonstrate that the value of the financed project exceeds the loan requested.

To demonstrate the value of the project to the lender, the film company must present a film package that lays out its existing collateral. Since filming has not yet begun, that will include the screenplay and story rights, legally binding commitments by the key personnel to participate in the film, and the production budget, including a draw-down schedule for the use of the proceeds as they are paid to the filmmaker throughout production.

Most importantly, the package should include legally binding guarantees for the territory sales, negative pick-up, or other financing arrangements. These contracts must specify the guaranteed minimum the filmmaker will be paid; that amount can be used as collateral to be pledged against the value of the loan. If the film's distribution agreements, negative pick-up contracts, or presales involve non-U.S. territories, the financing becomes a bit more complex. (Issues involving fluctuating exchange rates, governmental stability, and creditworthiness can frustrate the lending process.)

Finally, to get the collateral ready for the bank, there may be significant expenses, particularly with regard to key personnel—cast and crew who require an advance payment to legally bind themselves to the project. The bank will also require a security agreement that puts a lien against the developed (and the exposed) film stock and the copyright in the film, so that the lender can foreclose on the assets in the case of nonpayment.

Payments by film lenders are typically made weekly, upon proof of satisfactory progress during the prior week's shooting. This short-term bridge financing may be substantially more expensive than other financing sources, and the cost of the interest payments must be included in the budget for the project.

2. General Commercial Loans

All commercial banks provide other forms of commercial loans, including unsecured loans. Even though these lenders may lack a sophisticated team experienced in entertainment or media-secured financing, they may be of assistance to an independent filmmaker seeking modest additional funds. Unless the transaction is for an unsecured loan based on the filmmaker's personal creditworthiness, the lender will require the following elements to be in place before it will agree to finance the film:

- a reputable distributor that has entered into an agreement to distribute the finished film
- a completion bond company's guarantee that the film will be completed for the agreed-upon budget
- a budget that accurately reflects the anticipated costs of the film's production
- sufficient general liability, and other insurance
- adequate security agreements between the lender and the production company so that the lender holds a perfected security interest in both the physical and intangible property of the production company
- written, enforceable contracts committing the principal cast members to appear in the production

When the filmmaker can package these elements, lenders may be willing to provide credit to the film company.

For a company that has received significant cash investments, some lenders will be willing to provide small lines of credit. In these cases, the lender may reduce the demands for documentation, completion bonds, or other requirements because the risk to the bank is minimized by the investor's participation. The company's assets, including the copyright to the film and its cash reserves, provide sufficient security for the lender to accept the risk of providing the modest loan. The creditor will have priority for repayment over the investors, so in the event of default, the bank will be repaid in full before the investors receive any of their funds.

D. Nonprofit Financing

For guerrilla and digital filmmakers, nonprofit grants often go unnoticed. Many nonprofit organizations are willing to participate in independent film projects. Some invest in film as an art form regardless of content, while others support particular projects because they are interested in promoting the message of the filmmaker—this is particularly true for documentary film.

Another selling point of nonprofit investment in independent filmmaking is that the donors' return on investment is guaranteed. Given the number of independent films that never recoup any of the investors' principal, shrewd supporters may prefer the more general benefit provided by a charitable tax deduction than the unlikely chance that they will see an equivalent return on their investment. Moreover, the tax deduction occurs at the time of the donation, so the return is immediate and without risk. For first-time filmmakers, particularly documentary filmmakers, charitable support is a very legitimate way to enter the business.

For the filmmaker himself, a further benefit is the level of appreciation afforded by the sponsors. Nonprofits often recognize that most of the work done on an independent film is essentially volunteer time, donated to complete a worthwhile project. As a result, they may offer the filmmaker wide latitude and a great deal of respect.

A limitation on nonprofit fundraising is that the money is often quite modest. The donors may also lack any sophistication regarding the project, unlike sources connected with the film industry. When funds become available from industry sources, they may often lead to other opportunities to promote the film or to valuable connections essential to the casting or production of the project.

1. Sources for Nonprofit Financing

Organizations that provide resources to filmmakers include the Sundance Documentary Fund, assisting the development of documentaries on social issues; the Fund for Jewish Documentary Filmmaking, focusing on Jewish history and culture; the National Black Programming Consortium, focusing on films emanating from African American communities; the Astraea National Lesbian Action Foundation, addressing issues in the lesbian community; and many geographic programs, such as the New York State Council on the Arts, the Minnesota Independent Film Fund, the Pacific Pioneer Film Fund, and the Texas Filmmakers Production Fund.[2]

The Paul Robeson Fund is typical of the documentary funding model. Grants ranging from $2,000 to $15,000 are provided for documentaries dealing with relevant social issues. Filmmakers must complete grant applications that detail the project and provide samples of their prior work.

In many other cases, a nonprofit organization may not specifically be looking to finance a film project, but rather to provide funds for community outreach, training, or other goals. If the film being developed promotes those goals, the film project may become a valuable investment for the organization.

2. Fiscal Sponsorships

Nonprofit organizations may raise money from private donors or from grant organizations to fund those who support their exempt charitable purpose. As charitable organizations, they do not pay federal income tax, and they allow their donors to receive a charitable deduction against personal tax obligations. These charities are often referred to by their IRS tax designation, as *501(c)(3) organizations.*

A few 501(c)(3) organizations have the development of noncommercial film and video as their charitable purpose. Organizations such as the Independent Film Project (IFP), Film Arts, and others accept donor funds to promote film projects. Under the typical fiscal agency relationship, a filmmaker applies for fiscal sponsorship by providing information on the film project, the filmmakers, the budget, and the distribution strategy. If approved by the fiscal agent, that charity serves as the entity that receives the donations. The charity then provides the donated fees to the filmmaker. The fiscal agent typically charges a 5 to 10 percent fee for its services.

The filmmaker is responsible for careful financial accounting and for compliance with all applicable tax laws. For example, the donor cannot be given any financial interest in the film, because this would transform the charitable gift into a for-profit investment. Donors can be given tokens of appreciation, but if these gifts have any significant monetary value, then the donor must be informed of the value of the gift, and the donor must deduct that value from the value of the donation listed on her tax returns.

3. Partnership Projects and Agenda-Based Films

Fiscal sponsorships are not limited to arts organizations. Any 501(c)(3) organization may elect to serve as a film's fiscal agent, provided the film meets its charitable purpose. For example, a charity dedicated to promoting the elimination of a particular rare disease may find that a documentary highlighting the devastating consequences of the disease would help promote awareness and encourage pharmaceutical research to find a cure. A filmmaker hoping to make such a documentary could enter into a relationship with that charity by which it served as the project's fiscal agent.

The filmmaker would be responsible for attracting new donations to the charity earmarked for the documentary, and the charity would be responsible for assuring that the tax and reporting obligations were fully met. The agreement should provide for the filmmaker's salary, whether paid up front or deferred, and also stipulate that any donations in excess of the production and distribution costs be retained by the charity. The charity may charge a small fee to cover the expenses it incurs. The filmmaker retains the ownership of the film and its copyright, and all revenue from the film.

Even without becoming a fiscal agent, a nonprofit may serve as a conduit for additional funds donated by supporters of the film project. For example, if a church were willing to sponsor a production based on the life of one of its former pastors, the church would probably provide a modest grant toward the production costs (and perhaps provide the use of the church without charge as a shooting location). In addition, the church could collect funds for the film project from other donors. So long as the payments were consistent with the charitable purpose of the organization, a nonprofit could choose to use its resources to underwrite the film project.

4. Accounting and Accountability

As mentioned above, the fiscal agent is responsible for ensuring that the film project's fundraising meets its tax obligations. If the fiscal agent is a film arts charity, it will likely have little or no control over the content of the film. (Non-arts charities are likely to participate as fiscal agents only in those situations where the charity and filmmaker have agreed in general terms about the content.) To meet IRS regulations, however, the fiscal agent must have a legal right to control the project, to assure that the funds are used in a manner consistent with the agreed-upon budget and that financial record keeping and reporting occurs properly. Charities with ongoing fiscal agency programs will have operational guidelines that the filmmaker must agree to follow. The filmmaker remains responsible for any liabilities of the production.

The film company does not itself become a 501(c)(3) charity. Instead, it should receive an annual tax form from the fiscal agent identifying the funds donated to it. Since the amount should be offset by the costs of production, there should be no taxes owed on these payments. If the film company is a sole proprietorship, however, and the budget includes the filmmaker's salary, then this will constitute personal income to the filmmaker.

E. Other Opportunities for Financing and Cost Management

1. Product Placements

The most recent trend in independent filmmaking is financing opportunities generated by placing products strategically in the motion picture. While product placement opportunities have always been a part of film and television financing, declining television audiences have led advertisers to seek them out with greatly increased frequency.

Perhaps the most famous product placement story is the decision of candy manufacturer Mars not to work with Steven Spielberg to feature M&Ms in his movie *E.T.: The Extra-Terrestrial*. Instead, the director used Hershey's Reese's Pieces, and E.T. later starred in some Hershey advertising. Today, automobile companies including Audi and BMW have invested heavily in films featuring their vehicles. In addition to cross-licensing film content for Audi advertising and paying for product placement, Audi invested heavily in developing a concept car to be featured in the film *I, Robot*.

While independent productions are unlikely to receive this same level of support, advertisers are increasingly interested in product placement in independent films and even Internet shorts. The advertiser may pay a fee for having a product in a shot. Filmmakers can negotiate a larger fee if the product plays a featured role in the story. Generally, any such arrangement requires that the product be shown in a positive light. Advertisers will rarely pay to have their products disparaged.

Local advertisers may be the easiest to approach and the most willing to participate. Featuring a local coffeehouse or store as a location adds verisimilitude to the production and creates a potential windfall for the advertiser if the film is successful. Movie locations generate significant tourism, so featuring the actual name and location of a retailer can inspire a boom.

Moreover, if the film can generate a following on YouTube or other popular social networking Web sites, the opportunity may appeal to companies interested in viral advertising. The product placement agreement can include provisions that earn the filmmaker additional payments from the advertiser if video clips hit specified thresholds.

If the filmmaker hopes not just to receive payments for product placement but also to use the film content in advertisements, then she must ensure that the actors involved agree to their commercial participation. This should be clearly provided for in their contracts or, perhaps preferably, through a separate agreement. Of course, the advertisements could lead to additional revenue for the performers, so most actors will not mind, if the ads are done appropriately.

2. Sale of Incentive Tax Credits

As states compete to lure film companies into their jurisdictions in search of employment opportunities and the rise in tourism that can be associated with successful films, production companies are being provided with an additional financing tool. Some of the states provide incentive tax credits, and in certain jurisdictions these credits can be sold to other companies in the state.

An incentive tax credit allows the company to receive a portion of its budget back from the state as a credit. Credits are typically applied against taxes due, providing a significant tax benefit. Since the value of the credit is based on the employment practices and payment activities of the film, the value of the tax credit will be established by the end of principal photography and should be able to be projected with a fair degree of accuracy. With sophisticated accounting and legal assistance, the tax credit may be able to be sold in exchange for funding that can be used to produce the film. Such sales can only occur in those jurisdictions that permit the transfer of the tax credits, so advance planning and close cooperation with the state film office are required. In jurisdictions that allow for the sale of tax credits and provide high incentives, this may be a significant financial resource.

3. Noncash Contributions

Often the film company receives not only the cash contributions of investors but other forms of contributions as well: professional services, equipment, cast participation, locations, and many other attributes of the film. They can help alleviate the filmmaker's financial burden—but they may also have an unintended tax effect.

If a service provider receives shares or an interest in exchange for his services, this results in taxable income to the provider. If the service is exchanged for stock, partnership, or LLC interest, then the payment is presently taxable.[3] In contrast, a share of the film's future profits or revenue should not be taxed until the revenue is actually earned. The significant risk that no actual profits will be earned should be taken into account in structuring the transaction.[4]

Unlike contribution of services, contribution of equipment or property (but not its rental) in exchange for partnership or stock interest does not result in any tax liability. If an individual contributes camera equipment and computer equipment in exchange for its value, no tax liability is incurred. The same rule applies to intellectual property such as the screenplay. If the contributor receives a return on her investment within two years, however, the IRS may treat the transaction as a sale to the film company and assess additional tax liability, so the ultimate tax consequences may be affected by the time it takes for the film to begin to return profits.[5]

Both the timing and the characterization of noncash contributions are very important. If an existing screenplay is exchanged for partnership or stock interest, it will generally be considered a contribution in exchange for property not subject to immediate taxation, but if the same interest is given to a writer as payment for the obligation to write a new screenplay, the exchange will constitute a payment for services and be immediately taxable. Before signing any agreements, the filmmaker or an attorney should consult with a qualified accountant to ensure that the tax consequences are understood fully.

F. Self-Financing the Production

The simplest form of self-financing is for the filmmaker to take cash from her savings account and transfer it to her business account. While this certainly works, few filmmakers have sufficient savings to use this system. In addition to personal cash, filmmakers can seek nonprofit grants, personal loans, and other avenues to help complete their film projects.

1. Guerrilla Financing: Discretionary Money and Gifts

For a true guerrilla film, presale arrangements and studio financing—with its attendant studio control—simply will not work. A guerrilla film is not fully conceived until finished. The guerrilla artist thrives on the energy generated from the chaos that a lack of funding can foster, even if this environment takes its toll on everyone else.

A guerrilla filmmaker's primary source of personal financing will be *discretionary income*—savings that will not be missed—and loans. A guerrilla filmmaker who can finance a film exclusively from discretionary income needs little financial advice. Tell your story, make your movie, and suck as much of the marrow from the production's bones as possible.

Most guerrilla filmmakers, however, do not have the luxury of sufficient discretionary income. To raise additional funds, the best approach is to rely on small gifts. These need not be tax-deductible gifts to a nonprofit fiscal agent, but simply small checks from friends, family, and supporters of the filmmaker's work. For example, the guerrilla filmmaker can arrange a party at a local bar, and invite everyone she knows. Each guest pays a cover charge that provides at least a $20-per-person profit to the filmmaker. In addition, the filmmaker asks for gifts of $50 to $250, offering a "Thank You" credit and premiere tickets or a copy of the DVD. Even better, the filmmaker can ask a local band to play at the event and donate a copy of its latest CD to the film's larger contributors.

While offering to sell interests in the film is a clear violation of securities laws, requesting gifts or selling advance copies of the DVD is not. If the filmmaker offers advance copies of the DVD, however, the language of the offer should make it clear that the money is a gift and the DVD will be provided only if the movie is completed and DVDs published.

2. Personal Debt: Credit Cards and Home Loans

When self-financing without cash in hand, the filmmaker often turns to available sources of debt financing. Personal credit cards and personal collateral often provide emergency money for filmmakers. These sources are generally expensive, because they have high interest rates. They are also highly risky: the debt comes due whether or not the film is completed.

A common use of personal collateral is to obtain a *home equity line of credit*. In home equity lending, the filmmaker borrows money from the bank by securing her primary residence as collateral. Historically, a bank would only lend to someone who maintained at least 20 percent equity in the property. Although banks had substantially relaxed these rules, the mortgage crisis of 2008 compelled lenders to tighten all lending rules.

If the filmmaker is married, her spouse will typically be a co-owner of the property. The bank will require that all parties who own the property sign the loans. This makes both the filmmaker and the nonfilmmaking spouse personally responsible for the loan. In most states, the loan must be repaid even if the house is worth less than the value of the loan.[6] The danger of borrowing against one's primary residence is that if the film does not sell, the filmmaker's home is put in jeopardy. This is a significant burden for the filmmaker to impose on the nonfilmmaking spouse, particularly when added to the time commitment and personal sacrifice that the guerrilla filmmaker's work extracts from her family.

The filmmaker should carefully consider the expenses, both the interest and the principal payments required. If the only way the filmmaker can cover the payments from the loan is to successfully sell the film, then the filmmaker should restructure the budget or take other steps to avoid this risk. I have never given different advice to any student or client, nor have I ever heard of anyone who has gambled her house on a film and won. Change the budget, change the project, or find another way to tell the story. If, on the other hand, the filmmaker can cover the interest and principal payments, then using her home as collateral is merely an unwise, highly risky choice that should be avoided if possible.

The other personal source of funds for financing the film is *revolving credit*—credit card debt. Because of questionable lending practices, a moderately successful individual with a reasonable amount of personal debt could once be offered up to hundreds of thousands of dollars' worth of credit cards. The economic crisis has largely ended this practice, however, so access to credit from credits cards has suddenly become much more difficult.

Credit cards are unsecured and generally offered for personal rather than commercial use; the cards are usually in the filmmaker's name rather than in the name of the film company. The filmmaker should carefully consider the consequences before committing her personal assets by financing the film through short-term, high-interest credit card loans. While the attraction is obvious, and filmmaker Spike Lee built his early success on credit cards, the downside can be financial ruin.

If used at all, credit cards should be a method of last resort. The filmmaker may decide to keep a credit card available to serve as a rainy-day fund, to cover the final costs of editing when the investments and production expenses go slightly over budget. They should also be paid off first to avoid the high costs of the loans.

Finally, some guerrilla filmmakers convince the cast and crew to "lend" the production their credit cards. This practice is unethical and should be avoided, no matter how tempting the idea. The party named on the card is the person responsible for the debt, and even a promise or written agreement by the filmmaker to cover the costs on the card cannot change that fact in the eyes of the bank issuing the card. Since a crew member's credit card would not be used unless the production itself had no assets, the effect is to make the other participants in the film financially obligated for the debts of the project. If members of the cast or crew have the financial ability to become investors, then they should be properly informed and rewarded as such. The so-called borrowing of their credit cards offers them no protection while exposing them to significant financial risk.

G. Financing the Film Company: Organizing the Operating Agreement

The basic structure of the film business entity must provide the core ownership and management for the filmmaker with limited protections for the investor. Depending on the form of the business (see chapter 2, p. 13), organizational papers may have to be filed and submitted to the secretary of state along with a tax payment. In addition to this filing, a film company must have written and signed articles and bylaws or an operating agreement that sets out the rules for operations, governance, and payments.

1. Business of the Company

The first question to answer is whether the film company is being created for the purposes of the particular film project or whether it may be used for multiple projects—sequels, unrelated films, or other projects entirely. Today, a typical corporation's bylaws state that it can conduct "any lawful business," meaning any business that exists. For Disney, that makes sense. To protect small investors, however, the better choice is to limit the investment to a single film project. The filmmaker can always try to amend this decision at a later time—but, of course, the investors will then have a voice and a vote in such a modification.

If the purpose of the company is not limited, the filmmaker can continue making movies until the money runs out; even if the first film returns a nice profit, the income is retained for future films. In such a case, the investor may still receive nothing. Given the risks involved in motion picture investing, the more equitable approach is to limit the investment to the production or productions agreed upon at the time of investment.

2. Control

As described in previous chapters, the filmmaker must be the authority behind the film, and the documents organizing the business must reflect this authority. The filmmaker must retain management control, at least throughout the initial production and distribution of the project. The operating agreement of the film company should be drafted to guarantee that the filmmaker retains control of the film company's management to the greatest extent permitted by law. Even so, this authority cannot be absolute. The filmmaker will eventually die[7] or become unwilling or unable to manage the company's operations.

3. Personal Obligation of the Filmmaker

By nature, an independent film is a highly personal undertaking. As a result, the operating agreement should reflect the importance of the filmmaker's role and include specific provisions in the event the filmmaker becomes disassociated from the project. For example, the death or incapacity of the filmmaker may terminate the project. Similarly, if the filmmaker becomes professionally unavailable—whether it is because he has become too famous or too frustrated is irrelevant—the project should end. In many ways this also serves as a form of protection for the investor.

4. Project Milestones

It is not uncommon for independent films to languish for years while money is found to complete them. The operating agreement must be very clear regarding the rules about the availability of the investor's money. The investor should be obligated to pay immediately, and should receive no interest in the company until that payment is received. If the budget sets the minimum amount of cash available at $150,000, either the investor must agree that his funds can be spent prior to the company raising the entire $150,000, or the investor's purchase payment should be put in escrow and held until the film company has raised a specified amount (see chapter 8, p. 151).

Most typically, the terms of the operating agreement stipulate that the investors' funds will be released when there is enough to make meaningful progress. For example, if the film can be made for $150,000, then the agreement may provide that the funds will be released when $100,000 is received, because that is enough to get through preproduction and principal photography.

5. Management Fees

The filmmaker, as manager of the film company, may choose to receive some portion of the revenue as payment for services provided. The choice to pay oneself is neither a good or bad choice. So long as the payment structure is fully disclosed, rather than hidden in fine print or unstated, the investors can have no legitimate complaints. Such payments are akin to the producer's fees charged to a studio. However, if all participants in the project worked without pay and the investors assumed a very high risk, then it may be appropriate to forgo any producer's payment. Both approaches have been used. The key is for the operating agreement to explain specifically the basis for the investors' return on capital and participation in net revenue.

6. Wrap-Up of Ownership

The operating agreement should also provide for a mandatory repurchase of the investor's interests at some point in the future. For example, this may be triggered by a lack of production company revenues for a three-year period. Such a clause would provide that if the production company has not made more than a minor amount of income (say, $5,000), then the company can repurchase the interests of the investors by paying a preset fee, or by providing for mandatory arbitration if the parties cannot voluntarily agree on a price.

7. Deferred Compensation for Some Participants

Most independent film companies are unable to pay all their expenses. Instead, they rely on locations, cast, crew, and service providers to work on credit. (To balance the risk of nonpayment, filmmakers often promise revenue or profit participation to those parties as well.) The company must plan carefully regarding deferred payment obligations. They must be incorporated into the budgeting process and clearly identified when defining the revenue returns to which the investors are entitled.

For example, it is common to grant the investors a return of capital before the producer takes his portion of gross revenues. Often investors are entitled to as much as 125 percent of their initial investment before the producer receives payment. The operating agreement must specify whether the cast, crew, and other service providers are entitled to deferred compensation payments prior to the investor's payment. If the motion picture has a total cost of $150,000, an investor may think the film has a reasonable chance to return the majority of the investment and the potential to return far more. If instead, the picture has a "cost" of $150,000 because those are the expenses that could not be deferred, but an additional $250,000 in deferred compensation, then the investor may not receive his first dollar until after $400,000 in revenue has been earned. Deferred compensation dramatically changes the risk of an investment and is therefore highly material to the structure. The operating agreement should specify whether the deferred compensation is paid first, the investors are paid first, or both are paid proportionately at the same time.[8]

8. Limitations on the Managers

As the person in charge of a legally recognized business, the filmmaker undertakes business and professional obligations toward the investors as well as the employees and other participants of the project. And if the filmmaker enlists other individuals to serve as managers of the LLC or directors of the corporation, those individuals have a similar duty to act in the best interests of the business.

Further, the law does not like to vest unbridled discretion in a single businessperson's hands. State laws will protect the investors in some situations, requiring that the filmmaker provide the investors with information and an opportunity to vote on suggested changes. For example, if the company has insufficient funds to start its movie and another film company has insufficient funds to complete an unrelated picture, the filmmaker might wish to merge the two companies in order to receive producer credit and associate director credit on the second picture. Nonetheless, the merger can take place only if the shareholders or members of the LLC agree. Similarly, the filmmaker could not take the money invested in the first film to the second film, because that would breach his duty of good faith to the investors and the film company.

In the same vein, the operating agreement will generally limit the amount of debt the company can acquire without member approval, set the minimum and maximum amount of equity that the film company can raise, and prevent the sale of the company's assets other than through agreements to distribute the motion picture. In this way, the interests of the investors are protected from excesses of the manager or director.

Budgeting

THOUGH SOMETIMES IT is the most creative part of a film, a carefully crafted budget provides the pivotal road map for the entire film project. Whether the film is expected to cost $2,000 or $200 million, its budget must account for every dollar to be expended on the production. In addition, the budget serves as a comparative tool, assuring that all the pieces of the film are proportionate or at least carefully planned. If each cast member receives tens of millions of dollars, then the film should not have homemade special effects.

The budget will be shaped by the filmmaker's specific choices: locations, size and prominence of cast, stunts, and the effects needed both during and after principal photography. For independent and guerrilla filmmakers, the key is to identify the cornerstone elements of the film and build the budget around those items. If a particular location must be used to tell the story, a particular cast member becomes essential to the financing, or a certain special effect defines the film, then that element should be identified early and its costs determined. Thereafter, the remainder of the budget can be structured to keep the production in harmony with that item.

The budget process continues from the inception of the project through the completion of the finished negative. Neither the prints used to show the film theatrically nor the advertising and promotional budget are included in the budget numbers used for production. For studio films, print and advertising costs often equal the production costs, and for an inexpensive film, they may greatly exceed those costs.

There are excellent software programs to assist filmmakers with the detailed budgeting and accounting process, including EP Movie Magic Budgeting and Jungle Software's Gorilla. These programs can handle a great deal of detail and generate extremely helpful reports. The approach to the budget, however, must come from the filmmaker rather than the software.

A. Purpose of the Budget

The budgeting process is important for a number of reasons, both internal and external. The screenplay may be the most important filmmaking tool, but only the budget can set the financial framework for all the decisions regarding the film. It provides a material foundation on which every party involved in the project relies.

An accurate and complete budget must be provided to the investors, the lenders, the completion bond company, and the unions. Once the filmmaker obtains a commitment, few significant alterations can be made without their approval. A filmmaker may not unilaterally decide to film for an extra two weeks to capture the light, no matter how artistically compelling it may be. Nor can she drop a name star to pay for those two weeks, unless she has the permission of the lender and the completion bond company. Even investors might get upset by such changes, so the documents must be very explicit regarding which budget decisions are subject to change and which are not.

1. Independent Review of the Budget

Many of the recipients of the budget will undertake an independent review of its assumptions. For instance, if a low-budget production seeks to use WGA or SAG reduced-scale agreements (see section C, p. 136), the proposed budget is part of the document package provided to the unions. They assess the anticipated cost of equipment, locations, cast size, and number of days, and may reject the budget if they do not believe it accurately reflects the cost of the shoot. In addition, the unions will require the actual expenses to be submitted at the end of principal photography to ensure that the filmmaker has stayed within the financial limits of the low-budget agreements.

The completion bond company will also review the budget carefully, in combination with the script, to determine the feasibility of delivering the film within the projected budget. The company will only be willing to provide a completion bond if it believes the budget is reasonably conservative in its estimates of cost and schedule. Since the completion bond is a requirement for many entertainment lenders, this budget review can make or break a production.

2. The Budget as the First Disclosure Document

As will be discussed more fully in chapter 8 (p. 142), the film company is required to provide the investors with a series of disclosure documents that are accurate, complete, and sufficient to give the investor a full understanding of the risks involved in the production. No document is more important for this purpose than the budget. It details the costs to complete the film and acquire a distributor. If the film company seeks to raise substantially more money than this, the additional money raised will likely go into the pockets of the filmmakers. If the film company does not raise enough money to meet the budget, then the filmmakers must explain what combination of loans and personal funds they are committing to the film. Otherwise, the project is doomed from the start.

Investors have no information other than the budget to understand the relationship between their potential investment and the costs of producing the proposed film. Despite the ease with which the filmmaker can adjust the presumptive costs in the budget software, the filmmaker must understand that the budget represents a commitment to those parties who have relied upon the document.

3. Working and Reworking the Budget

Because a budget is an important source of information for investors, the time to adjust and experiment with the budget is before they have committed to the film. Until the budget has been presented to investors, lenders, or the completion bond company, it represents nothing more than numbers on a page.

Budgets often are changed during the planning stages of the project. For an independent filmmaker, there may be a variety of budget scenarios based on best-case financing and worst-case financing. Certain scenes may be noted for possible revision based on the financial outcome. Like a modern theatrical writer, the filmmaker writing a low-budget film must treat the financial limitations as a structural framework around which the story is crafted. If no flashback to the Eiffel Tower is possible, a close-up of a toy replica in a store window might do the trick.

If an independent film will be made on a minimal budget, then certain expenses must be eliminated. Because the budget cannot accommodate travel expenses or other costs, the movie may be filmed locally, or in areas that can easily double for other locations so that multiple scenes can be shot without moving. A high-speed car chase may need to be revised to take place on foot or on bicycles. The science fiction genre has become so effects laden that low-budget science fiction films have nearly disappeared.

4. Budget Coverage

When studios or production companies review scripts for possible purchase, the script is put through a *coverage review*. The result is a two-to-five-page report in which the potential purchaser quickly summarizes the project, assesses the strengths and weaknesses of the concept, story, and writing, and provides an estimated cost of production.

The estimate reflects what this particular production company believes it should spend to bring this script to the screen. Embedded in this analysis is the production company's choices regarding the quality and budget for lead cast members, scale of special effects and visual effects, and approach to international locations. A studio or major production company with a roster of A-list talent and films will incorporate those types of costs into the analysis and coverage. A small art house will assume a different pool of actors from which to choose and different strategies for managing costs. Each will provide budget coverage for the script that is accurate for that company's production, but that coverage will not necessarily be relevant to any other producer.

The majority of the coverage process is focused on the script rather than the budget. The coverage report will separately rate the script and the writer, as well as the key elements of the content: concept, plot, story structure, characters, dialogue, and visual impact. This grading, along with the company's own synopsis, will become the document used to assess the film.

B. When *Not* to Disclose the Budget

Although many parties to the financing of the film will rely on the budget, the filmmaker may not find it helpful to disclose budget figures when selling the distribution rights in a film market or film festival setting. The film company is seeking the largest possible advance for the rights to the film, because a large advance provides cash to the film company and motivates the distributor to work diligently to recoup its investment in the film. The distributor, in contrast, rarely wants to provide an advance greater than the budget of the film. Since the filmmaker would be violating her duty to negotiate in good faith were she to lie regarding the budget, the best strategy is to keep information regarding the budget secret and refuse to respond to inquiries regarding the budget during the negotiation process.

Nonetheless, no-budget films, such as Kevin Smith's *Clerks* or Robert Rodriguez's *El Mariachi,* do create a certain rough ambience about them. Even modest success can often result in large-percentage returns, which bolster the credibility and bankability of the filmmakers. In contrast, high-budget films must be blockbusters to justify the expense, resulting in ever more lavish productions and increasing expectations. As a result, while independent filmmakers often want to create the impression that their film cost more than it did when selling it, they frequently *understate* the cost once the film is being exhibited, to suggest that they are more creative and resourceful than the actual budget would suggest. For example, it was rumored that while the reported budget of *The Blair Witch Project* was only $30,000, Artisan Entertainment spent close to $1 million to finish the film.

C. Anatomy of a Budget

A budget consists of the summary page, known as the *top sheet,* and a series of department-by-department itemizations for that budget. Even if a film's expenses top $200 million, every roll of tape must be budgeted, receipted, and credited to its particular account. The numbers may get large, but the need for attention to detail never diminishes. Each day throughout the course of the production, the actual expenses are reconciled with the budget to calculate the production's accuracy in planning and to make the necessary adjustments to keep the project on time and on budget.

Every budget contains several different types of expenses. *Above-the-line expenses* are the major costs that set the scale of the production; they include the salaries of the director and leading cast members, the cost of the script, and the producer's fee. In the studio world, they are often negotiated in coordination, so that star salaries are proportionate and the director has a deal somewhat similar to those of the other above-the-line participants. *Below-the-line expenses* are typically the production expenses, which include the remaining cast, locations, sets, costumes, permits, and equipment rentals. These costs tend to vary less than above-the-line expenses; the cost of a location permit, for example, does not change based on the fame of the cast. The budget must also reflect postproduction expenses, including the editing, sound, addition of special effects, and titles.

In addition to the production and postproduction expenses, significant other budget items include the various forms of insurance which must be maintained, legal fees, accounting expenses, and a small budget for capturing film and video content to be used in the publicity of the film and as extras on the DVD or Web site.

Traditionally, the scale of a film was set by above-the-line costs, which represented the most significant portion of the budget. In today's moviemaking environment, however, this may not be the case. The visual effects added in postproduction can equal or exceed the cost of production and may represent expenses as great as the salaries of top-name star talent.

1. Deferred Compensation

Deferred compensation represents income earned but not paid to cast, crew, or other parties. In reality, deferred compensation represents a form of an unsecured loan made to the film company by its employees. If the film company does not obtain sufficient funding or earn sufficient income, then the employee will forgo this portion of her income.

Deferred compensation is an expense, and like all expenses it should be included in the budget, itemized in the appropriate category. If a film has cash needs of $200,000 and deferred compensation of $300,000, any contracts or other provisions reflecting return to investors would be based on a $500,000 budget amount rather than the $200,000 cash needs, so the budget should make this clear.

However, the budget should also identify deferred compensation as such. The average investor will be much more likely to respect additional royalties paid to the deferred income participants if he can see that it reflects the risk that they will not receive their $300,000 in earned income.

2. Special Considerations: Music

Music has always been an important part of filmmaking. The film score can influence the emotional impact of a scene, shaping audience reactions at a subconscious level. Featured songs can carry the audience's emotional associations with those songs into the film's world of suspended disbelief. For instance, when *Wall-E* incorporated a video clip from *Hello Dolly,* it helped to bridge the audience age gap and served as instant shorthand for the values learned by the main character, a self-aware robot, during his 700 years of isolation.

The details of music licensing for the film score, featured songs performed for the movie, and *needle drops*—prerecorded songs played during the film—are described in chapter 14, but because music has become not only a vital aspect of independent filmmaking but also an expensive one, the filmmaker should pay particular attention to its role in the budget process. The budget should separate out the payments to the composer of the film score from the budget for featured song and needle drops.

Budgeting for needle drops requires the filmmaker to identify the rights holder, which is typically the record label. The record label will want information on the planned use of the recording: "opening credits," "end credits," "background," or "featured in the scene." The label will also want to know the budget for the film and the planned distribution.

The record companies understand that motion picture promotion can lead to great sales for songs and records. But their goal is to maximize the revenue, so songs that are already more popular among filmmakers demand a high premium. In addition, it costs money for the companies to review the music license rights for each song, so they tend not to be particularly helpful unless the filmmaker already has a distribution agreement in place.

For filmmakers who do not have distribution agreements, the record companies' compromise is to offer a *festival license.* For a modest fee, the record company gives the film company permission to use its song in one or more film festivals. This gives the film company the authorization it needs to proceed, implying permission to copy the song onto the audio tracks of the film, edit the song to the appropriate length, and otherwise exploit the song enough to prepare the film for its festival release and screen a rough cut to potential distributors.

The significant downside to the festival license is that it does not state the cost the filmmaker will have to pay to use the song in theatrical distribution or in any of the other media for which a license will ultimately be needed. The festival license leaves the filmmaker at the mercy of the record label, perhaps even creating a risk that the film rights will be sold for a price below the cost of the music rights. Unfortunately, few record labels are motivated to provide complete fee schedules to low-budget filmmakers.

Filmmakers must anticipate the financial challenges of music acquisition. If they hope to use popular recorded music, they must set aside a budget for this purpose. Wherever possible, they should avoid relying on popular recorded music unless they can establish the price for the music's use. If the music is featured in a scene, then the film is put at great financial risk unless the filmmaker can rely on a fixed price to acquire the music. Filmmakers should use other music sources to the greatest extent possible to avoid the licensing trap created by the festival license.

3. Special Considerations: Low-Budget Union Agreements

To encourage low-budget filmmaking and promote the employment of union members, the various industry trade unions have authorized a series of low-budget agreements to reduce costs for production. A number of low-budget agreements exist for various trade unions, including SAG, WGA, and IATSE.

Under the SAG agreements, for example, all the work must be completed in the United States, and various budget caps set the eligibility to participate:

Short Film Agreement (35 minutes or less)—Total budget of less than $50,000
- Salaries are deferred
- No consecutive employment required (except on overnight location)
- Allows the use of both professional and non-professional performers
- Background performers not covered

Ultra–Low Budget Agreement—Total budget of less than $200,000
- Day rate of $100
- No step-up fees
- No consecutive employment required (except on overnight location)
- Allows the use of both professional and non-professional performers
- Background performers not covered

Modified Low Budget Agreement—Total budget of less than $625,000
- Day rate of $268
- Weekly rate of $933
- No consecutive employment required (except on overnight location)
- Reduced overtime rate

Low Budget Agreement—Total budget of less than $2,500,000
- Day rate of $504
- Weekly rate of $1752
- No consecutive employment required (except on overnight location)
- Reduced overtime rate
- Reduced number of Background Performers covered

The WGA low-budget provisions use a similar approach, reducing the minimum payments and allowing for some deferred compensation. Under these agreements, the production company must still provide payment to the writers for residuals and contribute to the union's health, welfare, and pension funds.

WGA Low Budget Agreement for films budgeted up to $500,000
- The screenplay purchase minimum of $39,290 due the writer may be deferred until the earlier of
  (1) commencement of commercial distribution or
  (2) recoupment of production costs

WGA Low Budget Agreement for films budgeted between $500,000 and $1.2 million
- The screenplay purchase minimum of $39,290 may be partially deferred as follows: $10,000 of the screenplay purchase minimum is due the writer upon commencement of principal photography and a $5,000 script publication fee is payable after writing credit is determined.

- ALL other amounts due the writer may be deferred until the earlier of
  (1) commencement of commercial distribution or
  (2) recoupment of production costs

WGA Minimum Basic Agreement for films budgeted between $1.2 million and $5 million sets the screenplay purchase minimum price at $39,290; projects budgeted above that amount must budget a minimum purchase price of $80,427.

The low-budget agreements provide considerable budget relief for low-budget producers, but also increase the need for accuracy in the budgeting process. Moreover, because the actual production expenses must be reported to the unions, the agreements put additional pressure on the filmmakers to stay under the budget caps set out in the various union agreements.

D. Managing Risk: Contingency, Insurance, and Completion Bond Requirements

In addition to the costs associated with the mechanical processes of filmmaking, the budget must account for other expenses that are part of the risk management of the production. It should set aside an amount of money, typically 10 percent of the total budget, to cover whatever contingencies may arise, and allot additional funds to insurance coverage and often a completion bond.

1. Insurance Coverage

Except for the tiniest of productions, each film company must carry a variety of insurance, including workers' compensation insurance; cast insurance; liability insurance on the negative and videotape, sets, equipment, and property; and errors and omissions insurance to cover problems with the script such as defamation or copyright infringement.

Liability insurance can cover many aspects of the production. The insurance is typically *short-term,* since the coverage is only necessary during principal photography. These policies may include:

- general liability
- rented equipment
- props, sets, and wardrobe
- negative and faulty stock
- third-party property damage
- extra expense
- automobile liability and physical damage
- umbrella
- certificates of insurance (including special certificates)

A film company may need only some of these policies. Every project should have general liability insurance, automobile liability insurance, and workers' compensation coverage. Other policies will depend on the nature of the shoot and the risks the film company is willing to undertake. Any specialty items such as boats, planes, or antiques require separate coverage.

2. Completion Bond

Many film projects must be protected with a completion bond, by which the bond company agrees to pay unforeseen costs in excess of the project's 10 percent contingency. This insurance is expensive in both financial and practical terms. The completion bond company retains veto control over cast and crew and can take over the production if either the shoot begins to fall behind schedule or reshoots are necessary. Its concern is focused on the budget, so an aesthetically bad but efficient production has little to worry about.

To obtain a completion bond, the production company must have full financing; complete, unambiguous ownership of the story and script rights; full insurance coverage for the production; agreements for use of the primary locations; and a feasibility study or coverage report showing that the script and budget balance. The steps necessary to obtain a completion bond make it significantly less likely that it will be needed, so for many filmmakers the process simply serves as an exercise in good planning. A completion bond is essential, however, if the film company requires a loan for cash flow based upon a distribution agreement.

E. Contingent Fees

Royalties, profits, and residuals are not considered deferred expenses of the production; instead, they come out of the income earned by the film. As a result, these various contingent fees do not need to be incorporated into the production budget. They serve as an effective tool to reduce the cost of completing the picture, but they must be spent carefully and wisely.

The order in which the various contingent payments are made to the parties must be clearly established in the employment contracts and disclosed to the investors. As owners of the film company, investors are generally the last parties to receive a share of income. To protect investors, it is not uncommon to treat the return of the investment as a separate category of obligation and to reimburse some or all of the production investment at the same time other contingent obligations are paid.

If the contingent fees are based on *gross income,* then the payments are due before money is paid to investors or other parties. If they are based on *net profits,* then the fees are paid only after all other expenses are paid. While this may seem clear, there is no standard definition of the relevant terms on which to rely. Instead, the definition of "income," "expenses," and "net profits" adopted by the film company will establish whether payments to the investors are expenses to be deducted before the film has earned net profits. The film company should adopt a single standard for these terms that is used in every disclosure document and agreement in which profits are distributed.

A better practice is to avoid the terms *gross* and *net* entirely, using terms like *adjusted gross* or *defined profits,* because these terms more clearly indicate that the order of payments will be derived from the project's agreements rather than from general accounting procedures.

The Investors' Package

FILM INVESTORS PURCHASE an ownership interest in the film company. Whether the interest is sold as shares of company stock or limited liability company membership interests, the transaction involves the sale of securities. This stands in stark contrast to selling (or preselling) the distribution rights in the movie. When the film company sells the distribution rights, it is selling the product the company makes, and the purchaser does not acquire any interest in the company.

If the filmmaker is going to finance his project independently by receiving investments from relatives and qualified individuals, he has to determine what he *must* tell and what he *should* tell the potential investors. The hardest decision is how to convey the story. Few professionals, and even fewer nonprofessionals, can read a treatment or screenplay and interpret what it will look like as a completed motion picture. As with the sale of distribution rights, the filmmaker may often elicit a greater visceral reaction by creating small poster mock-ups, or one-sheets, than by sharing the written treatment or completed script.

Regardless of how the story will be sold to the investors, there remains a great deal of information the investors should know.

A. Prerequisites to Soliciting Investments

Because investors are acquiring rights in the company in which they invest, the transaction is a complicated, sophisticated business arrangement involving securities laws, federal disclosure requirements, and complex tax and reporting obligations. The various documents provide information to the investors regarding the transaction and set out the terms of their ownership. Although quite common, selling interests in a film company requires careful planning, diligent execution, and ongoing maintenance. The basic rules discussed below apply to all formal business structures: corporations, limited partnerships, and limited liability companies.

1. Basic Requirements and the Meaning of "Disclosure": Making a Federal Case Out of Film Financing

Under both state and federal law, a business seeking to raise capital has as its first obligation a duty to provide full disclosure. In other words, the filmmaker must reveal all the material facts regarding the investment and its risks. This simple rule that the filmmaker must fully disclose all the terms of the investment is often overlooked, but at the filmmaker's peril. Failure to fully disclose all the material terms can result in the investor being entitled to a complete return of his investment directly from either the film company or the filmmaker herself, depending on which of the parties has assets. The filmmaker may also be held criminally liable for knowingly misrepresenting the risks involved in the investment. All the other planning done by the accountants and lawyers will be worth nothing if the filmmaker hides information or misrepresents the facts regarding the production.

Not only must all information provided to investors be accurate when made, but it must be updated as well. This means that the investors need to be kept informed throughout the life of the project.

One challenge for properly meeting disclosure requirements is identifying what facts and issues are material. At its heart, *material* means information that is important to the investor, information a reasonable person would consider important in deciding whether or not to invest.[1] Put another way, information is material if there is a substantial likelihood that this information would be considered to have significantly altered the "total mix" of information available to the potential investor. Thus, material issues include all the terms of any investment deal, but also information regarding the film, the production, the competition, and anything else the filmmaker thought was important to say when promoting the project to the investor. This also means that the filmmaker must avoid puffing up her resume, overstating the potential chances of profitability, or otherwise painting an unrealistic picture.

2. Overview of Federal Securities Restrictions

Because the sale of interest in the film company is governed by state and federal securities law, there are a number of important limitations on the way a filmmaker can raise investment funds. These limitations do not typically apply to presale arrangements and other distribution-based financing—which is yet another reason such financing is preferable to soliciting investor funds. Still, if Aunt Betty's investment is the only way the film can get made, this section will identify when it is fair to ask Aunt Betty for funds and when it violates the law even to ask.

Offers to sell and sales of securities are governed by the Securities Act of 1933 and the Securities and Exchange Act of 1934. Unless exempt from the federal rules (see subsection 3, below), an offer to sell securities must be accompanied by a detailed disclosure document called a *prospectus*. In addition, every state but Nevada has its own laws governing securities offerings and sales. The state laws set forth specific rules for the offers to sell securities and often allow the state to judge the fairness of the offering to residents of the state. Again, certain offers may be exempt from these rules (see subsection 4, below).

Because of the costs and difficulties involved with preparing these offering documents, virtually all film financing projects are structured to fall within one of the exemptions to the federal and state laws. Even if they are exempt from the documentation requirements, however, state and federal laws still protect the investor from fraudulent statements or failures to disclose material information.

Since the laws cover the *offers to sell* as well as the sales themselves, the filmmaker must be careful to avoid casual conversations about the availability of interests in the film. In other words, posting e-mails to newsgroups or listservs should never be part of the film financing strategy.

3. Exemptions for Certain Types of Securities Transactions

Although federal law covers all securities, it categorically exempts from documentation registration a variety of transactions. This means that if the offering falls into one of the exemptions, the documentation does not need to be reviewed by the SEC prior to the sale of the security. It does *not* mean that the film company should not provide documentation regarding the sale of the shares, membership interests, or limited partnership interests, merely that the form and content of the documents will not be specified by federal regulations.

Under federal law, the company does not need to register securities if they are offered by the company in a transaction not involving any public offering.[2] At a minimum, nonpublic transactions are those conducted directly by the issuer (the company) without any finder's fees or other fees paid for identifying investors, and without any public advertising, broadly defined. While this definition appears to cover a wide range of offerings, the interpretation of various state and federal securities laws and regulations limit it significantly.

Nonpublic offering exemptions often apply to securities sold to the company's senior officers, directors, or managers—individuals who are in a position to have sufficient knowledge of the company's situation because of their professional association. Similarly, the exemption may be available to close family members. A sale to Aunt Betty would most likely not be governed by the federal securities registration requirements if she were truly a blood relative. Were she a family friend called "aunt" out of respect, however, the answer under the securities laws would change. As a result, the nonpublic exception is rather narrow and difficult to rely on.

In addition to nonpublic offerings, the federal laws generally do not govern transactions that occur completely within one state.[3] To meet this test, the business entity must be formed in the selected state, every offer and sale must occur exclusively in that same state, a significant portion of the business activity must occur in that state, and the interest must come to rest in that state. For example, if all offers to finance the film took place in California, the sales were in California to residents of California who did not move during the next nine months, the film company was formed in California, and much of the production occurred in California, then only California law would apply regarding the sale of securities and no federal registration would be required.[4]

In addition, and perhaps most significantly, federal law exempts from documentation and registration transactions that are limited to *accredited investors,* those with the financial resources and personal savvy to take care of themselves. Accredited investors include the following:

- individuals with income of $200,000 annually in each of the two most recent years, or joint income with a spouse exceeding $300,000 for those years, and a reasonable expectation of the same income level in the current year
- an individual who has individual net worth, or joint net worth with a spouse, that exceeds $1 million at the time of the purchase
- a director, executive officer, or general partner of the company selling the securities
- a charitable organization, corporation, or partnership with assets exceeding $5 million[5]

This is not a complete list. Some banks, nonprofit organizations, and other entities are also accredited investors. Federal law presumes that these people and organizations are sufficiently sophisticated, that they will ask the right questions and protect themselves from poorly understood business transactions. The law also assumes that only those with substantial income can afford to take the significant risk involved with these types of small offerings. If someone falls within this category, federal law does not require that the information regarding the financing be in any particular form, as long as the information is fully disclosed to the investors' satisfaction.

In addition to these examples, the SEC has promulgated rules for a variety of transactions involving nonpublic offerings and sales of securities. Each rule has its own disclosure requirements regarding the amount of information that the issuer must provide to the purchasers, which vary depending on the size of the offering and the description of the individuals receiving the offers. Companies selling securities have substantially less risk of violating the law if they follow these SEC rules than if they rely on the general exemption for nonpublic offerings.

For example, the federal exemption known as Rule 506 provides a series of clear guidelines regarding persons to whom private interests can be sold without having to register with the SEC and without any limitations on the dollar amounts raised. Rule 506 allows for an unlimited number of accredited investors and up to 35 *sophisticated investors.*

A sophisticated investor is a nonaccredited investor who is nonetheless considered capable of evaluating the risks and merits of the investment under the SEC rules. As Rule 506 puts it, "each purchaser who is not an accredited investor either alone or with his purchaser representative(s) has such knowledge and experience in financial and business matters that he is capable of evaluating the merits and risks of the prospective investment, or the issuer reasonably believes immediately prior to making any sale that such purchaser comes within this description."[6] (The purchaser representative must herself be a sophisticated investor capable of evaluating the risks and merits of the investment.) For these sophisticated investors, however, the SEC rule requires that the film company make a more detailed disclosure of information, making the inclusion of one or two sophisticated investors potentially more difficult than their investment is worth.

Given the high-risk nature of film investment, private solicitations are better left with those in the accredited investor category, to the extent the filmmaker has that choice.

As an alternative, although generally a dangerous choice because of the lack of any limits on liability, general partnerships have one primary benefit. Because of their access to information and control of the organization, all general partners are usually treated as exempt for purposes of mandatory disclosure documents.

4. Additional Filing Required Under State Securities Law

The rules governing securities sales grow even more complex when dealing with state laws. For offerings not involving publicly traded companies, state law often plays the more important role in governing the nature of the transaction. Because state laws vary so greatly, there are few generally applicable rules.

The first step is to consult a qualified securities attorney in the state where the offering will take place. Generally, if the offering is nonpublic, with no advertising and no commissions or finder's fees paid, then the sale to sophisticated investors will require a minimum amount of mandatory documentation under state law. Similarly, if the interests are provided only to those people who have a direct working relationship with the project, there may be few mandatory requirements for documentation. As discussed below, however, the company always has the obligation to provide the investors with all material information. Many of the states' laws simply assist the filmmaker in meeting this obligation and should serve as a guide rather than a burden.

B. Requirements for Creating Nonpublic Offerings

The key to properly structuring disclosure documentation is that all the information is accurate, complete, and sufficient to give the investor a full understanding of the risks involved in the production. For the sake of both the investors and the filmmaker, the money should only come from people who can afford to invest the funds. The documents should properly alert potential investors to the significant risk involved with independent film financing.

The form and substance of the investment documents will depend on the legal structure of the film company, the amount of money sought, state laws, and the federal exemptions used to reduce or eliminate federal registration of the securities. As a result, no single document can be used for all film financing transactions.

1. LLC or Financing Agreement

For motion picture financing, the LLC serves as an excellent vehicle, because the operating agreement, which dictates the rights and interests of the managers of the company, can also serve as the disclosure document in many transactions. In corporations a disclosure document known as a *subscription agreement* or *financing agreement* must provide the same detail. Whatever the form, the guiding principle of the process is the need to provide full disclosure of all the material facts regarding the project.

Among the material details, the agreement must state the total amount of money to be raised and the ownership interest in the film company received in exchange for each payment. It must also state the ownership interest retained by the filmmaker and what was given in exchange for that interest (services, the screenplay, etc.). It must clearly state how these numbers can be modified by the film company if necessary.

The agreement will also provide information on the transferability of the interests, the payments to the managers (typically the filmmaker), the other income or deferred compensation paid to the managers and to other participants, and any other financial arrangements already made. If any presale arrangements have been entered into, any loans have been obtained (even credit cards), or any other material contracts have been signed, they should also be disclosed.

2. Private Placement Memoranda

Depending on the amount of money involved and the nature of the participants, the filmmaker may elect to use a private placement memorandum to describe the investment opportunity. This memo should be used exclusively for sophisticated or accredited investors who have the financial resources to risk a total loss of their investment in the film.

The private placement memo should include information regarding the business entity, the risks involved in the production, the film, the filmmaker, the production team, and the offering—including the financial opportunity and structure, the use of the investment proceeds, the allocations and distribution of revenue, and fees and expenses. It should also provide information regarding the independent film market in general and those films that are most comparable to the filmmaker's project in particular. Finally, the document should outline tax issues, procedures for the termination or dissolution of the company, conflicts of interest for the filmmakers or other principals, and the effect of taking on additional financing. Such a document is quite detailed and must be completed by an experienced attorney with the help of the filmmaker.

The private placement memorandum contains only disclosure information; the investor receiving it has no obligation to invest. Instead, in a traditional corporate stock transaction, the actual sales document is typically a *subscription agreement*. The subscription agreement provides contractual language for the obligations described in the private placement memorandum similar in detail to that of an operating agreement. Such terms may include limitations on the transferability of the stock, identification of the obligations of the investors, the rights and returns expected, and any other contractual protections offered by the film company or waived by the investors.

Private placement memoranda and subscription agreements provide much greater detail regarding the business and the transaction than may be necessary for a small-budget independent film. Ultimately the form of disclosure will depend on the amount of information necessary to explain the transaction adequately, the expectations of the investors, and the sophistication with which the investors spend their money.

The disclosure documents are *anti-sales* documents. By outlining all the details and highlighting all the risks, these documents should discourage investment unless the person investing has the financial ability to take a complete financial loss on the project and yet is still willing to back the film. The key must come not from the potential financial return—which is extremely speculative—but from the commitment to tell the filmmaker's story or otherwise support the filmmaker in his career.

3. Contingent Planning

Disclosures must be accurate, complete, and sufficient, but they need not be unduly limiting. If the film company has developed contingency plans, then it should explain them in the private placement memorandum or other disclosure documents. For example, all commitments by cast members are subject to the possibility that the cast member will become unavailable for health reasons or simply because the actor has changed her mind. Union actors cannot be bound to perform without being paid, and filmmakers cannot pay the actors until the funds have been raised, so the actors' commitment is always subject to change.

Another example of contingencies may involve the budget and the ability to raise funds. Filmmakers are often faced with the choice to shoot on 35mm stock, on 16mm stock, or with digital equipment. A filmmaker can disclose that on a budget of $1.5 million the film will be shot using digital equipment, but if the company brings in $2.25 million then the larger budget will be used to shoot with 35mm stock. By disclosing these options, the filmmakers can seek funds for the $2.25 million project but elect to go forward with as little as $1.5 million. This may be preferable to amending the offering documents and asking each investor to sign an amended agreement when the decision to change course occurs.

4. Other Documents

The investors' package must also include a finalized budget that accurately reflects the anticipated production expenses. A statement should be included to indicate the budget reflects the good-faith plans of the filmmaker, but that it is subject to change throughout the project.

Similarly, a production schedule should be provided to give the investors an idea of the time involved in preproduction, principal photography, and postproduction. The planned distribution strategy should also be outlined. Again, these documents must clearly explain that they are good-faith planning devices, and that the filmmaker expects them to change as circumstances dictate.

C. Optional Information

In addition to the requirements listed above, the film package can be augmented with additional information generally designed to encourage the investors. There is no standard or set package. If a movie is to be based on a play, then reviews of the play might be helpful. If the movie will be a documentary, then newspaper stories about the topic might provide the potential investors with insight into the project. The more the package is creatively tailored to the filmmaker's vision, the more likely it will elicit positive responses.

The information must meet the same test as the disclosure and contractual information: all information must be accurate, complete, and sufficient to give the investor a full understanding of the risks involved in the production. A document that says the play on which the film will be based was "stunning" cannot be taken out of context from a quote that found the play to be "a stunning example of what is killing Broadway." While the statement is accurate, it is not complete, and it materially misrepresents the true statements in the review. When added to the investor package, this puffery may invalidate the entire offering.

1. Director and Cast Information

Cast information and photographs are often a movie's strongest selling point, and investors react to them like any other audience. Even if the cast is relatively unknown, strong backgrounds may instill confidence. The same holds true for the director and other key production personnel; if a person has professional expertise that enhances the film, then that information should be included in the package. Nonetheless, remind the cast and crew that embellishing their resumes can be costly, and that all information they provide must be accurate.

2. Distribution Information

Any distribution guarantees must be disclosed, particularly if they affect the possible returns the film company will see. If there are no distribution agreements in place, then the film company may be wise simply to explain that it will seek distribution of the finished film in all media. Describing the best-case scenario would be misleading, and describing the range of possibilities would ultimately prove fruitless and depressing. Assuming that the risk has already been explained elsewhere, there should not be any need to identify the particular odds of selling the film or receiving an award from a film festival.

3. Comparisons with Other Films

Like the discussion of distribution possibilities, the comparison with other films is a dangerous addition to the investors' package. Offering documents that list the top five independent films and their return on investment is wholly inadequate unless the documents also provide information such as the average return or the number of films that do not receive any paid distribution at all (a number that has reached into the thousands annually). Like describing a lottery jackpot without disclosing the odds of winning, comparing the current project to the most successful independent films is misleading at best. For any sophisticated investor, it demonstrates a lack of professionalism on the part of the film company.

In contrast, comparisons with other films for the purpose of communicating the story, the genre, or the visual style have far fewer drawbacks. Describing a spoof comedy as "in the tradition of *Airplane!* and *Scary Movie*" does not suggest that it will have the same box office success, but it does convey the nature of the content well.

The filmmaker should include information in the film package based on what she herself would be informed by and would respect. Independent filmmaking is an incredibly high-risk financial proposition. Stress the passion and commitment rather than trying to sell the wild but quite rare successes.

D. Getting Hold of the Money

Whatever financing structure and disclosure strategy is selected, most of the money will not be used until principal photography commences. Only a modest portion of the financing should be allocated to the early preproduction process. As a result, most of the funds will not be needed until later in the project. This allows the film company time to continue raising funds while it is engaged in preproduction.

1. Escrow Accounts

The greatest risk for any investor is providing seed capital for a business that fails to get started. In that situation, the investor has no collateral to provide a return. Most investors, therefore, are less willing to provide funds to the production company unless they know that the other money sought will also be collected and the project can at least attempt to meet the specified targets.

Although promises are nice, nothing is as secure as cash in the bank. A subscription agreement often provides that each investor's participation is due when the minimum investment amount has been sold. When that milestone is reached, the company notifies all the investors, and they each send in their payments. This strategy may work well in a large commercial setting, but for most small ventures, the risk is simply too great that an investor will renege, whether for personal or for financial reasons, resulting in the filmmaker's failure to secure the minimum amount of capital.

An *escrow agreement* provides an excellent alternative. It stipulates that the funds raised from the investors will be deposited and held in a segregated account (or with a separate escrow company, if necessary), and that the funds can only be released for use once the milestones are met. The most typical milestone would be that the minimum capital investment has been raised. Milestones may also relate to casting or other key elements of the film.

The agreement need not require that every penny be raised before the funds are released. Instead, the agreement may provide that if the capital sought was $1 million, reflecting the amount necessary to complete the film, then the escrow funds could be released at $800,000, because that amount reflects sufficient finances to complete principal photography. Presumably, a filmmaker will have an easier time raising editing money if a high-quality shoot has already produced sufficient footage to create a good movie, and investors may feel sufficiently comfortable to agree to escrow provisions with such a clause.

Alternately, the reduction in budget may mean the elimination of certain scenes. The documents can give the filmmaker discretion to begin with a budget of a lesser amount or wait for the larger amount, as long as the investors can understand the choices involved.

The escrow agreement should also be tied directly to the contingencies disclosed in the offering documents. If the filmmakers reserved the option to shoot using less expensive equipment or otherwise save funds, then the escrow provisions should be drafted to allow the company to make that election and release the funds.

2. Waivers

While some investors may require the protection of the escrow accounts, others may be more generous. If an investor sees supporting the film project as the primary purpose and any return on investment as secondary, he may be willing to release his investment even prior to the funding of the entire minimum capital amount. The filmmaker may request that such an investor waive the protections provided by the escrow accounts. The investor should sign a waiver of any rights for the monies to be held in escrow and explicitly grant the film company permission to use the funds for the purposes of raising capital and conducting necessary preproduction activities. The filmmaker may consider structuring the offering so such investors receive a premium for their additional risk (such as their interest being sold at a 10 percent discount from the price of the other investors).

The access to funds and the ability to gather enough capital to begin the project should be the final business issue in the making of the movie. With full disclosure, complete financing, presales and loan agreements in place, and the investment money released from escrow because the target amount has been raised or waivers have been signed, the filmmaker is finally ready to add the creative process to the business process. The filmmaker is one step closer to making the movie.

Filming the Movie:
Preproduction and Production

Assembling the Production Team

WITH THE BUSINESS structure in place, the rights secured to the story, and the money raised, the next step in the filmmaking process is the lengthy but critical process of preproduction. An axiom of good filmmaking is that 90 percent of the work is good casting. This is true for the people both in front of and behind the camera.

The production team will be defined by the budgetary and creative choices the filmmaker makes for the film. For example, if he decides to sign union agreements and employ only union cast and crew, the salary expenses for the film will rise, but the film company will also be able to hire employees with greater experience. Low-budget and guerrilla filmmakers may not be able to afford union personnel, and many independent films elect to work with some unions but not others.

In structuring agreements with members of the production, there are only three significant points of negotiation: credit, compensation, and control. In the independent film world, the amount of compensation is necessarily modest. As a result, both credit and control become more important in the negotiation process for landing cast and crew. Fortunately, neither credit nor control has a direct effect on the cash available to complete the movie, so thoughtful choices by the filmmaker can still provide positive incentives for all the film participants.

A. Unique Opportunities as an Independent Filmmaker

The opportunity to make movies in new and different ways should be exploited whenever possible. In the independent filmmaking arena, filmmakers simply do not have the luxury of indulging in counterproductive, inappropriate discrimination on the basis of sex, race, or other insidious stereotypes. As a result, independent films may provide the most important vehicle for professionals looking to expand their skills into new areas and for women and minority filmmakers seeking the opportunity to prove themselves.

The odds for success in Hollywood are painfully low for all participants, and perhaps especially for women. There are role models, however, in every aspect of the industry. Sherry Lansing, Dawn Steel, Lili Zanuck, and Kathleen Kennedy, among many others, exemplify quality producers. Many other women have moved from actor or writer to producer or director or both. Again, strong examples abound: Liv Ullmann (*Faithless, Private Confessions*), Nora Ephron (*You've Got Mail, Sleepless in Seattle*), Diablo Cody (*Juno*), Sofia Coppola (*Lost in Translation*), Kimberly Peirce (*Boys Don't Cry*), and Jody Foster (*Flora Plum, Home for the Holidays*) are just a few of the many powerful women who have leveraged independent productions to redefine their career paths and overcome the additional hurdles faced in Hollywood because of gender stereotypes and residual discrimination.

Independent films have served the same role in helping filmmakers surmount racial barriers. Filmmakers such as Spike Lee, John Singleton, Robert Townsend, Mario Van Peebles, and Keenan Ivory Wayans have also staked their claim by creating strong identities in themselves and their work through independent film.

Documentary filmmaking in particular has felt the increasing influence of strong female and minority teams. And as the documentary genre itself expands, this helps develop talent and opportunity for feature films. Independent film projects in general are well situated to fostering the professional growth of individuals who are struggling against barriers to their development. Fortunately, the audience truly is colorblind and gender neutral. It sees only the sounds and images on the screen. The filmmaker controls those choices, but the audience responds only to the results of those choices. The opportunities are real.

B. Who, What, and When to Hire

Perhaps the single greatest flaw in American filmmaking is the overwhelming number of people involved in the production process. Independent filmmakers do not have this luxury, and, as a result, they can avoid some of the pitfalls of overblown productions.

The preproduction team creating the film should evolve as the project nears principal photography. Qualified individuals should be identified early and kept up to date on the preproduction process, but they should not begin employment on the film until their particular services become essential. This both reduces costs and streamlines the information flow of the project. Since most film shoots operate in barely contained chaos, the better the information flow, the less time is wasted on distractions or costly mistakes.

The initial team is typically made up of the producer, director, and screenwriter. On an independent film, these may all be one person, but to move forward on the project, even the solo filmmaker needs someone with whom to collaborate. The process is far too lonely not to share the tensions and triumphs with someone. Filmmaking teams such as Joel and Ethan Coen and James Ivory and Ismael Merchant have had longstanding success in part due to their healthy collaboration. On the other hand, many of the tasks identified for preproduction can be carried out by one or two people, if they have the skills to accomplish the task (or if the filmmaker cannot afford to hire anyone else to help).

The team should be expanded as the necessary preproduction tasks exceed the abilities of the personnel already in place. For example, if the producer cannot provide the skills necessary to estimate the scope and costs of the production, then the first critical hire on the project is someone to create the budget. After all, as described earlier, the accuracy and completeness of the budget is crucial to the film's operations. Similarly, since casting is often a long process, the person in charge of casting must be identified, and if it is neither the director nor the producer, then a casting director must be brought on board early in preproduction as well.

The next round of hires often involves locations for the filming. The settings are often integral to both the story being told and the costs of telling that story. A location manager and location scouts must be assigned the task of finding interior and exterior locations where the film may be shot, identifying the proper parties for arranging permission to shoot at those locations, and creating a feasible production schedule. On smaller films, the director typically serves as location manager, enlisting volunteer location scouts to help with the early legwork.

Next, the directors of the creative elements must be identified and incorporated into the process. If there is to be a director of photography separate from the director, her early input into the locations, lighting, and visual style of the film becomes crucial. Similarly, if costumes, sets, props, lighting, special effects, or stunts play heavily in the film, then the person in charge of each creative area should become a central figure in the preproduction planning. For low-budget projects, however, these departments are luxuries. Actors wear street clothes, apply their own makeup, and manage their own action. There is no need to add directors and designers when the scope of the project does not call for their services.

C. Introduction to the Key Unions

Whether because of the prevalence of people trying to break into show business or despite it, Hollywood remains one of the more heavily unionized industries. Nonetheless, production companies are not required to become signatories to union agreements, and the decision to become a signatory to one union agreement does not require a company to become a signatory to agreements with other unions.

The decision to work with union or nonunion labor will depend on the quality of the talent pool available, the costs to the production, and the benefits of working with an experienced workforce. Use of unions generally increases as the budget increases, since the complexity and visibility of higher-budget shoots tends to increase the need for experienced union members.

1. Unions' Benefits for Hollywood

Through collective bargaining agreements with the signatory production companies, the key Hollywood trade unions provide their members with guaranteed minimum payments for various jobs; contributions by employers to health, welfare, and pension funds; minimum health and safety procedures; and grievance procedures to simplify any disputes between a member and the production company that employs him. The unions provide important benefits to their members and to the professional quality of the entertainment industry.

2. Union Representation and Eligibility

Individual union members are free to negotiate deals with production companies that are more generous than the terms of the minimum agreements. The collective bargaining agreement merely serves as a floor for such contracts. In other areas, however, the unions exact more control. As described in section D (p. 165), the unions exert a good deal of authority over the form of screen credits, even in situations in which all the parties would prefer a result other than that dictated by union rules.

Many of the industry unions maintain very high membership standards. At the same time, under the *Taft-Hartley provisions* of the union collective bargaining agreements, if a person becomes a "principal performer" by performing dialogue in a film shoot governed by SAG or otherwise becomes employed by a production company in a position subject to a collective bargaining agreement, that person becomes eligible to join the union for 30 days. The production company cannot employ the person beyond 30 days unless that person joins the union, so the eligibility must be used or the person terminated. The production company may also face union sanctions for hiring a person who is not a member of the union, unless specified conditions are met.

3. Union Members Prohibited from Nonunion Work

A member of a union is barred by union rules from working on a nonunion production. If a union member works on a nonunion shoot, he may be permanently banned from the union. Usually, the union will give the member violating this rule the opportunity to convince the nonunion company to become a signatory company, curing the problem created by the member.

If this situation arises during production, the union member is likely to pressure the film company, arguing that unless the company signs with the union, he will have to leave the project. Particularly if the member is an actor, the costs associated with having to reshoot previously completed footage may put tremendous pressure on the production company to sign a collective bargaining agreement that would likely affect the employment and union status of the entire cast.

4. Listing of Key Unions

The following are brief introductions to each of the significant trade unions for the motion picture industry:

Screen Actors Guild (SAG) www.sag.org
- SAG represents the professional actors in film, television, industrials, commercials, video games, music videos, and other new media.
- SAG is the primary talent union for the film industry.

American Federation of Television and Radio Artists (AFTRA) www.aftra.org
- AFTRA represents performers in broadcast, public and cable television; radio (news, commercials, hosted programs); sound recordings (CDs, singles, Broadway cast albums, audio books); nonbroadcast and industrial material; and Internet and digital programming.

Directors Guild of America (DGA) www.dga.org
- DGA represents directors, associate directors, and stage managers in motion pictures and in broadcast, public, and cable television.
- DGA guarantees the right of a film director to provide the first cut of a motion picture.

Writers Guild of America East and West (WGA) www.wga.org
- WGAE and WGAW represent writers in negotiations with producers to ensure their rights in screen, television, and new media.

International Alliance of Theatrical Stage Employees, Moving Picture Technicians, Artists and Allied Crafts (IATSE) www.iatse-intl.org
- IATSE represents below-the-line film craft professionals such as camerapersons, lighting crews, sound technicians, editors, live-action storyboard artists, set designers, art directors, and scenic artists.

American Federation of Musicians (AFM) www.afm.org
- AFM represents musicians working in recording; broadcast, public and cable television; music videos; commercials; films; video games; and traveling theatrical productions.

Actors' Equity Association (AEA or Equity) www.actorsequity.org
- Equity represents actors and stage managers performing in live theater, such as Broadway, touring companies, professional theaters throughout the United States, and Disney World.
- Equity does not have jurisdiction over film productions, but its collective bargaining agreements may impose limitations on the ability to film works produced for the stage, as in a "Live on Broadway" movie.

The Animation Guild and Affiliated Optical Electronic and Graphic Arts, Local 839 IATSE (TAG) www.animationguild.org
- TAG represents cartoonists, animators, and animation writers.

International Brotherhood of Electrical Workers (IBEW) www.ibew.org
- The IBEW represents electrical workers in telecommunications and broadcasting as well as in construction, utilities, manufacturing, railroads, and government.

Motion Picture and Theatrical Trade Teamsters (Hollywood Teamsters Local 399) www.hollywoodteamsters.org
- Hollywood Teamsters Local 399 represents workers in motion pictures; broadcast, public, and cable television; commercials; and live theatrical productions. Members include animal trainers, autoservice personnel, casting directors, chefs, couriers, dispatchers, drivers, location managers, mechanics, warehousemen, and wranglers.

Alliance of Motion Picture and Television Producers (AMPTP) www.amptp.org
- The AMPTP represents motion picture and television producers. Member companies include the production entities of the studios, the broadcast networks, and certain cable networks, and independent producers.

Producers Guild of America (PGA) www.producersguild.org
- Although once a union, the PGA is now a trade association for producers of film, television, and new media, including producers, associate producers, line producers, coproducers, segment producers, and production managers.
- Since it is not a trade union, it is not involved in any collective bargaining agreements, but it may still provide a useful resource for independent filmmakers involved with contractual and labor issues.

D. Screen Credit

Providing an on-screen credit in a motion picture acknowledges the primal need for personal recognition. It serves as a thank-you and it permanently recognizes the work done by the person named. For professionals in the film industry, the size and placement of the credit on their most recent project plays a significant role in helping set their fee and credits in their next role. More generally, a screen credit works to promote the individual or company named, conveying the status of the entity to future employers and peers. As a result, it is a valuable commodity that should not be squandered.

Screen credits fall into two basic categories: those on "card" at the beginning of the film and those in the scrolling credits at the end of the film. End credits are usually provided in a single typeface, moving relatively quickly across the screen, and, as a result, there are few serious negotiations about the format of the end credits.

The opening credits are much more contentious. Accepted industry standards attach importance to the placement of individual names within the credit sequence. The first name shown is considered the "star" of a film—certainly the actor with the most clout regarding the production. If two names appear at once, the upper left is considered to be in first position. And names that appear before the film's title carry significantly more weight than the names that follow the title of the movie. Because these are industry standards, cast members, other professionals, and even audience members interpret the credits in this way, even if the filmmaker would like to ignore the implications.

In addition to rules regarding placement, the size of the typeface can also suggest importance. If the cast credits listed after the film title are in smaller type than the stars who precede it, the filmmaker is further highlighting the importance of the stars over the remainder of the cast.

Cast members are not the only parties who seek to have their names in the opening credits. Film producers (perhaps including individual investors), writers, and the director are all typically credited. Rarely do these names go before the stars or the title, but all placement is subject to negotiation.

1. Union Requirements

Credits are one of the most important keys to continued employment in the entertainment industry. For a writer, director, or actor, the receipt of a credit helps establish a benchmark for future employment negotiations. As a result, trade unions such as WGA, DGA, and SAG all set policies that require that their members receive minimum credit and, in the case of DGA and WGA, govern who can receive credit at all.

Under DGA and WGA rules, any dispute over directing or writing credits must be resolved by an arbitration process run by the applicable union. The Writers Guild Screen Credits Manual reports that the Writers Guild handles more than 150 credit disputes annually.[1] For WGA members, the writers must either agree unanimously as to the writing credit or submit the work for arbitration. The finished film and all the written submissions made by each of the authors are submitted to the arbitrator, who makes a determination regarding the contribution of each individual. For most writing credits, there can be no more than two writers credited. DGA uses a similar process for disputes among directors, but it is generally utilized much less frequently.

2. Optional Suggestions

For film companies that are signatories to union contracts, these rules must be followed. The good news is that the union arbitrator, rather than the filmmaker, must decide which writer or director deserves the name recognition for the work. For nonunion films, the union processes can serve as a guide, but making highly contentious credit decisions is likely to create trouble. Contrary to union policy, there is no reason for a nonunion film not to offer everyone who legitimately worked on the film some credit or recognition. If the movie was inspired by a person who did not otherwise participate in the film's production, feel free to give the "inspired by" credit, regardless of whether the WGA would approve.

The employment contract should, therefore, guarantee that the person's name will appear in the end credits of the film as long as that person was not in breach of the contract. The contract can also provide that the person will receive sole credit for the task, such as writer, if that person was the only one to provide the service, and that credit will be shared if others provided a similar service. The contract should also provide that the determination of the credits is solely at the discretion of the film company and not subject to appeal or arbitration. Taken together, a generous approach and clear contract provisions should limit the problems over credits for most independent film companies.

3. Credits as a Marketable Commodity

Credits can be valuable to a host of other participants in the filmmaking process beside the cast and crew. New York City, for example, requires that films using the valuable and free services of the New York City Film Office give the office an end credit. Independent films often offer a "special thanks" credit to the individuals and companies that provided service, but this undervalues their assistance and blunts the recognition provided. Being able to tell a lawyer, accountant, or restaurateur that she will be given a substantive credit in the film may have more than passing value. The promise of a screen credit for "legal services provided," combined with a promise of at least deferred compensation, is enough to convince some attorneys to assist independent filmmakers.

Again, a nonunion project need not be bound by rigid union credit rules, so if the film is based on a stage play, then prominent screen credit may be the way to induce the playwright to risk allowing an independent production company to have the film rights. The key is to recognize the high value and low cost that credits provide for the filmmaker. This is one of the few advantages nonunion movies have over union productions, and the filmmaker should take advantage of it.

E. Compensation Packages: Making the Deals

To many participants, an independent film project is a professional stepping-stone that provides concrete evidence of their professional skills and serves as their first paid work experience. As a result, offering even modest payments can be the key to securing many individuals' participation. Nonetheless, as mentioned in chapter 3 (p. 39), truly modest compensation raises legal concerns, because of minimum wage laws and other employment obligations. For many participants, however, these legal concerns take second place to the psychological and professional importance of working rather than volunteering on the film project. This need should be respected.

1. Salaries and Per Diems

The basic payment system for most films is a flat fee. The cast members and crew members involved in the entire production are guaranteed a certain amount of money for their work. Payments of the fee are typically apportioned based on the planned number of weeks for the production. Except for those production members actively involved in preproduction, payments generally do not begin until principal photography has commenced.

The norms for payments conform to the traditional structure for most filmmaking, which assumes little rehearsal time and tightly scheduled shoots. For independent filmmakers, these conventions may not reflect the production's actual schedule. To the extent the production differs from the norm, the payment systems should be adjusted to fit the actual employment experience. For example, if the filmmaker adopts a theater model for preproduction, extensive rehearsals of the entire script may be done over a period of four to six weeks. The filming can then take place over a period of a few days rather than weeks. This model works best in a film that uses few sets and camera setups. If the director will shoot with a handheld camera, walking with the cast through the sets as the scenes unfold, the filming process will need to be well choreographed, but once it is staged, the natural flow of the action will seem organic to the film. For such a shoot, the rehearsals become integral to the production process while the length of principal photography is substantially reduced. The timing of payments must be varied to reflect these choices.

In addition to salaries, the cast members and crew members may be paid *per diems*. These are modest payments based on the number of days worked. With the possible exception of the above-the-line participants, the per diems are the same amount for everyone on the film. The amount is intended to cover food, gas, and lodging (if the shoot is away from the production center). For nonunion productions, per diems are not required, but they often supplement craft services (food service on the set) or assist with significant travel to the shooting location. Even if salaries themselves are entirely deferred, per diems often help ensure that the cast and crew can afford the gas to get to the set.

2. Deferrals

One very effective way of extending the amount of money on hand to complete principal photography is to defer expenses. Theoretically, if all the costs were deferred, then the film could be produced for no money and all budget expenses would be paid from the film's future revenues. While this is not typically possible for all expenses, participants in the film project are often willing to defer all or part of their salaries. A true deferral simply puts the payments off until the film begins to receive revenues. Since the deferred salaries are budgeted costs, they must be paid before any capital is returned to the investors or profits are paid to any parties.

A common source of confusion is the order of deferral payments. If the film is sold for an amount greater than the total of deferred expenses outstanding, then everything is paid simultaneously. If, however, money trickles in, then it is important that the priority of payments be clearly spelled out in the employment contracts or in other agreements incorporated into the employment agreements by reference.

First, each class of deferment should be treated *pro rata,* or in proportion. This means that all salary deferrals for all participants are pooled together. If the film company receives $5,000 to be applied to the salaries, then the $5,000 would be distributed to all the participants on a percentage basis. If the total pool was $50,000 in deferrals, then each participant would receive a payment of 10 percent of the amount owed to that person. The filmmaker could instead choose to divide the deferrals evenly among all participants, but this would mean that some participants would be paid in full before others. Either approach works as long as the system is applied consistently and agreed upon in advance.

Second, any other classes of payments should also be spelled out. For example, it may be that all expenses, including equipment leases, credit card expenditures, invoices, etc., must be paid in full before any of the deferrals are paid. If this includes ongoing expenses such as office rent, then that must also be specified. Theoretically, all costs other than the deferrals should have been covered by the capital investment, but in case (as frequently occurs) there are budget overruns or not enough capital, the agreement should state whether the credit cards are paid before or after the deferrals. In addition, the producer's fee may be treated as a separate payment, to be made either before or after the other deferrals, depending on the needs of the producer.

Finally, the filmmaker may be receiving payment for many different aspects of the project. To the extent he is wearing different hats (director, actor, screenwriter, editor, producer, etc.), the tasks that entitle the filmmaker to additional compensation should also be clearly identified in advance. The filmmaker may specify that his producer's fee is deferred until after all the other deferrals are paid in full, but he will still be entitled to his deferred fee as a cast member and as the screenwriter. To avoid bad feelings and legal problems, such a structure must be quite explicit in both the budget and the contracts. As long as the system selected is clear, fewer problems will arise later.

3. Profit Participation

The other source of payment to the film participants flows from profit participation in the film. Studio films are notorious for definitions of profit participation 20 or more pages in length that make it almost unheard-of for even the greatest blockbuster to actually turn a profit as defined by the convoluted agreement. For independent films, however, the successful project will return a profit that is not hidden in the studio overhead or other charges to the film.

Profit must still be defined. As suggested in chapter 7 (p. 140), it may be preferable to use the term *defined profit* rather than *net* or *gross profit* to avoid unintended meanings of those terms. Defined profit is distributed after the expenses are paid in full, the entire investment is returned to the investors (often at 110 to 125 percent of the amount invested), and a reserve fund is made for ongoing operations of the film company. The remaining earned income should be profit. Except as provided in the profit participation agreements, all profits belong to the film company and, in turn, to the shareholders or members of the company. As a result, profit participation arrangements must be carefully specified in the offering documents for the film company.

Filmmakers may find it helpful to create a profit participation pool of some percentage of the profits, anywhere from 10 to 25 percent. In this way, the investors can be told that, say, 10 percent of all profits are apportioned among the members of the cast and crew. That number will not change

even though the exact participation within the pool may continue to fluc-
tuate as shares are assigned to particular individuals during negotiations.
The filmmaker designates that the pool has a certain number of points—
say, 100 or 1,000—which are then allocated to cast and crew in the employment agreements. The points not allocated can be returned to the investors,
retained by the filmmaker, or paid pro rata to the pool. Any of these options
work, as long as the choice is made in writing as part of the initial employment contracts.

Although even more contingent on the film's financial success than
deferred salaries, profit participation has the potential to be the most valuable aspect of the compensation package. For those rare blockbuster films,
the profit participation points can amount to exceptional income. The contract, therefore, should also be very clear about when they are earned—
upon successful completion of the employment task rather than upon
signing the employment contract. If an actor leaves the film because a paying job is suddenly available, that actor should not remain a profit participant. Instead, if the director can negotiate to shoot sufficient coverage to
work around the actor in exchange for keeping some of the deferrals and
profit participation, the contract provides the filmmaker with negotiating
leverage.

4. Union-Defined Minimums

For union productions, each union requires that a guaranteed minimum
amount be paid as compensation, consisting of salaries and per diems. The
collective bargaining agreements allow union members to negotiate higher
pay and profit or revenue participation above those minimums. Under their
low-budget agreements (see chapter 7, p. 136), the unions now allow for
limited deferrals.

Despite the flexibility afforded by the low-budget agreements, some
independent film companies still find they are unable to meet payroll and
complete principal photography. To fulfill both their obligations to the
union and the need to fund the film, union members may choose to invest
their entire net salary in the film. This should not be a condition of employment, but the film company can provide generous deferrals and contingent
payments for those union members who elect to invest in the production
in this fashion. Such an arrangement must be established early in the negotiations, and the union participants should receive both generous profit

participation in their compensation package and the same return as other cash investors.

Given that many actors working on low-budget films are more concerned with remaining eligible for union health benefits, financial concessions that protect those minimums are treated favorably. By reinvesting the actors' net income, all union financial obligations are met, the cast members do not risk jeopardizing their union status by working on a nonunion shoot, the professional quality of the production is generally improved, and the resources needed to make the film are not substantially reduced. Finally, as members of the production company, the participants should be sufficiently involved in the production to avoid most restrictions on the sale of securities.

F. Control During Production

The third primary negotiation point for most major hiring decisions concerns the allocation of control over the film project, and how the balance of control may change throughout the production process. Perhaps one of the most famous of film legends is that Sylvester Stallone received one or more offers from producers interested in his screenplay for *Rocky* that he turned down because those offers did not include a guarantee that he would play the title role. The studio offered him substantially more money to sell the script without that guarantee. His perseverance reflected his understanding that the role was far more important to his career than the credit and money he would undoubtedly have earned for the screenplay.

For the filmmaker, control should be the primary concern. In decisions involving the business structure, the hiring of the management team, financing, and distribution, the filmmaker should be sure to insist on control to the greatest extent possible. Control over the film should be the touchstone for all decisions unless the money or other rewards become so rich that the filmmaker is prepared to take them and run.

If the filmmaker assumes ultimate control, then the other participants in the filmmaking process necessarily will not have control. Nonetheless, the other professionals will have many of the same concerns that the filmmaker does, and as a result, reasonable authority and responsibility must be delegated by the filmmaker to these professionals as well. Further, to be successful the filmmaker must assemble a competent, professional team. Professionalism includes respect for others and requires that the filmmaker trust the assembled professionals to make competent decisions.

1. Artistic Control

The filmmaker, often the director, must establish the mood and tone of the film. As he shares this vision with others—the cinematographer, the location manager, the designers of sets, costumes, props, lighting, sound, and music—he should allow those individuals to suggest ways of achieving his goals. Even the writing must be shaped carefully to fit within the desired tone and mood. Casting choices are based on the decisions that shape or reshape the script, and will inform every choice in direction and editing.

If the filmmaker is not the director, then the collaboration must be even more closely structured. Directors are often hired to fulfill the vision of the producer or story writer, but this relationship can easily turn into conflict if the two visionaries do not have the same goals. Schedules for collaboration must be agreed upon in advance. If the director proves unwilling to accept the intrusion of the filmmaker, then the filmmaker should select another director early in the project, before such a choice dramatically affects the budget or morale of the film.

Artistic control should not be left to unspoken assumptions. In the larger-budget union films, rules of control have evolved over decades into complex provisions in the collective bargaining agreements that balance the interests of the writers, directors, crafts, and talent against the interests of the producer and financial backers. These models may not be relevant for independent films and are particularly unrepresentative when the filmmaker plays more than one of these roles. Nor are these norms laws. They simply will not govern the film company's employment relationship if the film company is not a signatory to the collective bargaining agreement in question.

The film company should instead adopt explicit job descriptions for the key participants, clearly explaining to whom each employee reports. The contracts should specify that the employment is "at will." Although the compensation is most likely based on a fixed amount, the contract should provide that if the employee is terminated prior to completion of the project, then only the portion of the fixed amount that has accrued to the date of termination is paid. This is true for both paid salary and deferred salary.

The filmmaker should also specify whether or not the proportionate amount of any revenue or profit participation accrues.

Once the filmmaker has adopted a structure, he must then follow the authority vested in the employees as much as possible. The director should work closely with the cast, directors, and designers. The directors and designers, in turn, should be responsible for and have full authority over the workers within their areas. For example, if the job descriptions place the job of costumers as being supervised by the costume designer, then the director should work through the designer rather than giving inconsistent orders directly to one of the costumers. In this manner, the information flow is maximized, confusion is minimized, and the designers are given the courtesy and professional respect they deserve, while the director retains ultimate control and the ability to terminate employment, if necessary.

2. Management Control

Like artistic control, management control requires a strong command system. In a very short period of time, a company that did not previously exist will suddenly employ dozens (or hundreds) and spend thousands or even millions of dollars, only to once again collapse down to a few people with little or no activity. The most popular person in the company becomes the person with the checkbook. The most important person becomes the *comptroller,* the person supervising the accounting and financial reporting for the film company.

Professional titles should be matched to business duties, since legal obligations attach to titles such as "president of the corporation" or "managing member of the LLC." Such positions should be reserved for the people who have the authority to carry out their obligations on the project; they should not be used as "credits" with which to bargain or reward. To clarify the ultimate management and control of the production, the filmmaker should hold a key management position in addition to his artistic title, putting all other employees within his professional jurisdiction.

The producer has the business responsibility for managing the organization. If the filmmaker is the director of the film, and holds the position of president of the film company, then the producer may be a vice president. Where the filmmaker is not the producer, the company's operating agreement must be explicit that the filmmaker still has primary authority, with the producer deriving her authority from the filmmaker.

As a practical matter, however, the director will have his hands full making the movie. The producer must manage the business decisions. This may include coordinating with the line producer, location manager, and others to ensure that schedules continue to function, that each expenditure is within the budget and fully authorized for payment, and that all laws, regulations, and agreements are signed and followed.

Occasionally, decisions will meld the art and commerce of filmmaking. Weather can wreak havoc on film schedules, and decisions to postpone, relocate, or eliminate scenes are necessarily a compromise between business and artistic interests. Most decisions, however, tend to be either artistic choices (e.g., the color of a set) or management ones (e.g., the budget to build a set). The producer and director must both know when they must consult each other. They should also meet regularly to keep each other apprised of the ongoing progress. Separately, each one then manages the people and decisions for which he or she is responsible. In this way, the structure encourages the most efficient and least contentious planning process possible. This is not to suggest there will not be problems, merely that the problems will not be caused by simple confusion and misunderstanding.

3. Resources to Outsource

Some of the more important but mundane tasks of the film can be readily outsourced for arguably less money and certainly greater efficiency. The management of the film company remains responsible for these outside providers, but their services make the process more professional and better structured.

The most important area to outsource is the payroll function. As mentioned in chapter 3 (p. 39), payroll has a host of legal obligations regarding taxes, insurance, withholding, and reporting requirements. All of these obligations can be transferred to a payroll house rather than being handled internally. There are many firms that handle basic payroll, including a number that specialize in the motion picture or entertainment industry. Their services should be able to accommodate any union obligations the film company has undertaken, and some will be able to continue to provide residual payments that will come due as income flows from nontheatrical media.

Either as part of the bundled payroll service or separately, employment taxes should be outsourced as well. This increases the chance that proper tax filings will be made not only in the first year of the film production but in years to come, when fewer people remain professionally associated with the project. Similarly, services provided by lawyers and accountants are typically outsourced as well.

To the extent that any management function can be provided by a professional who has experience in the motion picture industry and who can provide that service for a price comparable to that of internal personnel, the filmmaker should consider outsourcing the task. If the failure to perform the task will result in legal liability or risk of injury, then the choice to outsource becomes the better course of action.

G. Insurance

In addition to the completion bond (see chapter 7, p. 139), there are a number of other types of insurance that should be considered by every film company. Ultimately, the amount of insurance purchased depends not only on the budget but also on the level of protection the participants in the film deserve.

1. Workers' Compensation

Required in many states, workers' compensation insurance provides automatic medical insurance for work-related injuries. In some jurisdictions, this coverage is mandated by law and must be included in the production budget. Even where voluntary, participation in a state workers' compensation system provides an essential protection for the cast and crew at a cost much lower than that of most private insurance systems. In some states, workers' compensation insurance will extend to volunteer crew members. In others, supplemental coverage can be purchased to assure that the unpaid members of the company are provided this minimal level of protection. Workers' compensation also protects the employer from lawsuits resulting from personal injury. It is an extremely inexpensive and valuable form of insurance that should be purchased to extend to all participants on the set.

2. Property Damage Liability Insurance and Auto Insurance

For any production shooting on location, property damage liability insurance must be purchased to protect the film company and the locations on which the company operates. For each private location, the property owner will be added to the policy as an additional insured. Most municipalities will also require this protection for the use of public areas.

Similarly, for production vehicles used both on and off camera during filming, comprehensive general liability and auto liability insurance remain a necessary part of doing business.

3. Equipment Insurance

The rental cost of film and lighting equipment represents only a tiny portion of the total value of the equipment. As a result, the rental fees may include equipment insurance. If not, the equipment owner will invariably require that the film company purchase its own insurance to protect these assets. Given the number of things that can go wrong, this is certainly valuable coverage for most productions. As digital equipment drops to consumer prices, however, the particular nature of the equipment used will dictate whether or not this precaution is necessary.

4. Errors and Omissions Insurance

Errors and omissions insurance protects the distributor (and potentially the exhibitors) from liability based on the content of the film. The insurance company defends lawsuits and indemnifies or pays for the cost of any losses that arise from defamation, invasion of privacy, or copyright liability claims, as well as other claims based on titles, piracy, plagiarism, or theft of ideas. Particularly given the more controversial nature of many independent films, the purchase of errors and omissions insurance is critical.

Often, this purchase may be left to the distributor or at least until the time of distribution. The danger with deferring the purchase is that any script changes required by the insurance company may cause minor inconveniences during the shoot but will be extremely costly and difficult to make after the cast has dispersed and the sets are no longer available.

5. Other Coverage

In addition to the four categories of insurance listed, there are a number of other policies that may be necessary depending on the shoot and the budget. These include specific insurance policies for aircraft, watercraft, animals, and flights. These additional protections may be useful—and occasionally even required—but only in select situations.

The elements of the production may also be insured, including the props, sets and wardrobe; the cast; the film negative; and other media. Finally, insurance may even be available against the weather. Given the size of the investment, the filmmaker can select what degree of risk she feels appropriate for the production. Considering the other risks involved in an independent film production, however, these insurance policies are not particularly popular with independent filmmakers.

The Key Members of the Independent Film Company

ALTHOUGH MANY OF the jobs that must be filled have already been introduced in the context of financing and planning the production, brief job descriptions may be helpful to understand the broader role each of them plays in the filmmaking process.

The variety of jobs does not necessarily require the same variety of personnel. A truly guerrilla documentary can be created by a single person. Nonetheless, that filmmaker still fills each role, alternately serving as his own producer, director, writer, and editor. The cast, sets, costumes, and other elements are taken as they are found, but decisions regarding their inclusion are continuously being made by the director. As a result, the filmmaker has many of these tasks imposed on him as well.

Every production will mix and match the personnel hired and the roles that must be filled, depending on the skills of each individual and the depth of the budget. Regardless of who performs each activity, most of the activities themselves are essential to the successful completion of the picture.

A. The Producer

1. Job of the Producer

The producer provides the key leadership, management, and supervision for the entire film project. This includes the "creative, financial, technological and administrative [process] . . . throughout all phases of production from inception to completion, including coordination, supervision and control of all other talents and crafts, subject to the provisions of their collective bargaining agreements and personal service contracts."[1] Like the CEO or president of a corporation, the producer is responsible for all final executive decisions and personally participates in many of the choices made in every aspect of the project.

A good producer must have a solid grasp of the financial, artistic, and technical aspects of filmmaking. Often the task requires that the producer bring strong-willed professionals together to make hard decisions that balance the filmmaker's vision against the financial resources and technical limitations of the project. Experience, problem-solving skills, and strong management techniques are the essential qualities of a good producer.

Executive producers, on the other hand, are generally involved in the project only indirectly, helping raise funds or coordinating multiple films at the conceptual level. Few independent films have executive producers, except as a way of securing additional capital by providing the credit to inactive but essential financial participants. Occasionally, executive producer credit is provided to important cast members who use their influence to sign the remaining members of the cast and crew. By taking an extra hand in the production, these actors empower the film to go forward.

Associate producer is a title that is often liberally distributed to production participants who undertake many of the producer's duties, whether in coordination with the producer or by their own initiative. Although this credit is sometimes used in bargaining, independent filmmakers may wish to grant associate producer status to the individual who stands out throughout the production process, the unsung hero who went well beyond the job description or who paid to ensure that the project was completed.

2. If the Producer Is Not the Filmmaker

The Producers Guild of America distinguishes between entrepreneurial producers and employee producers. In the independent filmmaking context, the *entrepreneurial producer* is the filmmaker—the person who takes it upon herself to initiate the project. An *employee producer* is a person hired by the financier of the project to manage the film's production.

If the filmmaker is not an entrepreneurial producer, then she must entrust the producing responsibilities to an employee producer, and take pains to ensure that he is under her direction and employ, rather than under the authority of the distributor or other financier of the project. The producer's control of the budget gives him primary authority over the film, so the filmmaker can retain control only to the extent that the producer answers to her and no one else.

This is not to suggest that the filmmaker should not employ a producer at all. If she (like most artists) lacks the experience, problem-solving skills, or management strength to do the job herself, an independent professional will add perspective to the project, enabling the filmmaker to make prudent, responsible choices. Even if the producer can be overruled, his advice and alternative viewpoints will prove invaluable.

3. How to Select

Unlike some other independent film roles, an employee producer is only worthwhile if truly qualified. On-the-job training can occur, but an experienced producer adds incalculable value to the production company. If no such individual is willing to work within the production budget, it is better to forgo the employee producer and spend whatever money is available (whether in salary, deferrals, or revenue participation) on an experienced consultant who can provide some regular guidance throughout the film project.

If no experienced producer is available, the job will fall to the filmmaker. There is nothing inappropriate in the filmmaker retaining the credit as sole producer—or credit as coproducer if that is the reality of the production—as long as the sole producer credit has not been granted as part of anyone else's employment agreement.

When choosing to hire a producer, the filmmaker should do more than review the candidate's prior credits. A producer's level of participation in a particular project can vary dramatically, so have extensive conversations with the producer's former directors and other colleagues. These conversations should help the filmmaker better evaluate whether the producer is qualified, and whether his style and approach to filmmaking is compatible with the filmmaker's goals and expectations. More than any other relationship on the film, the compatibility between producer and director is critical; it will set the tone for the rest of the production. The filmmaker may find it helpful to meet with the prospective producer on a few occasions, discussing the project and soliciting advice.

A prospective producer should be willing to invest a little time up front as a way of doing his own due diligence on the film. (Remember, the producer also has to decide whether this is a film and filmmaker with whom he wishes to be associated.) This trial period provides a good opportunity to test the strengths and styles of both the producer and the filmmaker, so that each can assess whether the combination will be successful. The most successful producer/director relationships can last decades, enhancing the careers of both participants.

4. Deals for the Producer

The entrepreneurial producer is invariably among the most highly compensated participants in the film project. Often the producer's salary is relatively modest, but the producer will seek a significant percentage of the revenues. A filmmaker who can serve as her own producer should expect to see a much larger return than one who works with an employee producer.

Producers are committed to the project for the long haul. They should agree to be available for all of preproduction, principal photography, and postproduction, and, as reasonably necessary, to oversee all the marketing and distribution issues thereafter, including the supervision of the foreign language versions, dubbed editions, special edits, and other longer-term projects.

A producer may be interested in a long-term relationship as well, including a right of first refusal on the director's next project, or at least on any sequel or prequel undertaken during the three years following the initial theatrical release of the film. The compensation package may even extend to a small portion of any sequel and prequel rights or rights exploited in other media, such as television or live theater.

B. The Writer

1. Job of the Writer

The motion picture writer may be the loneliest person in Hollywood. Although the job may include the development of the story, the preparation of the treatment, or the writing of the shooting script, each of these tasks is done in relative isolation. To protect its members from loss of credit and status, the Writers Guild insists that the writer's work be highly restricted and noncollaborative. While this does not stop collaboration from occurring, it does illustrate the solitary nature of the writer's role in the process. The job for the writer will depend significantly on the relationship of the story to the screenplay. The writer of an original screenplay will typically play a much more central role than a person adapting a novel or dramatizing a true story.

a. Spec Script

When a screenwriter creates a script on speculation (i.e., a *spec script*), she crafts a finished draft of a complete screenplay on her own initiative, then offers it to producers, directors, and companies to produce. A spec script may be based on a story idea original to the writer or an existing story in the public domain. Occasionally, the spec writer will actually purchase the literary rights to a copyrighted source work herself—but given the low chances the project will be produced, the costs associated with purchasing the underlying literary rights make this approach infrequent and rarely successful.

Many independent projects use another form of spec script. In this case, the filmmaker approaches a writer and offers her the opportunity to write the script for the project. Any payments for the script are dependent on whether the filmmaker likes the submission. This form of writing on spec is prohibited for members of the Writers Guild, since the screenwriter assumes all the risk of the script not being accepted, and if the finished script is rejected the writer cannot take it to a different producer, since it is based on the story provided (hopefully, in writing) by the filmmaker.

b. Original Screenplay

For the majority of film projects, a screenwriter is hired to write an original screenplay based on an idea of the filmmaker's. The screenwriter works as an employee of the film company. In this process the writer usually submits a first draft, meets with the producer or the producer and director to review their thoughts and ideas on the script, and, based on their notes and the subsequent discussion, revises the script into a final draft. There may be multiple interim versions before the screenwriter considers the work the final draft, although multiple submissions are not contemplated under the Writers Guild minimum structure.

In this scenario, the production company is the copyright holder of the script, and the writer is paid for the submissions pursuant to the agreed-upon payment schedule, whether or not the film is eventually shot or distributed.

c. Nonoriginal Screenplay

A nonoriginal screenplay differs from an original screenplay in that the story idea or source material already exists. If the film will be based on an existing stage play, for instance, then much of the story and dramatic structure will already be in place. Even some of the dialogue may be taken from the play. The film adaptation may be significantly different from the stage version, or it may change only the physical attributes of the project, opening the scenes up from the confinement of the stage.

In order to develop a nonoriginal screenplay, the production company must own the rights to the source material or at least have nonexclusive permission to use it. The company may have purchased the film rights from the playwright or novelist or be using true life stories compiled from newspaper accounts. In any case, the screenwriter bases her work on the materials and rights acquired by the production company.

d. Rewrites and Polishes

The writing process seems never to end. Final scripts are often revised on a daily basis for a variety of reasons. Casting and location choices each dictate certain script changes to better reflect the people and places that will actually appear in the film. Cast members frequently offer suggestions to reshape and grow their characters. Humor that works in print sometimes fails to translate to the screen.[2] Personnel changes among the producers, directors, designers, and cast can alter expectations. Finally, some people always tinker, not knowing when to leave well enough alone.

The difference between a rewrite and a polish is that a rewrite may be a substantial reworking of another writer's "final" script, while a polish should be focused on details: refining particular lines of dialogue, or punching up the script with some added humor. Both rewrites and polishes are often provided by additional screenwriters who revise the earlier writer's final draft of the script. The process can continue indefinitely.

Invariably, even filmmakers who do not serve as their own screenwriters become involved in script revisions, at least to some extent. For union productions, advance notice and other guidelines exist to protect union writers from losing screen credit to this tinkering, but true collaboration or rewriting by the filmmaker can meet union muster, if done properly.

2. Protecting the Filmmaker as Story Writer

Often, the filmmaker will write the initial treatment for the project well before engaging a screenwriter. The filmmaker must be cautious, however, to protect himself from losing any advantage in the creation of the work. Stories abound in which similar projects by different production companies race through production to be first to market. This can happen because public domain literature has become popular on stage and in print, because historical stories gain modern relevance, or just by random chance.

If a filmmaker were to meet with a writer and suggest a story for the writer to create as a spec script, there is no legal limitation on the writer regarding the script eventually created. Instead, the filmmaker must take concrete steps to protect himself in that situation. First, the more concrete the story provided by the filmmaker, the more likely the story will be entitled to copyright protection. As explained in chapter 4 (p. 59), copyright law does not extend to ideas, merely their expression. The law will protect a detailed plot or treatment but not a mere story or idea. In addition, copyright will protect the filmmaker to the extent that the treatment is written down in a tangible form, so an oral pitch will not be entitled to copyright protection, but the written treatment will. The filmmaker may wish to register the treatment with the Writers Guild (see chapter 4, p. 72), because it provides dated evidence of the treatment's content. Writers Guild registration does not provide any additional legal protection.

In meetings with prospective screenwriters, the filmmaker should also make it clear that he is retaining "story by" credit. The filmmaker should be willing to share that credit if the story is significantly enhanced or altered by the screenwriter, and should explain this to the prospective writers as well. A written invitation to the meeting—even in the form of an e-mail—should be enough to document this position. The e-mail or other written note explaining the "story by" credit will help clarify the agreement between the film company and the writer when a contract is ultimately drafted.

Finally, in rare cases the filmmaker may wish to require that the writer (as well as producers and others) sign a nondisclosure agreement (see chapter 5, p. 89). The nondisclosure agreement merely provides that the information disclosed will not be used except for the filmmaker's benefit, unless the information becomes generally available to the public through no fault of the recipient of the disclosure.

Nondisclosure agreements are not common in Hollywood, but they have become ubiquitous in the software industry and other fields devoted to intellectual property. Realistically, few producers, distributors, or financiers will be willing to sign a nondisclosure agreement, but the spec writer should be willing. For the filmmaker, it provides protection for the idea behind the film in addition to the copyright protection that extends only to the expression.

3. How to Select

The selection process for the writer or writers depends on where in the production cycle the film presently stands. The best way to know whether to buy a script is to read it—to commission a spec script and hire the writer only if it meets the production's needs. Despite the position of the Writers Guild, many writers are willing to write scripts on spec, even for a production company that owns the underlying story idea and rights. In fact, the writer's speculative risk is not significantly different from the risk taken by the filmmaker who will sell the finished film through a film festival only if the audience receives it warmly. However, the filmmaker should not commission a spec script from more than one writer at a time. To do so shows a lack of respect, if not bad faith, on the part of the filmmaker. The writers should not be bidding or competing against each other.

The primary alternative to commissioning spec scripts requires that the filmmaker evaluate prospective writers on the basis of previous screenplays and credits received. When applicable, the filmmaker should compare the writer's script to the finished film to better gauge the work actually contributed by that screenwriter. Since screenplays are rewritten constantly, judging a screenwriter by her filmed work may not show the true picture. Many new writers, however, are not likely to have produced many films with credits. By reviewing their own spec scripts (as opposed to a newly commissioned spec script), the filmmaker can assess their writing styles and skills.

To help evaluate the body of work submitted by the screenwriter, the filmmaker may request sample pages for the current project rather than a full script. In this way, the writer can demonstrate her take on the filmmaker's materials and directions but not be forced into the labor-intensive process of creating an entire screenplay. This allows the filmmaker to assess the timeliness of delivery, the style of writing, the ability of the writer to listen to suggestions, and the artistic sense of the writer for the filmmaker's material. Otherwise brilliant writers may fail on any given project if they do not have the right eye for the imagery, ear for the dialogue, or taste for the story. The request to review sample pages works particularly well with an up-and-coming screenwriter who has only a modest body of previous work. In contrast, for a seasoned veteran writer, such a request may not be appropriate.

4. The Role of the Union

If a writer is a member of the Writers Guild, then union rules prohibit her from working with a nonunion company. Whether the individual writer chooses to follow this rule, however, is her choice rather than the concern of the production company. The only danger in working with a union writer on a nonunion production is that she could change her mind and refuse to deliver a script unless the film company signs the WGA Theatrical and Television Basic Agreement (commonly called the Writers Guild Minimum Basic Agreement, or WGA-MBA). A film company may become a signatory to the WGA-MBA simply by contacting the Writers Guild. The WGA-MBA provides an excellent structure for negotiations whether or not the writer is actually a member of the union.

5. Deals for the Writer

The minimum writer's fees outlined in the WGA-MBA can help the film company determine appropriate compensation. Fees are linked to the type of writing requested, with the writer earning a greater amount of money for writing both the treatment and the screenplay than for writing the screenplay alone. Similarly, writing an original screenplay is worth more than writing a screenplay based on literary rights owned by the production company.

The payment should be based on delivery of both a first draft and a final draft. The number of iterations between them should be specified in the contract, such as a *first draft, intermediary draft,* and *final draft.* If the production has cash available, then the writer should be paid a portion of the total amount at the delivery of each installment. A schedule should be used that offers incentives for early delivery, and stipulates the right of the production company to reduce payments for late delivery or to terminate the agreement.

Even if the majority of the screenwriter's salary will be deferred, she should receive some cash payment at each delivery point, unless all other salaries are also deferred. The screenwriter should not be singled out for complete deferment. When all or most of the writer's fees are deferred, depending on the size of the budget, it may be appropriate to provide some percentage above WGA-MGA minimum. In this way, the writer may earn, say, 150 percent of minimum in the event the film fully covers its deferred costs.

Under the WGA-MBA, the screenwriter's minimums are automatically increased if the production budget exceeds the low-budget minimum. Even with a nonunion writer, tying the deferred salary to the production budget (with both a floor and ceiling) allows the screenwriter to benefit proportionately from any significant increase in the project's scale. Though highly imprecise, paying the screenwriter a minimum of 1 percent of the film's total production budget may reasonably approximate the negotiated fees for films in the low-budget and blockbuster range alike.

As mentioned in chapter 9 (p. 165), another important provision of the WGA-MBA provides a means for establishing writing credit in the event there is a controversy over which writers contributed to the finished film. The WGA-MBA includes mandatory arbitration provisions, but even without a union writer, the filmmaker should retain the right to award credit based on each writer's contribution; limit the number of parties entitled to screen credit (perhaps subject to the producer's discretion); and incorporate an arbitration clause, so that the determination can be made without resorting to a court proceeding in the event of a dispute. Additional interests, such as profit or revenue participation, should be available only for the credited screenwriters. The total participation may be divided among the credited writers, or earned by a single writer if that writer receives sole writing credit.

In addition to salary minimums and credit guidelines, the WGA-MBA also provides that the screenwriter should have some access to the shooting set. A nonunion contract should retain this provision as a professional courtesy to those writers who receive writing credit. Similarly, the writers receiving credit should be afforded the opportunity to screen the movie at a time when any feedback may still be valuable to the filmmaker and the editors. The writers should also be included in the promotion of the film:

they should be mentioned in all written materials and potentially included in junkets and film festival appearances as well.

Despite some competition between writers and directors over the paternity of a project, the writer is often a highly dedicated part of the creative team who provides a great deal of additional, uncompensated assistance to help get the project completed and distributed. Industry custom provides much helpful guidance, but participants and resources should not be lightly dismissed simply because of those customs.

C. The Director

1. Job of the Director

According to the Directors Guild of America, the job of the director is "to contribute to all of the creative elements of a film and to participate in molding and integrating them into one cohesive dramatic and aesthetic whole."[3] This somewhat vague description nonetheless captures the essence of the director's role. The director (typically the filmmaker but not always, as described previously), supervises all the creative elements of the production, imprinting his vision of the story, sound, design, and essence of the film onto the project. Technically, the director need only be responsible for the actions of the cast and the camera; in reality, the director remains integral to the entire production.

Unlike with screenwriters, the use of multiple directors occurs rarely and results in significant confusion in those unfortunate situations where it is required. The director is usually attached to the project early and thereafter participates in all the other employment arrangements for the production. The director should know about, or help decide, virtually all issues involved with the production, including the casting, employment of other creative personnel, and creative decisions involving script, locations, set design, scheduling, and postproduction editing. The producer generally has authority over the director, but throughout most of preproduction and principal photography, the director has practical control over much of the project.

If the director joins the production after a final screenplay has been delivered, there is a strong chance that he will request additional script revisions. The director will work with the producer and location manager on locations, revising the budget to accommodate the choices made. The director should also participate closely in the casting decisions. During principal photography, the director will coordinate the creative elements of the film, directing the action and filming each day and typically reviewing videotape or rushes of the day's shooting each night.

When the filming is completed, the director will assemble his cut of the film. If the director is someone other than the filmmaker, he may not have the right to determine the final cut of the film, but he should be given the opportunity to create an initial version. The producer or filmmaker should provide comments to the director, who may wish to act on those comments to revise his edit of the finished film. If not, the director will have completed his work, leaving final tweaking (or more significant editing if the parties do not agree on the film) to the filmmaker. The director will also participate in the promotion of the film in all venues.

2. How to Select

If the filmmaker is not the director, then the selection of the director becomes a critical step in the production process. The wrong choice can cripple or kill the project. Because of the practical difficulty in terminating a director, the filmmaker must work closely with the candidate to determine whether their visions are compatible.

There is no meaningful way to conduct a tryout for the filmmaker's particular project. Filming is dependent on too many choices, and early work may not be indicative of later decision making. Instead, the filmmaker should review the previous projects helmed by the potential director. She should speak directly with the producers on those projects, along with cast members, production crew, and others.

Thorough due diligence is a must. The filmmaker should pay particular attention to the comments of former cast members who have worked with the director; they may be in the best position to gauge his effectiveness. If a former cast member is reluctant to work with the director again, or has significant doubts about his abilities, the filmmaker should be very active in determining whether problems may come to her project as well.

3. The Role of the Union

Since its inception in 1939, the role of the Directors Guild has traditionally been to provide representation on issues of credit, control, and finances. The DGA represents directors, assistant directors, and unit production managers. Because the motion picture has evolved into a director's medium more than the medium of any other artist, the union focuses primarily on its relationship with the studios. Within the independent filmmaking arena, the filmmakers are typically the directors, so the union has little to do in that respect. Nonetheless, the DGA Minimum Basic Agreement can serve as a useful guide even in the context of low-budget nonunion filmmaking, and is mandatory for any union production. The DGA-MBA provides for compensation minimums, mandatory credit, and rules on the relationship between the director and the production company.

The DGA also offers a *side letter* that serves as a rider to the DGA-MBA, providing reduced director minimums. The side letter has changed in recent years to improve the opportunities for union directors to participate in low-budget productions. The side letter, available on the DGA Web site at www.dga.org/contracts/agreements_ctr_low.php3, provides various minimum fees depending on the budget of the production. It also allows for the deferral of some of the director's payments.

4. Deals for the Director

Whether or not the production is governed by the DGA-MBA, the agreement provides useful guidance on the proper relationship between the director and the filmmaker. To the extent that a nondirector filmmaker wishes to retain control of a nonunion project, certain protections may be modified, but most of the director's creative rights are essential to a quality production and should be honored.

Before hiring the director, the filmmaker and the candidate should go over the key issues of the production. Unless the director comes into the project knowing these issues, the relationship may get off to a rocky start. The DGA-MBA provides excellent guidance on the important discussion points:

1. budget for the film, or at least its top sheet (see chapter 7, p. 133)
2. proposed shooting schedule
3. names of creative personnel already employed
4. shooting methodology
5. any rights of script approval or cast approval contractually reserved to any person other than the filmmaker and producer
6. story and scripts presently available
7. any other artistic and creative commitments

These points really detail the significant issues that the director and the filmmaker must agree upon when structuring the film project. The scheduling, budget, and creative decisions will dictate as much about the film as any choices made during the filming process. A director who does not participate in these decisions is at a severe disadvantage, one that he may be unable to overcome.

In addition to forging a common understanding, the filmmaker must also address the director's concerns regarding issues of compensation, credit, and control. The director's compensation package will most likely include some combination of salary (paid and deferred) and either profit participation or revenue participation. Unlike producers, directors only occasionally participate in revenues rather than profits. If the filmmaker is attempting to lure a well-respected professional director to work on a low-budget independent film, she can offer revenue participation to make up for substantially lower budgets and resources than the same director has traditionally had available. On the other hand, she can offer very modest compensation to a relatively inexperienced director, who will likely jump at the opportunity to prove himself as the director of a feature film.

Director's credit has not historically proven controversial. If a director must be replaced partway through production, a choice must be made as to who is awarded the credit. The general assumption is that the second director is the person with the greater influence on the final look of the film; invariably, he's the person who has the better relationship with the production company. A subsequent director who shoots as little as 25 percent of the footage may still dramatically reshape the project and therefore be awarded shared or even sole directorial credit. The DGA-MBA requires that the initial director receive credit if he has completed at least 90 percent of the film, though a choice can be made to award credit to both. Similarly, a nonunion contract should provide that the first director will be guaranteed director credit only if he has completed 90 percent of principal photography and is not in material breach of any contractual obligations. Otherwise the filmmaker should retain discretion on how to award the credit.

Unlike a straightforward director's credit, the "a film by" credit has proven to be highly controversial. Increasingly, this credit has been granted to the director, but the slowly developing trend is to provide this credit only to directors who are also credited on the script. Given the procedural hurdles of a director receiving script credit, however, it may also be appropriate in those situations in which the director is a substantial uncredited writer on the project. In the independent filmmaking world, "a film by" should be the credit of the filmmaker, if anyone.

The most controversy involving directors' contracts stems from issues of control. The producer controls the budget and authorizes expenditures, while the director is responsible for determining the *need* for all expenditures. The same division of authority applies to hiring, selecting locations, and many of the production decisions. As a general matter, the contract may simply provide for consultation by the director with the producer on these issues, but that contract will be highly unsatisfactory if relied upon. For salary expenses, the DGA-MBA identifies which support staff can be selected by the producer (such as the unit production manager) and which by the director (the first assistant director). To be effective, the producer must provide more than cursory consultation with the director and instead collaborate closely so there is a common understanding of the film's budget as it is used to shoot the film. Consultation rights also extend beyond the budget. For example, significant changes to stunt work require advance notice to the director, who may object to them if he has a legitimate reason. Perhaps more important than the right to consult on significant changes is the right to be notified in advance of any producer-ordered changes.

Finally, under the DGA-MBA, the director must have some assurance regarding his participation in the postproduction process. The union agreement requires that the director be allowed to assemble a *first cut* of the film, without interference from producers. Once this initial edit is done, the director may or may not have *final cut* authority over the film; if he does not, the producers may step in and reedit the film. Regardless of the director's final-cut authority or the union status of the film, he must be allowed to create the first cut and should be invited to participate in the rest of the postproduction process. Since the final look of the film is so essential to a director's future, offering him anything less than reasonable consultation seems highly inappropriate. Unless he has been terminated for cause or has become an obstruction in the editing process, he should at least serve as an advisor to the producer or filmmaker throughout postproduction.

D. The Production Team

1. Jobs of the Unit Production Manager and First Assistant Director

The team of unit production manager (UPM) and first assistant director (AD) fill out the senior management of the film production. The UPM implements the decisions of the producer, and the first AD implements those of the director.

The UPM oversees the logistical details of the production, working through the budget, scheduling, finance, travel, and myriad additional issues that affect the film. She will negotiate many of the agreements for the production and arrange (and rearrange) the production schedule. On union productions, despite their budgetary role, UPM positions are governed by the Directors Guild.

A related position to the UPM is that of *line producer*. On an independent film, there is likely to be only a line producer or a UPM, but not both. In a larger production, the UPM may be a standing employee of the producer who moves from one film project to the next, serving each project exclusively while the producer provides nonexclusive services to a number of films at various stages of development. In this situation, the film company may also hire a line producer who has on-set operational responsibility for the film's expenses.

The first assistant director runs the set, ensuring that each day's schedule is ready for the director—that the call times for shooting, costuming, and makeup are coordinated so each cast member can be costumed and ready in time for his scheduled appearance. The first AD works with the cast and serves as an intermediary between cast and crew whenever necessary.

Any significant changes made by the UPM or line producer must be filtered through the first AD so that the production can continue to operate smoothly. Like the relationship between producer and director, the relationship between UPM and first AD must be one of respect and constant communication, to set the tone for everyone else.

Although the two team members' tasks are interrelated, they are not interchangeable. The first AD must monitor and participate in the ongoing production and coordinate each day of the shoot. The UPM, in contrast, will often be working on what comes next, adjusting production schedules to account for weather or other uncontrollable variables, revising the budgets as expenses come due, and preparing for the design and logistics issues that are on the horizon throughout the production.

Even on the smallest of films, both of these roles must be filled continuously. To reduce the number of participants on a film project, the filmmaker is more likely to succeed by merging of the roles of producer and UPM, or the roles of director and first AD, than by collapsing the UPM and first AD into a single role.

2. How to Select

The primary criteria producers consider when they choose the UPM or line producer and that directors consider when they choose the first AD are the qualities of trust, respect, and confidence in the relationship. More than any other positions, these two roles are extensions of the needs of their supervisors. A personal rapport is essential, so wide latitude should be given to individual preference in the selection process.

If someone is to be hired who has not worked with either the director or producer before, the key is to look for a track record of organization, efficiency, initiative, attention to detail, and experience on film sets. These two roles serve as the engine of the project, propelling the cast and crew late at night, early in the morning, and into long weekends when exhaustion is setting in. They are also the face of the production, because the producer and director do not spend as much time among the rank-and-file production personnel as they do. Their capacity for tact, respect, and professionalism—or lack thereof—reflects directly on the director, producer, and production company. The employer should be concerned about these attributes as well.

Often, production assistants move up through the ranks to become second ADs and eventually first ADs. Others may follow a similar track to become line producers or UPMs. By identifying these climbers early in their career, even a low-budget project may be able to employ someone with strong potential and a reasonable amount of experience.

3. Deals for the Production Team

Both the first assistant director and the unit production manager are covered by the DGA. For a union shoot, the DGA-MBA provides the minimum compensation and credit obligations. As with the director, a side letter agreement may be used to reduce the costs to employ union talent in these roles. The side letter may also allow for limited nonunion personnel in these areas, particularly if an experienced director or producer can use the opportunity to train and promote someone who has worked on prior union productions.

E. Cast

1. The Actor

The actors portray the characters in the film. More formally, acting may be defined as "the performing art in which movement, gesture, and intonation are used to realize a fictional character for the stage, for motion pictures, or for television."[4] The task is as simple as that, but it remains perhaps the most difficult role in the creative arts. Some film roles may be portrayed by experienced professionals with years of training to project their emotions on film. Others are portrayed by untrained individuals who simply appear onscreen in the manner sought by the director of the film. Casting choices are often the most fundamental to the success of the entire project.

As mentioned earlier, the independent filmmaker may be a cast member rather than one of the other participants in the film. When an actor has achieved some degree of fame, an independent film may provide an opportunity to both star in the film and direct the project, as Ed Harris did so successfully with *Pollock*. For less well-known actors, it may be a chance to star in a role that no other producer would offer. Particularly for minorities and women, independent films offer the ability to create opportunities rather than to wait for Hollywood to offer them. Many independent films may be fueled, at least in part, by the desire of actors to play these hard-to-find parts.

a. Casting Directors

Except on productions with the most modest of budgets, filmmakers rely on casting directors to provide them with information and advice on the actors to be sought, based on suggestions made by the producer and director and *breakdowns* of the script—brief synopses of each character in the film. An experienced casting director has access to talent agents representing union talent, a database and personal knowledge of potential cast members' experience, and some insight into their income histories and box office appeal. By analyzing information about the actors' prior film contracts, the casting director can help negotiate reasonable salaries for the cast and avoid unnecessary delays or unrealistic choices.

For many independent films, the producer and line producer or UPM fill the role of casting director, soliciting the talent agents of potential cast members. To the extent that the producer and director have personal working relationships with any of the preferred cast members, these relationships may serve better than any formal process to interest the actors in the project.

b. Breakdown Services

To inform actors and their agents of the roles in need of being filled, casting directors rely heavily on script breakdowns. For over 30 years, Breakdown Services, Ltd., has been the leading provider of these character synopses, which are available free to casting directors and producers. Breakdown Services' staff writers read and analyze approximately 30 scripts daily.[5] Talent agents download the casting information they produce directly from the Breakdown Services Web site. Based on the breakdowns, agents may submit cast members for the production. In some situations, with the producer's approval, Breakdown Services also allows the actors themselves to access the breakdowns directly.

In addition to Breakdown Services, Ltd., new Internet-based companies are beginning to provide similar services.[6] The growth of the Internet and rapid changes in Internet business may lead to significant changes in how casting information is distributed over the next decade, as well as shift the participants in the industry.

Breakdown services provide an efficient method of providing cast information to the talent community at little cost or trouble to the producer. The true work comes next: sorting through the potentially thousands of submissions to narrow the field and begin the process of auditioning.

2. Talent Agents and Managers

For union projects, the primary official contact flows between the casting director or producer and the agents for the talent. Talent agencies will receive the breakdowns of the script and, at the same time, the casting director will be contacting the agents for the star talent that the filmmaker has in mind for the key roles. Occasionally, the agent will be interested in the project. More often, filmmakers pursue stars that prove to be outside the budget for the project, unavailable for the scheduled production period, or simply uninterested in working on an independent film. With tremendous perseverance, however, the production will begin to generate interest from actors whom the filmmaker might wish to cast.

The talent agent's obligation is to maximize her client's income and professional opportunities. (Which coincides with the agent's own financial interests; typically, she is entitled to 10 percent of the client's revenue.) Occasionally, a talent agent will find an independent film script that she believes will transform her client's career. More often, however, the agent will regard her client's participation in an independent film as the loss of the opportunity to work on a higher-paying, higher-profile project. As a result, talent agents may often be a hurdle rather than an aid to independent film production.

An agent will typically suggest a number of other, less-established clients who may be appropriate for the roles identified in the breakdown sheets. Among these less-known performers may be some stellar talent. One of the true benefits of the independent film process is that it provides opportunities to undiscovered talent both behind and in front of the camera.

To attract strong, well-recognized talent, however, the filmmaker should use whatever resources he has to contact potential cast members through informal means. This is where personal and professional relationships make the largest difference. On a low-budget project, a single known star may guarantee at least a DVD distribution agreement. Such a "bankable" star will encourage financing, improve press coverage, and lend credibility to the project. Once an actor becomes interested in the project, the negotiations will still be conducted by the talent agent. It is important, therefore, that the filmmaker work to keep the talent agent somewhat positive toward the project, so that she does not convince the actor not to pursue the role.

Some talent also have personal managers. For nonunion actors, a personal manager may be the only professional willing to assist them. If an independent film role exposes an actor to a broader range of opportunities or might serve to reinvigorate a stagnant career, the manager may see long-term value in such a relationship. Managers, therefore, are a useful avenue for the filmmaker to attract talent. However, managers should not negotiate contracts or actively pursue job opportunities; that is the exclusive domain of talent agents. Filmmakers should be leery of any manager acting as an agent. Such a manager may not be in compliance with union rules or financial limitations imposed by agreement on registered agents. Particularly in states that regulate talent agencies, such activity is inappropriate, and may lead to complications if any dispute arises involving the talent agreements. As a result, the filmmaker should always work directly with the actor or through her agent, if represented.

3. Advertisements

In addition to the formal casting processes, using casting directors and breakdown services, a myriad of online databases have developed that allow actors to submit their pictures and resumes for review. Unless the film requires someone of truly unique talent (such as a 4'9" soprano or a sword-swallowing juggler), these databases may be of limited value. On the other hand, some of these sites allow the filmmaker to post casting requirements or breakdowns directly. For nonunion shoots, this may greatly expand the range of possible talent available.

One of the premier traditional casting resources now boasts not only a newspaper presence but also Internet resources. *Back Stage East* and *Back Stage West* (which acquired its Los Angeles competition, *Drama-Logue*) publish short cast descriptions for both union and nonunion productions. These listings are free and widely read (see www.backstage.com). For many independent projects, most of the cast members come either from personal relationships or these advertisements.

4. Auditions and Casting

For motion pictures, casting can take one of three general forms. For well-known performers, no true audition is required. Instead, a meeting or interview will be held between the actor and director to discuss the part and give both parties a chance to get acquainted. While there will be some discussion of the character and the vision of the director, the actor will not be expected to perform the part. This meeting may include some readings from the script, but they are not necessarily required.

For less high-profile actors, a more formal audition may be held. In this setting, the director, casting director, and perhaps the producer or line producer/UPM will observe as an individual actor presents a scene from the production, often together with another actor who has already been cast. If, for example, the film is to star a particular female lead, she may be willing to read the part with a few different actors in the role of the male lead so the director can better judge the chemistry between the actors.

At the other extreme is the *cattle call*. This invariably humiliating experience allows the producers and director to observe potentially hundreds of unknown actors reading for roles in the production. Actors with any modicum of success will not participate in cattle calls, but for unknown actors, cattle calls represent an opportunity (admittedly much like a lottery ticket) to land a smaller part on a production. Casting directors who submit breakdowns through Breakdown Services, Ltd., may not then use a cattle call to review the talent submitted. It should really only be used as an alternative to requesting that actors submit resumes directly. Also, since the process is painful for both the actors and the producers watching the process, cattle calls should not be used unless the production seriously plans to cast from the process. As a backup plan, it is far too time-consuming and disrespectful of the actors. Where it will result in actual casting, however, many, many actors are willing to endure the indignity.

5. The Role of the Union

The Screen Actors Guild not only provides for minimum salaries, pension, and health care benefits for its members but also governs work conditions on productions. SAG represents both film actors and extras. Regardless of whether a union contract is signed, the independent filmmaker should abide by the SAG requirements designed to provide a safe working environment. Almost every major film accident occurs because work schedules were violated or safety rules ignored. Most independent films do not have the resources to survive even a modest accident, and no film is worth risking the lives of cast or crew.

Under a SAG agreement, the minimum salary for actors depends on the production budget, the amount of time the performer will be in principal photography, and the specific contract signed with the union. SAG provides a range of agreements ranging from major studio production contracts to contracts designed for student films shot for academic credit. Because of the number of different contracts available—and because they are constantly fluctuating—the filmmaker should contact the closest SAG office early in the preproduction process to determine whether a union agreement can be arranged. The obvious benefit of shooting under a SAG agreement is the ability to cast professional actors. If even one of the preferred cast members is a member of SAG, then the production must enter into a SAG agreement.

Perhaps the biggest drawback to a SAG production manifests itself if the film is to be made outside of a traditional SAG market. SAG operates approximately two dozen regional offices, each covering a carefully mapped geographic zone. Shooting outside those zones can increase the costs under the SAG agreement considerably, so locations should be selected with this in mind. Alternatively, if a particular out-of-zone location is central to the film, the filmmaker may instead opt against using union talent.

6. Extras

SAG now provides for union representation of extras, having merged the former Screen Extras Guild into the SAG union. The union agreement requires that a specified number of union extras be hired before nonunion extras can be employed. The particular number depends on both the contract under which the production is authorized and the location of the shoot. For contracts involving low-budget projects, this requirement is often waived.

7. Deals for the Actors

In addition to the primary issues of compensation and credit, cast members are generally concerned about their obligations to the production, mostly regarding the production schedule. The filmmaker usually will be required to accommodate the schedules of the key cast members, particularly if they are working below their normal salaries to participate in the film. In addition to the dates of principal photography, the contract must provide that the actors will be available for any necessary reshoots and for postproduction looping, or redubbing. The contract will typically include a minimum number of days of looping and establish a pay scale for any additional days needed.

Financially, the independent filmmaker also needs to take into account the cost of agents and managers. An agent's 10 percent of her client's revenue cannot reduce a SAG actor's pay below the minimums of the collective bargaining agreement, so the film company will be expected to pay union minimum plus 10 percent. Moreover, because the contract between actor and agent requires that the all funds be paid to the agent and then disbursed, the 10 percent is also subject to the health, welfare, and pension obligations of the film company to the union. Because agents recognize that the payment amounts for union-minimum, low-budget shoots provide little income but important goodwill, many are willing to waive their commission if the actor asks them to do so in advance of the production. As long as this is planned, and the film company has made it clear to the actor that waiver of the commission is a part of the prearranged agreement, budget surprises can be avoided.

The talent agreements should also include contractual obligations to promote the film. For stars working below their normal salary, a contractual commitment to promote the film may be difficult to negotiate, but it should be part of the package for other cast members. Even a small amount of promotion may be critical to the success of the film, so the filmmaker should work to encourage participation, contractually or otherwise.

If there is a possibility of generating additional revenue through ancillary products, soundtrack albums, or other merchandise, then the contract should specify that the film company has the right to use the names, likenesses, and publicity rights of the actors on these products. The provision should limit the use of each actor's publicity rights to products directly associated with the film, and should include a royalty payment to the actor. The royalty typically will be based on a percentage of the income paid to the film company for that item or items. The filmmaker should avoid agreeing to pay a percentage amount unless the percentage is based on the income of the filmmaker himself. If the filmmaker were to offer a percentage of retail sales, for example, the filmmaker might well owe more than he earns, and he might have no method for auditing that obligation.

If the company has contracts for product placement, the manufacturers providing those products may have hopes to use actors to promote the products in television commercials or Internet ads. Any such arrangements are best negotiated directly between the actor and the manufacturer. SAG provisions will govern the use of its members in commercials, so these provisions will need to be added by separate agreement. The film company should be paid for the use of the film footage in any such advertising, which is in addition to the use of the actors. The agreement between the manufacturer and the film company may include these provisions or they may be negotiated later, if the manufacturer decides to expand beyond product placement into commercials.

Equipment and Locations

THE LEGAL AND business choices in this chapter should be secondary to the aesthetic production goals of the filmmaker. The digital revolution has dramatically affected the range of equipment available, and the business practices are slowly adapting to that change. The ability to digitally alter locations during or after the shoot creates an entirely new set palette with which to paint the images. Each choice affects every other choice.

A. Types of Equipment and Contracts

1. Cameras and Lights

The production company will rent a package of camera equipment and lighting equipment, plus stands, electrical generators, and other related equipment for the film production. Perhaps the hardest choice to make at present is the medium on which the "film" will be shot. For the first time, the independent filmmaker has a choice of formats, including 35mm film stock, 16mm film—the traditional staple of the independent filmmaker—and a number of competing digital media. The choice of medium will be based on cost and ease of use, as well as the overall look being sought.

The medium chosen will dictate a number of other choices. Because 35mm film requires significantly more lighting power than any other format, the film company must select lighting equipment that complements the shooting format. The size and weight of the 35mm camera will also require that most moving shots use dollies or similar equipment. The production can rent *Steadicam* equipment, which allows a 35mm camera to be operated in a fluid, "hand-held" fashion, but this choice also requires that the camera operator be experienced wearing and operating this large piece of equipment.

Increasingly, digital options are rendering the 16mm format obsolete. Digital's ease of shooting, low-light capabilities, and instant recording ability all make it a strong contender for independent filmmaking. Of course, with digital equipment comes the attendant issues of hard drive failures, computer error messages, and other information-age obstacles. Sophisticated digital equipment is readily available in some cities, but it remains hard to rent in other areas.

Whichever format is chosen, rental prices will vary significantly from company to company and region to region. Be sure to shop around. In some areas, it may be cheaper to travel considerably to rent the equipment than to pay local prices. The rental contract should always be between the production company and the equipment supplier. The filmmaker should try to avoid accepting personal liability for rental fees or for any damage to the equipment.

Often the fee will include equipment insurance. Be sure to include this and other costs when comparing potential suppliers. If the production company carries adequate insurance already, it may offer to include the rental company as an additional insured on its own policy rather than paying for an additional policy. Flexibility on this point will vary from company to company.

Finally, some suppliers have weekly rates that offer significant savings over the base cost of daily rentals. They may apply a weekly rental fee equivalent to three or four days of rental. Careful planning is necessary, however, because most contracts do not allow for extensions to convert a daily rental into a weekly rental. It may more be cost-effective to rent for a full week rather than renting for two days, in case the production schedule proves to be overly ambitious.

2. Firearms and Other Weapons

Filmmakers often wish to use real weapons in the creation of certain scenes. While this is commonly done, independent films that intend to use fewer personnel and guerrilla filming techniques should nonetheless be ready to comply with detailed, time-consuming regulations and supervision. A handgun or rifle is subject to licensing and permit requirements even if it is not operable on the set. While temporarily disabling the weapon is a good idea for safety purposes, it will not change most licensing requirements. If it has been permanently disabled—the interior components rendered unworkable—then it may not be subject to licensing requirements, but even that will vary from jurisdiction to jurisdiction. Swords and other weapons may not have the same licensing requirements, but they may still create a public disturbance if brandished on the street.

In most jurisdictions, even if no film permit is required for the production under the local rules, the production company must still have a film permit if a firearm will be used. And not without reason: In one instance, a shot was fired as part of a lawful, independent shoot on a private farm. The police were called to the scene of the "shooting," the production was shut down, and the production company was assessed substantial fines for the false alarm. Had the production obtained a permit, the police would have had a record of the planned use of gunfire on the set, and the production could have continued.

Since the September 11 terrorist attacks, state and federal laws have tightened access to both real weapons and look-alikes. This makes access to these props more difficult and requires more planning for the production. If firearms or other weapons are part of a scene, filmmakers should contact the film office in the jurisdiction where the filming is scheduled well in advance of the scheduled shoot. Filmmakers may wish to take advantage of services licensed to provide weapons and pyrotechnics rather than try to borrow props for the filming.

3. Stunts and Special Effects

Stunts and on-set special effects both involve specialized activities with significant degrees of risk. Stunts typically include fight scenes, falls, or other highly choreographed movement. Special effects typically involve pyrotechnics—explosives or fireworks—that in most jurisdictions require state licenses and local permits, even on private property. Both should be conducted under the supervision of experienced professionals, no matter what the production budget.

Attempts to create homemade pyrotechnics can result in serious injury. Unlicensed attempts may void the production's insurance coverage and will certainly make the participants in any accidents personally liable for the losses. If injuries or expenses related to an unlicensed accident disrupt the production budget, the filmmaker might conceivably be personally liable to the investors as well, because her personal negligence cost the production its opportunity to be completed. Needless to say, unlicensed pyrotechnics should be avoided.

Even relatively simple stunts should be done only under the careful supervision of a stunt coordinator. Of course, the line between action and a stunt is not always clear. Common sense should serve as a guide. If the action, done improperly, could result in one of the actors being seriously hurt, then it should be treated as a stunt and conducted only after it has been well rehearsed and all risks have been minimized.

4. "Renting a Crew Member"

Just as stunt coordinators and special effects experts are employed for specific tasks, so are specialized technicians such as the *gaffer* (electrical expert) or *key grip* (individual in charge of the movement of lighting and camera). For nonunion projects, these professional trade union positions may be unnecessary. Particularly on small, digital productions, the filmmaker may reduce the need for such specialists by using handheld cameras and limited professional lighting.

In certain situations, however, a gaffer or key grip may be required. Rather than hiring the person for the entire project, it may be possible to enter into a special arrangement that covers only the particular scenes needed. However, this is not necessarily compliant with the expert's union obligations. Asking a professional union member to work on a nonunion project runs the risk that the person could be forced to leave the set if requested by a union representative, or may simply change his mind. This risk can be minimized if the person is hired for a short duration to assist with particular segments of the film.

Alternatively, the producer may determine that the project is complicated enough to require a union crew. The International Alliance of Theatrical Stage Employees (IATSE, or IA) provides locals for all below-the-line production personnel. Generally speaking, IATSE does not cater to independent films and provides few accommodations for these productions.

Other professionals, notably the director of photography and the sound mixer, are often package rentals along with their own equipment. If the production rents the equipment, the operator is supplied. Producers should be sure, however, that the production requires the professional services in addition to the equipment. The producer will have far less control over these packages than she would if she were hiring the equipment from a rental house and employing the professional separately. On occasion, this can limit the producer's discretion over the quality of either equipment or personnel. The producer must carefully scrutinize the references of anyone offering a package. Nonetheless, experienced sound mixers and directors of photography provide welcome efficiency and cost-effectiveness for the independent filmmaker.

B. Selecting Locations

In a visual medium, location choices convey much of the story. Each location should be treated as one of the characters in the script. Independent filmmakers often choose to blur the locations represented in the film or otherwise render them unrecognizable, but this denies the filmmaker one of his chief assets. Instead, effective use of the film permit process and solid legwork will allow the filmmaker tremendous flexibility in the locations represented in the picture.

1. Use of the Soundstage

The Hollywood of the 1930s built tremendous soundstages where controlled environments could be used to create any set imaginable. The obvious benefit to such spaces is control. Soundstages are enclosed, providing for excellent sound and allowing the production company to reproduce exactly the settings envisioned by the filmmaker. In addition, small portions of rooms or areas can be constructed, allowing even a 35mm camera to move into spaces that it could never enter in the real world. Soundstages also provide certain efficiencies because all the production facilities center on a single location.

The film industry has witnessed another transformation as the soundstage of the 1930s has been augmented by non-Hollywood locations such as the Long Beach geodesic dome (former home to Howard Hughes's *Spruce Goose*) and other major facilities in which film locales can be built. This trend blurs the distinction between soundstage and location shooting. These spaces are not owned by the studios and exist outside of Hollywood. They are typically rented on a long-term basis so that multiple sets can be constructed in the space.

Dedicated soundstages, however, may be too expensive for all but the largest of independent films. The independent filmmaker may instead create his own temporary soundstage, by using a larger space as a one-stop location for multiple sets. In a shuttered warehouse, a school building during summer break, or a similar structure, the filmmaker may enter into a single lease that provides him with a range of environments that can be adapted to various scenes needed throughout the film. Legally, the issues are the same as with any location shoot (see below).

2. On-Location Shooting

The modern trend for filmmaking—both independent and studio pictures—has been to move out of the studio and into natural locations. Location filming adds realism to movies and expands the range of tools available to set designers even when the designer modifies the location to represent other spaces (such as using futuristic architecture to represent science fiction settings). Location shooting necessarily includes a certain amount of set decoration. If a filmmaker is shooting a film set in the 1950s, and he selects a neighborhood because of its period houses, then modern attributes must be hidden or removed. A period film cannot retain visual credibility if the featured exterior has a satellite antenna.

Location shooting agreements enable the production company to use the property for the purposes of filming, to portray it in the film, and to alter its name or image in any manner. The film company generally will pay for the right to use the property. Any planned alterations to the property should be specified very carefully in the agreement. Usually, the film company will agree to restore the property to its original condition. When appropriate, however, the film company can agree to make modifications to the property that the owner is permitted to keep, such as repairs to the exterior, repainting, etc. The filmmaker should identify the property owner and the tenants (if different) and add each one to the film company insurance as an additional insured, regardless of whether the party is included in the contract.

In Los Angeles, property owners are very sophisticated about the use of their properties, while in other parts of the country, even the smallest of feature films is a rarity. In any event, the filmmaker should be prepared to discuss other details of the shoot. The property usage agreement may need to specify the use of electricity, telephone, water, or other utility services, provide for late-night access that could entail asking the residents of a residential property to stay at a hotel, and detail the parking requirements. Filmmakers should also be prepared to negotiate with commercial property owners regarding business loss during the period of production. If a filmmaker proposes to shut down a retail business during filming, the business owner will want to be compensated for the lost revenue. Even if the film's eventual release will result in improved traffic to the store, most shop owners will insist on current payments.

Although property owners have very limited rights to stop the use of photographs taken of their property, the same location agreement should also grant the film company the right to make photographs and films of the location. Additionally, a paragraph should be included that acts as a general release of all claims against the film company for use of the images (such as defamation or rights of privacy or publicity)—just in case.

Famous buildings require slightly different agreements. Although an owner may have no right to the copyright in a publicly visible building, if it serves as a visible symbol of a corporation, it may enjoy trademark protection. In addition, the building may have ornamentation—sculpture or murals—that are protected by copyright. In such cases, express permission from the copyright and trademark holders are highly recommended. The First Amendment may serve as a valid defense to any claims for a documentary filmmaker, but for a feature film, there is ample opportunity to secure the shooting rights. Finally, it should be noted that the copyright and trademark rights holder in this situation might not be the same as the tenant of the building who has the exclusive right to grant access. Instead, the building owner must be contacted (usually through the property management company), and perhaps the original artist as well, to gain full permission for the filming.

3. Permits and Requirements

In New York, California, and major metropolitan areas throughout the United States, a filmmaker must obtain a film permit in order to conduct any commercial filming. This often does not apply to news filming and may be inapplicable to documentary filmmakers under either the terms of the particular film ordinance or the First Amendment. As a general rule, film permit requirements are designed to protect the community from the disruptions caused by large productions, and a small digital camera is an advantage as it will generally go unnoticed on a city street.

Whether a film permit is necessary from a practical standpoint, the permit process in most major areas has become increasingly simple, and the filmmaker may find that the local film commission provides significant assistance in the making of a film. Most film offices have libraries of available locations for shooting. They may also have experience with various locations throughout the area, and they can work with the filmmaker to minimize the disruption that may be caused to areas in which the filming takes place.

There are very few requirements for obtaining a film permit. The nature of the production must be specified, with particular attention to the number of trucks and amount of parking the shoot will require. Any weapons or pyrotechnics must be detailed, and their use processed through the fire marshal or other specified authority. Finally, there will be a minimum insurance requirement. If the filming will take place on city, county, or state property, then the film office will also require that fees are paid for the use of the property, usage restrictions are met, and the jurisdiction is named as an additional insured on the film company insurance.

As cities and states have begun to recognize the enormous economic value filmmaking offers to local communities, most film offices have streamlined the permitting process and provide very helpful resources that are fully available to the independent filmmaker. Film offices—particularly that of the Office of the Mayor of New York City, the California Film Commission, and FilmL.A., the L.A. film office—all provide tremendous resources for independent filmmakers. Other city and state film offices, attempting to compete with L.A. and New York, have also grown in scope and resources. Independent filmmakers should take advantage of these resources to the greatest extent possible to reduce costs and improve the quality of the production.

C. Tax Incentives for Location Shooting

As states and cities recognize the value to local incomes from the payments made by film companies and the long-term benefits for tourism by having films use locations for filming, more and more states provide tax incentives to film companies as a way to lure them into the jurisdiction to film or keep them from leaving for Canada or overseas. These reimbursements vary greatly from state to state, but because they can be considerable, filmmakers should take them seriously when deciding where to film.

These incentive programs tie tax benefits to production costs spent in the state or employment opportunities offered to state residents or both. Some programs require the film company to maintain offices in that jurisdiction, while others focus more heavily on itinerant productions. Incentives range from exemption from paying sales taxes or hotel taxes to significant tax credits. Tax credits provide the film company with an offset of its production expenses that can be applied to its future earnings. Some states have tax credits as high as 50 percent of the production budget—which would allow half of the production expenses to be paid from tax credits in years of future revenue. Other states even allow for the credits to be sold to other companies, providing an asset that can be used to finance the film. The programs in each jurisdiction vary significantly from each other, and states modify the terms almost annually. The local film office provides the best resources for understanding how to maximize the potential tax benefits, and every program is available on the Web site of the film office or office of economic development.

Tax credit opportunities should be considered early in production planning, when deciding in what locations to shoot the film. However, because these programs limit eligibility based on whether payments are made within or outside the state, and may set similar limits for the employment of personnel, their benefit must be weighed against the project's overall location and personnel needs. If these needs are not harmed by the limitations of the incentive program, then the use of tax credits to finance the film creates some very nice opportunities.

Shooting the Film

A WELL-ORGANIZED production should anticipate most legal and practical issues before arriving on location. To accomplish this, the film company must practice good planning and professional organization. Typically, these responsibilities fall to the location manager, working in conjunction with the line producer, UPM, or producer.

A. Scheduling

Filmmakers rarely have the luxury of filming the script in chronological order. They must schedule the film around those resources that cannot be controlled. First, stars often have only limited dates available to shoot—particularly for the low-paying independent filmmaker. Their availability will set the start and end dates of the shooting schedule. Second, if certain locations are only available during a particular week, then other locations must not be scheduled during that window. Third, weather cannot be controlled, but it can be prepared for. Indoor shooting days should be left until the end of the production so that if inclement weather prevents a scheduled outdoor shoot, those indoor days can be moved up and production will not be shut down waiting for the weather to change. Fourth, budget constraints must be considered. There is no reason to pay people who are not working, so, typically, the larger production days are grouped first and cast and crew are slowly let go as the shooting schedule calls for fewer and fewer people.

Because weather constantly changes, as does the availability of cast and crew members, even the most rigid schedule is likely to be changed throughout the production process. Proposed changes must be evaluated against the other constraints of locations, cast, and budget, and the UPM must be sure that everyone involved in the production is kept constantly aware of the changing schedule. Contracts for locations and equipment should specify target dates but allow the filmmaker to adjust those dates as the production requires.

B. Preparing Locations

Well in advance of the day of filming, the location manager must provide the property owner with a contract that specifies exactly what changes are to be made to the location and how they are to be made. Typically, all modifications to the property will be temporary, so the contract should provide a schedule that includes preparation time, a period of filming, and a period for striking the set and returning the location to its original condition.

1. Working the Neighborhood

If the changes are significant or the filming will otherwise affect neighbors, then the location manager should contact them as well to let them know what is happening and, to the extent possible, enlist their support. This is particularly important if the production will shut down traffic to streets, even for short periods of time. Even a guerrilla filmmaker working with a single handheld camera will need neighborhood support, and a modestly sized independent film project can be quite an intrusion into a neighborhood. Trucks carrying lighting, electrical generators, film equipment, sets, and costumes, and the cars of cast and crew, add up to a logistical invasion larger than most construction projects. The need to remove cars from street parking for exterior shots can become quite a complex task, particularly if the individuals refuse to move their cars voluntarily, and the film company requires the city to close the street to parking.

To minimize disruptions, the filmmaker must communicate closely with those who may be inconvenienced by the filming. At least two weeks prior to the scheduled shoot, the location manager should contact the owners of all the properties that may be affected. She should inform the property owners and occupants of the dates of the proposed shooting; the scheduled starting time and approximate end time; the nature of the film and that it is an independent feature (it may be helpful to include some promotional information); the particulars of the shoot (if it involves exteriors, interiors, moving vehicles, etc.); and the needs of the company. If sound matters, then she should request that no lawnmowers be used. If a historical period is being recreated, then modern cars may need to be removed.

Be sure to give the name, telephone number, and e-mail address of the film company's contact person—and respond immediately to any request. A follow-up should be made the day before the shoot. For most locations, the neighbors typically will be quite helpful.

Business owners will be concerned about interference with their customer traffic. Filmmakers must be prepared to avoid disruption or to work with affected store owners. In some cases, this may include negotiating with a local chamber of commerce on behalf of a large number of retailers. Here, timing becomes critical: interrupting business is much more expensive in December than in January.

2. Closing Streets

If an exterior shot using closed streets is planned, then the city and the police department must be involved. The film company will be most successful if it can minimize the disruption. Given the start-and-stop nature of filming, the filmmaker should consider using intermittent traffic stops. Rather than closing the street, production could stop traffic only while the cameras are running. For many films, intermittent traffic stops are all that will be needed to capture the necessary shots.

If a street must be closed for any significant period of time, the film company must work closely with all the regular users of that street. To close a street, a local film permit is absolutely required, unless the jurisdiction does not issue such permits. The permit is typically conditioned on the film company providing alternative parking, patrolling the intersections to control traffic (or hiring off-duty law enforcement personnel to do so), and gaining the permission of the affected residents or businesses. To get such permission, payment is sometimes necessary, but a tactful request, permission to observe the filming, or an offer to provide pastries or cold drinks often suffices.

C. Daily Production Requirements

Independent filmmakers should utilize the community surrounding their locations to the greatest extent possible. By working with local vendors, the film company may reduce its expenses and improve its relationships—particularly important if the location in question will be used for an extended period. The area Lowe's or Home Depot often benefits tremendously from location shooting. Film companies may also opt to provide cast and crew with prepaid vouchers from local restaurants in lieu of craft service, if it can be arranged in a cost-efficient manner.

1. Set Preparation: Utilities Basics

All but the smallest sets require significant electricity, water, and sewage capability, and the ability to control sound. Unfortunately, these needs are not necessarily compatible. Each of these elements must be planned in advance with careful attention to local regulations.

Electrical power may be obtained through portable generators or temporary *power drops* attached to utility poles (provided by the local electrical utility), or by tapping into the existing electrical service of the location. The choice of electrical source will depend on the size of the production, the resources available, and the duration of the shoot. If an agreement has been made in advance, a small guerrilla shoot should be able to plug lights directly into the location's power service. A large production will need to bring its own generators, unless it plans to use the location for a significant length of time. In that case, arranging a power drop with the local utility will become more cost-effective. A second advantage of using a temporary power drop is the avoidance of the noise and fuel consumption of portable generators.

If portable generators are selected, the location must be carefully mapped to park the generators sufficiently far from the shooting that their noise does not interfere with the production sound. Large power lines will snake from the generators to the lights and production equipment. The scale of this equipment increases the complexity of location shooting considerably, and adds to the size of the crew.

Water and sewage are also important considerations with any location filming. Water availability varies dramatically from area to area. In urban areas, water hookups are often provided by the location, because the cost to the landowner is not significant. Where well water is used (and in areas facing drought conditions), access to water may be costly and difficult to obtain. If the location will not provide water, then the local utility must be contacted to connect a hose to a fire hydrant, if available, or to provide other suggestions for temporary connections.

The same approach applies to toilets and sewage. The scale of the production will dictate the size of the facility necessary. If the location has facilities, arrange to use them. If that cannot be done, or if the size of the production makes it impractical, then the company will need to rent a *honey wagon*—a trailer with built-in dressing room and bathroom facilities. Most honey wagons will need water and sewage hookups, although honey wagons with storage tanks are also available. In addition, portable toilets that do not use local water may also be rented if no other alternative is available. These options are all more expensive and cumbersome than making arrangements with the location, so the contract with the property owner should be negotiated with these needs and expenses in mind.

2. Parking

Often overlooked, crew parking is a significant logistical component of location shooting in some areas. Even a small production may require extended parking for 10 to 20 vehicles. Larger production should include a "campsite" area with enough space for individual cars; cast trailers (mobile homes starting at 35 feet in length); a honey wagon ranging from 35 to 65 feet in length; a 35-foot trailer for wardrobe, makeup, and the grip truck; and a much larger truck for lighting and electrical production equipment. Add the portable generators and the parking area can grow to the size of a small college. Locations must be selected that can provide support for these needs. If necessary, the automobile parking can be moved to a remote location and the production can use a van or car as a shuttle between the parking and the rest of the camp.

D. Staying in Control

To keep the location operating smoothly, the location manager must work closely with the line producer or UPM and first assistant director to ensure that the location is used as efficiently, productively, and legally as possible. Efficient use comes from coordinating the shooting schedule and the activities of the cast and crew on the set. Productive use comes from maximizing the amount of usable film shot—by creating multiple scenes at each location so some areas can be prepped while others are being used for filming. Legal use includes compliance with the location permit and its restrictions and with any location agreements.

1. Logistical Planning

Coordination is the key to controlling the logistics on the set. When dealing with rental of equipment for the film location, scheduling and availability of equipment is critical. In areas familiar with the motion picture industry, equipment rental companies have a great deal of expertise. In other areas, however, local vendors may not be familiar with the production company's needs. The UPM must be sure to negotiate with these companies and put the dates and times for each piece of equipment into the contract. The location owner must be fully apprised of the equipment that will accompany the shoot so that there are no surprises the morning of filming when the trailers and equipment roll up.

To be cost-effective, timing each piece of equipment is also critical. It may be more affordable to rent a location for an extra day, allowing the set designers and crew more time to prepare the set before the grips and electrical are scheduled to arrive. The honey wagon might not appear on location until the third day. By staggering the activities, costs can be controlled, but the UPM must truly understand the activities occurring on the set at any given moment in time. Scheduling should take place on an hour-by-hour basis rather than day-by-day.

2. People Planning

Hour-by-hour scheduling is also essential for effective management of locations and personnel. Idle cast and crew reduce efficiency, while a missing cast member can bring the entire production to a halt. Since the UPM manages the crew and the first AD manages the cast, the two must carefully coordinate call times and the day's schedule to be sure that the right people are always available and planning to work on the same scenes.

Independent productions are generally less structured than larger-budget studio films, and crew members may be willing to pitch in to help with needs outside of their primary responsibilities. If crew members are given the ability to work on both today's and tomorrow's shooting schedule, they can be kept involved more effectively than in traditional shoots.

3. Budgeting and Cost Control

The original budget for the film should be treated as a historical document, retained in its original form as a tool for comparison. Actual expenditures will begin to deviate from that document before filming even begins. As a result, the budget will need to be updated constantly to reflect the actual expenditures and to project the additional expenses necessary to complete the film. For example, if the screenplay requires an additional, unbudgeted polish, the money for it must come out of some other area or the total cost of the film must be increased. Most independent films cannot afford to increase the budget, so something else must go. If the choice is to eliminate a location and its associated costs, the set budget must reflect this change, or the elimination of one location will merely allow the set designer to spend more on other locations. Both the budget and the schedule must reflect every change, and interim budgets should be kept on file.

The need to account for actual expenses becomes most pronounced during location filming. In the heat of the shoot, crew members are often sent out to buy necessary but forgotten items. These last-minute expenses can add up. For a small independent film, such expenses can overwhelm the budget. Receipts should be turned in within minutes of the expenditure and must be turned in by the end of each day. Even on the largest studio shoots, every dollar spent must be accounted for with a receipt, and every receipt must reflect a particular budget item. If someone is sent to Target, Walmart, or Home Depot to pick up various items, he should ring up gaffer's tape on one register receipt and wood screws on a second, so the accounting properly reflects which departments are charged with the expenses.

Just as he reviews each day's shooting, the filmmaker must look at expenditures daily to ensure that the production remains on time and on budget. If either the schedule or the budget starts to go awry, the filmmaker should make adjustments. The earlier adjustments are made, the smaller they generally need to be. Careful management can keep problems to a minimum.

4. Costumes and Props

Movies with any significant budget will provide that all costumes be purchased by the production company and can be worn only on the set. To assure that a film sequence is not ruined by the destruction of a costume, every significant character's costume will have a backup. Even if the perfect pants for a major character can be purchased for $5.00 at the Salvation Army, the film company may still have to spend hundreds of dollars to reproduce an exact copy by hand. If a costume is used in scenes involving dirty, outdoor activity—running through thick woods or climbing rough mountain terrain—the production should probably have three or four duplicates so that the filming can continue quickly if a costume is torn or heavily soiled.

Not all costume damage comes from the scenes being shot. When the cast helps out on the set, it adds another risk to the maintenance of costumes. Clothing can get very dirty while helping with lights or moving equipment. Great care must be taken to protect the clothes used for filming.

Properties or *props* also require great attention and care. These are the nonfixed items on the set that are handled by the characters. If a photograph rests on a mantel, it is set decoration. If that photograph is picked up for a moment by one of the characters, it becomes a prop. Actors take a strong, proprietary view of the props they use, and may become very particular about the nature of the props. Like costumes, any props subject to wear and tear need to be backed up by identical copies to ensure that filming will not be held up if something happens to the item.

Managing the props can take a lot of time and energy, far more than first-time filmmakers may expect. Every item needs to be catalogued and carefully noted when it is checked out to the set, so that all the props are returned every night. Some props are only on loan to the film company and need to be returned to their owners once they are no longer required. Failure to return these props can create a significant additional expense for the film company.

Finally, film shoots generate a lot of interest in souvenirs. When members of the public watch filming, they may want to pick up props as small mementos. Cast members and extras often want personal souvenirs, and the props they used are available and important to them. If people are allowed to steal these items, the film company loses all control. If scenes need to be reshot, or if sequences are shot out of order, the missing props may be needed later in the production.

Even the cast and crew may not realize the importance of keeping all props available, so film companies may want to manage their expectations by allowing them to request props and take them as souvenirs at the end of production. Keeping a log of requests for those items the producer is willing to give away will let the cast and crew know that there is an acceptable way to earn a memento and help discourage the casual pilfering that can become very costly on some productions.

E. Managing the Content in the Frame

Although film is an expressive art form, it is also an increasingly international and highly commercial business. As a result, filmmakers should be very selective regarding choices to use a third party's property—copyrighted works, trademarks, readily identified individual names or corporate names—without express permission. Permission is not always difficult to come by. Without the express permission, the errors and omissions insurance (see chapter 9, p. 176) may be drafted to exclude any liability for the use of such content, and the lack of coverage may discourage distributors or exhibitors from buying or showing the work.

The issues regarding clearance become more difficult in the context of international film distribution. Different countries have very different approaches to censorship and to the kinds of content deemed inappropriate. In some cases, this relates to third-party ownership rights, and in other cases it relates to the action being filmed. In the United States, filmmakers risk changes to their MPAA ratings for depictions of smoking. In countries where alcohol is banned, the exhibition of drinking may be discouraged or banned as well. In some cultures, religious images may not be photographed. For example, images of the prophet Muhammad are banned from exhibition in some countries. And depictions of nudity are treated very differently from country to country and from medium to medium.

1. Script Clearance

When a shooting script is prepared, it should be sent for *clearance review,* to ensure that the filmmaker has acquired all the rights necessary to film it. (See appendix F, p. 424, for the names and contact information of script clearance services.) The resulting script clearance identifies all the script elements that may give rise to third-party ownership claims. It will identify the potential legal issues, and will instruct the film company to consult with the production attorney to resolve those issues. Many of the topics of the report are discussed elsewhere throughout this book: acquisition of literary rights, purchase of life-story rights for fictional works and documentaries, acquisition of music, and location agreements. The report should be reviewed carefully by the film company and its lawyer to identify the rights that must be acquired and the situations that can be avoided.

Script clearance should be undertaken well before principal photography begins. This provides the production company with sufficient time to make any script changes necessary and to acquire permission for all items that will be included in the film. If some of the permissions are not forthcoming, it is helpful to have enough time to seek permission from alternative sources.

Documentaries have a very different set of demands for clearance. Because a documentary filmmaker generally does not create the content of his shots, he may rely much more heavily on the fair use privilege, which allows the incidental inclusion of copyrighted material. Nonetheless, documentary films should also be subject to a clearance process, and documentary filmmakers should minimize conflict with other rights holders when practical. The unique considerations and processes are dealt with in chapter 13 (p. 232).

2. Coverage Shots

Whenever a scene may involve content that is owned by a third party or that may include content banned in various markets, the filmmaker's best strategy is to also shoot an alternative version of the scene that omits the questionable material. Scenes involving nudity can be shot with total nudity, then again with highly suggestive costumes. If the director wishes to shoot a scene that includes a billboard in the background, he should also shoot a version of the scene that removes the billboard from the frame.

By shooting coverage shots, the filmmaker captures the footage as he most desires it but also captures sufficient footage so that the film company has choices if faced with clearance problems or censorship. This is far preferable to making the inclusion or exclusion of a scene an all-or-nothing battle. With good coverage footage, any objections can be addressed with relatively inexpensive editing rather than the much more costly reshooting.

3. Location Names

Script clearance reports will identify any overlap with identifiable locations. For example, a fictional locale may coincide with the uncommon name of a real city or region, and the institutions in that location may be unintentionally named in the film. If a script is set in the fictional town of Garonsburg and there happens to be one or two such towns in the United States, then references to Garonsburg High School, Garonsburg General Hospital, and the Garonsburg Police Department may all identify real institutions even though the screenwriter had never heard of them.

The film company does not necessarily have to revise the script to change such conflicting names. As explained in chapter 4 (p. 61), the use of an identifiable name will only interfere with the rights of another party if it defames that party or invades that party's privacy rights. A casual reference that a character attended a high school or was born at a particular hospital is unlikely to defame any person or business. At the same time, however, film companies should try to avoid exclusions to their errors and omissions insurance coverage. Even an unfounded lawsuit can be very expensive. If the fictional location can be changed to a city that has a common name, it is less likely that the fictional name will be identified with one particular city. Within the fictional locale, the choice of institutional names should similarly be reviewed to avoid direct references, unless such references are intentional and important to the film.

4. Background Copyright and Unlicensed Art

For feature films, copyrighted materials should only be used with the express permission of the copyright owner. The claim that a filmmaker has a fair use privilege to show another party's copyrighted work generally has little support if the work is being used as background or foreground decoration on a feature film or television show. Since there is a ready market for licensing images, the courts are quite reluctant to allow unauthorized copying of copyrighted works. Moreover, copyright owners tend to be very protective of their content, so the likelihood of litigation is high even in those situations in which the merits of the case would favor the filmmaker.

Obvious copyrighted materials may include stock footage, playback footage on television or in films, images that the set designer would use to decorate the set (artwork, posters, computer software screenshots), and pictures on T-shirts, jackets, or other costumes. Less obvious materials include the artwork on product packaging and billboards or public artwork that is visible on the street where one is filming.

There are exceptions to this general approach. For example, if the filmmaker is shooting cars driving on public freeways and incidentally captures the images of billboards, she should generally be protected by fair use, provided that their screen time is brief and they are only in the background. Some copyright owners are much more aggressive than others, however, so there is always a risk of litigation. Even with the background billboards, the errors and omissions insurance coverage may put an exclusion into the coverage for copyrighted images that are not *cleared,* or licensed.

5. Consumer Products and Identifiable Brands

Consumer products may be subject to strong third-party ownership rights. The names of goods are often trademarked, and their packages often feature copyrighted images. Scenes showing children playing games or characters eating prepackaged food will typically incorporate both copyrighted works and trademarks.

The best strategy is to seek express written permission to depict the product. The second-best strategy is to show the product itself but not its packaging. Once a soda has been poured into a glass, Coca-Cola no longer has any trademark or copyright ownership of the caramel-colored beverage. The actual product will be given far less legal protection and lend itself to much stronger claims of a fair use privilege than the depiction of the packaging.

Tobacco companies do not provide product placement permission, so film companies are strongly encouraged never to show the brands or use brand names in dialogue. Depending on the jurisdiction, the tobacco companies may be barred by legislation or court orders from providing their products to filmmakers in this fashion, and may even be required to defend against such use. Filmmakers should avoid brand references to tobacco products to the greatest extent possible, and use such content only after weighing the risks against the importance of the scene.

Despite these cautionary recommendations, filmmakers may rely on fair use to depict trademarked products or to use the name of such products and services in dialogue. A trademark owner cannot automatically stop a film company from showing its brand name in a scene. If the trademark is said or depicted accurately, the use in the film will not give rise to a successful legal action. Using trademarks without authorization will raise concerns for the insurance company, however, and could make eventual distribution more difficult.

6. Misuse of Products in the Scene

Particular care must be exercised when a trademarked product is used in a dangerous or offensive manner. Manufacturers may feel compelled to take legal action to show their displeasure and send a message to the public that such use is unauthorized, even if there is only a weak legal basis for the action.

For example, in a 2006 episode of the NBC drama *Heroes,* a character mangled her hand in a garbage disposal on which the In-Sink-Erator brand name could be seen lightly etched into the metal. In-Sink-Erator claimed that the scene "casts the disposer in an unsavory light, irreparably tarnishing the product," when in fact such a dangerous act would injure any person. NBC ultimately chose to digitally alter the shot to remove the trademark rather than face litigation. While NBC had done nothing legally wrong, and would very probably have won the resulting lawsuit, the costs required to defend the suit would have been higher than the costs of editing the episode prior to rebroadcast or DVD sales.

7. Nonproblematic Trademark References

The clearance review will respond to any trademark referenced in the script. As a result, clearance reports often include a number of "false positives" if the writer has used a brand name in an action paragraph to describe the use of a product that will appear onscreen. Thus, if a character grabs a facial tissue but the script says he grabs for a Kleenex, the clearance report will identify a potential conflict with Kleenex. Depicting the product is not the same as using the brand, so these descriptions in the script do not raise issues for the film.

8. Character Names

The screenplay should use only fictional character names. If the script uses a real, living person's name but fictionalizes certain elements of the character, that only increases the likelihood that that the person can claim the use is defamatory, since the fictionalization means the use is knowingly wrong. To avoid liability for characters that are not intended to represent living persons, the script must not use a living person's name, particularly in cases where

- the name is taken from real persons known to the writers, director, producer, or other senior members of the film company;
- the name relates to the locations or situations in the film; or
- the name is sufficiently unique that the person named can reasonably believe the film relates to that person without any other direct relationship.

When a first or last name is used alone, it is much harder to associate it with a particular person than when first and last names are used together. Clearance companies suggest that a full name should not be used unless there are at least five individuals who can quickly be identified as having that name. A quick Internet search is a helpful tool to identify common names.

If real persons' stories are used, then additional reviews and releases are required. The character names should be authorized, particularly if there is an attempt to depict real persons. Finally, names of performers in any of the unions to which the production company is or will become a signatory should not be used.

F. When Things Go Wrong

Even if the filmmaker makes the best possible choices and works as carefully as possible, the complexity of a motion picture almost guarantees that things will go wrong. Locations that have been contractually secured suddenly become unavailable, cast members get sick, sets that looked perfect as scale models do not allow the action to take place properly, the weather will not cooperate . . . the list of possible problems is endless.

Financial contingencies can be anticipated. The budget should include a contingency amount—typically 10 percent of the budget—that cannot be used unless a true emergency develops. Solutions to other possible problems should be prepared in advance by the filmmaker. Backup locations should be identified for all the major locations selected, so that there is someplace to go when things go wrong. The filmmaker should also identify simple scenes that can be shot in readily accessible locations if a day's scheduled scenes fall through entirely.

Other circumstances benefit less from advance planning. If a key cast member becomes unavailable, a double can be used and the dialogue later dubbed in, but this solution has limited effectiveness. Often, it is better to adjust the script than to try to hide the missing cast member.

The most important aspect of crisis management is quick communication throughout the production team. The filmmaker and key personnel must agree upon a strategy to solve the problem as quickly as is reasonable. All of those key personnel must understand the final decision made, and must communicate it to the cast, crew, and vendors affected by the change. Today, e-mail and Web pages can be used to give everyone a place to look for the latest information, call sheets, and changes. If a Web page is used, it must be kept up to date. Confirming telephone calls should be made to the cast and crew so that no members of the production are left unaware.

If the communication works effectively, even significant changes can be made with a minimum of intrusion. Things will go wrong, but good producers and filmmakers count on these moments of change to energize the creative muscles of the production. If the practical and legal needs are met, then the creativity can be unleashed most effectively.

Special Considerations for Documentaries and Films Based on True Life Stories

↓

IN THE PAST decade, documentaries have become powerful voices in both the artistic and commercial worlds. Films like *Fahrenheit 9/11*, *March of the Penguins*, *An Inconvenient Truth*, *Bowling for Columbine*, and *Sicko* were all able to garner critical and commercial success. The success of documentaries created a rush to produce more such films, so the market has temporarily become oversaturated.

Despite the short-term glut in the market, documentaries have become an increasingly important part of the film industry as well as tools of public discourse. Since documentaries only rarely receive national theatrical distribution, audiences do not treat nontheatrical distribution as an aesthetic judgment against the film. They expect to find relevant documentaries through Netflix, Amazon, or PBS. In addition, crafting short-form documentaries is becoming part of the core competence for journalism majors, since the ability to write the story, film the content, edit the narrative, and publish the work reflects the fundamentals of multimedia journalism today.

Since documentary films hover closer to the news media business than narrative theatrical motion pictures do, documentary makers may wish to consider using traditional and nontraditional news publishers to obtain credentials and gain access to some of the content they wish to cover. Having press privileges may be quite helpful for certain documentaries, and producing shorter news pieces alongside the full documentary may serve as a way to promote the eventual release of the film and improve the access for the camera crew.

Finally, it is important to remember that U.S. law provides all speakers and writers, including the press and documentary filmmakers, much greater legal protection to publish material than the protections afforded by most other nations. Particularly if the individuals identified in the documentary are residents of Europe, the Middle East, or Asia, the filmmakers should at least be aware of the significantly different laws regarding standards for defamation, invasion of privacy, content with religious overtones, and content that may be considered political advocacy. The information in this chapter does not extend to the challenges faced by filmmakers producing content that may be deemed scurrilous or denigrating—and may even be banned outright—under the laws or standards of other countries or cultures.

A. U.S. Documentary Film Clearance

The filmmaker has significantly less need for licenses and approvals to shoot a documentary than to create a feature film. He relies upon the truthfulness and accuracy of the film presented as much as permission for the legal rights to film the locations, people, and other elements that make up the story.

1. Accuracy in Storytelling: Overcoming Defamation

The greatest legal protection for a documentary filmmaker is indeed the truthfulness and accuracy of the film presented. The primary concerns raised come from complaints regarding defamatory presentations or invasions of privacy by individuals or companies. Under U.S. law, a party claiming that she was defamed must prove the falsehood of the information. This is much more protective than a rule establishing that truth is a defense, because it puts the burden on the plaintiff to prove that the statements are falsehoods. In so many situations, proof of truth or falsity is extremely difficult to establish. Moreover, if the documentary features individuals who are public officials or public figures, then the filmmaker would only be legally liable if he knowingly used false material or was reckless in the choice of material presented. Even if the featured individuals are private figures, the filmmaker would have to be at least negligent in the use of the false material.

Since litigation is expensive, most distributors want to know that they can win any lawsuit without going to trial. Therefore, documentary filmmakers must be able to demonstrate readily that they were not negligent in the making of their film or in its depiction of any persons or companies. This is a higher threshold than the law requires, but it reflects a degree of caution on the part of the distributors not to be caught in expensive and drawn-out legal battles.

To assist in establishing the accuracy of the filmmaking process, the filmmaker should take careful notes regarding all his sources, and record all the statements made by his sources as faithfully as possible. If sources are videotaped or audiotaped, however, the filmmaker should be sure to request permission at the time of each taping. Every statement of fact should be verified to the fullest extent possible. This includes the ages of individuals, their educational backgrounds, their work history, and their relationships with the parties in the documentary.

If one party makes serious allegations against another, the documentary filmmaker will need to investigate and corroborate those allegations. Often, the lawyers for the distributor will ask for evidence of corroboration, just as they would expect it from network news crews. And unlike the nightly news or newspapers, documentary filmmakers are assumed to have had sufficient time to investigate leads and corroborate information. For example, if a filmmaker is given a story about dangerous working conditions at a slaughterhouse, he should find out enough about the source to know if the person was recently denied employment at that plant, fired from that plant, or otherwise had a personal grudge that could color the accuracy of the complaints. This does not make the information inaccurate, but it does highlight the need for corroboration by multiple sources. The whistle-blower may very well have been part of the misconduct before deciding to tell his story, and his motivations and behavior must be carefully investigated to show that the filmmaker has taken reasonable care in researching the story.

By maintaining logs, writing down the sources of leads, capturing interviews on tape and retaining those tapes, and confirming times, dates, and locations of all the major events, the filmmaker can show he has taken appropriate care in researching the story and presenting each detail so that there can be no claim of defamation.

2. Avoiding Invasions of Privacy

Perhaps nowhere does the law protecting the rights of the filmmaker differ more greatly from the industry practice than in the area of invasion of privacy. Under the law, if the information is newsworthy or of public interest, then there can be no invasion of privacy for accurately depicting the story. Minors may be afforded slightly greater protection, but as long as information is public and of public concern, the news reporter and documentary filmmaker are free to use that information. Despite the law, by practice, some distributors demand a signed release proving permission from every person depicted on the screen. Documentary filmmakers must balance the need for documentation and caution with the need to capture the footage necessary to tell their story.

Privacy laws are discussed in greater detail in chapter 4 (p. 65), but several of them are of special concern to documentary filmmakers. In most states, the laws include (1) false light, (2) publicity rights, (3) intrusion into seclusion, and (4) publicity given to matters of private concern. Statements which put persons into a false light are legally very similar to defamatory statements. The false statements need not be as contemptuous as those required for defamation, but the statements must still highly offend an ordinary person. In some states, the rights of publicity are also included as a form of privacy, but publicity rights have increasingly been treated separately as a commercial interest and are discussed elsewhere throughout the book.

Protections again intrusion into seclusion primarily protect against physical intrusion, such as trespassing and planting hidden cameras or microphones in the home of a subject. The use of a high-powered lens used to view through windows might qualify in some jurisdictions, and voyeurs' use of electronic equipment to see under women's skirts or peek into bathroom stalls has extended notions of physical intrusion into public venues. These are obvious invasions of personal space, and such offensive techniques simply should never be used.

The most important and challenging privacy consideration for documentary filmmakers is the protection against publicizing matters of only private concern. A filmmaker should not publicize a private fact if that information is not of legitimate public concern and the publication of that fact would be deemed highly offensive to the ordinary person.

There is little clarity regarding the legal point at which a matter becomes a matter of public concern. Criminal activity is generally considered public, and almost any activity by elected officials and entertainers is fair game. Stories that disclose misconduct or highlight important matters of public policy are all likely to qualify as being of legitimate public concern. On the other hand, a newspaper's casual reference to a student-body officer's previous sex change operation was deemed not a matter of public concern since it was unrelated to the news story.[1]

Similarly, if a 12-year-old is competing in a spelling bee not open to the public, such a private endeavor, despite the inherent drama, does not become a matter of public concern. On the other hand, if the spelling bee is a public event that anyone can attend, then there can be little claim that taping the competition itself violates the privacy of the participants. This would not, however, extend to the private areas of the competition, such as the green room or the rooms in which the students were waiting along with their parents. A filmmaker does not get to publicize a personal story merely because it makes for good drama.

Fortunately, public concern is not the only test. For the private facts disclosed to be actionable, they also must be highly offensive to a reasonable person, not merely to the particular person who was the subject of the documentary footage. Graphic film footage of accident victims may fall into this category, if the accident was not a matter of public concern and the victims' bloody bodies, personal agony, and vulnerable state were such that a reasonable person would find the broadcast highly offensive. If the rescue is newsworthy, however, then the filmmaker has much greater leeway.[2]

Simply put, filmmakers should pay attention to the privacy rights of the people in their documentaries, being careful to ensure that if individuals depicted have not consented to be in the documentary, they are involved in matters of public concern or their depictions are not highly offensive.

3. Using Consent Agreements to Acquire Rights

Since privacy laws are so ambiguous, the overwhelming practice is to seek permission to film individuals or at least to inform them that filming will be taking place. An actual permission agreement is the most effective tool available to the filmmaker and distributor to eliminate the potential for lawsuits. If the distributor can remind the offended individual that she signed a release, most often she will drop her objections.

Amazingly, most people will sign such releases.

The release used can be very vague or extremely detailed. The release used by the makers of the mock-documentary *Borat: Cultural Learnings of America for Make Benefit Glorious Nation of Kazakhstan* was very specific. In this highly controversial film, individuals who were unaware that the movie was a parody were included in scenes that were turned into grotesque situations. The release they signed gave the film company clear and unambiguous rights and has thus far withstood a number of legal challenges from participants who objected to being the unwitting butt of star Sacha Baron Cohen's jokes:

1. The Participant agrees to be filmed and audiotaped by the Producer for a documentary-style film (the "Film"). It is understood that the Producer hopes to reach a young adult audience by using entertaining content and formats.

2. The Participant agrees that any rights that the Participant may have in the Film or the Participants contribution to the Film are hereby assigned to the Producer, and that the Producer shall be exclusively entitled to use, or to assign or license to others the right to use, the Film and any recorded material that includes the Participant without restriction in any media throughout the universe in perpetuity and without liability to the Participant, and the Participant hereby grants any consents required for those purposes. The Participant also agrees to allow the Producer, and any of its assignees or licensees, to use the Participant's contribution, photograph, film footage, and biographical material in connection not only with the Film, but also in any advertising, marketing, or publicity for the Film and in connection with any ancillary products associated with the Film.

. . .

4. The Participant specifically, but without limitation waives and agrees not to bring at any time in the future, any claims against the Producer or against any of its assignees or licensees, or anyone associated with the Film, that includes assertions of (a) infringement of rights of publicity or misappropriation (such as any allegedly improper or unauthorized use of the Participant's name or likeness or image) . . . (d) intrusion (such as any allegedly offensive behavior or

questioning or any invasion of privacy), (e) false light (such as any allegedly false or misleading portrayal of Participant), (f) infliction of emotional distress (whether allegedly intentional or negligent), . . . (k) defamation (such as allegedly false statements made on the Film). . . .

The *Borat* film producers were accused of burying the waivers in voluminous boilerplate, including much less likely defenses to claims for an "act of God" and damages from "terrorism or war," but only those two waivers were unrelated to the crass conduct Sacha Baron Cohen had planned for the unwitting participants in the film. Although the original waiver paragraph used on *Borat* included waivers for items not listed above, this slightly shortened list is a useful and appropriate example of the waivers that can be used by documentary filmmakers.

4. Acquiring Location Permits

Although some jurisdictions exempt news companies from the need to acquire location permits, film permit offices and other local authorities generally consider documentary filmmakers to have an obligation to obtain film permits just like feature filmmakers, reality television producers, and commercial still photographers.

In practice, film permit obligations are not that onerous. If a documentary filmmaker plans to interview dozens of individuals in a public park or municipal parking lot, then the activities of the filmmaker have the potential to interfere with the ordinary operation of that venue and will likely attract the attention of the police or the municipality. Having taken the steps to acquire a film permit will protect the filmmaker from interference at the location.

At times, however, the documentary filmmaker operates more like a news crew. In a film such as *Hoop Dreams,* for example, the filmmaker follows the regular activities of its subject. If the subject of the film is meeting friends in a public park or hanging out in a municipal parking lot, it would be unreasonable to demand that the filmmaker avoid the location until a film permit has been arranged. To a certain extent, the filmmaker will rely on good luck to avoid police interference. In most situations, however, the police will accept that the film crew is doing a "news story" in the form of a documentary and allow the filming to proceed.

In a situation where the subject of the film is expected to sporadically but often visit a location that would require a film permit for a prearranged shoot, the documentary film company should try to work with the local film office to obtain some form of permit waiver. For example, if the documentary is following an attorney in a high-visibility trial that means frequent filming outside the courthouse, the film company may find that it is much more successful gaining access if it has the support of the film office to sit beside the members of the media waving their press credentials. Alternately, the filmmaker may improve his access to the story by offering to provide footage to a press outlet and thereby gaining his own press credentials.

B. When Purchasing a Life Story Helps

In certain situations, the documentary filmmaker may wish to have substantially more access to and control over a story than provided under the law or through a simple release. In these situations, she may decide to acquire the rights to the subject's life story. The purchase of a life story should increase the access to information and provide exclusive control of the story. With the agreement to pay the rights holder may come a perception that the filmmaker is no longer independent, however, so she must carefully weigh the benefits and limitations the relationship might entail.

1. Access

Purchase of a life story generally requires the subject of the story to do more than simply acquiesce to the filming of an interview. The filmmaker may need access to private records, to the names of other individuals associated with the subject, and to details not available to the public. The language of the purchase agreement should obligate the person selling the story rights to actively assist the filmmaker in gaining access to records and information under his control.

Where third parties hold confidential information about the subject, it can only be properly disclosed to the subject himself. With his permission, however, it can also be disclosed to the filmmaker, acting as an agent of the subject. The subject's doctors, lawyers, and accountants will only be able to disclose information with the express written authority of their patient or client.

The express permission of the subject of the documentary may also change the manner in which others with knowledge of the story will confide in the filmmaker. If the request to interview friends and family is accompanied by a letter from the subject asking for full cooperation with the filmmaker, it is likely that their candor will improve.

2. Exclusivity

Often the most important reason to purchase a person's story is to ensure that the information remains exclusive to the filmmaker. Under an exclusive agreement, the filmmaker becomes the sole individual to whom the subject can provide personal information. The contract should make it clear that this is not merely a confidentiality provision. The contract limits the access to the filmmaker only, affording the filmmaker a preferred position for those stories of significant public interest and multiple film projects.

Exclusive agreements will not prevent any of the filmmaker's potential competitors from accessing public information about the subject. It will merely prevent the subject from assisting those competitors himself. Nonetheless, if a filmmaker is documenting a public event, acquiring the personal stories of the key participants will improve her ability to tell that story and reduce competition. Anyone else covering the event will be forced to rely on public information alone and will not have access to the unique content provided by the exclusive arrangement.

The filmmaker needs to determine the scope of the exclusive rights being acquired. They may be limited to the filming of the documentary or to a particular period of time, or they may cover a much broader period of time and range of media. If the filmmaker acquiring the rights sees potential both for a documentary film and for a fictionalized retelling, then she should be explicit that the agreement covers the fictionalized use of the story as well.

The contract may provide additional compensation for such use to provide an incentive for the person selling the rights to continue to feel bound by the agreement. Since such contracts may prove hard to enforce, provisions that encourage the seller's compliance, support, and participation may be very useful to ensure the effectiveness of the agreement.

C. Fair Use for Documentaries

For documentary filmmakers to accurately depict their stories, they invariably need to rely on copyright's fair use provisions significantly more than other filmmakers. This is particularly true if the documentary focuses on literary or visual works or incorporates copyrighted materials as background content, although the situations in which the documentary filmmaker may rely on fair use are not limited to these two categories.

1. Fair Use Basics

Fair use represents a limitation on the exclusive rights held by copyright holders. Under certain conditions, it allows third parties to use copyrighted content without the copyright holder's permission. Broadly speaking, fair use is available for "for purposes such as criticism, comment, news reporting, teaching, . . . scholarship, or research."[3] In addition to these broad categories, fair use has also developed to protect the rights of researchers, such as documentary filmmakers, to make personal copies of entire works for their research archives, to enable owners of copyrighted works to make backup copies of materials, and to allow consumers to temporarily copy music, television, and film for personal enjoyment at a later time or in a different place.

Fair use is a very fact-specific balance between the rights of the copyright owner and the rights of the person seeking to make copies or to use content without permission. Because it is fact specific, the exact limitations of fair use are often subject to conjecture. Moreover, because of the significant cost of lawsuits, there is a tendency to be unnecessarily cautious regarding the interpretation of the law. Since filmmakers, producers, and distributors must manage not only the legal rights involved but also the costs associated with defending those rights, documentary filmmakers often feel pressured not to use content in ways in which lawyers would reasonably expect to be considered fair use. Nevertheless, fair use is not blanket permission to take copyrighted works that are readily available for licenses. A low production budget is not a basis for fair use.

The statutory provision of fair use emphasizes four factors to help courts determine whether the party copying material has acted legally.

In determining whether the use made of a work in any particular case is a fair use the factors to be considered shall include—

1. the purpose and character of the use, including whether such use is of a commercial nature or is for nonprofit educational purposes;
2. the nature of the copyrighted work;
3. the amount and substantiality of the portion used in relation to the copyrighted work as a whole; and
4. the effect of the use upon the potential market for or value of the copyrighted work.[4]

The four fair use factors are balanced in the context of the fair use provision's goal of providing public broad access to public discourse and a statutory tool to ease the tension between the Copyright Clause of the Constitution and the First Amendment. No single factor is determinative.

Broadly speaking, the law favors documentary film's goals of public comment, so the first prong of the four-factor test will generally weigh in the favor of the filmmaker. This does not mean that the documentary must be ponderous or academic to benefit from the clause. Irreverent or polemic, comical or studious, all works improve public knowledge and thereby benefit the public. However, the first prong also specifies that to be considered fair use, a work's appropriation of copyrighted material must be *transformative* in nature. A transformative use is one that changes the character of the copyrighted material. Quoting dialogue or showing a short clip as part of a critique of the material is transformative. Merely reproducing the content without comment does not transform it. Thus, if the documentary provides insight or criticism through the context in which the copyrighted material is used, it is much more likely to be considered fair use.

The second prong of the test reflects the fact that stronger copyright protection is given to fictional or highly creative works than to those that are factual. While ideas, facts, formulas, and processes are not even protected by copyright, the manner in which they are expressed is given modest copyright protection. Fair use offers very wide latitude to make use of such factual expressions, because copyright should never create a monopoly over facts or ideas.

For most documentary filmmakers, the most important aspects of the fair use test are the last two prongs. Under the third prong, the law makes clear that less is more. The smaller the portion of a copyrighted work one uses, the greater the chance it is considered fair use. Short quotes are more likely to be fair use than recitation of extensive passages; 30-second clips are more likely to be fair use than 5-minute sequences.

Similarly, the fourth prong balances the economic interests of the copyright holder with those of the documentary filmmaker or others who seek to use copyrighted works without permission. To the extent that the documentary film serves as a competing product with the copyright holder's own work, it is less likely to be considered fair use. If the documentary filmmaker's work does not threaten to replace the copyright owner's work in the market, the documentary will more likely be considered fair use.

2. Documentaries About Media and Culture

The greatest challenge in the application of fair use provisions relates to documentaries that focus on media and culture. To effectively communicate, these documentaries often make extensive use of materials copyrighted by third parties. To the extent that the documentary filmmaker uses the source to illustrate his own editorial content, such clips generally do not require the copyright holder's permission. However, the documentary must not become a direct competitor for the copyright holder's work. For example, if a Three Stooges short is shown in its entirety, followed by footage of interviews with comics who learned their craft by watching the Three Stooges, the use of the short would not be fair use. In this example, the documentary filmmaker's original content would have only a loose relationship to the copyrighted work, and the use of the entire short would turn the documentary into a commercial competitor of the original. If instead the filmmaker interspersed his original interviews with brief clips of the Three Stooges directly tied to the content of the new material, and each clip was no longer than was reasonably necessary to illustrate the original content, that would more likely be considered fair use.

Though not a legal standard, a practical standard that applies to other forms of research can also be applied to documentary filmmaking. Students are taught that using a single source is plagiarism but using five sources is research; the same practical rule may apply to the use of film clips. A documentary that takes all its clips from a single source is much more likely to feel the wrath of the copyright holder than a documentary that draws content from a number of sources. If the documentary's emphasis is the impact of television comedy on pop culture, focus on a range of modern television comics rather than only on Jerry Seinfeld. If the real subject is Jerry Seinfeld, use a broader range of material than just his network television series.

3. Background and Incidental Content

Since a documentary filmmaker implicitly represents that his film is accurate and truthful, he should not alter the content of footage. He must avoid falsifying the trademarked goods, copyrighted materials, and other content captured while filming scenes as they unfold. This creates a significant challenge. Billboards, sculptures, posters, television broadcasts, ring tones, T-shirts, and other copyrighted works are ubiquitous. To strip these elements from a documentary would essentially falsify the film's content.

At the same time, the filmmaker should take reasonable steps to limit these elements when practical and appropriate. If, for example, he is arranging sit-down interviews, then the space behind the interviewees in the frame should not include copyrighted works. If the interviews are taking place in the field and the camera operator has the opportunity to stand facing any direction, then she should move to the extent practical to avoid capturing a copyrighted work in the background just as she moves to control sunlight and shadow. In addition, the filmmaker should not try to use fair use as an excuse to incorporate material for which he did not get a license—say, by turning on a television in the background or otherwise staging the appearance of copyrighted material.

4. Documentary Filmmakers' Statement of Best Practices in Fair Use

In 2005, a coalition of lawyers, law schools, and film industry advocates came together to help outline many of these principles. The effort served both to clarify the practices commonly used by professional documentary filmmakers and to help advocate that those practices meet the legal guidelines for fair use. The result of that project is the *Documentary Filmmakers' Statement of Best Practices in Fair Use*. The report is available from the American University Center for Social Media and reprinted here as Appendix E (p. 411). (The Center for Social Media also has other projects related to online video and teaching.)

The *Statement of Best Practices in Fair Use* outlines appropriate and inappropriate applications of fair use by documentary filmmakers. Like the advice offered throughout this book, the report's recommendations can only lay out the various choices filmmakers can make. Ultimately, fair use remains rather fact specific, and filmmakers must decide for themselves when to seek permission and when to risk legal conflict.

Perhaps the most significant impact of the *Statement of Best Practices in Fair Use* has been its acceptance within the insurance industry. Coauthors of the statement have written about its impact: "The theory behind the Statement is that courts respect the views of responsible professionals about what kinds of uses are fair in their area of practice."[5] As a result of the industry acceptance, insurance companies are demonstrating stronger support for including fair use content in documentaries. "The four companies most used by U.S. documentary filmmakers—AIG, MediaPro, ChubbPro, and OneBeacon—all announced programs to cover fair use claims between January and May of 2007."[6] The result of the widespread support of the statement and adoption of its standards within the insurance industry is a normative change for acceptable practice that provides documentary filmmakers concrete guidance regarding the scope of risk associated with fair use claims.

D. Acquiring Access to Archive Materials

Documentaries often require archival material to illustrate the filmmaker's story. Fortunately, most television networks operate film archives that sell footage to third parties, and other materials may be obtained from commercial film and television archives. The cost for obtaining archival footage usually includes fees for copying the material and separate fees for licensing the material for use. The licensing costs are typically based upon the length of the film clip, the popularity of the clip for licensing, the nature of the film project, the project's production budget, and the anticipated distribution or projected revenue of the film. Each archive sets its own rates and policies.

1. Sources

Fair use applies to archival footage in precisely the same manner it applies to other content. Moreover, to the extent that important historical events are only available from limited archival sources, the basis for fair use might improve. On the other hand, if the only restriction on access to archival footage is a disagreement regarding a reasonable license fee, then a filmmaker should be cautious before deciding to claim fair use instead. The owner of the copyright is not obligated to assure filmmakers that they can meet their budgets.

In addition, the film archive may require that the filmmaker enter into a contract before footage is released to her. In the contract, she may be asked to agree to pay a licensing fee for the usage of any clip and agree to other terms in the license. Depending on the terms of the license, the filmmaker risks waiving her ability to later claim fair use for any of the archive's footage. The archival agreement may also limit the filmmaker's usage of the acquired content in other ways. The filmmaker should review these agreements carefully to ensure that the contract offers her sufficient rights to meet the film's distribution needs.

2. Government-Owned Materials

Works authored by the U.S. government are not protected by copyright and are free to be fully utilized by any party. The same is not true, however, for works created by companies or individuals not working for the government, even if the copyright in these works are later transferred to the government. Similarly, the ownership by the U.S. government of a copy of a work does not have any effect on the copyright. U.S. military film footage is often in the public domain, because it was filmed by the U.S. government and its employees acting within the scope of their employment. Military film footage shot by news companies would not be in the public domain, even if the Library of Congress is the owner of the copyright or of the copies of those materials.

One of the most valuable public domain collections consists of works created by the Works Progress Administration or WPA, a federal agency established during the Great Depression to create gainful employment for individuals in a vast number of professional fields. WPA artists were federal employees, so their murals, plays, films, and other expressive content were all created with the U.S. government as its owner and without the benefit of any copyright protection. The Library of Congress maintains an extensive archive of WPA materials.

The Library of Congress also maintains a large library of film and television content. This material is not necessarily in the public domain, however, and the library does not provide any licensing services. As a result, the Library of Congress Motion Picture and Television Reading Room can be used only if the filmmaker has already obtained clearance from the copyright holders for use of the particular clips. With written permission to use the clips, the filmmaker can obtain quality duplicates by paying the Library of Congress's processing fee.

For modern national political content, C-SPAN is an important resource. The cable network is a private company, so much of its content is protected by copyright law. But C-SPAN does provide that "all uses of the video of the House and Senate floor proceedings are permitted because it is in the public domain."[7] For documentary and other similar uses a license is required.

Even more interesting is the Universal Newsreel collection, which contains newsreel segments that were produced twice each week from 1929 to 1967. The collection was released into the public domain by Universal City Studios and made available online.[8]

U.S. states and governments outside of the United States do not have the same legal limits on their ability to vest copyright in their original works of authorship as the U.S. federal government. As a result, film footage and most other copyrightable works created by states or foreign governments may have the same copyright protection as those works created by nongovernment authors.

3. Sufficient Rights

Stock footage often refers to existing film or television material that has been cleared for licensing to filmmakers and media companies. In contrast, archival resources include both stock footage and footage that may not be ready for commercial exploitation without additional licenses.

In a narrative or fictional film, for example, an archival shot of an actor's performance would require the license from the copyright holder in the work and from the actors. Assuming the original movie was made pursuant to a SAG collective bargaining agreement, then the SAG members in the archival footage would be entitled to at least the minimum compensation provided under the agreement. For a documentary, the union obligations and publicity rights claims would not apply. The documentary should be able to use the clips without the actors' express permission.

Nonetheless, for a documentary filmmaker seeking specific archival footage, the film company must conduct full copyright research and clearance to use the film footage itself and all the content within the frame of the film. Copyrighted works captured within the archival footage will need separate copyright licenses or a determination that fair use is appropriate for each work. In the same manner, synchronized music associated with the archival footage will require separate clearances. Again, fair use may apply. The fair use analysis, however, must be applied separately to each copyrighted work captured within the archival clip.

E. Partnerships for Financing and Distribution

Documentary films and nonprofit organizations often have a common agenda of trying to educate the public on particular issues and shaping public opinion. *An Inconvenient Truth* has had a profound impact on energy and environmental policy throughout the world, while *Sicko* helped push health care reform to the forefront of the presidential campaign that immediately followed its release.

1. Using a Nonprofit Alliance to Fund Projects

In 2004, the *New York Times* extensively covered the relationship between two political organizations and the Robert Greenwald documentary *Outfoxed: Rupert Murdoch's War on Journalism*. Funded by contributions "in the range" of $80,000 from both MoveOn.org and the Center for American Progress, the movie attempted to document that Fox News had systematically favored conservative and Republican positions.

The film financing strategy also included a significant distribution strategy. Each of the two political organizations used the film as the focal point for events and urged their membership to view or purchase the film. The twin contributions of direct financing and market financing illustrate the very powerful potential of an alliance between documentary filmmakers and political organizations that share the message of their films.

2. Need for Disclosure of Financing Partners

Every documentary filmmaker should ensure that the credits of his film include a list of the financial investors or charitable contributors who may benefit from the claims of the documentary or with whom a conflict of interest over content might exist. Just as journalists mention when a story involves their employer or a company owned by their employer, sound ethical practice requires that this information be made available in the credits of the documentary. In addition to the ethical obligation, there may be a legal obligation under the laws of various jurisdictions, including the rules governing U.S. television broadcasts.

3. Issues of Partnership Autonomy

In some cases, support from a nonprofit partner can raise more than disclosure issues. A documentary filmmaker oftentimes has the subject of his film in mind but finds that his point of view regarding that subject changes during the filmmaking process. But a nonprofit partner with a particular agenda may not agree with that change. The parties to the agreement need to specify the extent to which the contributing nonprofit has control over the content or tone of the documentary. While documentary filmmakers would prefer that the funds they receive have no strings attached, the organization providing its name and financial support correctly insists that it has an ethical duty to ensure that its contributions are being used in a manner that furthers the mission of the organization.

If the alliance is a distribution strategy, such as a guaranteed minimum purchase of copies of the film or rentals for public exhibition, then the arrangement can be based on approval after seeing a final version of the documentary. The initial agreement can be more specific than that, specifying that the "nonprofit can only withdraw from the distribution agreement if the completed documentary varies substantially from the outline of the film attached to the distribution agreement." In this way, the filmmaker does not have to renegotiate the distribution from scratch, while the nonprofit is protected from being forced to fund a project that no longer supports its position.

If the arrangement is a financing strategy, then either the investor must trust the filmmaker to keep to the message based on his track record and passion, or the investor can contribute funds in stages, tying them to opportunities to see a rough cut and a preview copy of the film. Again, the contract should be specific enough that the investor can only withdraw in the event that the documentary substantially deviates from the project proposal in a manner that adversely affects the mission of the nonprofit or its strategy in supporting the documentary. If the nonprofit desires to wait until the film is finished before deciding to financially support it, then the agreement should make that clear and not establish a contractual relationship that cannot, in fact, be enforced.

Music

MUSIC HAS BECOME an integral element of the cinematic storytelling process. Music can be used to accentuate the action. Evoking the emotional response sought by the filmmaker, it can come from natural sources, such as a car radio shown onscreen, or it can be created directly by the characters in the film. Each of these different types of music not only plays a different role in the story but also has a different legal relationship with the filmmaker. Music performed by the characters in the film is labeled *foreground music*. In contrast, both the original musical score composed for the film and any recorded songs played in the film are considered *background music*. Because acquiring the rights to music for film, television, and video games has become the most intricate licensing of any copyrighted works in the law, each type of music must be treated separately.

A. Licensing Prerecorded Music and Published Music

Since *American Graffiti,* the modern film musical has been reinvented as a greatest hits collection of popular or cutting-edge genre music. But if a filmmaker wishes to use recordings of popular songs, she must enter the byzantine world of music licensing. The filmmaker takes on the role of a record album producer, assembling the right mix of sounds and artists—collected from a variety of songwriters, singers, music publishers, and record labels. Each party has an interest in the copyright of the songs to be used in the film, and each must be represented in the licensing process.

1. Two Different Copyright Holders

The recording of a popular song is protected by two separate copyrights. First, the *composition* (the lyrics and the written music) is protected by a copyright held by the composers. The composers may consist of a songwriting team, such as Lennon and McCartney; a composer and a lyricist, such as Rodgers and Hammerstein; or a single person. Regardless of the number of composers, they jointly hold a single copyright. In most cases, the composers have assigned these rights to the music publisher, so the publisher is the party with which the filmmaker must negotiate to obtain rights to use the music and lyrics in the film.

Second, the *sound recording* of the song is protected through a copyright held by the producer of the song or the record company that manufactured and distributed the song. The performers on the recording are not protected by copyright but look to employment contracts with the record company for participation in the song's revenue.

If the filmmaker wishes to use a particular recording, then both the composers (or the music publisher to which the composers have assigned their rights) and the producer or record company must license it. For instance, Motown Records owns the recording of "Trouble Man," while singer and composer Marvin Gaye owns the composition rights. If the filmmaker wishes to play the Motown version of the song, then both the representatives of Marvin Gaye as composer and Motown as owner of the sound recording will need to grant permission to use the work. In addition, because of a long, strained history, there are a variety of different rights that must be identified and licensed separately. Failure to include any of these discrete rights in the contract can create substantial problems when distributing the film, or it can result in the entire film being unmarketable in some or all markets.

Every film distributor today intends for each film to be shown theatrically and via premium cable, broadcast television, standard cable television, nonnetwork broadcast television, home recording machines (DVD, Blu-ray, etc.), and online downloads and streaming performances. To exploit these markets worldwide, the distributor must acquire a number of different music rights. Most distributors expect that the acquisition of all these rights has been accomplished or arranged by the filmmaker.

2. Rights from the Music Publisher: Public Performance, Reproduction, and Synchronization

To properly use a piece of music, the filmmaker needs to acquire three specific rights from the composer or music publisher. Typically, all three rights are acquired in the same license agreement. Together, they give the film company the right to make its own recording of the song for use in the film. To use a prerecorded song, the film company needs these rights from the composer or music publisher plus rights to reproduce the prerecorded song from the record label.

a. Public Performance

In music, the public performance right protects the copyright holder for the composition from any unauthorized public performance of his work. The performance of the songs in the movie theater, on television, or streaming over the Internet constitutes public performances, so the filmmaker must acquire this right before the movie can be played in such venues. Historically, this right was reserved only for the composers in the song, not the record company in the sound recording. Recently, however, digital sound recordings were granted a limited public performance right.

For the theatrical distribution of motion pictures, the public performance right must be obtained directly from the copyright holder, typically the music publisher. For other public performances of music, the rights may also be obtained through a license with a performing rights society, such as ASCAP, BMI, or SESAC.

b. Reproduction of the Composition

Because the film will be licensed to sell copies on DVD or other physical media or via digital downloads, the music and score also need to be licensed to allow the film distributor to make multiple copies of the composition. The license to reproduce the song is also known as the *mechanical license*.

c. Synchronization

In addition to the statute-based rights of public performance and reproduction,[1] copyright also recognizes a distinct right to associate a song with a particular audiovisual image. Whether a song is used in films, television, video games, or other multimedia works, the right to synchronize the pictures with the sound is a distinct legal right that must be separately protected. The synchronization or *synch rights* are also provided by the publisher (or the composer, if there is no publisher).

3. Rights from the Record Label: Master Use License

The right of reproduction protects not only the composers but also the recording companies from unauthorized creation of copies of a sound recording in any medium. Most consumers view this as the rule against taping radio broadcasts or ripping CDs, but in a commercial context, it applies to duplicating songs and sound recordings in each print of a film and, more importantly, in every copy of the DVD.

To use a particular prerecorded version of a song, the film company will need to acquire the rights to that particular performance from the record label that owns the copyright in the master recording. If the filmmaker contemplates a soundtrack album, then the reproduction right must extend to use in that format as well.

B. Utilizing Noncommercial Music

Every Hollywood studio has a team of lawyers and paralegals who focus exclusively on the music licensing issues for their productions. The independent filmmaker must find a way to accomplish this same task. Through creative planning, she can bring the same artistic vision and entrepreneurial approach to the film's music as she has to every other element of the film.

If the filmmaker is willing to use more generic music, a music production library will be a helpful source of musical content in a wide array of styles, instrumentations, and arrangements. These production libraries own both the composition and the sound recording copyrights, so they provide one-stop shopping for the musical needs of the production. Another type of bureau acts as a clearinghouse service. These companies do not own any rights in the music, but they serve to locate the rights requested, help establish the pricing, and ensure that the appropriate rights are identified.

1. Royalty-Free Music

There are many royalty-free services available that, for a fixed fee, provide prerecorded music and the unlimited right to use that music. Filmmakers must be careful to acquire the rights to use both the song (music and lyrics) and the prerecorded version of that song. They must also ensure that the royalty-free license includes theatrical distribution of the film, synchronization with the motion picture, and rights to reproduce the song and the particular recorded version of the song in all media. If all these rights are included, then this will be the easiest way to provide songs for the film.

2. Public Domain Music

The independent filmmaker will often choose to avoid licensing songs altogether. The costs and administration simply outweigh the benefits to the story and film. Such a choice will not prevent the use of music; it will only change its source. One alternative is to exploit songs no longer protected by copyright because the work is in the public domain.

All songs published in the United States before 1923 are now in the public domain. Many other songs did not have their copyright renewed, so those compositions are also in the public domain. Filmmakers must be careful when using public domain songs, however, because a particular recording of the song may still be protected by copyright. Different legal rules were in play during various time periods, so it is impossible to make any general statement regarding the copyright status of sound recordings, but filmmakers should not assume a sound recording is in the public domain just because the music itself has fallen out of copyright. To sidestep this difficulty, the filmmaker may choose to record a new version of the public domain music using film company employees.

3. Other Alternatives

Filmmakers may also create original songs for the movie, or purchase the copyright to the music outright. In these cases, filmmakers commonly choose to record the music specifically for the motion picture. Regardless of the source of the song, original recordings greatly reduce the scope of rights to be licensed.

Independent films can achieve both artistic and commercial success by identifying bands that are not yet signed to recording contracts. Their songs are not available as commercially licensed music, but the rights can easily be acquired directly from the composers and the band. By featuring their songs, the film may help launch successful careers for new talent and greatly reduce the cost and complexity of acquiring the music necessary for the film.

C. Commercially Licensed Music

Industry tradition has developed a byzantine series of contracts for each of the types of rights, rights holders, and media.[2] The practice has created an absurd number of separate contracts and confusion regarding the use of the music over the life of the film. For some of these choices, the costs may be prohibitive and the filmmaker must choose to either do without the desired song or risk buying something less than all the rights he may need to exploit.

For example, as described in chapter 7 (p. 135), the use of a festival license creates significant risk that the film company will not be able to secure ongoing rights to some or all of the songs important to the sale of the film. At a minimum, the filmmaker should note which songs have not been acquired, so that there is no contractual obligation to deliver the rights to particular songs to the distributor of the film. The distributor should provide the filmmaker some leeway to acquire the songs used in the festival release version of the film or mutually agreeable alternatives.

For nonfestival contracts, the following are the key provisions of the music license.

1. Term

The rights should last in perpetuity. Although some contracts provide for five-year terms, this means that future sales of the film rights can be frustrated by the inability to acquire (or even identify) the music rights. At a minimum, the contract should include renewal provisions that guarantee the right to renew and specify the renewal fee. Otherwise too much can go wrong—for example, a new owner of the music rights (say, a company that purchases the music library in a bankruptcy sale) could demand exorbitant fees for the new grant of rights.

Of course, if the movie is never released or has only a short run, then the cost savings of the shorter term will be worthwhile. Since this is generally not the bet being made by independent filmmakers, a short music license term is probably the wrong place to save unless the savings is truly dramatic.

2. Territory

The territory should specify "the universe" rather than any particular region or even "the world." Given the growth of the International Space Station and the increasing length of copyright, which could well extend to over a century, the universe may be the more appropriate territory. There is no reason to license anything less than worldwide, because even short delays in licensing the soundtrack at the time of foreign distribution may frustrate the distribution agreements.

3. Media Covered by License

The standard contracts will typically require a list of media. Given the rapid development of technology and the fact that technological growth is highly unpredictable, the media should be "all media now known or hereafter developed." This should prevent future conflicts regarding various forms of distribution over the Internet and whatever will come after.

Older contracts may list theatrical exhibition, television (be sure to include free and pay or further identify the various tiers of broadcast, satellite, and cable television), foreign distribution, and specialty markets (16mm prints, airplane cuts), but will often omit some of the home distribution technologies, which include DVD, Blu-ray, etc. The list of media for both the public performance category and the home use category are evolving, and both should be defined broadly.

4. Public Performance Rights

Most music license agreements are drafted very narrowly. As a result, traditional contracts recognized that the public performance rights were only necessary in those media that were screened publicly. The license of a song in a film extended public performance rights only to theatrical exhibition and television broadcasts. Home presentation of a DVD does not involve a public performance, so many contracts do not give any public performance rights for DVDs or similar products. Nonetheless, videos are often shown in schools, community centers, and other smaller public venues. Without the public performance rights in DVDs and the like, the filmmaker cannot authorize any such performances. For some independent films, the guerrilla marketing strategy could be frustrated by the failure to secure public performance rights across all media.

In addition, the need for public performance rights in digital sound recordings is relatively new and virtually untested under the law. If the Internet or other interactive digital technologies grow in bandwidth and sophistication, the digital performance interests in sound recordings may become a significant right. All filmmakers, but particularly those digital filmmakers hoping to exploit the Internet for some portion of the film's distribution, must purchase the limited digital performance rights available from the record company.

5. Reproduction or Mechanical Rights

The right to reproduce a song is often limited to the home media market (DVD, Blu-ray, etc.). Nonetheless, each print of the film also includes a mechanical reproduction of the sound recording and the composers' song, so this mechanical license should include all media. The mechanical license applies to both the composer and the record company if the record company's original recording is to be used.

6. Synchronization Rights

The right to use the song in conjunction with the visual image is an aspect of the public performance right. As such, this provision is essential in the composers' agreement, but because of the new digital performing rights, it is advisable that it be included in the license from the record company as well.

7. Scope of Usage

The contracts will narrowly limit the way in which a song may be used. First, the song may not be altered (although it typically can be used in part rather than in its entirety). This means that the lyrics cannot be changed. If a song is to be featured in the foreground as a parody sung by a character, or if it will otherwise be changed for dramatic effect, then this particular usage must be separately negotiated, and such permission will not be granted lightly.

Second, the song can only be used in the film as a whole. Permission to use a song in the film's commercials or trailers must be negotiated separately. The use of the song as part of a music video based on the film must also be separately negotiated.

Third, the filmmaker must provide credits for the composers, publisher, performing artists, and record company from which the rights were licensed. They generally appear in the end credits.

Finally, the filmmaker's rights will be nonexclusive, allowing the copyright holders to license the song to other films as well.

8. Fees

The range of fees can vary greatly, depending on the popularity of the song, the budget of the film, whether the music is used in the foreground or background, whether the music is featured in the story, and what other songs are being licensed. Typically, the U.S. theatrical and television broadcast rights are contracted on a flat-fee basis. Outside the United States, theatrical performances are covered by licenses provided by performing rights societies. The mechanical rights are increasingly based on a royalty fee tied to the number of units manufactured or sold. To get a general idea of the range of licensing fees and structures, the filmmaker or his attorney may wish to consult *Kohn on Music Licensing* by Al and Bob Kohn (see bibliography, p. 431), which provides a list of licensing ranges for the various types of licenses needed.

D. Composers and the Film Score

The original film score is the background music written specifically for the motion picture. Composers such as Elmer Bernstein, John Williams, and Danny Elfman have created intricate orchestral works for film that rival the great opera scores and symphonies of past centuries. Generally, after a series of meetings between the filmmaker and the composer regarding the goals for the music both overall and for each scene, the filmmaker provides the composer with a rough cut of the edited film. The composer creates the score, which is then modified and refined until the musical beats within each measure align perfectly with each frame of the picture. Arrangements are made—either for a live orchestra or for an electronically created performance—and the music is recorded as the finished cut of the film is played. Like Foley artists (see chapter 15, p. 269), the musicians carefully play to match the timing of the action on the screen, accompanying the film as an orchestra would accompany a ballet or opera.

Low-budget filmmakers should consider hiring composers who can not only write the music but also arrange and play the music on digital equipment. There may be as many untried film composers finishing music school as directors finishing film school. The musical triple threat—composer/arranger/performer—can significantly enhance the overall production at a far lower cost than any other solution.

The musical track is recorded separately so that it may be incorporated into the final prints of the film. For foreign distribution, the sound and dialogue tracks are delivered separately so that the original dialogue can be replaced with a dubbed soundtrack.

The filmmaker must also consider the legal status of the film score. It should be created as a work for hire or its copyright should be completely assigned to the film company.

1. Work-for-Hire Productions

Under copyright law, certain types of works vest their copyright in the employer rather than the employee. The first of these two situations occurs when an employee creates a work in the regular scope of his employment. So, for example, if the film company were to employ the composer for a reasonable length of time for the purpose of writing compositions for the motion picture or pictures created by the film company, then the film company, rather than the composer, may be considered the copyright holder of those compositions. Courts look at the nature of the employment relationship, with heavy emphasis on tax status, withholdings, and insurance; the ability to control the work; the actual control of the work; and the ability to add additional projects without additional pay. It would not be good planning to rely exclusively on the employment relationship to define a composition as a work for hire. At a minimum, the employee should have an employment agreement that carefully specifies that the compositions are created on behalf of the employer and are intended to be treated as work for hire.

The second category of work for hire provides greater certainty. For nine categories of work, a party can specially commission works from non-employees. Among the nine categories are contributions to motion pictures and other audiovisual works. This is very important, because most other musical commissions are outside the scope of this category. The filmmaker can specially commission the film score as a work for hire. The agreement must be in writing and signed by both parties. The agreement should be signed before the work is begun, but certainly the earlier the better.

2. Assignments of Copyright

If the film receives worldwide success, the score's work-for-hire agreements may create additional difficulties. Some countries do not recognize the work-for-hire concept, rendering any such arrangement unenforceable. To protect against this problem, the employment agreement or agreement for the special commission should also include a paragraph stating that any rights not granted as a work for hire are irrevocably assigned by the composer to the film company in perpetuity. This means the composer cannot reclaim the rights, and the grant will last forever. (A reversionary right in U.S. copyright law makes this contractual promise limited to approximately half the life of the copyright. This is why work-for-hire provisions are more useful in the United States, while copyright assignment is more effective abroad.)

The composer may insist on a third alternative: licensing the score for the motion picture but retaining all other rights. In this situation, the rights of the score's composer would be the same as those of the composers of any single featured in the film. If the film company plans to release a soundtrack album, then it should retain at least a nonexclusive right to release the music separately from the film.

In addition, however, the filmmaker should be sure to provide the composer with the ability to use the score on record albums and to distribute the music. The film company can retain all rights to the synchronization of the score, but provide a license back to the composer to use the score for other purposes.

E. Performers

In the United States the singers and musicians performing on a song have no copyright interests. As a result, no particular language in the performer's contract is necessary to protect the filmmaker's copyright in the work. Despite this, however, a performer may protect herself from the unauthorized use of her performance. As a result, the film company should be sure that every singer and musician has signed a contract that specifically authorizes the film company to record the performance and assigns any copyright interest to the film company.

As an added precaution, the language should also include work-for-hire and copyright assignment statements in the form suggested for the composer's contract. The assignment language may help avoid problems involving the interpretation of the contract in foreign jurisdictions, and the work-for-hire provisions may negate any additional changes to the legal status of possible copyright holders.

F. Soundtrack Albums

One of the most common additional revenue sources for filmmakers comes from sales of soundtrack albums. If the movie uses a significant amount of music, particularly popular songs, then a collection of that music as performed in the film may be quite marketable.

Like the movie itself, a soundtrack album requires the licensing of many different rights. They include the rights to the songs (music and lyrics), and the particular recordings of the songs that appear on the album. The license to use the music and lyrics is known as the *mechanical recording right,* which can be acquired by paying the statutory rate to the U.S. Copyright Office or by licensing it through the Harry Fox Agency (see appendix F, p. 424). The right to use the particular recording of the song is another provision of the master use license, and it should be negotiated at the same time that the rights to use the recording in the film are acquired.

If the recording was made by the film company during production under a license from the music publisher or other composition rights holder, then the film company already owns the recording rights. If the film company recorded the music itself, then it must also comply with any union obligations regarding royalty payments to the musicians for additional uses of their work on the soundtrack album.

The soundtrack album may include original music composed exclusively for the film. This copyright may be owned by the film company or may have been retained by the composer, and in the latter case a mechanical license must be obtained to produce the albums from the film soundtrack or new recordings of the score.

Negotiating the licenses to produce a soundtrack album is much simpler when done at the time the music is originally selected for the film. All of the same parties must give permission to use the music in the movie, so little additional effort is required to license the soundtrack album as well. To avoid increasing the cost of the film, these licenses should be based on a royalty paid on the number of soundtrack albums sold. In this way, the filmmaker avoids any costs until there is revenue.

Postproduction

WITH A TREMENDOUS amount of coordination, communication, and concerted effort—not to mention a little bit of luck—filming has been completed, and postproduction can begin. Realistically, however, some of the postproduction work often begins even while principal photography continues.

A. Editing

Editing is an artistic process. The proliferation of "director's cut" editions of popular films illustrates that there are many different choices that can legitimately be made within the editing process. It also shows that directors often continue to think about the editorial choices they had to make on their films. In any case, the process of editing allows the director to find the horse hidden in the marble, cutting out all the footage that does not help tell the story.

1. Timing the Editing Process

During principal photography, the director often identifies particular shots and begins assembling a very preliminary cut of the film. Particularly for tightly budgeted independent films, compiling a preliminary edit will allow the filmmaker the opportunity to determine when she has shot enough film to tell the story. Many compelling scenes never make the final cut of a film, and independent filmmakers simply do not have the luxury to waste time and money on anything that will not ultimately appear onscreen. If the script has a scene that is interesting but not essential, slot it later in the production schedule. That will allow the filmmaker to drop the scene if time and funds require hard choices.

Once principal photography ends, the real editorial work begins. Following the wrap of principal photography, the director should take a short break to recover some physical strength after the rigors of filming and gain some perspective on the material shot. She must look at the footage as a fresh observer rather than responding to the conditions of the filming. If there is a separate film editor working on the project, the director should begin to work with him as soon as she can treat the film with renewed enthusiasm and new objectivity.

2. The Editor's Role

The role of the editor will vary dramatically, depending on the budget of the film project. In larger productions involving International Alliance of Theatrical Stage Employees (IATSE) union crews, the editor (or editors) must also be a member of the union. At the other extreme, many independent films are edited by the filmmaker herself, either on an Avid editing system or with Final Cut Pro or another software package. When a professional editor is employed, the director and editor will typically work closely throughout filming so that the director can identify the scenes she prefers from the dailies and explain the nature of the shots. As this process continues, the editor can work to compile the film as the director focuses on shooting it, allowing the first cut to be completed within days following the end of principal photography.

3. The Director's First Cut

If the filmmaker is not the director, then the role of the director must be carefully determined when the director is hired. Directors Guild of America (DGA) union rules obligate the producer to allow the director to deliver a cut of the film. Even if the production is not governed by union requirements, this obligation serves as a good minimum standard. The director should have the best ideas about the film that's been shot and the story being told. As such, he should provide the primary structure to the final film. If the producer and filmmaker do not like what they receive, then they are free to change it.

4. Rough Cuts

Once the director and editor have viewed the first cut, the real work of sculpting the film begins. Scenes are deleted, reordered, and tightened. The running time starts dropping dramatically. Ultimately, the final rough cut must be made to meet all contractual requirements. To conform to distributor demands, for example, the length of the film may need to be adjusted, and the content may need to be trimmed to achieve a particular MPAA rating (such as R or PG-13).

The editing process should also anticipate the need for multiple versions of the film. Alternate shots should be identified for the broadcast television version of R movies, airplane edits, and foreign jurisdictions (where censorship rules may vary considerably). Identifying the coverage shots as part of the original editing process may save significant time and effort—if not sanity—when the distributor calls.

Whether to open the editing process to others remains a highly individual choice. Producers will wish to see the film early in the process, but it may be more dangerous to share an uncompleted film than even the screenplay. Relatively few observers have the experience to judge a film that still needs minor adjustments and lacks a score and sound effects. The editing process has been further complicated by the evolution of digital editing technology. Traditionally, directors relied on scratched work prints to show off rough cuts, and they created a particular image that was quite distinct from that of a final film. But a digital file will look perfect, even if the edit is unfinished. As a result, digital viewing may be even more misleading than the scratched print once relied on.

B. Final Cut: Control of the Final Picture

When the director has finished the film and made those adjustments suggested by the producer, he delivers his final version of the film. At this point, the producer has the ability to make additional changes to the film without the permission of the director. In rare situations, the director negotiates for final cut, which affords him the power to control the theatrical version of the film. This is the ultimate power in the production hierarchy and it is granted only rarely, to the most powerful of directors.

The filmmaker may retain final cut for her independent film in a number of situations. If the filmmaker is the director and has financed the film without entering into a negative pick-up or distribution agreement, then she retains this power by default. The filmmaker should not relinquish such control to the producer unless he demands it as a condition of financing the film. Even then, the demand may make the cost of the financing too great.

1. Contractual Control

Depending on the contractual arrangement, the director's influence over the final project will vary. The most successful or most influential of directors negotiate the final approval rights over the content of their films, but even these rights are not absolute. The director must meet all contractual preconditions to exercise such control. Typically, this means that the film must be edited to an agreed-upon length (typically somewhere between 93 and 120 minutes), conform to an agreed-upon MPAA rating (most likely PG-13), come within budget (including all preapproved overages), and substantially contain the same scenes and dialogue as provided in the final shooting script.

Woody Allen is famous for his absolute control over the content of his films and his ability to deliver a film every year on schedule. Steven Spielberg exercised such a degree of control over the final cut of *Schindler's List* that he retained the right to personally supervise the film's adaptation into every foreign language and every foreign censorship edit. Because disputes over final cut are covered by the Directors Guild collective bargaining agreement, these cases are not typically reported.

2. Control of Final Cut

The most significant benefit to directing an independently financed film is the autonomy it affords. Because there is no distributor financing, there rarely is the type of editorial pressure on the filmmaker that occurs with studio pictures. Nonetheless, distributors will sometimes insist on changes to films as a condition of purchasing them for distribution. In this way, the director is never completely free from outside influences.

If the filmmaker is the producer, then she should retain control over the hired director. If possible, she should consult with the director when preparing the final cut, so that all of the participants in the process walk away satisfied with the outcome. This becomes critical when it is time to market and promote the film. Nonetheless, the contracts must be explicit regarding who retains the ultimate control of the film. Only one person can have the final cut. Absent any contractual language to the contrary, that person is the producer of the film, the CEO of the production company that owns the copyright in the final motion picture. If any variations are required, they must be spelled out very carefully in the employment contracts.

Even control of final cut will not end all editing of the film. Censorship needs will differ in various media and markets. Certain words cannot be spoken or images shown on broadcast television or in many countries. The distributors will demand control over the editing to make the film salable in those markets.

C. Sound

Music, dialogue, and sound effects combine to create a critical part of any film. Each of these three different audio elements plays a separate role. Music, as discussed in the previous chapter, can dramatically alter the emotional impact of a scene. Sound effects can emphasize action, turn small visual effects into overwhelming events, or even add characters to the scene. The off-screen cry of a baby, for instance, changes any moment, whether a romantic tryst or an attempted carjacking. The audio quality of the dialogue should remain natural and balanced throughout—the bare minimum for a competent production.

1. Separation of Soundtracks

Each of the three audio elements—music, dialogue, and effects—must be kept separate to allow the sound editor to shape the project and the production company to deliver the film to international distributors. Occasionally individual segments of dialogue must be changed—either for effect or to meet censorship obligations. In other situations, the entire dialogue track must be replaced with rerecorded dialogue in Spanish, Mandarin, or another foreign language. Choices of music may need to be changed for either artistic or legal reasons. As a result, most distributors will insist on receiving the three separate tracks for dialogue, music, and effects. Separate tracks are required to facilitate such changes. Each of the three tracks should be recorded in stereo or some proprietary enhanced stereo system such as Dolby, if available.

Although it may seem somewhat counterintuitive, part of the sound editor's job is to separate out some of the recorded sound into the separate tracks. Dialogue is typically further separated into separate tracks by character.

2. Source Music

Given the need for separate soundtracks, source music—music recorded live as part of filming—can create difficulties for the later mixing of the film. For very low-budget productions, recording source music may make sense because the filmmaker takes what he finds, and one benefit to recording music on location is that it is easier to match the sound with the location's background environment—the ambient noise that exists in every location. For most productions, however, studio recording may be preferable.

To synchronize a studio recording to the performance of the musicians on the set, a previously recorded studio session will be mixed and played during filming. The performers will play along to that reference track, matching their physical movements to the earlier recording. The reference track will be replaced with the studio recording in the final mix.

3. Score

The musical score cannot be finalized until the cut is locked—until all edits have been made so that the timing of the music can be exact. The traditional process involved matching the score to a print of the film. Today, the composer can time the score directly to the digital file playing on a computer.

4. Cue Sheets

If the film includes a traditional score, the composer must provide different musical notations for that score. First, the composer will develop musical timing sheets that provide descriptions of the scenes and the associated music associated with each beat. More important, the composer will refine these notations into musical cue sheets, which track each musical moment.

Cue sheets also include the cues for the score, effects, and dialogue. Each cue is tied directly to the edited film by footage or frame number. The musical cue sheets are part of the written sound description and will be required by most distributors. The cue sheets are critical for foreign distributors to be able to dub the dialogue without disrupting the remainder of the film.

5. Sound Effects and Foley

The original on-set recording may include many of the sounds necessary to make the film feel realistic—or stylistic—as required by the filmmaker: footsteps, doors opening and closing, glass breaking, etc. Nonetheless, a good many of these sounds need to be enhanced by the effects editor. The choices for sounds dramatically shape the impression of each scene and the overall film.

Foley is a particular type of sound effect created by working in a sound-proof stage. The Foley artist works with a variety of props and floor surfaces to create the sounds to match the action on the screen. She acts out the sound effects, synchronizing them to the film.

6. Looping

Often, filming conditions simply do not provide for good on-set sound recording. An actor dangling from a building buffeted by wind may be difficult to mike. Even without stunts, background noise like car traffic can obscure the audio. In such situations, the sound editor will use looping, or *ADR* (automatic dialogue replacement or additional dialogue recording), to loop, or rerecord, the missing dialogue. In other situations, ADR may be needed to correct mistakes in the dialogue or make other necessary changes.

If significant use of ADR is anticipated, the production schedule should be organized to ensure that the cast members are available for the duty. Matching dialogue is difficult enough without losing the cast to other projects and delaying the sound editing. For smaller films, scheduling may make ADR a difficult choice. To the extent possible, the filmmaker should rely on good location sound over ADR. Spending a small amount of additional production time to make sure the sound is recorded effectively during the filming can save the filmmaker substantial time and money.

7. Background Sound

Equally important, the sound editor needs to record ambient sound for every set. The background sounds of a silent set create the baseline for later dialogue editing and whatever looping is required. The investment in this 60 seconds of audio production can save significant money in the long run and should never be neglected.

D. Testing the Picture

Film directors often feel that audience testing exemplifies the worst excesses of corporate Hollywood, giving a kid with a response card veto power over their vision and integrity. While this perspective overstates the importance of particular response cards, test audiences play a highly controversial role in the completion of a film.

An audience test involves screening a nearly completed film for an audience demographically selected to fit the film's target age and gender. (Studios also select geographically, which refers both to regions and, unfortunately, to race or ethnicity.) These representatives of the target audience view the film and comment on what they have seen on small response cards. The audience is also carefully watched to gauge its reaction.

If the audience is representative and the questions on the cards are appropriate, the filmmaker can learn a great deal about whether the choices she made have the desired effect on the audience. If the audience is not representative or the wrong questions are asked, the process can lead to a frustrating round of counterproductive edits and reshoots. Unfortunately, there is no way to know whether the audience is right or wrong.

In the studio system, the greatest problem directors face with test audiences is that the producer controls the process and the outcome. Directors often invite their own preview audiences—friends, colleagues, and others—to watch the early edits of the film and provide comments. These previews are not significantly different from test screenings—except that the director is able to accept or reject each criticism.

Similarly, since the primary benefit of working on an independent film is the control it provides the filmmaker, the filmmaker should control the testing process as well. That does not necessarily mean rejecting a test screening if the distributor offers to provide one, but the filmmaker should retain control over what will be done with the information the test audience provides.

E. The Ratings System

The acquisition of an MPAA rating is a voluntary step for the production company. The rating is a designation provided by the MPAA Classification and Rating Administration (CARA) that suggests the appropriate audience for the film based on whether and how it depicts sexuality, violence, mature subject matter, tobacco use, etc. Each rating designation (other than X) is an MPAA trademark. No filmmaker can designate his film as having achieved a particular rating without the certification of the MPAA.

Although obtaining a rating is voluntary, the ratings system has tremendous influence on the marketing and sale of films in the United States. Exhibitors treat the ratings as legal obligations and will generally not allow minors under 17 years of age to attend movies rated R without adult accompaniment or to attend movies rated NC-17 at all. Many newspapers and television outlets will not accept advertising for NC-17 or X-rated films. Consequently, most distribution sales agreements require that the film be rated and receive the particular rating listed in the contract.

To obtain a rating, the filmmaker applies to CARA and pays a relatively modest fee. If the rating is higher than that sought, the rating can be appealed. Appeals are difficult to win, however, requiring a two-thirds vote of the CARA Appeals Board to overturn the initial rating. More frequently, the filmmaker makes small changes to the language or to the length of offending scenes and resubmits the film, satisfying the ratings board's concerns and allowing a lower rating to be applied.

Independent filmmakers should be able to require the domestic distributor to shoulder the cost and administration of the ratings process. There is no value to rating a film until it is ready for commercial promotion, so any expenditure before this is premature. By the time a rating is necessary, the distributor is better equipped to initiate the process.

Occasionally, filmmakers may choose not to rate a film. If the use of violence, nudity, or language will result in a rating that will strongly discourage the attendance of the film's intended audience, then the filmmaker may choose not to apply for one. This will make it much more difficult for the film to be shown in previews or on television, but may still be better than, for example, having to sell an R-rated film as a literary work to high schools. Had the R-rated *Schindler's List* been distributed as an independent film, the distributor of this powerful Holocaust film may have chosen not to rate it rather than lose the ability to promote it to schools.

F. Finalizing Credits: Contractual Obligations and WGA Assent

As part of the postproduction process, the final credits for the film should also be locked and repeatedly checked. Mistakes in the spelling of names or omission of earned credits can be very costly to fix. The credits should be reviewed by the production attorney to be sure all contractual obligations are met.

If the film company is a WGA signatory, then it has an obligation to send the tentative writing credits to the union immediately after principal photography is complete. If there is no conflict regarding writing credit, then this process is merely a formality. If multiple writers have been employed on the project, however, and several of them are seeking credit, then the WGA will require a cut of the film and copies of the various writers' drafts of the script so it can determine which of them have the right to be listed in the credits.

G. Delivery Elements

Independent filmmakers face a difficult choice when selecting a medium for delivering the final film, because certain distributors will insist on a full panoply of traditional delivery requirements. Fortunately, as digital filmmaking becomes more common and more sophisticated, distributors are increasingly willing to accept the delivery of digital files rather than film elements. But this will be a key negotiation point during the sale of the film.

The list of elements to be delivered to the distributor must be at the forefront of the film company's attention. If the company does not have the material available, it cannot meet its contractual obligation to the distributor. This would allow a distributor to claim the film company was in breach of the distribution agreement and cancel the arrangement, and possibly result in the film not being distributed at all.

1. The Negative

The most critical delivery item is the original negative of the cut, finished film and the accompanying optical soundtrack. In addition, distributors typically request an *internegative*—another copy of the negative that is used to strike prints and protect the original negative. Some distribution agreements will also call for an *interpositive*—a print of the film used to make the internegative. If the film is shot on 16mm, the filmmaker must first transfer the film to 35mm before creating the other elements. The internegative and interpositive apply only to celluloid film, whether shot on 16mm or 35mm. For a digitally created film, the digital image of the final cut is used to create the negative from which the prints are made. If the original negative becomes torn, another can be created from the electronic file.

Filmmakers should be sure not to agree to deliver elements that they do not need to create and do not have the money to make. Since the number of prints needed for an independent film is often very small, the additional expenses are unnecessary.

2. Sound and Music

The delivery of sound is a critical component of the final delivery requirements. As described above, the filmmaker must work carefully to separate the sound into its three separate tracks. The typical distributor will require a magnetic track on 35mm film, separated for dialogue, music, and effects. The distributor may additionally request a stereo or Dolby version, resulting in a six-track mix.

In addition to the recorded sound, the written materials necessary to create the sound mix must be delivered. They include copies of the music cue sheets with the necessary timing, the title of each composition, and copyright clearance information such as copyright owner and publisher.

Distributors will also require the actual music license agreements for each licensed composition used in the film. Every song used, regardless of length, will require an accompanying license from the music publisher and, if the film uses a prerecorded version of the song, from the record label.

3. Titles and Credits

Just as the distributor demands various formats of the print, it will also typically require that the titles be made available both in the final film and as a separate negative and interpositive. Of course, the filmmaker's list of contractual credits must also be complete and supplied to the distributor in writing to assure the distributor that the filmmaker has met all her legal obligations.

4. Other Media Formats

Some distributors require a version of the film on one-inch videotape that can be used as the videotape master. While creating it should be the distributor's obligation, the filmmaker will want to control the transfer to the narrower 1.33:1 (4:3) analog television ratio. During filming, she may actually create coverage shots so that certain scenes are composed differently than in the wide-screen 1.85:1 aspect ratio. Although the United States is converting to the HD screen ratio of 1.78:1 (16:9), which is the international high-definition standard, there will likely be the need for the conversion for some time. Even widescreen television ratios are slightly different from film ratios and require a modest conversion.

If the filmmaker has shot additional coverage scenes for the video format, then the distributor will request access to the additional material for its own editing. Similarly, the distributor will want coverage shots such as cut-outs, trims, and second takes if it has any right to edit the final film for distribution in foreign markets, television, or other arenas where different content or language issues may arise. In this case, the distributor will also require the accompanying sound effects, dialogue, and music that apply to that material.

5. Lab Access Letters

Many of the production elements are stored in a film laboratory rather than with the filmmaker. This facilitates production and distribution. The labs act as an escrow agent, holding the negatives and other elements of the film so that the distributor or distributors can gain access without gaining ownership. To grant the distributor access to a lab's stored materials, the filmmaker signs a simple letter to that effect. The letter grants the lab permission to produce whatever versions of the material are necessary for the distributor, and requires that nothing will be removed from the lab without both the filmmaker and the distributor being notified. In this way, neither can disrupt the business of the other.

6. Promotional Material

The independent filmmaker typically has little ability to help with the promotional requirements of the distributors. Although most distributors will cut their own trailers, they will expect that the filmmaker has cleared the music for such use. They will also seek a variety of photographs of the cast and the shoot to be used in the promotion. Typical requests include 25 to 100 color slides of the film and as many in black and white; contact sheets and negatives of additional photographs of the production; color and black-and-white negatives and prints of the cast and key production employees; and press books or press kits, if any exist. The filmmaker should remember to shoot a few rolls of film during the course of production so that at least some marketing materials are available, but she must also remember to be clear with potential distributors about what is available so no demands can be made after the contract is signed.

More important than production photographs, the filmmaker may be requested to provide the artwork and materials for the one-sheet poster of the film. While the distributor may wish to control all the marketing, the filmmaker should try to meet this demand as a way to control the style and tone of the promotional materials. On the crass assumption that people are generally lazy, the filmmaker may be able to control substantially more of the marketing campaign if she voluntarily creates the initial materials as part of the distribution package.

7. Documentation

The required range of documentation will vary considerably from distributor to distributor. The filmmaker should be prepared to provide a certificate of copyright and a statement certifying that the distributor has exclusive rights in the territories granted under the agreement. The transfer of exclusive rights to the territories should be filed with the Copyright Office, and copies made available to the distributor upon request. Distributors will also require a copy of the final screenplay and shooting script.

If the distribution agreement provides that the film will receive or not receive a particular rating or ratings (e.g., G or NC-17), then the film company must provide documentation from the MPAA. For independent films, the filmmaker should try to negotiate the distribution agreement to require the distributor attend to this obligation.

The distribution agreement will often establish which party is obligated to obtain errors and omission insurance. The film company will be required either to submit a copy of the insurance policy or the documentation necessary for the distributor to purchase the insurance. In addition, the film company must provide documentation relating to the filmmaker's valid ownership of the film and its constituent elements. But, as mentioned, the specific documentation requirements will vary greatly, and they should be treated as subject to negotiation.

H. Storage and Delivery

The designated film lab should serve as the repository for the original negative of the film, the final soundtracks, and the alternate scenes and other footage that could conceivably be used in the distribution of the film. Digital films should have an off-site backup at a secure data warehouse facility.

Everything else will reside with the film company—or more likely in the garage of the filmmaker. If the film is shot on 35mm, then hundreds of hours of undeveloped film stock may be stored there (at high risk of damage and decay). Similar hours of images will be stored on removable hard disks or other digital storage media. Material that may be necessary for distributors in additional markets or territories should be included in the lab storage, while the remainder can be kept at home.

The lab access letter serves as the primary vehicle for delivery. Rather than providing physical copies of most materials required by distributors, the filmmaker can simply authorize access to them. By limiting the ability of both the distributor and the filmmaker to remove the film without notice or permission, the lab help protects against any unscrupulousness by either party.

The filmmaker must assume that the distributor could go bankrupt or fail to make payments at any point. Although this most likely will not happen, the mere possibility that the original negative could be handed to the distributor and lost or destroyed invokes a filmmaker's nightmare that no amount of money could rectify. The filmmaker must be careful to give only copies of film elements and documents. If the distributor breaches its contract, the filmmaker must be in a position to grant the rights in the film to a new party. If the first distributor has physical custody of the film, the filmmaker is at its mercy.

Finally, the production budget should include the cost of a long-term lease of a storage facility for the documents, film, and other materials. Film must also be archived with particular attention to temperature and humidity, so the types of storage must be carefully selected. Ironically, the good news is that most independent films will succeed or fail rapidly after their release, and the extra storage can be either justified or eliminated shortly after the film comes out.

Special Considerations for the No-Budget Production

For today's aspiring filmmakers, the low cost of television-quality digital production equipment and improved access to distribution channels makes the appeal of no-budget filmmaking stronger than ever. A no-budget film may provide novice filmmakers with a demo reel to show off their abilities, a trailer to help fund feature projects, or simply an outlet for the filmmaker's creative ambitions.

The approach to the story should be crafted to fit the resources of the filmmaker. The budget creates a constraint that challenges the filmmaker, and the film must be made within those limitations if it is to be completed. The film must also meet the filmmaker's goals to tell the story and attract an audience. By keeping both filmmaking goals and the constraints of the production in mind, today's no-budget filmmakers have the opportunity to tell a broader range of stories than they would ever have been able to tell before.

A. Differences Between No-Budget and Conventional Independent Filmmaking

No-budget filmmaking is truly a subset of independent filmmaking. Every aspect of planning, budgeting, principal photography, and postproduction discussed in previous chapters is just as applicable to the no-budget film. Nevertheless, there are unique concerns for filmmakers who have such little financial support.

Ironically, no-budget filmmakers are under greater pressure than other independent filmmakers to plan carefully, rehearse diligently, and film efficiently. No-budget films have little or no money set aside to fix mistakes in postproduction or to reshoot sequences. As a result, the filmmaker must be more vigilant when preparing each scene.

In contrast to typical studio projects and even other independent productions, the cast and crew of a no-budget film are likely to be local and willing to spend time together to rehearse scenes, develop the script, learn which props are essential, and walk onto the set ready to capture the film. This sense of solidarity is the reason theatrical casts can move so readily from a community theater onto a movie set. Similarly, this is why cast and crew can come together to create such effective horror movies. No-budget filmmakers should capitalize on this camaraderie to enhance the filmmaking process.

While the motivations behind making a no-budget film may seem self-indulgent, the practice of such filmmaking must be highly disciplined. Whether filming on weekends in locations that can be carefully controlled for continuity or filming very quickly, the filmmaker must know what he is seeking in each shot and keep experimentation to a minimum. The reliance on volunteers, the lack of backups for costumes and props, and the limited ability to fix things financially should propel the no-budget filmmaker to move quickly from scene to scene, capturing as much footage as he can each day.

By starting with detailed planning and working with quick, exacting deliberation, the no-budget filmmaker will gain the confidence of his cast, crew, and supporters. The successful completion of the project will then serve as professional proof that the filmmaker and his team can be trusted with funding for increasingly larger projects.

B. Contingent Professional Assistance

One option for no-budget filmmakers is to find less experienced attorneys, accountants, and other professionals who are willing to work on contingency. Early in their career, many professionals are willing to invest their time and effort to learn the movie business by accepting deferrals for their pay. For lawyers, filmmakers may identify volunteer attorneys through the Volunteer Lawyers for the Arts network of legal referral services (www.vlany.org). While these professionals may not have the depth of experience of seasoned veterans, the price is right and the services will make a tremendous difference to the filmmaker.

An expanded strategy would include hiring as an "executive director" someone with a strong legal background who could review the work of the young attorney. On occasion, experienced professionals in the film industry are willing to work on contingency in exchange for screen credit and revenue participation. Of course, such a negotiation begins with the script and requires confidence on the part of the experienced professional in the talent, vision, and resourcefulness of the filmmaker.

C. Financial Essentials

The business of filmmaking focuses on minimizing professional risks while maximizing distribution opportunities and revenue streams. These goals may appear at odds with guerrilla and no-budget filmmaking, but they remain goals to keep in mind when shooting a no-budget film.

Even no-budget filmmaking costs money. The purchase or rental of a camera involves some expense. If the shoot lasts three or four weeks, the cost to provide drinks and food on the set can add up. The key to reducing the costs is to cut out any nonessential expenses, combine expenses with other activities, and set realistic goals for the project.

1. Risk Management

Filmmakers face direct financial risk that the funds invested in the film will not result in any financial return, or worse, will not result in a completed film project. If the filmmaker commits to spending up to $15,000 of his own money on food, equipment, insurance, rights, and music, then he will lose all $15,000 if the money runs out and the project is not completed. On the other hand, if the filmmaker can accomplish the same tasks by using an investor's $15,000 capital investment, then he incurs no personal financial risk.

The second form of risk stems from liabilities that occur while filming. The filmmaker or film company will be responsible for any contractual obligations or liabilities for accidents such as property damage or personal injury. This form of risk is minimized through the purchase of insurance (see chapter 9, p. 175) and the creation of a formal business structure (see chapter 2, p. 13).

Business planning can reduce risk, but it cannot eliminate it. If a filmmaker creates a corporation with no assets, the courts will ignore that corporate entity and continue to hold the owner of the company personally responsible for the contractual and tort liabilities of the company. In the case of a no-budget film, the use of a corporate structure or LLC to create limited liability will only have limited effect.

Purchase of general liability insurance, therefore, becomes the most significant single purchase a no-budget filmmaker can make. It protects both the filmmaker and the parties who might be injured. The filmmaker must also be prepared not only to pay for the goods and services he orders by contract but also to purchase insurance on the cameras or other more expensive items.

2. Loans and Investors

Because of complex federal and state securities laws, the cost to properly document even the simplest of investor agreements can greatly exceed the budget for many no-budget films. On the other hand, seeking investors in violation of state and federal securities laws hardly seems to be an appropriate approach. As a result, no-budget filmmakers often struggle with their financing. The recommendations for nonprofit fiscal sponsorship and receipt of gifts discussed in chapter 6 (pp. 116 and 122) are particularly helpful for no-budget productions.

Instead of seeking investors, very small budgets can be raised either through gifts or loans. A loan document can be drafted in extremely simple language. As discussed in *Own It: The Law and Business Guide to Launching a New Business Through Innovation, Exclusivity and Relevance*, a simple loan can provide the funding necessary to pay for the costs to start a business—here the film company—without significant documentation. The example below was written about the funding of a retail boutique, but can be adapted easily by replacing "boutique" with "film."

Personal loans are not uncommon for start-up businesses. Generally, they are nothing more than oral agreements in which the parents of the entrepreneur provide some money in exchange for vague promises that "I'll repay this as soon as I can." With family, these are often considered "gifts" that the lender expects never to be repaid.

The process of formalizing these relations may be more trouble than it is worth. At a minimum, however, the entrepreneur should specify the expectations of the loan with some written document. While a contract or note would be preferable, even a receipt letter would go a long way to avoid the problem of disputes. For example, one such letter could include the following:

[Date]
[Name]
[Address]

Dear Mom,

Thank you very much for the non-recourse loan of $5,000 last night, which I plan to use for the start of my new boutique. This letter will confirm the terms of that loan as we discussed them. As I said last night, all the money will be used for the business. Among other things, your loan will help me buy merchandise and begin advertising.

Just as I explained when you provided me the loan, I intend to repay you the entire amount of the loan plus 5% interest. I hope to repay you over the next three years—beginning the first payment a year from now, but if you need the money earlier, I will repay it within a month of your asking. I also appreciate that you will only ask for the money from the money I make in the boutique.

If I misunderstood any of the terms of the loan, please let me know immediately. Your confidence in me and in the boutique means a great deal to me. Thank you for your generosity and your faith.

Love,
[Signature]

Admittedly, this letter leaves much to be desired. Still, it serves to clarify the financial transaction and will serve as a clear reminder of the actual terms long after the exact memories of the offered loan are forgotten. As such, it will discourage disputes more than resolve them—an extremely important part of managing a business.

To be effective, the letter should be dated and signed. As this example does, the letter should state that it reflects the oral understanding between the parties. It should be sent very soon after the loan is offered (or received) so that it is contemporary with the funds, rather than drafted months or years later, once the parties are in the middle of a dispute. The letter may seem awkward, an unduly formal way to speak to one's mother (or aunt or friend), but the letter achieves a number of very important goals.

First, the letter clarifies that the funds were not a gift or an equity investment. It binds the recipient to understand the loan obligations, and it clarifies to the lender that no ownership interest in the company is conveyed as a result of the loan.

Second, the letter identifies the exact amount of the loan, the interest payment due and the payment schedule. These are the same terms any commercial loan would require. The purpose again is to set the rules of the relationship in place. Because the letter allows the lender to call the loan on thirty days' notice, it is drafted as a demand loan. By omitting the phrase "but if you need the money earlier I will repay it within a month of your asking" the demand nature of the loan can be removed.

Third, the letter establishes the loan is a "non-recourse" loan both because it describes the loan as non-recourse in the first sentence and because it explains the term with the phrase "you will only ask for the money from the money I make in the boutique."

The letter is not intended to serve as a legal contract. Rather, it is evidence of an oral conversation and contemporary understanding of the parties. It captures the essential terms of a loan agreement in three simple paragraphs rather than the two pages of formal text used by banks and commercial lenders. While any of these key terms can be adjusted, each should be addressed in such a letter.

In managing a start-up business, a little goes a long way. A simple letter like this provides much of the same protection as does a properly drafted and complex loan agreement. While it would be better to have a lawyer draft the loan agreements, the letter sent by the entrepreneur achieves many of the same goals at little cost. For family and close friends, this may be enough. As the complexity of the transaction increases, however, or the relationship moves beyond family, more formal documents are increasingly important to protect the entrepreneur from misunderstandings.[1]

Using nonrecourse loans instead of investments makes a good deal of sense in the context of guerrilla or low-budget filmmaking. The dollar amounts invested are very small, and the chances of repayment are quite low. Most contributors in this situation are acting for the benefit of the filmmaker rather than for their own financial gain, so this approach will generally meet their needs.

3. Values of No-Budget Filmmaking

Since no-budget filmmaking does not provide meaningful financial compensation for its participants, the filmmaker must take particular care to provide a positive experience for everyone involved in the filmmaking process. As film attorney and producer Dan Satorius put it, "No-budget filmmaking depends on the goodwill of others. You do yourself a favor and you will do a service to those low-budget filmmakers who follow you by treating people fairly."

Among the practices important for no-budget filmmakers, the most critical include following through on all promises made to cast, crew, investors, locations owners, and others; picking up after the film company at all locations; treating everyone with respect and appreciation; being generous with credits; and always remembering that the success of the film relies on the kindness of strangers.

4. Food and DVDs

Most beginning actors and crew members are ready to apprentice themselves for free. This is the reality in Hollywood and in most other locations throughout the country. It is the reason the professional unions protect jobs so aggressively. There is no end to the number of people who will accept less than minimum wage, if given the chance to work in the movies.

The new filmmaker must appreciate that if she cannot afford to provide any payment to her cast and crew, she must go out of her way to provide some benefits to them for working on the production. At an absolute minimum, the set should always have ample food and refreshments for everyone working on the production. The filmmaker is also responsible for maintaining a positive, energetic, and supportive environment on the set for all the cast and crew.

If the film company can find a few more dollars, then T-shirts, hats, or some other item of memorabilia can provide a value to the cast and crew that vastly exceeds its actual cost. Given the choice between a $25 payment or a T-shirt available exclusively to those people who worked on the film, most members of the cast and crew will take the shirt over the check. And all will remember the shirt long after the money has been forgotten.

Finally, a thank-you note and copy of the DVD should be given to everyone credited on the film or in any other way responsible for the film's completion. This is a sign of courtesy and respect to those who worked on the project. The DVD also provides a positive sign to supporters of the filmmaker that the movie resulted in a tangible success. Even if the movie did not return any financial reward, the existence of the DVD greatly increases the chance that the cast, crew, and financial supporters will be ready to work with the filmmaker on her next project.

D. Personnel Agreements

A no-budget film company remains responsible for meeting its legal obligations regarding minimum wage, tax withholding, and other hour and wage laws. If the film company does not have the resources to abide by these obligations, then at a minimum the company should use a formal business structure to make the company's best-faith efforts to meet its obligations.

1. General Partnerships

A general partnership provides an obvious business structure for the no-budget production company, and in fact will be formed by operation of law if the filmmaker takes no additional steps. Participants working closely with the filmmaker could be treated as general partners unless they are clearly identified as employees, independent contractors, or volunteers (see chapter 2, p. 17). In a general partnership, all the parties are jointly responsible for the business and share equally in the potential for its losses.

The general partnership model automatically provides every general partner with equal authority and ownership, but the authority and ownership interests can be varied by written agreement. As general partners in the business, the participants are owners rather than employees. The partnership agreement should specify the rights and responsibilities of each partner, including the structure for allocation of profits, which of the partners have decision-making authority, and which partners have primary responsibility for debts.

The same agreement should also set forth the partners' ability to enter into the agreement, confirm their availability during the shoot, and provide that the partners grant to the partnership the rights to use their name and likeness in association with the film and its marketing, as well as all other key employment provisions.

In the absence of a written agreement specifying the rights and interests of the parties, a general partnership provides shared ownership of all interests and risks among all the parties. For the filmmaker, this may result in parting with a great deal of ownership and control of the project in exchange for relatively small contributions from the other members of the film company. This may be a very high cost, given the filmmaker's own hard work, and thus a general partnership should be undertaken with caution. The use of a written agreement can provide some significant protections.

2. Independent Contractors

Since a general partnership exposes the partners to unlimited liability for the obligations of the company, many cast and crew members will be unwilling to become general partners. Bona fide independent contractors hired by the film company need not become general partners, provided the filmmaker documents the independent contractor agreement as described in chapter 3 (p. 41). For cast members and many of the crew, however, acting as an independent contractor will not work. State employment laws and federal tax laws provide detailed rules regarding the characterization of workers as employees or independent contractors, and the film company has little power to vary these classifications. However, no-budget films shot on an intermittent schedule may require little full-time commitment by the participants. Under these conditions, more of the participants may qualify as independent contractors.

3. Nested LLCs and Joint Ventures

No-budget film companies may consider a variation of the nested-LLC model described in chapter 2 (p. 27). Under this variation, the filmmaker forms an LLC for the purpose of making films. The LLC enters into a joint venture with a general partnership composed of the cast and crew, under which the LLC is responsible for all financing and budget while the general partnership is responsible for all personal services. In this way, all contracts will be executed by the LLC rather than the general partnership, and the LLC will be primarily responsible for all obligations. Along with sufficient insurance, this structure should minimize the potential for personal liability among the cast and crew.

E. Genres Well Suited to the No-Budget Film

The no-budget film has been around since the Edison Trust acquired Woodville Latham's patent on the shutter gate and started the motion picture business. But modern no-budget productions owe their paternity to filmmakers like Edward D. Wood Jr. and Roger Corman. As an art form, the no-budget film may be considered a genre unto itself, but this is misleading. Several different genres are particularly well suited to small-budget productions.

1. Horror and Suspense

In the 1970s, the homemade films *Halloween* and *The Texas Chainsaw Massacre* redefined the horror and suspense genre. The genre was reenergized in the late 1990s by the success of the low-budget *The Blair Witch Project*, and it continues to provide a potentially large financial return on very small investments. In no-budget horror films, the lack of polish only adds to their subconscious believability. Moreover, the pressure is on the characters, not sophisticated special effects, to convey the tension in the films. For beginning filmmakers, horror and suspense movies continue to be excellent training vehicles.

2. Documentaries

Documentaries are particularly well suited to shooting with small budgets. Since they do not require sets, costumes, or paid actors, documentaries can eliminate many of the expenses of the filmmaking process. Most documentaries are not released theatrically, so a first-time documentary filmmaker may choose to shoot with less expensive equipment, making the size of the crew and the cost of the equipment rental much lower. In addition, unless he stages reenactments or asks his subjects to perform on behalf of the film, the documentary filmmaker is not responsible for the activities of those individuals being filmed, so he can film high-risk activities such as motocross or hang gliding without incurring liability. As soon as the film company begins to stage events, however, it takes on the same obligations as with a narrative film project.

The documentary filmmaker is in the best position to hire the limited and often intermittent crew as independent contractors, to serve from time to time when the production is on location. Even if the documentary film has a few full-time employees, the film company can likely use a payroll service and meet its obligations readily even on a low budget.

3. Cinematic Nonunion Theater

Nonprofessional theater continues to be a mainstay of art and culture throughout the world. More than a source of endless productions of *Our Town* or *Grease,* many small, nonunion theaters provide the first opportunity for new playwrights to develop their craft. Most of these productions run for a few weekends and are never seen again.

No-budget filmmaking can provide an extremely useful opportunity for these playwrights and their directors, producers, and casts. By working with a small theater to film original plays and musicals, the filmmaker can capture a version of the production for posterity. These productions can be shot either on stage or on more realistic sets, and they can range from filmed stage performances to full movie adaptations. They usually land somewhere in between.

While members of the Equity actors union will generally not agree to such productions, most other performers would jump at the chance to participate in the film version of the show. Similarly, original plays and musicals produced under union-approved Broadway agreements generally preclude this technique, but there are many original productions that would benefit from the opportunity no-budget filmmaking provides to increase their audience.

Contractually, the rights in the play and the script need to be clarified. Often the theatrical director is also the filmmaker, combining the projects into a single activity and using the same actor and crew contracts. These contracts need to provide for both live and filmed versions of the production. The playwright will generally not consider the no-budget movie to be the definitive motion picture version, so her contract will likely allow the film company to produce only this one version of the motion picture. The writer will retain all other rights, such as the rights to create sequels or remakes. In this way, she may use the no-budget version as a demo reel for promoting the sale of the play and eventually a more professional film version.

F. Building on Film School

New filmmakers often create their first feature as part of their graduation from an undergraduate or masters of fine arts film program. While tuition costs a considerable amount, the value of an education extends well past the technical skills developed in one's field—it represents a transformative experience for every graduate. As such, the investment in film school may be a very strategic method for financing one's first film.

Moreover, for the no-budget filmmaker, great value may be found in the video and digital filmmaking programs of community colleges. For the cost of a few thousand dollars, the filmmaker will receive access to equipment, insurance, cast and crew, locations, editing equipment, professional discounts, and a host of other resources. A person seeking to make his first documentary or feature would benefit tremendously from utilizing the resources of these community college programs. Oftentimes the availability of community college resources will not be limited to the particular courses offered. This means that by signing up for the program, the filmmaker may gain immediate access to many of the resources necessary to begin production on projects chosen by the filmmaker rather than selected as part of course requirements.

P A R T

3

Selling the Movie:
Distribution and Marketing

Theatrical Distribution

THE CHAPTERS IN part 3 apply only to filmmakers who did not enter into a negative pick-up or other arrangement that sold the entire marketing of the film to the film's financier. Once the filmmaker has sold the marketing and distribution rights, his role, except his capacity to participate in marketing events for the film, is usually finished. In the current film economy, however, most filmmakers are left to scratch up sufficient funds to create the film, then use the finished print to sell the distribution rights.

Distribution of films has never been easier. Through Amazon, YouTube, eBay, and personal Web sites, filmmakers have direct access to the public. On the other hand, these same services are joined by dozens or even hundreds more in providing free content to the public. As a result, building an audience, and most essentially making money, for independent films has never been more challenging.

Where theatrical distribution is concerned, over the past decade the number of movie screens has continued to increase while the range of content has narrowed. More troubling for independent films, the length of a movie's theatrical run has also dropped considerably. Many movies do all their business in a two- to four-week period, with tremendous drop-offs in sales after the opening weekend. The general strategy for independent releases has been the opposite approach of building word of mouth and slowly increasing availability. The independent distribution strategy is now competing for an audience increasingly likely to see films either in the opening week of release or on DVD. This will impose ever-greater challenges to independent film distribution.

A. Distribution Economics

The rental of films from distributors to theatrical exhibitors is a complex transaction, defined by historical relationships and years of legal conflict during the 1930s through the 1950s that continue to shape the transactional practices today.

1. Exhibitors' Participation in Revenues

The average film provides very roughly half of its box office revenue to the exhibitor with the other half returning to the distributor—but this is not how the contracts are structured. Instead, the theater is guaranteed a *nut,* or minimum revenue for showing the film, and the distributor is guaranteed a *floor,* or minimum revenue of the next monies earned above the nut. Assuming the film has done well enough to fulfill both guarantees, both the distributor and the exhibitor split the revenue from ticket sales on a sliding scale.

In the first week the percentages may range from 90:10 to 70:30 in favor of the distributor. As the weeks continue, the percentage begins to become more balanced toward the exhibitor, creating an increasing financial incentive for the exhibitor to keep a film longer. The distributor, in contrast, is encouraged to spend aggressively on marketing to maximize the ticket sales in the first week or two of distribution. Increasingly, marketing efforts have devoted greater and greater emphasis on attendance on a film's opening weekend.

The exhibitor enjoys higher attendance and other benefits from the front-loading of the audience into fewer weeks. The overhead for running a theater includes the movies' projectionists, ticket takers, popcorn sellers, and cleaning crew. These employee expenses over a given period of time remain largely the same regardless of a film's popularity during that period. Since the overhead is inelastic, the greater the revenue, the lower the overhead as a percentage of gross income, resulting in a greater profit. Movie theaters also have a very high profitability on their concession items and the distributors do not receive any percentage of this income, so movie theaters earn higher revenue from the greater attendance generated by a succession of big openings and short runs than the modest attendance generated by a single film's extended run.

2. Change in Audience Expectations

Audience behavior has both followed and encouraged this trend. As the number of screens grows and reviews, blogs, and clips quickly proliferate, theatergoers feel increased social pressure to attend a film when it first opens. The fear of plot spoilers on television, the Internet, or in newspapers puts pressure on the audience to see a movie before the experience is ruined by the positive or negative influence of the media. Finally, as films disappear from movie theaters more quickly, theatergoers begin to fear that the movies will not be available for long, so they decide to go to a movie as soon as it opens or to plan to see it later on DVD or cable.

3. Relationship to the Independent Film

This broad, national distribution strategy is only one way to sell a movie. There remain theater chains dedicated to independent and foreign films and other movies that benefit from more niche marketing. Unfortunately, the high cost of marketing does not favor these theaters, which rely on much smaller but loyal audiences and marketing through Web sites, newsletters, and word of mouth.

Theatrical distribution continues to provide important marketing support for DVD sales and other media, so these alternative distribution channels remain extremely important for the independent film industry. Whether they are a critical part of a particular film's strategy depends on the costs of production, the advertising budget, and the expectations of the filmmaker and distributor.

B. How to Entice and Select a Distributor

For most theatrical distribution, the film company must enter into an agreement with a film distributor that will promote the film and negotiate with theaters in each of the exhibition markets. The distributor will be responsible for shaping the marketing and publicity strategy, paying for marketing, striking prints of the film, and promoting the film in each market in which it is shown.

If the filmmaker is highly adept at writing, directing, or editing films, then she should not have to invest years learning how to sell them as well. The filmmaker and the film are both better served if she works to create movies and allows the distributor to perform its obligations to promote and market its films.

The duty of the filmmaker is simply to create the best possible market opportunities for the distributor. This requires that the filmmaker take certain strategic steps to prepare the film for sale to the distributor and to ensure that the distributor can meet its obligations. Each of the following steps helps to increase the odds that the film will be sold to an enthusiastic and experienced distributor.

1. Show Only Final Product

The filmmaker should show only the completed film unless there is no feasible alternative. Few people have the ability to watch a film with the sound incomplete, the color not balanced, or cuts missing, without judging the overall quality of the film based on its missing elements. Worse, distributors will not recognize that they do not have this ability. Many of the subtle techniques used to give polish to the final version operate below the audience's consciousness. If the techniques were noticeable, they would detract from the film. Thus, the more polished the final film, the more misleading the unfinished preview.

If the filmmaker cannot afford to finish the film, she would be better advised to present an extended trailer of the film, along with a one-sheet poster and production stills. The distributor needs a good trailer and promotional material to sell the film; the quality of the film itself is secondary. For the filmmaker faced with the hardest decisions regarding the last few dollars in the production budget, the trailer and promotional materials should be the priority unless the film can be completely finished—not just rough cut.

2. Sell the Biggest Market First

Distribution costs for a studio film often exceed the total costs of independent films. Each 35mm print of the film may cost $3,000 to $5,000, so a wide distribution of 3,000 screens can run as much as $1 million in print costs alone. If a film is to open nationally, advertising costs often run between $20 million and $50 million, depending on the size of the release and the intensity of the campaign.

Although independent films are rarely treated to this level of marketing, the filmmaker should not ignore the long-term impact of any substantial market investment. A strong advertising campaign may not result in theatrical ticket sales, but the same film that bombs at the box office may soar to the top of the video sales or rental charts with almost no additional marketing. A distributor who controls both theatrical and video distribution should be much more willing to invest in promotion than a distributor that owns only one of those markets. The combined budget of the two markets distributed separately will invariably be less than what a single distributor would spend on them.

The filmmaker should incorporate this marketing reality into the sales strategy. Early in the selling cycle, the filmmaker should insist that the U.S. market be sold only to distributors who can exploit all or most of the domestic markets. Only if the filmmaker can close on complete domestic deals should she start to market the film to distributors who specialize in smaller media.

3. Know the Film

Perhaps the hardest job of the filmmaker is to realistically assess the value of the film. The filmmaker knows intimately what the film cost to make but has little idea how many people would be willing to pay full price to see it at the movie theater. If she wants to have realistic conversations with film distributors, she must develop some perspective on the film. A lack of perspective can cut both ways: Early in the sales process, the filmmaker may believe that her work should win all the Oscars. After a few months of distributor rejections, she may think that the film should not be allowed on public access television, even at 2:00 A.M.

Realism helps build credibility with the distributor, assists in properly positioning the film within the distributor's catalog of films, and creates a solid basis for the contract negotiations. Without these attributes, even the most marketable film may go unseen.

Knowing the film is most critical when the filmmaker has choices regarding the distributor. If the filmmaker receives multiple distribution offers, this knowledge will enable her to match the film to the strengths and successes of the distributor.

4. Enter Film Festivals Selectively

The independent film marketplace is something of a community. For filmmakers who consistently create independent work, the premier film festivals are the professional equivalent of the Academy Awards—an opportunity to move among peers as leaders in the industry. New filmmakers can learn a great deal about the realities of the industry.

Participating in film festivals serves as an efficient way to get the filmmaker's work in front of potential distributors and a paying audience. Most films are made to be viewed in social settings. Comedies, for example, are always funnier to a viewer laughing along with a live audience. Film festivals provide a powerful marketing opportunity and a chance to display the film to a distributor in a far superior setting than on a television in an office.

The filmmaker must still be careful. Not all festivals are alike. While some are stellar events, others are of less value. Filmmakers must be selective or the submission fees and time commitments may undermine any value of attending the festivals. The filmmaker should learn what films have previously come out of each festival, whether the festival serves as a true marketplace for distribution deals, and in what regard a festival is held by the independent film community. Local festivals in the filmmaker's hometown may be given special consideration. They can create opportunities for press coverage, and travel fees are eliminated.

The more prestigious North American festivals include the Sundance Film Festival, the New York Film Festival, the Toronto International Film Festival, the Montreal World Film Festival, the South by Southwest Festival (SXSW), and the Telluride Film Festival. These festivals are highly competitive, but the exposure should help improve the chances of distribution for most films. That is not to suggest that getting into one of these festivals will guarantee a distribution deal. The New York Film Festival shows approximately 50 films annually, while the Sundance Film Festival screens approximately 120. Only a small percentage of the films shown even at these festivals go on to theatrical distribution.

Even if the percentages seem hopeless, there is a silver lining. Film festivals put the filmmaker in a room with thousands of other filmmakers, producers, distributors, and others with the same profession and passion. Even if the film does not end up in theatrical release, it may impress producers looking for talent on other projects or actors willing to take a risk on new material. The opportunities are real.

5. Go Where the Buyers Are: Attend Film Markets

In addition to the competitive film festivals, many films debut at film markets such as the American Film Market, held every November in Santa Monica, or the Cannes Film Market, held in conjunction with the Cannes Film Festival. Typically film markets are huge, weeklong affairs with thousands of participants. While there may be some panels, mixers, and other secondary activities, the primary goal is to screen films for sales agents and distributors seeking to purchase content. These markets are likely to be more financially rewarding than film festivals, since the former are geared to film buyers more than the general public.

Filmmakers may try to be strategic about participation in film markets as part of an overall distribution strategy. The filmmaker may reduce the film's marketing guarantee if he sells his film at a film market prior to winning a significant festival award. On the other hand, the distributor may anticipate a better response from competitions than what ultimately occurs, so that the guarantee advanced would be higher. Ultimately, such timing is a matter of luck or serendipity.

C. Knowing the Distributors

Distributors tend to specialize in a particular strategy they use for distribution. Major studios specialize in the distribution of nationally released and heavily marketed films. They do not regularly use the tools that drive smaller marketing campaigns, so they are less familiar with such campaigns and less competent at carrying them out. Small distribution companies, on the other hand, do not have the staff or experience to handle the distribution of over 5,000 prints, a simultaneous worldwide release, and a $50 million advertising buy. When seeking distributors, rather than focusing on the size of the distribution company, the filmmaker should consider whether its distribution strategy will help the film find an audience.

The filmmaker should know who the significant distributors are so that when one expresses an interest, he can quickly assess the credibility of its enthusiasm. He should look carefully at films that have a similar audience demographic to his movie and identify those projects that were effectively released by their distributor. Both the filmmaker and the potential distributor will be more successful if they share a common vision on how the film can best be marketed and supported.

1. Majors

Each major motion picture producer operates as a major motion picture distributor as well. The vast majority of films produced in the United States are released domestically by these companies. They are vertically integrated telecommunication giants, which own production and distribution companies, and even the manufacturing facilities for DVDs.

Although the corporate ownership has varied considerably over the past century, the roster of film studios has not varied significantly since the early days of the MPAA. The companies are Warner Bros. (Time Warner), Universal Studios (NBC Universal), Sony Pictures Entertainment (formerly Columbia Pictures Entertainment), Paramount Pictures (Viacom), 20th Century Fox (News Corp.), and the Walt Disney Company. Metro-Goldwyn-Mayer (MGM/UA) was the seventh original member of the MPAA, but it was marginalized by a number of mergers. At present, the studio has plans to reemerge as a producer and distributor.

2. The Mini-Majors

What was once a growing roster of new production/distribution companies has largely disappeared due to production costs and industry risk. The strongest contender was DreamWorks SKG, the modern answer to Mary Pickford's United Artists. Formed by Steven Spielberg, Jeffrey Katzenberg, and David Geffen in 1994, DreamWorks challenged the majors in feature films, animated movies, music, and television production. But the company abandoned its independent status in 2006, becoming a division of Viacom.

All of the majors also own smaller film production companies. Although each company is operated in its own idiosyncratic fashion, these smaller, wholly owned companies often make their own purchasing decisions. Recently, however, the major studios began closing or consolidating these companies, so many will become simply in-house brands of their parent studios, without separate purchasing staff or distribution strategies. Others, such as Miramax, will continue to develop, produce, and distribute a strong slate of films independently from their parent company. Like Miramax, Focus Features, Fox Searchlight, and Destination Films are likely to be strong buyers in the market.

3. Leading Independent Producer/Distributors

In addition to the companies owned by the majors, a few independent producers have become havens for independent films. These include Lionsgate Entertainment, the Weinstein Company, Overture Films, Summit Entertainment, Samuel Goldwyn Films, Pathé International, Canal Plus Group, Wild Bunch, Media Asia, and a host of increasingly smaller companies that have less theatrical impact.

Also important in the mix are the television powerhouse companies of Showtime and HBO. These two companies purchase a tremendous amount of content for premium television distribution, including a significant amount of independent fare. Showtime and HBO do not compete for theatrical distribution, so a filmmaker can leverage a sale to either of them as validation of the marketability of the film with theatrical distributors that otherwise might not have been interested.

4. Everyone Else

There are hundreds of independent film distributors working in the United States, but few of the remaining distributors have significant impact on the theatrical market. While most independent filmmakers do not have the opportunity to distribute their films theatrically, the possibility should not be conceded without a fight. If no experienced theatrical distributor offers a contract, the filmmaker should begin to work with the remaining distributors on how best to maximize the impact of the film.

D. The Importance of International Distribution

Throughout the filmmaking industry, the larger growths in revenue have come from Asia and Central America, with some modest growth coming from Europe as well. Filmmakers who fail to distribute in these markets may easily forgo half the film's potential revenue. At the same time, independent filmmakers have few resources to carefully monitor distribution activities across the globe, so it is critically important that they work with companies that have established track records.

If a film is successful in attracting the interest of a large distribution company, that company is likely to seek worldwide distribution rights. Assuming the company has an established record for selling its films overseas, this one-stop shopping arrangement is likely to provide the filmmaker with the greatest opportunity to earn international revenue, while allowing her to return to producing works. Moreover, a single distributor is likely to craft domestic and foreign marketing strategies that complement each other.

As an alternative, the filmmaker should seek out an international sales agent, which can work to sell the film in the various territories that have yet to be sold. As with every other distributor, the key to selecting the international sales agent is the track record it has had with sales of similar films.

In addition to providing access to foreign markets, the international sales agent should provide the filmmaker with guidance regarding the distribution requirements and censorship standards in each market or territory. The filmmaker should be able to rely on the international sales agent to know how the movie will fit into the standards and practices.

Whether negotiated directly with the distributor or through an international sales agent, the distribution agreement should specify that any modifications to the film must be approved by the film company, rather than being made unilaterally by the foreign distributor, and it should provide the film company with the authority to withhold the film from any market that would require unacceptable changes to the content of the film.

E. The Distribution Deal

Every distribution agreement, large or small, covers the same fundamental issues. The distributor must promote the film in various media, collect payments, and share those payments with the film company. In addition to the filmmaker's delivery obligations, discussed in chapter 15 (p. 272), additional concerns should also be addressed.

1. Media and Territory

The territory of the film includes both the media markets and the geographic area in which the distributor is acquiring the right to show the work. The United States and Canada are usually sold as a single territory, referred to as North America (which may or may not also include Mexico, depending on the definitions in the agreement).

Unless the agreement provides for worldwide distribution in all media, this provision must very clearly spell out what countries and what media markets are covered by the agreement so that additional contracts can be negotiated with other distributors to build up the worldwide distribution of the movie. For example, the provision for domestic television should include pay-per-view, pay cable, network, syndication, free cable, satellite, and any and all forms of television transmission now or hereafter existing. The section should specifically include or exclude home video. It should also specifically include or exclude interactive services like the Internet or consumer devices other than television, such as home computers.

2. Term

The term of the distribution agreement will vary depending on the range of markets covered by the agreement. If the agreement is limited to domestic theatrical distribution, then there should not be significant activity more than one year after distribution begins. Recognizing that the distributor may need some flexibility regarding the start of the campaign, the term in such a situation should be limited to from two to five years.

Further, the filmmaker may wish to insist that the distribution rights terminate if the film has not been released in any of the listed markets within 18 months of delivery of the finished film to the distributor. This short drop-dead provision may be somewhat difficult to negotiate, but it provides significant protection for the filmmaker properly concerned about his film being left in the back of the distributor's catalog.

3. Advances and Payments

With significant debts generated throughout film production, the filmmaker may be most concerned about the up-front payments to be made by the distributor. These payments serve as advances against the future income generated by the film. As income flows in from the various markets, the distributor will withhold any additional payment to the filmmaker until the filmmaker has earned an amount equal to the advance. Advances act as a minimum payment, because the filmmaker will be entitled to keep the entire amount, without regard to the total income generated by the distribution.

If the filmmaker does recoup his advance, he will then be paid a percentage of the revenue generated by the film. Payment will be determined based on the total gross income generated. The distributor will keep 20 to 30 percent of the theatrical and video income, and 40 to 50 percent of the income from other markets. After the distributor deducts this fee, it deducts its expenses for the marketing and promotion of the film, often including its costs in attending national marketing conventions and other general overhead costs. The remainder of the net proceeds is then paid to the filmmaker.

Because of distributors' ability to manipulate the reporting of gross income and expenses, the filmmaker should focus primarily on the advance. Industry practices reduce the net proceeds paid to the filmmaker to a relatively small portion of income generated.

4. Distributor's Guarantees of Marketing Expenses

Almost as important as the advance is the distributor's guarantee regarding the size of the marketing campaign. Even though the costs of the marketing campaign ultimately come from the filmmaker's portion of the revenue, the larger the campaign, the more likely the film will be viewed. Without the guarantee, the distributor will have no particular incentive to get behind this picture and push for its distribution. The filmmaker can always ask the distributor to cut back on the campaign if he feels the payments are no longer needed, but invariably he will want a larger campaign than the distributor is willing to provide. Without a contractual obligation from the beginning, the filmmaker is at the mercy of the distributor.

5. Audits

Given the importance of the advance, payments of guarantees, and accounting of the marketing expenses, the filmmaker must be able to monitor or audit the books of the distributor. More specifically, the filmmaker must have the right to have the books made available to his own accountant. Often a distributor will seek to limit access or limit the amount of time the filmmaker has to conduct an audit or bring action on one, but the filmmaker should resist limiting this legal protection.

6. Foreign Sublicensing

If a distributor does not have the ability to fully exploit some markets or territories, it will often sublicense them to other companies. This sublicensing arrangement can be an efficient substitute for the filmmaker's own attempts to track down those markets and cover them with different distributors. Often, however, the sublicensee is actually a company owned by the distributor itself, meaning that the distributor is making the profit as the sublicensee and charging the filmmaker a premium for its own licensing fee. Unless the total fees are capped, an unscrupulous distributor can claim twice the revenue by sublicensing to its own subsidiary. Filmmakers should be careful to cap the sublicensing fees to limit the revenue that can be lost to this practice.

In addition, to the extent possible, the filmmaker should seek advances for each territory exploited, because foreign royalties may be difficult to negotiate. Beyond theatrical distribution, the ways in which foreign markets are exploited may be mandated by the laws of the country in question. In many countries, for example, if a film is broadcast on terrestrial television—over the airwaves—then cable operators are allowed to carry that broadcast simultaneously on local cable systems in exchange for paying into a national fund. The owner of the film is then eligible to receive a portion of those funds.

Each country may have its own revenue sources for such a national fund, including cable retransmissions royalties (described above), surcharges on blank videotape, rental royalties, educational royalties, theatrical box office levies, public performance royalties for video, and many others. Typically, the money is collected by a national rights society similar to ASCAP and divided among the registered content owners. This means the filmmaker must register with dozens of collection societies in hundreds of counties.

Fortunately, the Independent Film and Television Alliance (IFTA) provides a collection service that acts as both registration agent and collection agent for these funds. Registration is far simpler when handled by the IFTA, and filmmakers are much more likely to receive royalties through the collective powers and efforts of IFTA than through a distributor or sales agent in a particular country.

F. Rights to Withhold from the Distributor

The distribution agreement should also be quite explicit regarding limitations on the distributor. No rights should be granted unless the distributor can exploit those rights and the filmmaker can be assured that he will see a return. In addition, there are certain legal controls that distributors often request, but these requests should be carefully limited or refused.

1. Copyright and Ownership

The distributor may need the right to edit the film for certain markets, particularly foreign markets. Nonetheless, the distribution agreement should not be an assignment of copyright and should not grant the distributor the right to remake the film or create new projects out of the story or related rights. The editing rights must be limited to those changes required by local censorship laws or changes for accommodating foreign languages. These accommodations may also include translating the title in either a literary or a conceptual fashion. Except for these specific changes, the distributor should have no power to modify the film. This limitation may not apply if the film project is purchased outright by a major studio's distribution arm, but for all other purchasers, the copyright and ownership in the story should be retained by the filmmaker.

2. Marketing Materials

The marketing campaign often defines the film in the public's mind, but as mentioned earlier, the distributor is typically the party that creates this campaign. In deals involving small distributors, the filmmaker can negotiate to have significant participation in and ownership of the marketing. Particularly in a situation in which multiple distributors will distribute the film in various markets and media, each distributor must agree that the filmmaker will own any marketing materials. This way, the materials from the theatrical campaign can be used to promote the video sales of the film, even if the two markets are licensed to different distributors. This arrangement is also helpful if the distribution agreements expire and later interest in the film requires the filmmaker to promote the picture again. In addition to legal ownership, the agreement should provide that at the end of the contract term any remaining materials be given to the filmmaker or destroyed, at the filmmaker's discretion.

G. Staging the Domestic Theatrical Distribution

Distributing the film requires tremendous coordination and a good deal of cooperation on the part of the exhibitors. Exhibitors are entitled to bid on each film separately and may choose not to show a particular film. In addition, theater chains buy films for each screen (or at least each theater complex) rather than for the chain as a whole. These rules have developed over the years to protect independent theaters and small chains from the larger chain competitors.

1. National Release

Studios generally release their films nationally, meaning in each major market in the United States and Canada on the same date. This allows them to maximize the impact of paid advertising and drown out negative reviews with a well-financed campaign. Increasingly, international campaigns are opened simultaneous with or closer to the opening dates of U.S. release to reduce the window of opportunity for video piracy. Although the exhibitors negotiate individually, a large national campaign tends to announce an official release date, which forces exhibitors to participate or be left behind. A small theater chain wishing to be part of the release of *Titanic II* must be willing to stop showing whatever film it otherwise would play on that date to make room for the blockbuster release. Independent film distribution strategies must carefully consider the national release dates of major studio pictures, lest the independent film be forced out of theaters to make room.

2. Markets Sold in the Presale Agreement

Depending on the financing techniques employed, some distribution choices may already be settled. For example, if the presale agreements (see chapter 6, p. 108) call for exhibition in certain territories at specified times, these terms will dictate all other agreements. Presale agreements may allow some flexibility regarding the scheduling of actual release dates. A small film's release in overseas territories should not have a material impact on its domestic release, and good international reviews can even be exploited as part of the domestic marketing effort. Outside the United States, dates for theatrical distribution generally have little impact on the overall marketing campaign. There is no need to hold up the distribution in India while awaiting Europe, or to make sure Japan has the film before Korea. Audiences do not travel to see films abroad, the problems of piracy are not diminished, and distributors are generally not sufficiently sophisticated to create any meaningful strategy for international release dates.

If a portion of the presale agreement comes from DVD distribution, the filmmaker should be able to delay the release in that media for a specified period of up to one year so that he can take every opportunity to release the film theatrically first.

3. Platform Release

The best-known strategy for distributing an independent film is known as a platform release. The film is opened in one city (often New York, Chicago, or Los Angeles) selected for the size of the market, the influence of the critics, and the opportunity for word of mouth to spread to other areas. Assuming positive reviews and good word of mouth, audiences for the film should grow, and its per-screen revenue may well equal or exceed that of the top blockbusters playing at the same time. Exhibitors are far more interested in the per-screen revenue than the national grosses, because per-screen revenue translates into ticket sales and concession traffic.

After two to four weeks, press and audience reaction may generate interest sufficient to move to additional markets. If the campaign is highly successful, additional prints will be ordered and new theaters will be added to the original showings. Typically, however, the existing prints are shipped to the new markets, keeping the total print cost down. In this way, a movie may play 5 to 10 major markets on 1 to 3 prints.

If the film is doing well in 10 markets, then the distributor may choose to expand still further, adding an additional 10 markets, and so on, until national distribution has been accomplished. More likely, the expansion stops being an efficient strategy well before the first 100 markets have been hit, but the film will still have had a very successful theatrical run and will be positioned well for DVD sales built on theatrical word of mouth.

The timing and geography of the platform release is highly dynamic, reacting not only to the success of the film in question but also to other film openings throughout the country. This allows exhibitors to gain confidence in the film and gives them the flexibility to add it to their schedule when the blockbusters begin to fizzle.

4. Four-Walling

A filmmaker without any other options may still buy the opportunity to have a film shown in a commercial theater. In a four-wall arrangement, the distributor or filmmaker rents the theater, rather than licensing the picture to the theater. Typically, only a filmmaker who could not otherwise attract a distributor would do this. The filmmaker pays a rental fee for the theater for a specified time period and receives all income from ticket sales; the concession income may be either kept by the theater or apportioned, depending on the cost of the rental and the agreement between the parties.

Four-walling may seem like an act of vanity, but it can be much more than that. Sometimes the limited run will be enough to get the local critic to see the film and elicit a positive review. It may result in generating some interest among potential distributors.

Four-walling may even be profitable, particularly if the film is uniquely attractive to a specific local audience. For example, four-walling may do very well when a film is promoted exclusively within a geographic region, to a concentrated religious community, to the local gay and lesbian community, or on a college campus. Other exhibitors will not be able to promote within those communities nearly as effectively as a filmmaker who has created a work geared to that particular audience.

Nontheatrical Commercial Distribution

THEATRICAL DISTRIBUTION IS the goal for almost every filmmaker, but it is not a goal that will be accomplished by most. Moreover, whether or not a film has earned eligibility for the Academy Awards by premiering in theaters, the filmmaker must shape a marketing and distribution strategy that supports the film's continued viability long after the theatrical run has ended.

A. Shaping the Marketing Campaign

Marketing of the final motion picture is every bit as important as the film's content in creating an audience for the picture. Marketing is not a science. Spending $50 million and opening in 3,000 theaters will certainly generate millions of dollars in revenue, but it often generates far less than the print and marketing fees, let alone the film's production costs. In addition, few independent films have the marketing budgets to simply open wide and hard. Instead, the filmmaker must work with the distributor to guide the marketing campaign and build audience interest.

1. Marketing Begins Before Principal Photography

With the rise of social networking Web sites, the marketing for a movie now begins well before principal photography. Film companies must spend considerable time and effort cultivating an audience that will be receptive to a film's release.

Audiences are drawn to films because of subject matter, writers, directors, and cast, and because of affinities based on geographic community, age, race, ethnicity, religion, hobbies, and vocation. The independent film producer should work with the writers and director on the project to identify which of these elements will be emphasized in the marketing of the film, and the corresponding audience communities must be courted as soon as the film company has confidence in its message. For example, San Diego's Comic-Con has become a critical stop for the launch of genre films such as *Star Trek, The Dark Knight,* and *Terminator Salvation.* The online "virtual world" Second Life may become a screening room for films based on video games, graphic novels, and similar content (see chapter 19, p. 339). And religious conventions and communities may be an effective launching pad for films of interest to those groups. Mel Gibson's *The Passion of the Christ* broke new marketing territory by courting religious communities well before the film was finished, encouraging group sales, advance home video purchases, and written praise of the project.

The film company should maintain a Web site with select photographs and stories that emphasize the central marketing elements of the movie. The writers, director, and producer may wish to make selective event appearances to promote those same central elements.

Film companies tend to get caught up in the details of making of the movie, but marketing is about reinforcing the reasons to attend the finished film. Rather than providing a weekly update on principal photography, an e-mail newsletter should focus on reminding the core audience why the forthcoming movie will benefit their community and be worth the wait. Since the film will be available almost everywhere eventually, on DVD if not in theaters, the investment in this audience will be very helpful.

2. What to Sell

The content of the prerelease campaign will probably resemble the content of the Playbill at a Broadway play. It will include information on the cast and crew, a history of the movie's development, and a dramaturgic study of the movie's meaning and impact. The prerelease materials should be accurate, but since they are available to the general public, they should encourage and support the financial investors without becoming part of any financial offering.

There are risks when an independent film company creates a prerelease direct marketing campaign. If the prerelease campaign presents the film poorly, then it may discourage distributors from purchasing it. On the other hand, if thousands of people are signing up for the e-mail newsletter and millions of viewers have watched the trailer on MySpace or YouTube, then the distributors know the film has attracted the audience's interest.

For the independent filmmaker, the primary benefit of a prerelease campaign is the control it provides over the nature of the message. The film *Innerspace* was a broad comedy initially sold as a science fiction thriller. The audience reaction to the movie as a science fiction film was utter disinterest. The film was so unanimously ignored that the distributor actually rereleased the movie with a new campaign focused on its comedic aspect, and the movie finally gained some revenue and credibility.

The filmmaker must know the tone of the film and reflect that tone in the prerelease marketing. Small features on the cast, writers, and director are invariably safe and encourage audience interest. If the story is based on a book, comic book, or video game, then short articles regarding the translation to the big screen generally promote interest. If the story is closely based on a true life story, then material that provides information on that connection is also helpful.

3. What Not to Sell

Prerelease materials must be balanced between revealing so little that they annoy audiences and so much that they make the movie feel old when it is finally released. "Teaser" campaigns that reveal nothing about the film have very short shelf lives, so they should only be used in the weeks leading to the film's release. Similarly, footage from the shoot should rarely be provided. Without color correction and special effects, the scenes may present a far less professional image than that hoped for by the film company, and it would be very expensive to polish the footage sufficiently. Moreover, if the scenes tell too much of the story, then they stop encouraging audiences to come.

Clips of documentary films may be more effective than clips from narrative films at attracting an audience. Documentaries rarely have surprise endings anyway, so clips reflecting aspects of the movie being developed may encourage the audience and perhaps even improve access to individuals who have content relevant to the film. For many documentaries, there is less postproduction work than for narrative films, so the cost of readying clips should also be less.

B. Protecting Academy Award Eligibility

Filmmakers may wish to protect their eligibility for the Academy Awards. It could happen. The Academy of Motion Picture Arts and Sciences requires that to be eligible for the prestigious Oscar, a movie must be a feature film of more than 40 minutes in length, publicly exhibited exclusively for at least seven days for paid admission in a commercial theater in Los Angeles County. The rules are very clear about activities that will make a film ineligible for consideration:

> Films that, in any version, receive their first public exhibition or distribution in any manner other than as a theatrical motion picture release will not be eligible for Academy Awards in any category. (This includes broadcast and cable television as well as home video marketing and Internet transmission.) However, ten minutes or ten percent of the running time of a film, whichever is shorter, is allowed to be shown in a nontheatrical medium prior to the film's theatrical release.[1]

Additional rules regarding theatrical exhibition inside the United States state that previews and festivals do not affect eligibility.[2]

Film companies should be very careful regarding the development of their marketing materials to be sure that any clips posted from the film do not exceed the 10 percent or 10 minute rule. And if the film has an opportunity to play theatrically in Los Angeles, then the Academy Award rules may have an impact on the timing of the nontheatrical distribution strategy.

C. Controlling a Distributor's Campaign

The filmmaker may have no voice in the distributor's marketing campaign unless the distribution agreement provides contractual rights to the filmmaker. Even if the filmmaker initially supplied the one-sheet, the production stills, and the other tools of the marketing campaign, the distributor may still have absolute control.

1. Reviewing the Distributor's Obligations

As described in chapter 17 (p. 304), a healthy distribution agreement is likely to include some key milestone obligations for guaranteed promotion on the part of the distributor. As with every contract, the language in the agreement means little unless those obligations are followed by the parties.

To have confidence in the marketing campaign, the filmmaker should insist that a few key protections in the distribution agreement be carefully documented and the film company regularly updated—at least for the film's initial market (whether that be theatrical, DVD, or something else). A schedule should be provided for the money the distributor must spend on printed materials and advertising for marketing the film. The payments must be for costs exclusive to the film company's film or carefully apportioned among multiple projects being simultaneously marketed. Otherwise, the distributor can simply spend a great deal of money to promote its catalog of films, which includes the filmmaker's project but does not highlight it. The more detailed the type of spending documented, the stronger the filmmaker's confidence will be.

Ideally, the distribution should provide the film company approval rights for all the marketing materials. Since this is seldom granted, the filmmaker should at least be guaranteed the right to consult on all such materials. While consultation serves only as a good-faith gesture, it does obligate the distributor to work more closely with the filmmaker.

2. Following the Plan of Distribution

The distributor and filmmaker should also agree to a written plan for the distribution of the film prior to signing the distribution agreement. Although it would be unreasonable to make such a plan part of the contract, it should serve as the basis for discussion. The marketing plan must be highly opportunistic and therefore quite flexible, but the fundamentals should be explicit. Like any battle plan, the distribution plan will need regular updating as markets outperform or underperform expectations and the strategies are refined. A written plan provides an excellent communications tool for the filmmaker, the cast and crew who have an interest in the film's success, and the investors who are waiting for their returns.

3. Meeting Credit Obligations in Marketing

Negotiations with the film's stars and key personnel may also give rise to contractual obligations regarding the film's marketing efforts. At a minimum, both the filmmaker and any distributors must respect the obligations regarding credit size and placement granted to particular cast and crew members. Additionally, some cast members may have negotiated for picture placement in the marketing campaign. In that case, the filmmaker and distributor must use the photograph of the particular cast member in the posters and marketing material.

If other cast members negotiated "favored nations" provisions in their employment agreements, then they also are entitled to the photo placement. These contracts can severely limit the flexibility of the marketing campaign. If the distributor creates a great campaign that would violate the contractual rights of an actor, then the filmmaker must seek that actor's permission to waive the contractual obligation and use the campaign.

The original contracts for the cast and crew members should have included a provision granting the filmmaker the right to use the person's publicity rights, including name, likeness, voice, and signature, as part of the marketing and packaging of the film. If written permission was not provided, then it should be obtained prior to using any person in the marketing of the film.

D. Marketing Campaign Independence

Distributors generally work by playing the odds. A distributor will "buy" a number of movies and then support only the movie that proves easiest to sell. If one of the movies is bought without any payment of an advance or contractual obligation to spend money, then that film may sit in the distributor's catalog without any marketing effort. If that film begins to gather interest, however, then the distributor will start to actively promote it.

Therefore, the producer or other members of the film company must help promote the film. This may duplicate a small distributor's job, but realistically it will help the filmmaker's film to stand out from the rest of the distributor's catalog. A side benefit is that promotion often promotes the filmmaker as much as her particular film, an angle that is far more valuable to her than to the distributor. On the other hand, the time spent in active promotion pulls the filmmaker away from developing her next motion picture and can easily sidetrack a career.

1. Critics and Festivals

Perhaps the easiest step in the filmmaker's own campaign is garnering positive reviews for the film. She simply needs to screen the film where critics will see it and wait for some of those critics to write strong, laudatory articles about the film. The good news is that some people like brussels sprouts. No matter how quirky or idiosyncratic the film, as long as it is not a technical disaster, there will be some critic out there who will rave about it.

The hardest thing about working as a filmmaker is that the corollary is also true. No matter how brilliant the film, some critics will find it repugnant and many will find it old hat. Criticism goes with the territory. To manage the criticism, the filmmaker should be a bit selective. The less famous film festivals will often generate a good deal of regional press hoping to boost the films on exhibit. These festivals may be useless for attracting a distributor, but quite valuable in drawing a few solid reviews.

If the film is to be shown in a one-newspaper town, the paper's film critic must be invited to the opening. Often critics' reputations for the types of movies they like and dislike are well known, but do not think an unsympathetic critic can be avoided by snubbing him. He is likely to show up anyway—just with a chip on his shoulder. If the local critic has written that he despises gladiator movies, do not premiere the newest gladiator epic there. Unless the opening is national, open in that town after some positive press has been generated elsewhere.

2. Hometown Press

When a local resident makes good, that makes local news. Often the stories are very kind, designed to make everyone feel good about their neighbors. Do not ignore the opportunity. Every bandwagon has to start somewhere, and the lightest piece of hometown fluff will still serve to pad the publicity package. If the article compliments the film itself, then so much the better.

3. Specialty Markets

Independent films often tell stories that speak to small communities rather than the mainstream. Although Spike Lee's *Do the Right Thing* and Steven Spielberg's *Schindler's List* were nationally recognized films, most niche projects fizzle at the box office and as a result do not receive studio financing. Still, independent filmmakers create these movies as powerful testaments to their heritage and culture. Having made such a film, a filmmaker should turn to these communities for its first audience.

This strategy involves both the institutions of a community and the community itself. First, within each self-identified community are organizations that serve as the focus of that community's public outreach. Enthusiastic support from the leadership of these organizations may open doors to mainstream distribution and will certainly enhance media attention. These organizations are typically part of national and international coalitions of similar organizations that share common interests. Letters of introduction from local leadership may expand the potential to reach national boards.

Second, these community organizations may be able to deliver interested audiences for the filmmaker. Particularly for a film in a small platform or four-wall release, a strong, positive endorsement by the local community newsletter or paper will do far more to sell tickets than any paid ad. The filmmaker may even consider encouraging the community group to four-wall the film directly for only a modest fee. Let the local church underwrite the costs of the evening and keep the proceeds as a fundraiser. The filmmaker will have made a modest profit and generate substantial word of mouth regarding the film.

4. Distribute Advance Copies

Nothing tells the story better than the story itself. No one sells the film better than those who believe in it. The filmmaker can combine these two truisms into a powerful marketing tool. Every member of the cast and crew has acquaintances who will be interested in seeing the project. Some of them may be helpful in finding a distributor or soliciting a positive review. While most independent filmmakers offer a copy of the final film on DVD to each member of the cast and crew, most forget that the combined contacts of cast and crew may create a powerful base of people willing to screen the film. Add the investors to this group and the list begins to have some potential as a marketing tool.

Rather than distributing DVDs without introduction, the contact person from the cast and crew should draft a letter that explains why the person is receiving the film and by whom the mailing was initiated. Follow-up information should also be included so that interested recipients can get additional information. At worst, this technique serves as a nice community-building tool within the film company. At best, it may open doors the filmmaker never knew existed.

5. Promoting the Eventual DVD Sales

DVDs and Blu-ray discs of a film are sold to rental outlets such as Blockbuster or Netflix, which offer movies to consumers based on a per-disc rental or a monthly subscription. The rental outlet purchases the discs outright from the distributor and does not pay a royalty based on the number of units rented. Increasingly, DVD direct sales have also become a significant part of the market, with national discounters such as Target, Walmart, Kmart, Amazon, and Sam's Club leading the way. Best Buy and other electronics stores also enjoy a significant share of the market. Children's titles and holiday films do particularly well in the direct-sales market, because they are well-priced gifts and are often purchased on impulse. Blockbusters also have success in this category.

The public gains far greater access to independent films through DVD sales, Netflix, and other Internet venues than through the typical theatrical platform release. This means that the DVD/Blu-ray market is much more critical than the box office to the film's ultimate economic return. The filmmaker should be very focused on the tools available to promote the eventual sales of DVDs well before the film is actually available at the video store.

The two most significant tools are the ratings system of Netflix and the commentary system of the Internet Movie Database (IMDb.com). In both cases, strong ratings and positive comments on the film will make it more visible to others. The filmmaker should encourage everyone who has seen the movie at festivals, in previews, and in the initial release to promote the film as positively as he or she is willing. Following this same strategy, the film company should be using its Web site, e-mail list, or blog to let interested viewers know when the DVD is available for preorders on services such as Amazon or Barnes and Noble. Often, the number of reviews is very small, so a few passionate fans can have a powerful impact on the ratings—and sales—of the films in prerelease.

E. Staging the Nontheatrical Markets

The traditional cycle of film distribution starts with domestic theatrical distribution; approximately six months later the film is released on DVD or other home video media and pay-per-view; then six months following that it is released on premiere cable channels such as HBO or Showtime. After that, the largest films get network broadcast premieres, then free cable screenings. This cycle releases the film in the most expensive markets first. Since theater tickets are the most expensive option for the audience, common wisdom holds that once a film has been made available on HBO the chance for a theatrical release is over. While the logic may be generally sound, for independent films there are opportunities to schedule against the model.

1. Simultaneous Distribution on DVD

Films with small platform releases or four-wall theatrical releases have very modest marketing budgets. The paid advertising and positive film reviews will remain in the audiences' minds for only a short time. Filmmakers utilizing these sorts of theatrical releases are very likely to benefit from DVD distribution staged simultaneously with the platform release. The contractual arrangements for such a strategy will depend greatly on the relationship between the theatrical distributor and the DVD distributor.

If the film is quickly gaining momentum, then the DVD distributor may wish to hold back, hoping that greater box office revenue will increase initial orders by DVD rental and direct-sales companies. For a modestly successful film, however, the opportunity to place more copies in Blockbuster stores will be outweighed by the chance to add "DVD available on Netflix and Amazon" to the bottom of theatrical advertising and to fliers distributed at theaters showing the film.

As filmgoers become accustomed to being able to add interesting movies to their Netflix queues, they will identify which movies they will try to attend in the theater and which movies will end their runs before they can conveniently see them. Since the independent theater circuit does not have a large geographic footprint, filmgoers may prefer to add an independent film to their queues instead of traveling great distances to see it theatrically. For that reason, it may be naive to forgo immediate DVD sales in hopes that the theatrical run will foster breakout demand. If the demand does grow, the contract with DVD rental and direct-sales companies should enable them to add additional copies and carry the film in additional stores.

While the simultaneous distribution strategy has not been widely adopted yet, the economics suggest that it will eventually extend throughout the film industry.

2. Cable Premiere as Catalyst

Short distribution windows can create a momentum of their own. Disney regularly cycles its classic animated films on and off of television and in and out of stores, so that every showing is a new premiere. (Because these films are directed at younger viewers, a large part of the audience changes every five years, and the youngest viewers have never before been exposed to the work.) Similarly, a short "premiere" on HBO or Showtime creates tremendous exposure, but that exposure may not destroy the film's marketability in smaller art house theaters around the country.

Less than half the potential audience will be exposed to the film if it premieres on a single premium cable channel. Therefore, there may be a significant number of viewers willing to pay theater prices to see the film, and those viewers will be exposed to considerably more marketing as a result of the film's brief television appearance than if it had gone directly into limited theatrical release. Of course, such a distribution scheme requires the consent of the television network and the theatrical exhibitors that primarily show new releases, but for the right movie, it is a viable alternative.

One unfortunate consequence is that the film loses its eligibility for Academy Award consideration. As mentioned earlier in the chapter, to be eligible for the Oscars, the film must play for at least one week in Los Angeles County theaters before being distributed in any other medium.

3. PBS

Like the premium cable networks, Public Broadcasting Service stations show movies unedited and uninterrupted. Each public television station purchases its contents individually, however, which creates two separate PBS markets for the filmmaker. First, the filmmaker may be able to sell the film to the production companies that create or buy content for use on the PBS stations, such as *Nova, National Geographic,* or *Great Performances.* The filmmaker's work may sometimes be appropriate as content packaged for such a series—particularly if it is a documentary. Second, the filmmaker may license the work to any particular PBS station. This creates hundreds of possible sales, and the PBS stations can work like the premium cable stations to promote the film and expose it to a potential theatrical audience.

4. 16mm Format and DVD Community Showings

Although community showings are becoming less common, they remain unique opportunities to screen independent films. In these showings, the 16mm format is increasingly being replaced by DVDs and projection TVs. The DVDs are specially marked to designate that their license extends beyond private home viewing and they may be used for public performances under license. Smaller projectors allow films to be shown in organization-sponsored events and school-hosted screenings. Screenings are typically licensed through specialty distributors who control the public performance rights of the films exclusively in these formats. For the appropriate content, this market may create a great deal of interest and could lead to a cult following.

F. Direct to DVD Without Theatrical Distribution

Ultimately, most independent films must forgo theatrical exhibition and move directly into DVD and Blu-ray distribution. Given this reality, makers of very low-budget films may consider avoiding the costs associated with producing a film of sufficient image quality that it could be shown theatrically. A direct-to-video project can be made for a few thousand dollars, even while following most of the legal guidelines identified throughout this book, and can sometimes be highly profitable.

Independent films may fit well within this marketing strategy if the content compares to the other types of films sold successfully. An independent filmmaker's retelling of *Pinocchio* may or may not garner a theatrical distributor, but it will likely generate some interest from home video retailers.

Unfortunately, the home video market may become more difficult as distribution moves from physical discs to downloads using desktop devices. Netflix and Blockbuster both have direct-to-TV devices while Sony and Microsoft have enabled such services through their video game systems. The ability for consumers to easily find less-famous movies on these systems will depend on the navigation and recommendation algorithms used by each system. The good news is that the distributors tend to keep a larger portion of the profits from sales via these systems, so the filmmaker may be able to recoup more money on fewer sales.

For most independent filmmakers, success should be measured as it is for fighter pilots. A successful landing, or feature film, is any project you can walk away from. If DVD sales allow the filmmaker to recoup all costs while sharing the story with the audience, he has outperformed most in the field.

G. Back to Video with the Director's Cut and Unrated Versions

As a marketing method for getting attention for DVD and Blu-ray sales and rentals, distributors have taken to rereleasing films as unrated versions, extended editions, or so-called director's cuts. In some cases, these are significantly different movies with dramatically longer running time or additional adult content. In many situations, however, these are modestly edited versions intended merely to add "New and Improved" to a product's label.

The strategy works. Director's cuts sometimes generate additional reviews or new-release press coverage, helping to publicize the film's availability and boost sales. "Uncensored" versions of risqué movies tend to sell well and promote both versions of the film.

Contractually, the alternate cuts should not be treated as new films and should not require new payments to the various parties involved in the project. Instead, they count toward any royalty or residual obligations. Some care should be taken, however, to ensure that the film company has control over the distributor's use of this technique and that any marketing is accurate. If the distributor wishes to release a director's cut, the version released should have been prepared by the director, or at a minimum, have the approval of the director. If an unrated version featuring nudity is released, the filmmaker must have either had nudity releases from the cast members involved or obtain such clearances before the film is rereleased.

H. Additional Revenue Sources

For films that have been successfully distributed, additional revenue opportunities may present themselves. For all additional sources, the filmmaker must be sure to have secured the legal rights to the film's marketing materials for such uses. This means signing contracts with the creators of those materials to cover not only the film in every media but also all products related to the film. If the distributor of the film created the marketing materials, then the distribution agreement should include a license to use those materials in distribution markets not controlled by that distributor—and in all potential product markets.

1. Novelizations

While many films derive from novels or short stories, the story as told in the film often makes for good reading as well. As a result, films are increasingly the source for new novels. Assuming the film company properly purchased all the elements of the story, no additional contracts are necessary to create the novel of the film. Many screenwriters view the novelization as an opportunity to maintain control of the story, and they may seek the right to be the writer of the novel if they so choose. (This is referred to as a *right of first refusal;* the filmmaker is obligated to ask the screenwriter before asking anyone else.)

One compromise on the awarding of the right of first refusal to the screenwriter is to condition the grant on the screenwriter receiving sole screen credit, pursuant to the film's credit dispute policy. In this way, a single screenwriter who truly wrote and controlled the story will receive that same opportunity with regard to the novel, while screenwriters who may have contributed to the story in a less exclusive way can be politely told no. Of course, the filmmaker can still offer the opportunity to write the novel to one of the screenwriters who received shared credit, but there would no longer be a contractual obligation to do so.

The novelization rights will be sold to a publishing house, which will typically distribute the novel only in a mass-market paperback or trade paperback edition. If the film is an original story, and a particularly compelling one literarily speaking, the filmmaker may seek to use the novel to promote a theatrical distribution deal.

2. Merchandizing and Licensing

Perhaps the biggest windfall for motion pictures today is the merchandise tie-in. *Star Wars* (perhaps the largest-budget independent film ever created) spawned an empire of toys, games, dolls, and paraphernalia that now spans three decades. Like the creation of the soundtrack album (see chapter 14, p. 260), the key to merchandizing is control of the necessary elements. First, the filmmaker must control the marketing rights to the title, artwork, and photographs used to promote the movie. Second, the filmmaker or the product manufacturer must license the publicity rights of the actors.

An action figure cannot be created using the likeness of an actor without that actor's express permission. While these publicity rights are typically assigned to the film company for the ability to make and market the film, that contract would not cover dolls or games. These items must be separately licensed, and the actors will generally receive a small royalty or profit participation from these agreements.

Even a small film is likely to develop posters and T-shirts. These items are certainly popular among the cast and crew, but they might develop some market interest. The popularity of these items has as much to do with the cast or the artwork as it does with the film, so it should be treated as a slightly different business opportunity from the film itself. The sale of these items is not covered by the actors' publicity rights provisions in their employment agreement, so additional permission will be required.

3. Story Rights

Finally, the filmmaker may sell the story itself. It is no longer uncommon for Hollywood to remake movies that are still available on videotape and played often on television. *Planet of the Apes* and *Rambo* illustrate the temptation to remake a film that continued to be popular in its original incarnation. In addition, filmmakers are often haunted by the difficult choices imposed by very low-budget filmmaking and may wish to revisit the material later in their careers.

Story rights may include simple remakes or provide for the expansion of the original story through sequels, prequels, and spin-offs. Sequels are not limited to action stories like *Star Wars* or characters like James Bond. Children's characters naturally lend themselves to multiple adventures. Character-driven stories such as *Terms of Endearment, The Godfather,* and *Chinatown* opened the door for continuing sagas.

The ability to exploit the story rights in new projects brings the legal analysis full circle to the beginning of the book: The ability to create these works will depend on what rights were initially purchased, which entities own the rights, and how the financing was structured. The filmmaker should have made these original choices with an eye toward the film being produced and the future stories yet to be told. By controlling these rights, the filmmaker can increase the chances that she will continue participating in the lives of the characters she created and nourished throughout the filmmaking process.

Self-Distribution and Self-Promotion

↓

ALMOST CONSTANTLY THROUGHOUT the fundraising, preproduction and principal photography phases of a project, independent filmmakers will be asked what happens if the film fails to find a distributor. Given today's technology, filmmakers never again need to store their film stock in their parents' garage and give up. Some of the self-distribution strategies now available may result in substantial sales and opportunities for new projects. In fact, all of the theatrical and nontheatrical distribution strategies available to distributors are available to the film company if it wishes to self-distribute.

This chapter highlights the most important strategies for self-distribution, and outlines particular uses of new technologies that help to maximize a low-budget or self-directed distribution plan. Even if an indie distributor is working to distribute and promote the film, many of these steps will help the campaign and give the filmmaker an important role in the process.

A. Introduction to Self-Distribution

Just as technology has transformed self-published literature from the world of vanity press into a viable commercial alternative, it has turned self-distribution into a legitimate commercial choice independent filmmakers should consider seriously. As the filmmaker shops the film to distributors, he must weigh these companies' offers against the potential to achieve nearly the same results on his own.

1. When to Self-Distribute

The benefits of self-distributing are improved compensation, concentration, and control. The filmmaker who chooses this option does not have to give a substantial percentage of his revenue to a distributor that invests little time or personal effort on the film. The downside is little support from other professionals and no additional marketing budget. The opportunities open to self-distributors are often very modest strategies—strategies unlikely to interest distributors interested in quick returns. Finally, the filmmaker can avoid having to compromise with the distributor regarding the distribution strategies or messages of the film. While the filmmaker may be forgoing broader distribution and greater gross revenue, these considerations should be weighed carefully before deciding to go with a distributor.

The self-distribution alternative becomes most attractive when the distributor's offer provides no advance, no guarantee of a marketing and promotion budget, and no rights of approval or consultation regarding the marketing campaign. If the distributor is unwilling to commit on these three points, then self-distribution may be a sound alternative. The largest downside to self-distribution in this situation is that it requires the filmmaker to devote substantial time and effort to the distribution of the film rather than to the development of new projects.

2. Quasi-Self-Distribution: Two Models

For the film company that has received no offers to distribute the film or only offers with unacceptably weak commitments on the part of the distributor, there are two strategies that will allow both the movie and the filmmaker to move forward.

The filmmaker may choose to employ a "film placement executive." Working part-time as an independent contractor, and earning a percentage of the grosses from the film's sales, this person would be provided with posters and other promotional materials, detailed strategies regarding the distribution plan for the film, and the authority to act on behalf of the film company in distributing the movie in various markets and media. The contract may specify that prior approval from the film company is required for premium cable, cable, or broadcast television sales. As a practical matter, the film placement executive may be one of the former production assistants on the film who is willing to devote some time and effort to making calls, sending e-mails, developing Web materials, and continuing to encourage the viewership of the film.

The filmmaker may also choose to create a separate company devoted to distributing the film. This new distribution company would be particularly effective if it could operate on behalf of a number of similarly situated colleagues. For example, if the filmmaker became familiar with a group of other filmmakers while participating in the festival circuit during the initial attempt to promote the film, he might want to solicit their interest in a collaborative approach to distribution. If each filmmaker in the group was willing to provide the distribution rights and a small amount of funding, then the new company could support all of their efforts. The filmmakers themselves could even take on different roles within the company: one could be in charge of DVD distribution, another could build a YouTube and MySpace strategy, a third could work to promote college campus releases, and so on. Particularly if the groups' films complemented one another, this arrangement would help foster an artistic and commercial community.

3. Initial Steps for the Self-Distributor

One of the harder aspects of self-distribution is the obligation to undertake the distribution effort as if the film being distributed is someone else's work. The filmmaker cannot return to the film to tinker with the editing or music. During the distribution cycle, everything must be done as if the film is owned by a third party.

The steps for self-distribution are essentially the same as those the film company would expect from an outside distributor:

1. Prepare a strong press kit with log line and synopsis, photographs, and background information on the story and the writers, director, and cast; include any positive reviews; and have video clips available.
2. Contact theaters and chains that specialize in independent films to explore a theatrical release. Concentrate on theaters in the film-

maker's hometown and theaters located in communities particu-
larly interested in the film—urban communities for an urban film,
San Francisco or St. Paul for gay and lesbian films, New York and
Los Angeles for Jewish or Israeli films, etc.

3. Consider running a four-wall theatrical opening if you can guarantee some press attendance and a hometown or supportive local
audience who will ensure that the event at least breaks even. This
official opening will help considerably with the investors, cast,
crew, and supporters, who can see their hard work on the silver
screen in front of a paying audience. Particularly off-season, such
openings should be relatively inexpensive and can be quite a
boost to the film. Moreover, if the film screens theatrically for a
week in Los Angeles, it will be eligible for an Oscar (see chapter
18, p. 314).

4. Develop a strategy for packaging the DVD, including the artwork
and credits on the front and back of the DVD package. Determine
the pricing for a modest-sized print run, including the costs for
copies to give to the many individuals who supported the making
of the film.

5. Update the press kit and approach the major buyers of DVDs,
including regional discount retailers, Blockbuster, and Netflix.

6. Continue to work the film markets to meet with international sales
agents. If the film company is having no luck with paid distribution, then selling foreign markets in any media will bolster the
potential for the film to grow in the marketplace and encourage
later U.S. sales.

These steps may prove time-consuming, but they represent the essential steps for preparing the film for market. Most of the revenue for self-
distribution, however, will come not from a limited theatrical run but from
the new opportunities for self-promotion described below.

B. Internal Networking

When selling the film on DVD and Blu-ray or promoting it on various Internet download services, the most important job of the distribution company

is marketing. For an independent film, this means providing the fans of the film with information that they can use to encourage others to seek it out. Hopefully, if enough individuals become interested, it will create a "buzz" that results in an exponential growth in interest. Even if the buzz does not grow so large that the film is covered in *Entertainment Weekly* or the *Wall Street Journal*, there are steps the film company can take to help generate ongoing sales.

The most important people for the sale of the film are the people already committed to its success. The film company will give a DVD of the film to each member of the cast and crew, to the investors, and to the various individuals or businesses that provided locations or significant props. The film company should take a second step and offer bulk-rate discounts to any of these parties who might be interested in reselling the DVDs. For example, if stores at which the film was shot carry copies of the film, consumers interested in supporting their local store will be introduced to the title.

Similarly, all the cast and crew members should be encouraged to promote the film through their personal blogs, Web sites, and e-mail lists. If the film company's order fulfillment process can either track referring Web sites or just include a simple box that asks, "How did you hear about us?" the film company can share a portion of the sales income with the party that referred the purchase or download.

The film company may wish to send out regular marketing updates to the fans on its e-mail list, providing them with the latest information regarding the best places to obtain the film and word on new reviews or other positive promotional activities. A day in advance of sending an update to fans, forward a prerelease copy to the film's cast and crew so they can update their own e-mail lists, Web sites, and blogs. In addition, the film company will gain friends if it mentions the future success of its cast and crew as part of these news updates. Nothing can reintroduce an obscure film faster than the sudden fame of its star.

C. Introduction to Digital Distribution

Since the first edition of this book was published in 2002, its observations regarding the Internet have largely become outdated. Likewise, this second edition, written in 2008, describes practices that are likely to disappear within a few years, and probably fails to anticipate the developments that will shape the future of motion picture distribution in new media. Despite this risk, these sections will attempt to describe new methods for thinking about the relationship between the filmmaker and the audience. Some of the strategies described below may survive beyond the particular Web sites or companies that pioneered them. As technology improves and new companies enter the market, they can be updated to take advantage of the new technologies and build further on the important direct relationship between the film company and its viewers.

1. Methods of Distribution

Netflix redefined "digital distribution" when it began providing DVDs through the mail. Today, digital distribution refers to films delivered by a variety of Web-facilitated methods, but the content remains somewhat limited:

- conventional delivery of physical products rented or purchased over the Internet from retailers such as Amazon, Netflix, Walmart, or Best Buy
- direct download of content to computers, via systems such as Netflix, Hulu, MySpace, or YouTube
- download to computers and portable devices via systems such as iTunes, Sony Playstation, and most cellular telephone carriers
- download from kiosks in which the user inserts a USB drive and selects the content; the drive is then inserted into a computer or television set-top box
- download to digital set-top boxes using systems such as Roku/Netflix, Internet-equipped Blu-ray players, Microsoft Xbox 360, and Sony Playstation

An increasing amount of content is available for computer desktop and laptop viewing. Although older distribution agreements may not cover such a method of distribution, most modern film distribution agreements are drafted very broadly and pose no legal restrictions on such distribution.

The amount of content provided in this manner will only increase. Improved bandwidth and compression technology are enabling the migration from the computer to the television to occur with increasing speed.

The ability of video game systems to operate as distribution channels will add significantly to the number of devices that bridge the gap between computer systems and TVs. It may become increasingly common for consumers to replace smaller televisions with computer screens, to watch content on their computer instead of on cable or via an over-the-air television broadcast.

2. Access to the Public

Many of the digital distribution methods are quite open to user-generated content. At a certain point in the distribution cycle, or in those situations in which no distribution cycle ever gets off the ground, the film company could choose to stream the entire film directly from its Web site. Short segments of the film can be made publicly available on MySpace and YouTube. DVDs can be distributed through Amazon and its affiliated companies. As a result, the modern film company can always reach the public.

In most cases, these various strategies do not require exclusive agreements. This allows the film company or distributor to place video clips on a wide variety of sites, make DVDs available through multiple direct-sales companies, and work to make the film available on every platform from which content is regularly downloaded. The potential audience has more opportunities to access content than ever before.

3. The Challenge of Monetization

There is an important difference, however, between having access to content and buying content. While audiences generally prefer professionally made content to homemade video, there is not yet a significant shift in the payment for films. Theatrical ticket sales and DVD sales/rentals account for the vast percentage of motion picture revenue. Paid downloads represent only a small portion of the marketplace. It will continue to grow quickly, but it will not grow as fast as music downloads did in comparison to CD sales.

Very few Web sites pay filmmakers for downloadable content. A small number provide filmmakers with a portion of the advertising revenue associated with the download of the content. For most independent films, this revenue will reflect only a tiny fraction of their production budget. The real challenge for digital distribution is finding a model that pays any significant returns.

D. Selling It Online

Since most of the download strategies do not pay significant revenues at present, the best solution for self-distribution is for the film company to sell the film itself. Once a film is released on DVD, the film company's Web site should always have it available for purchase. The company can choose whether to refer the purchaser to a commercial Web site like Amazon.com or incorporate an online store function directly into the film site's software. This section outlines the logistics involved in these and other online sales opportunities.

1. Fulfillment Services

A fulfillment service provides a range of services, from pressing discs and printing packaging to full-service order control and customer shipping. Larger companies such as Technicolor and Deluxe have the capacity to handle millions of units of a particular movie. Other companies are much smaller but have the ability to provide the "back end" framework of the film company's online store. This allows consumers to purchase the DVD directly from the Web site for the movie.

In today's digital environment, producers of books, software, CDs, and movies can provide small-volume print-on-demand services for cost-per-unit prices that historically would have been available only for print runs of at least a thousand copies. For digital media, a print-on-demand order may consist of the burning of a DVD just as it would be burned using a computer hard drive. The disc then has a label printed on the other side to complete the process. In contrast, large-volume orders are pressed rather than burned. A pressing places the content of the media in the mechanical process as one of the physical elements, along with the plastic, aluminum, and lacquer of the disc. The aluminum image is formed with the content etched into it from the beginning rather than being modified through a laser burning process.

For the consumer, there is no appreciable difference between discs that were pressed and those that were burned in smaller lots. There may, however, be considerable financial benefit to producing small numbers of discs until the sales demand greater volume. Even at $5.00 per unit, a 1,000 minimum means that the first run of DVDs costs $5,000 (and the minimum orders for pressed discs are substantially higher than 1,000). Small-order fulfillment may increase the price per unit considerably, but eliminating large minimums may still make for better value and allow a return to be earned much sooner.

2. Video-on-Demand from the Web

There are a large number of sites on the Internet that allow content creators to upload video for users to download. The market for sale of downloaded videos over the Internet is presently dominated by iTunes. The iTunes strategy, however, emphasizes commercial content primarily distributed through only the largest and most successful of theatrical distributors. The service includes films from Lionsgate, Disney (with subsidiaries Touchstone and Miramax), Warner Bros., Paramount, Universal, and Sony. The actual range of distributors available may be somewhat larger, but at the time of publication, none had developed an independent film distribution strategy via iTunes. Such a strategy would likely entail the creation of an independent distribution umbrella company into which the smaller distributors could submit content for a fee. Until this occurs, however, the largest of Internet distributors is simply unavailable for independent films, particularly those without significant distribution.

Other video sites, such as GreenCine, host both features and shorts. GreenCine provides an alternative to Netflix, providing both a video-on-demand feature and a direct mail program. EZTakes uses a model by which users download movies to DVD themselves. None of these companies compare to the distribution size of Netflix or Blockbuster, but each commands a portion of the market. The various feature length video sites tend to pay a portion of the proceeds to the film company. The agreements tend to provide 50 percent royalties, but they vary considerably from company to company.

On the assumption that audience members do not comparison shop among the various Web sites, a filmmaker may elect to make the movie available to each of the sites. Almost none of the sites insist on exclusive distribution. The film company's Web site should highlight the company that provides the highest percentage royalties and most appropriate pricing. In this way, the film will be available to as large an audience as possible, but any traffic generated by the film company will be directed to the download services that maximize the film company's revenue.

3. Amazon's CreateSpace

Amazon.com continues to attempt to corner the market on online sales and physical distribution. The company's growth strategy provides an impressive opportunity for self-distributing filmmakers. Through its print-on-demand subsidiary CreateSpace.com, Amazon provides full DVD duplication services, packaging services, and UPC bar code labeling (see the next subsection) at costs that compare quite favorably to other DVD fulfillment houses.

CreateSpace and Amazon also provide for Web sales of the products. The DVDs will be sold directly through Amazon.com, and the film company can also sell them through a CreateSpace online store. Though the financial particulars are likely to change, when a film company currently sells a DVD through the online store, the DVD sells for the list price determined by the seller, from which CreateSpace deducts a $4.95 fulfillment price and a 15 percent royalty. Under this model, a movie retailing for $25.00 would earn the film company $16.30, with CreateSpace earning $4.95 in manufacturing revenue and $3.75 in sales royalties. Amazon also operates Unbox, a video download service, which provides a 50 percent royalty on sales and rentals of downloaded films.

Whether the film company chooses to sell through Amazon or through a DVD fulfillment house, the direct revenue it earns through these ventures is likely to be considerably higher than the traditionally small sales the company would have earned had the DVDs been sold through a small nontheatrical distributor.

There are a number of other Web sites that provide retail film sales. These sites charge the filmmaker relatively low fees and commissions to host the film, but the costs may add up rather quickly. Moreover, these sites may not generate many sales. It is often quite hard to really know whether these sites have strong traffic and should be reviewed carefully before the film company provides money to these sites.

4. UPC Codes

Regardless of how the film company chooses to distribute the DVDs, it is important that the film have a UPC (Universal Product Code)—a bar code that allows the sales to be tracked. Particularly if the sales grow and some of the copies begin to be sold in retail stores, having the UPC is important. The UPC is a 12-digit number and a corresponding box of black lines that can be read by product scanners.

The UPC may be purchased through a number of resellers. Some fulfill-ment services will include the UPC in the pricing, while others will require the film company provide its own UPC number. Because the organization that manages the UPC system, GS1 US (formerly the Uniform Code Coun-cil), sells bar code numbers in bulk, the cost to obtain bar codes from the company are higher than the cost of purchasing through resellers.

The first few digits of the bar code designate the company that sells the product. When a bar code is purchased from a reseller, it is the reseller that is designated as the originating company. When the DVD is manufactured by Amazon, it is Amazon that is designated. If the film company wants to sell the discs in Walmart and Kroger stores, those stores require a certifi-cate confirming that the company information embedded in the DVD's UPC is the company information for the distributor. They will not sell products with UPC codes that have been purchased from UPC resellers. As a result, film companies wishing to sell to these retailers would need to take the extra step and purchase the UPC directly from GS1 US.

If the film company is using a print-on-demand service to sell a DVD that was originally pressed by a different distributor, it will not be able to use the original bar code number for new copies manufactured by burn-ing the DVDs. The pressing process and burning process are sufficiently different that under the GS1 US rules and retailers' policies, these prod-ucts would need separate bar codes.

E. Exploiting the Web Beyond Direct Sales

In addition to selling the DVD directly (or through Amazon downloads), there are other online strategies that might increase the potential for sales and expand the audience of the film. All of these strategies should be seen as part of a more general campaign, building on the direct-sales efforts through the film company's Web site and Amazon.com.

1. eBay Rights Auction

On occasion, filmmakers use the online auction house eBay.com to sell the rights to distribute their films. The site cannot be used to sell ownership in the film company, because such a listing would constitute a public sale of securities and violate state and federal copyright laws. Selling the exclu-sive distributions rights is not the sale of a security. The distribution rights are a copyright license, and therefore the method is legal. However, unless the film was made on an extremely low budget and the filmmaker is very lucky regarding the auction, it is quite unlikely that such a strategy will do much good. There have been limited exceptions, but distributors need to see a film before they will consider buying it, and the bidders need to be ready to commit to the movie for such a strategy to work.

In contrast to selling the distribution rights or film company shares, using eBay as an outlet to sell copies of the DVD makes perfect sense. People shopping on eBay are looking for bargains, and if the film company's DVD comes up, it may attract potential viewers. It also provides another low-cost distribution channel with the additional benefit that the potential audience is different from the audience that regularly logs on to video sites.

2. Film Company Web Site: Public Performances

As mentioned earlier, an actively maintained Web site is an essential tool for every film actively being sold. If the film is in limited theatrical release, the site should provide the schedule and locations. If the film is in a limited public performance run of community organizations, colleges, or similar public venues, then not only should these screenings be listed but the Web site should also include the information necessary to help a person running a community organization book the movie for that organization. This information should include:

- a press kit and supporting materials related to that community's interests
- pricing information
- information on the formats available for their distribution, such as DVD, 16mm, 35mm, VHS, or one-inch videotape
- any unavailable markets in which the film has already been exclusively distributed

Armed with this information, the person interested in the booking can decide rather quickly whether the film meets her organization's programmatic and logistical needs.

3. Informational Web Sites

The Internet is home to a great number of Web sites that talk about films. Many of these allow the public to provide information about specific movies. The film company should take advantage of this and actively post information about its own movie. In particular, the company should be sure the film is properly listed on the Internet Movie Database (IMDb.com), a powerful search engine that provides detailed cast and crew information.

All postings about the film should include links back to the film company's Web site. The number of external links pointing to a Web site is one of the primary methods of gauging the popularity of that site, so the more people link to the film company's site, the higher it will appear in Google and Yahoo searches, and the more visible the film will become. At a minimum, the filmmaker himself should make every effort to link to the site, but he can also ask cast, crew, and other supporters of the film to post links, further improving the film's visibility.

4. Social Networking

Social networking has become a powerful online tool, connecting professionals on sites such as LinkedIn or friends on sites like Facebook and MySpace. The film company should create accounts on each of the major social networks to help encourage interest in the film and build an e-mail list of potential viewers. A sizable social network for the film may help attract distributors, and the community will be an excellent way to promote sales and rentals of the DVDs.

There are also a large number of sites on the Internet, most notably YouTube, that allow members of their communities to upload videos for other users to watch. Even some of the social networking sites, including Facebook and MySpace, support video uploads, so the film company can post content and link it to the accounts of the cast and crew and the film company. Most video sites prefer that only shorts are posted. YouTube, for example, limits the length to 10 minutes. Because such sites combine the audience-gathering power of social networks and the ability for the filmmaker to directly control the content posted, they have become a critical part of independent film distribution, and will only grow to play a larger role as the networks continue to expand.

5. Virtual Worlds

Virtual worlds are online communities based in graphical environments that look like video games, where users create characters called *avatars* to interact with other members. Environments range from fantasy realms to settings that closely mirror the real world. Virtual worlds such as Second

Life reflect what will eventually become a primary site for commercial, educational, and social activity on the Internet. These sites are still in their formative phase, but they foster a great deal of experimentation.

Virtual worlds may have the ability to show video in environments that look much like movie theaters or arenas. The viewers can interact among themselves using their avatars, giving friends in different physical locations the ability to watch a movie together, whisper or text to each other during the screening, and then discuss the film when it is over. The virtual worlds will eventually present the opportunity to monetize these events, enabling exhibitors to sell tickets to the virtual screenings and distributing their earnings. This possibility has not developed in any commercially relevant manner yet, but it is a trend for which independent filmmakers should be prepared. Given the importance of social networking Web sites and the highly visual nature of film, it is only a matter of time before virtual worlds grow to become a significant part of film distribution.

F. Return of the Cliff-Hanger: Webisodes

The Internet has reshaped the music industry and will do the same to both television and motion pictures. In recognition that much of the content on the Internet is transmitted in shorter segments of two to six minutes, television companies have already begun producing "webisodes" of this length to distribute over the Web. These webisodes complement existing programming and increasingly will replace it. For example, animated webisodes have been released to maintain interest in the *Iron Man* comics franchise, and *Star Wars* animated shorts were released between feature films.

Webisodes are reintroducing an old dramatic form. During the 1940s and 1950s, cliff-hangers were the very popular shorts presented before feature films. Saturday-morning audiences would come to see their favorite characters struggle through chases, crashes, and other life-threatening situations—but each short would end in the middle of just such a crisis. The open-ended conclusion kept the kids wanting to come back the following week. Eventually, however, these shorts lost ground to the weekly television episode and were dropped from theatrical bills.

Webisodes return to the cliff-hanger formula, and may constitute an alternate manner for a filmmaker to tell a story. In some cases, a previously completed film can appropriately be edited into a series of 20 six-minute episodes. At the end of each episode, the filmmaker appends the Web address for the film and a short ad encouraging the viewer to buy the DVD. Webisodes may also be an opportunity to further develop the story of the film, providing additional content that explores the backstory of the main characters, side stories relating to minor characters, or mini-sequels that keep the characters and central themes of the movie in front of the audience.

Webisodes may begin to replace independent filmmaking. Shooting a two- to six-minute movie requires far less time and effort than a feature length film. At the same time, telling a complete and fulfilling story in six minutes is more challenging than doing so in two hours. The short will not generate significant revenue, but a series of such shorts can provide filmmakers with a sample reel to help open doors.

Ultimately, webisodes are a different art form than feature length filmmaking. But, hopefully, each medium will help improve the other.

P A R T

Appendixes

Format for the Feature Screenplay

FOR THE NON-WRITER, a brief guide to the screenplay format may be useful. The American motion picture screenplay format differs from its British counterpart and from the television equivalent in small but important ways. Although the rules are quite specific, they are also quite easy to follow.

The text of a screenplay should be in 12-point Courier, Courier New, or an equivalent monospace typewriter font. Most script doctors strongly recommend never using bold or underlining for textual emphasis.

For margins, different sources provide slightly different recommendations. The following guidelines are based on David Trottier's suggestions in his book *The Screenwriter's Bible,* with some small alterations:

Page Margins
- Left and right: 1.25 inches from edge
- Top and bottom: 1 inch from edge

Margins of Screenplay Elements
- Scene header: 1.5 inches from left edge
- Scene description/action: 1.5 inches from left edge
- Character name: 3.7 inches from left edge
- Dialogue: 3.5-inch-wide block beginning 2.5 inches from left edge
- Parentheticals: 3.1 inches from left edge

The format and content of each of these elements is described below.

1. Scene Header

Each scene begins with a line in all capital letters, aligned on the left, that has three components. First, the header indicates whether the scene is an interior or an exterior, written as "INT." or "EXT." Second, the location of the scene is presented. The name of each location should be sufficiently clear and consistent so that all designers know where and in which room the action takes place. Finally, after two hyphens, the time element of the scene is given. This may be as simple as "MORNING," "NOON," "DUSK," or "NIGHT," or if it is necessary for the script, the actual time can be indicated, as in "6:25 A.M." The scene header looks like this:

    INT. TONY'S BEDROOM--NIGHT

The scene header is also where information such as the camera's point of view ("P.O.V.") or camera angle would be written. Such camera instructions should be used sparingly, if at all, in a screenplay prior to preparation of a shooting script.

A new scene should be used whenever the action moves to a new location or specifies a change in camera setup.

2. Scene Description and Action

Descriptive paragraphs lay out the action and the location of each scene. Film is a visual medium, so the descriptions are often more important than the dialogue. However, they are only a guide for the production designer and art director. The writer must find a balance between descriptiveness and brevity, while keeping in mind that the length of the paragraph will indicate the length of the shot.

These paragraphs should be left justified. Each character's name should be capitalized the first time it appears in a screenplay. Important sound information should also be capitalized, such as "GUNSHOTS ring out." Here's a typical example:

```
TONY stands in front of his dresser. He begins to get
dressed, pausing to clasp the chain around his neck.
Carefully, he dons his plain white shirt, then ties the
black obi to hold it in place. SHANE walks into the
room, knocking as he enters.
```

3. Dialogue

The name of the character speaking should be in all capital letters. Immediately below the name, place any "stage directions," in parentheses. These stage directions, or *parentheticals,* should be used only when the action and the dialogue do not suggest the emotion or intent of the text. Besides, almost no actor has ever admitted to following the parentheticals.

The actual dialogue is written in paragraphs with extra-narrow margins. If the same character continues to speak after another block of scene description, the parenthetical "(CONT.)"—for "continued"—should accompany the character's name before the next block of dialogue.

Here is another scene from the film script:

```
INT. TONY'S KARATE SCHOOL--LATE MORNING


Tony stands inside a large karate studio. From the top
of the ceiling hang "Grand Opening" banners. Half a
dozen karate instructors, men and women wearing karate
dress similar to Tony's, stand near the doorway,
waiting. Shane and MARY stand with Tony as 25 or 30
spectators watch.


                    SHANE
          Let's get this show on the road. I
          know this is a newsworthy event and
          all, but this isn't the only news
          that's fit to print.
```

TONY

Okay. I think we're ready.

Tony bows to the karate instructors. They bow in return, then kneel in a straight row in front of the rest of the audience, watching Tony.

TONY (CONT.)

Ladies and gentlemen, thank you very much for coming today for the opening of my fifth studio. What we do here is both art and sport, dedicated to discipline, strength, and endurance.

4. Editing Cues

The last technical element in the script is an editing cue, which may be included at the end of a scene. Editing cues include "CUT TO," "DISSOLVE TO," or "FADE OUT." Such cues should also be used sparingly, and editing choices left to the film's director, director of photography, or editor. Occasionally, however, a cue will be necessary to explain the transition between scenes. Editing cues should be in all capital letters, justified right. If they indicate a jump to another scene, they should be followed by a colon.

An editing cue looks like this:

DISSOLVE TO:

The four elements described above highlight the mechanical requirements of the screenplay. There is no other magic to the mechanics of script writing. The writer simply needs tremendous literary and visual creativity, the ability to tell a story, and a strong, interesting point of view.

5. Additional Tricks and Techniques

In addition to proper screenplay format, there are a number of even more minute details that make a script seem professional and mainstream. Since most investors and producers are looking for reasons not to get involved with a particular project, it is important to avoid the small problems that give rise to such excuses. One of these issues is the method of binding a screenplay. Each script should be three-hole punched and held together with No. 5 brass brads. This is not the best way to keep a script in good condition, but it remains the proper etiquette. An even more sophisticated variation is to eliminate the center hole and brad, binding the script with two brads only.

Another point of etiquette is the cover page. The cover should be the same white bond paper as the rest of the script. The title should be in normal, 12 point type, centered on the upper third of the page. The phrase "screenplay by" and the name of the author can be centered under the title. However, etiquette is giving way to desktop publishing on the matter of title size. While larger titles are not considered proper form, they are no longer considered distasteful, and since the large type size attracts attention, many scripts are beginning to use larger titles.

Finally, know the difference between a preliminary draft and a shooting draft of the script. The shooting draft includes scene numbers, camera instructions, indications when a scene continues on the next page, and certain other details that do not belong in a script until much further into the production process. Do not write the script in shooting draft format until you are preparing for principal photography.

APPENDIX

Library of Congress
Copyright Circulars

↓

1. Circular 45 (Excerpts): Copyright Registration for Motion Pictures, Including Video Recordings

General Information

Statutory Definition

Motion pictures are *audiovisual works* consisting of a series of related images that, when shown in succession, impart an impression of motion, together with any accompanying sounds. They are typically embodied in film, videotape, or videodisk.

How Copyright Is Secured

Copyright in a motion picture is automatically secured when the work is created and "fixed" in a copy. The Copyright Office registers claims to copyright and issues certificates of registration but does not "grant" or "issue" copyrights.

Only the expression (camera work, dialogue, sounds, etc.) fixed in a motion picture is protectible under copyright. Copyright does not cover the idea or concept behind the work or any characters portrayed in the work. Works that do not constitute a fixation of a motion picture include:

- a live telecast that is not fixed in a copy
- a screenplay or treatment of a future motion picture

Publication

Publication of a motion picture takes place when one or more copies are distributed to the public by sale, rental, lease, or lending or when *an offering* is made to distribute copies to a group of persons (wholesalers, retailers, broadcasters, motion picture distributors, and the like) for purposes of further distribution or public performance. Offering to distribute a copy of a motion picture for exhibition during a film festival may be considered publication of that work.

For an offering to constitute publication, copies must be made and be ready for distribution. The *performance* itself of a motion picture (for example, showing it in a theater, on television, or in a school room) *does not* constitute publication.

Publication of a motion picture publishes all the components embodied in it including the music, the script, and the sounds. Thus, if a motion picture made from a screenplay is published, the screenplay is published to the extent it is contained in the published work.

Copyright Notice

Before March 1, 1989, the use of copyright notice was mandatory on all published works, and any work first published before that date should have carried a notice. For works first published on and after March 1, 1989, use of the copyright notice is optional. For more information about copyright notice, read Circular 3, *Copyright Notice*.

Copyright Registration

Advantages of Registration

Registration in the Copyright Office establishes a public record of the copyright claim. Before an infringement suit may be filed in court, registration is necessary for works of U.S. origin and for foreign works not originating in a country that is a party to the Berne Convention for the Protection of Literary and Artistic Works. For details about the Berne Convention, see

Circular 38a, *International Copyright Relations of the United States.* Timely registration may also provide a broader range of remedies in an infringement suit. See Circular 1, *Copyright Basics,* for more information on the benefits of registration.

Registration Procedures

An application for copyright registration contains three essential elements: a completed application form, a nonrefundable filing fee, and a nonreturnable deposit—that is, a copy or copies of the work being registered and "deposited" with the Copyright Office.

Here are the options for registering your copyright, beginning with the fastest and most cost-effective method.

NOTE: **Copyright Office fees are subject to change. For current fees, check the Copyright Office website at www.copyright.gov, write the Copyright Office, or call (202) 707-3000.**

Option 1: Online Registration

Online registration through the electronic Copyright Office (eCO) is the preferred way to register basic claims for literary works; visual arts works; performing arts works, including motion pictures; sound recordings; and single serials. Advantages of online filing include:

- a lower filing fee
- fastest processing time
- online status tracking
- secure payment by credit or debit card, electronic check, or Copyright Office deposit account
- the ability to upload certain categories of deposits directly into eCO as electronic files

NOTE: **You can still register using eCO and save money even if you will submit a hard-copy deposit. The system will prompt you to specify whether you intend to submit an electronic or a hard-copy deposit, and it will provide instructions accordingly.**

Basic claims include (1) a single work; (2) multiple unpublished works if they are all by the same author(s) and owned by the same claimant; and (3) multiple published works if they are all first published together in the same publication on the same date and owned by the same claimant.

To access eCO, go to the Copyright Office website at *www.copyright.gov* and click on *electronic Copyright Office.*

Option 2: Registration with Fill-In Form CO

The next best option for registering basic claims is the new fill-in Form CO. Using 2-D barcode scanning technology, the Office can process these forms much faster and more efficiently than paper forms completed manually. Simply complete Form CO on your personal computer, print it out, and mail it along with a check or money order and your deposit. To access Form CO, go the Copyright Office website and click on *Forms.*

Option 3: Registration with Paper Forms

Paper versions of Form PA (performing arts works, including motion pictures) and Form CON (continuation sheet for paper applications) are still available on paper. These paper forms are not accessible on the Copyright Office website; however, staff will send them to you by postal mail upon request. Remember that online registration through eCO and fill-in Form CO (see above) can be used for performing arts works.

Effective Date of Registration

A copyright registration is effective on the date the Copyright Office receives all the required elements in acceptable form. The time the Copyright Office requires to process an application varies, depending on the amount of material the Office is receiving and the method of application.

If you apply online for copyright registration, you will receive an email notification when your application is received.

If you apply on a paper form, you will not receive an acknowledgment of your application (the Office receives more than 600,000 applications annually), but you can expect:

- a certificate of registration indicating that the work has been registered,
- a letter or a telephone call from the Copyright Office if further information is needed, or
- if the application cannot be accepted, a letter explaining why it has been rejected.

The Copyright Office cannot honor requests to make certificates available for pickup or to send them by Federal Express or another express mail service. If you want to know the date that the Copyright Office receives your paper application or hard-copy deposit, use registered or certified mail and request a return receipt.

Deposit Requirements for Registration

In addition to registering electronically through eCO or completing Form CO, you must send a copy and a description of the work being registered. The nature of the copy and description may vary, depending upon the factors indicated below.

For All Published Motion Pictures

1. *A separate description* of the nature and general content of the work— for example, a shooting script, a synopsis, or a pressbook; and
2. *One complete copy of the work.* A copy is complete if it is undamaged and free of splices and defects that would interfere with viewing the work.

For motion pictures first published in the United States. *One complete copy of the best edition.* Where two or more editions are published in the United States, the best edition is the one preferred by the Library of Congress. Currently, the Library accepts in descending order of preference:

A. Film, rather than another medium
   1. Preprint material, by special arrangement
   2. 70mm positive print, if original production negative is greater than 35mm
   3. 35mm positive prints
   4. 16mm positive prints
B. Videotape formats
   1. Betacam SP
   2. Digital Beta (Digibeta)
   3. DVD
   4. VHS cassette

For motion pictures first published abroad. *One complete copy as first published or one copy of the best edition.*

For Unpublished Motion Pictures

1. a separate description of the work and
2. a copy of the work containing all the visual and aural elements covered by the registration. An alternative deposit option is available for unpublished motion pictures. For information, contact the Copyright Office at (202) 707-8182.

Requirements for Motion Pictures That Cannot Be Viewed by the Copyright Office Staff

The Copyright Office does not have equipment to view motion pictures in certain formats, including 1" open-reel videotapes and HDCAM, D2, and 8mm videocassettes. If you send one of these formats, please include the credits in the separate written description. If the work was first published before March 1, 1989, the Copyright Office must examine the work for the required copyright notice. In this case, please send the best edition copy and a copy that the Copyright Office can view—for example, a ½" VHS videocassette.

Exceptions to the Normal Deposit Requirement

Special Relief

Where it is unusually difficult or impossible to comply with the deposit requirement for a particular motion picture, you may submit a written request for special relief from the normal requirement. The request, addressed to the *Chief of the Performing Arts Division*, must state why you cannot provide the required copy and describe the nature of the substitute copy being deposited. This letter should be included with the registration material. The decision to grant or deny special relief is based on the acquisitions policies and archival considerations of the Library of Congress and the examining requirements of the Copyright Office.

Motion Picture Agreement

The Motion Picture Agreement establishes several alternative deposit procedures for published motion pictures. How well it serves a particular applicant depends on a number of factors, including the frequency of filing registrations. For detailed information, call the Motion Picture, Broadcasting, and Recorded Sound Division (MBRS) at (202) 707-5610, or write to:

Library of Congress
Motion Picture, Broadcasting, and Recorded Sound Division
ATTN: Reference Assistant
101 Independence Avenue SE
Washington, DC 20540-4805

Mandatory Deposit for Works Published in the United States

Requirement Under Mandatory Deposit

The owner of copyright or the owner of the exclusive right of publication of a motion picture published in the United States has a legal obligation to deposit in the Copyright Office within three months of publication in the United States one complete copy of the best edition and a description of the work. Failure to deposit this copy after the Copyright Office demands it can result in fines and other penalties.

Satisfying Mandatory Deposit Through Registration

Depositing the required copy with an application and fee for copyright registration simultaneously satisfies any mandatory deposit requirement for the motion picture. Satisfying the mandatory deposit requirement alone does not provide the benefits of copyright registration.

The Motion Picture Collection at the Library of Congress

The Library of Congress is the nation's central collection of books, recordings, photographs, maps, audiovisual works, and other research materials. Many of the Library's acquisitions are obtained through copyright deposits. The material acquired by this means is critical to the Library's recognized success in maintaining superior and comprehensive collections.

Motion pictures form an essential part of the Library's holdings. As feature films, television programs, videos, and other audiovisual media become increasingly popular as a means of communication, education, and entertainment in our society, they also form a greater part of our historical record. The preservation facilities and bibliographic control provided by the Library ensure that many of these works will be available to future generations.

Motion Pictures First Published Before 1978

Works first published with notice before 1978 had an original 28-year term of copyright, and registration had to be made within that first term. It could then be renewed in the 28th year for an additional term. Legislation enacted in 1992 made renewal automatic for works copyrighted between January 1, 1964, and December 31, 1977, and made it possible to register such works during their renewal term provided they were published with an acceptable notice. Such registrations must be made on Form RE accompanied by Form RE/Addendum. If such works were registered during their original term, their registrations can be renewed at any time during their renewal terms with just Form RE. The RE forms are available on the Copyright Office website. They must be completed on paper and mailed to the Copyright Office with the appropriate fee and deposit. It is not possible at this time to register motion pictures first published before 1978 through online registration (eCO) or on Form CO. See Circular 15, *Renewal of Copyright, for more information.*

Deposit Requirement

To register a claim in a motion picture first published before 1978 on Form RE and Form RE/Addendum, deposit *one copy of the work as first published*, that is, one of the first prints or tapes made from the master and distributed. If that is not available, send a dubbed copy of the first published edition that displays the original copyright notice. Read Circular 3, *Copyright Notice*, for notice requirements.

Form GATT

Under a 1994 amendment to the U.S. copyright law pursuant to enactment of the Uruguay Round Agreements Act (URAA), copyright in certain foreign works that had previously been in the public domain (including those that had entered the public domain because of publication without the required notice) was restored as of January 1, 1996. Works whose copyrights have been restored may be registered on Form GATT. Read Circular 38b, *Highlights of Copyright Amendments Contained in the Uruguay Round Agreements Act*, for more information.

2. Circular 22 (Excerpts): How to Investigate the Copyright Status of a Work

In General

Methods of Approaching a Copyright Investigation

There are several ways to investigate whether a work is under copyright protection and, if so, the facts of the copyright. These are the main ones:

1. Examine a copy of the work for such elements as a copyright notice, place and date of publication, author and publisher. If the work is a sound recording, examine the disk, tape cartridge, or cassette in which the recorded sound is fixed, or the album cover, sleeve, or container in which the recording is sold;

2. Make a search of the Copyright Office catalogs and other records; *or*

3. Have the Copyright Office make a search for you.

A Few Words of Caution About Copyright Investigations

Copyright investigations often involve more than one of these methods. Even if you follow all three approaches, the results may not be conclusive. Moreover, as explained in this circular, the changes brought about under the Copyright Act of 1976, the Berne Convention Implementation Act of 1988, the Copyright Renewal Act of 1992, and the Sonny Bono Copyright Term Extension Act of 1998 must be considered when investigating the copyright status of a work.

This circular offers some practical guidance on what to look for if you are making a copyright investigation. It is important to realize, however, that this circular contains only general information and that there are a number of exceptions to the principles outlined here. In many cases it is important to consult with a copyright attorney before reaching any conclusions regarding the copyright status of a work.

How to Search Copyright Office Catalogs and Records

Catalog of Copyright Entries

The Copyright Office published the *Catalog of Copyright Entries (CCE)* in printed format from 1891 through 1978. From 1979 through 1982 the CCE was issued in microfiche format. The catalog was divided into parts according to the classes of works registered. Each CCE segment covered all registrations made during a particular period of time. Renewal registrations made from 1979 through 1982 are found in Section 8 of the catalog. Renewals prior to that time were generally listed at the end of the volume containing the class of work to which they pertained.

A number of libraries throughout the U.S. maintain copies of the *Catalog*, and this may provide a good starting point if you wish to make a search yourself. There are some cases, however, in which a search of the *Catalog* alone will not be sufficient to provide the needed information. For example:

- Because the *Catalog* does not include entries for assignments or other recorded documents, it cannot be used for searches involving the ownership of rights.
- The *Catalog* entry contains the essential facts concerning a registration, but it is not a verbatim transcript of the registration record. It does not contain the address of the copyright claimant.

Effective with registrations made since 1982 when the CCE was discontinued, the only method of searching outside the Library of Congress is by using the Internet to access the automated catalog. The automated catalog contains entries from 1978 to the present. Information on accessing the catalog via the Internet is provided below.

Individual Searches of Copyright Records

The Copyright Office is located in the Library of Congress James Madison Memorial Building, 101 Independence Avenue SE, Washington, DC 20559-6000.

Most Copyright Office records are open to public inspection and searching from 8:30 AM to 5:00 PM, eastern time, Monday through Friday, except federal holidays. An exception is the area containing copyright applications from 1870 to the present, which is open from 9:00 AM to 4:30 PM. The various records freely available to the public include an extensive card catalog, an automated catalog containing records from 1978 forward, record books, and microfilm records of assignments and related documents. Other records, including correspondence files and deposit copies, are not open to the public for searching. However, they may be inspected upon request and payment of a search fee.*

*NOTE: **Copyright Office fees are subject to change. For current fees, please check the Copyright Office website, write the Copyright Office, or call (202) 707-3000.**

If you wish to do your own searching in the Copyright Office files open to the public, you will be given assistance in locating the records you need and in learning procedures for searching. If the Copyright Office staff actually makes the search for you, a search fee must be charged. The search will not be done while you wait.

In addition, Copyright Office records in machine-readable form cataloged from January 1, 1978, to the present, including registration and renewal information and recorded documents, are available for searching from the Copyright Office website at *www.copyright.gov*.

The Copyright Office does not offer search assistance to users on the Internet.

Searching by the Copyright Office

In General

Upon request, and at the statutory rate for each hour or fraction of an hour consumed, the Copyright Office staff will search its records covering the records of registrations and other recorded documents concerning ownership of copyrights and will provide a written report. If desired, an estimate can be provided. Estimates for searches are based on the information furnished and are provided for a set fee that is applied toward the cost of the search and report. Fees for estimates are nonrefundable and are good for up to one year. Requests must include an address and telephone number where you may be reached during business hours and an email address if available.

Certification of a search report is available for an additional fee. Certified searches are frequently requested to meet the evidentiary requirements of litigation.

Preferred payment is by personal check or credit card. Contact the Copyright Office for information regarding payment with money orders or by overseas banking institutions.

For information, correspondence, or payment, contact:

Library of Congress
Copyright Office, Mail Stop 6306
101 Independence Avenue SE
Washington, DC 20559-6000
PHONE: (202) 707-6850 (M–F, 8:30–5:00 eastern time)
FAX: (202) 252-3485
TTY: (202) 707-6737
EMAIL: *copysearch@loc.gov*

What the Fee Does Not Cover

The search fee does not include the cost of additional certificates, photocopies of deposits, or copies of other Office records. For information concerning these services, request Circular 6, *Obtaining Access to and Copies of Copyright Office Records and Deposits.*

Information Needed

The more detailed information you can furnish with your request, the less expensive the search will be. Please provide as much of the following information as possible:

- the title of the work, with any possible variants
- the names of the authors, including possible pseudonyms
- the name of the probable copyright owner, which may be the publisher or producer
- the approximate year when the work was published or registered
- the type of work involved (book, play, musical composition, sound recording, photograph, etc.)
- for a work originally published as a part of a periodical or collection, the title of that publication and any other information, such as the volume or issue number, to help identify it

• the registration number or any other copyright data

Motion pictures are often based on other works such as books or seri-alized contributions to periodicals or other composite works. *If you desire a search for an underlying work or for music from a motion picture, you must specifically request such a search. You must also identify the underlying works and music and furnish the specific titles, authors, and approximate dates of these works.*

Searches Involving Assignments and Other Documents Affecting Copyright Ownership

For the standard hourly search fee, the Copyright Office staff will search its indexes covering the records of assignments and other recorded docu-ments concerning ownership of copyrights. The reports of searches in these cases will state the facts shown in the Office's indexes of the recorded doc-uments but will offer no interpretation of the content of the documents or their legal effect.

Limitations on Searches

In determining whether or not to have a search made, you should keep the following points in mind:

No Special Lists • The Copyright Office does not maintain any listings of works by subject or any lists of works that are in the public domain.

Contributions Not Listed Separately in Copyright Office Records • Individual works such as stories, poems, articles, or musical compositions that were published as contributions to a copyrighted periodical or collec-tion are usually not listed separately by title in our records.

No Comparisons • The Copyright Office does not search or compare copies of works to determine questions of possible infringement or to determine how much two or more versions of a work have in common.

Titles and Names Not Copyrightable • Copyright does not protect names and titles, and our records list many different works identified by the same or similar titles. Some brand names, trade names, slogans, and phrases may be entitled to protection under the general rules of law relating to unfair competition. They may also be entitled to registration under the provisions of the trademark laws. Questions about the trademark laws should be addressed to: *Commissioner of Patents and Trademarks, U.S. Patent and Trademark Office, PO Box 1450, Alexandria, VA 22313-1450*. Possible protection of names and titles under common law principles of unfair competition is a question of state law.

No Legal Advice • The Copyright Office cannot express any opinion as to the legal significance or effect of the facts included in a search report.

Some Words of Caution

Searches Not Always Conclusive

Searches of the Copyright Office catalogs and records are useful in helping to determine the copyright status of a work, but they cannot be regarded as conclusive in all cases. The complete absence of any information about a work in the Office records does not mean that the work is unprotected. The following are examples of cases in which information about a particular work may be incomplete or lacking entirely in the Copyright Office:

- Before 1978, unpublished works were entitled to protection under common law without the need of registration.
- Works published with notice prior to 1978 may be registered at *any* time within the first 28-year term.
- Works copyrighted between January 1, 1964, and December 31, 1977, are affected by the Copyright Renewal Act of 1992, which automatically extends the copyright term and makes renewal registrations optional.
- For works under copyright protection on or after January 1, 1978, registration may be made at any time during the term of protection. Although registration is not required as a condition of copyright protection, there are certain definite advantages to registration. For further information, request Circular 1, *Copyright Basics*.

- Since searches are ordinarily limited to registrations that have already been cataloged, a search report may not cover recent registrations for which catalog records are not yet available.
- The information in the search request may not have been complete or specific enough to identify the work.
- The work may have been registered under a different title or as part of a larger work.

Protection in Foreign Countries

Even if you conclude that a work is in the public domain in the United States, this does not necessarily mean that you are free to use it in other countries. Every nation has its own laws governing the length and scope of copyright protection, and these are applicable to uses of the work within that nation's borders. Thus, the expiration or loss of copyright protection in the United States may still leave the work fully protected against unauthorized use in other countries.

Sample Agreements

↓

1. Author Agreement (for WGA Members, Modified Low Budget Agreement)

When countersigned below, the following will constitute the terms and conditions of the agreement ("Agreement") between Productions, LLC ("Company"), and the writer identified below ("Author") in respect to the motion picture tentatively known as "The Picture" ("Picture").

1. **Employment and Services.** Company hereby employs Author in connection with the development of the Picture pursuant to the terms and conditions hereof and Author hereby accepts such employment.

    1.1 Author will render the writing services set forth in this Agreement on behalf of Company or such other parties as may be designated by Company and in accordance with Company's instructions.

    1.2 Author shall render all services as are customarily rendered by writers of first-class feature length theatrical motion pictures in the motion picture industry, as, when, and where required by Company, and shall comply with all reasonable directions, requests, rules, and regulations of Company in connection therewith, whether or not the same involve matters of artistic taste or judgment, and will incorporate into his written material the changes, revisions, deletions, or additions as may be required by Company or any representative designated by Company.

2. **WGA Low Budget Agreement.** Company shall undertake to become a signatory to the Writers Guild of America Minimum Basic Agreement (MBA), and shall produce the Picture as a low-budget picture at $1,200,000 or less. Provided Company becomes a signatory to the WGA, all provisions of the then-applicable MBA as modified by the Low Budget Agreement shall be incorporated by reference and shall take precedence over any conflicting provisions of this Agreement.

3. **Compensation.** Upon the conditions that Author fully performs all services and obligations required hereunder and that Author is not in default or material breach of any obligation due to Company, Company shall pay Author as full and complete consideration for such services and for all rights granted hereunder, the following sums at the following times:

   3.1 Company shall pay Author a purchase price of $_____.

   3.2 Company and Author have agreed to defer payment of one hundred percent (100%) of the screenplay purchase price owed to Author. It is presently anticipated that the budget shall remain at or below $500,000. If however, the budget exceeds $500,000 (while remaining below $1,200,000 upon commencement of principal photography) Company shall pay $10,000 to Author and apply this against any deferred monies owing on the screenplay purchase price.

   3.3 Company shall offer Author the opportunity to perform any rewrites or polishes on the script requested in writing by Company, which shall be compensated at the MBA minimum.

   3.4 Company shall pay Author a script publication fee of $5,000, which is due thirty (30) days after final determination of the writing credits on the Picture. If the Picture budget remains at or less than $500,000, then Author agrees to request the publication fee be deferred along with the screenplay purchase and/or first rewrite compensation.

4. **Term.** The term of this Agreement shall commence on the date hereof and shall continue thereafter until Company has fully completed all services required hereunder, unless sooner terminated or abandoned in accordance with the provisions of this Agreement.

5. **Credit.** Provided Author completes all services required hereunder and the Picture is completed by Company, then Author shall receive credit on the screen, in motion picture trailers, and in paid print advertising issued by Company and under Company's control which is at least 10 inches or larger.

   5.1 The credit shall be "_____" or such other credit as determined exclusively by the WGA.

   5.2 No casual or inadvertent failure to comply with the provisions of this clause shall be deemed to be a breach of this Agreement by Company. Author shall notify Company of any breach of this paragraph, after which Company shall take reasonable steps to correct all new prints, copies, and advertising on a prospective basis, but Company shall not be required to recall or alter any prints, copies, or advertisements in production or distribution. No monetary damages are available for breach of Company's duties under this paragraph.

6. **Work for Hire and Assignment of Rights.** Author acknowledges that all of the results and proceeds of Author's services in connection with the Picture, the Material (as such term is herein defined), is created by Author as a "work made for hire" specially ordered or commissioned by Company with Company being deemed the sole author of all the results and proceeds. To the extent such Material is not treated as work for hire, it is hereby assigned, granted, licensed, and conveyed to Company for all purposes in perpetuity. For purposes hereof, the "Material" shall include, without limitation, Author's Screenplay, any drafts thereof, characters, plots, names, locations, themes, trademarks, or other literary or intellectual property associated with the Picture or relating to the Picture that have been created or written by Author at any time prior to the date of the Agreement or during the term of this Agreement.

   6.1 Without limiting the foregoing, Author acknowledges that Company is and will be the sole and exclusive owner of the Material, including all rights of every kind and nature in, to, and with respect to Author's services in connection with the Material, the Picture, and the results and proceeds of the Picture, and that Company will have the right to use, refrain from using, change, modify, add to, subtract from, and exploit, advertise, exhibit, and otherwise turn to account any or all of the foregoing in any manner whatsoever and in any and all media whether now known or hereafter devised throughout the universe. These rights include, without limitation, remakes, prequels and sequels, trailers, making-of specials, featurettes, Web sites, promotional material, Author interviews, all forms of television, radio, stage, home viewing devices, portable viewing or listening devices, phonograph and sound recordings, print and electronic publications, and game rights in all languages, as Company in its sole discretion will determine.

6.2 Author waives any and all "droit moral" or "Moral Rights of Authors" or any similar rights or principles of law of authors to the greatest extent allowed by applicable law that Author may now or later enjoy in the Material. It is agreed that Author's consideration for the Material is included in the compensation to be paid pursuant to the Agreement.

6.3 In addition to all other right granted herein, to the extent necessary, Author irrevocably assigns, licenses, and grants to Company throughout the universe, in perpetuity, the rights, if any, of Author to authorize, prohibit, or control the renting, lending, fixation, reproduction, distribution, exhibition, display, or other exploitation of the Picture by any media and means now known or hereafter devised as may be conferred upon Author under applicable laws, regulations, or directives, including, without limitation, any rental and lending rights pursuant to any European Union ("EU") directives or enabling or implementing legislation, laws, or regulations enacted by the member nations of the EU.

7. **Name and Likeness.** Author grants to Company the right, in perpetuity and throughout the universe, to use Author's name, likeness, activities, attributes, or biography in connection with the production, exhibition, advertising, publicizing, and other exploitation of the Picture and all subsidiary and ancillary rights therein; provided, however, that in no event will Author be depicted as using or endorsing any product, commodity, or service without Author's prior written consent. Notwithstanding the foregoing, Company's use of Author's name in a billing block on any item of merchandise or other material will constitute an approved use of Author's name that will not require Author's further consent.

8. Representations and Warranties. The Author hereby represents and warrants as follows:

8.1 The Material has been and will at all times be written solely by and is original with Author; no element of the Material infringes upon any other literary property.

8.2 The Material is wholly fictional, no portion of the Material has been taken from any other source (other than the public domain), and the Material does not constitute defamation against any person or violate any rights in any person, including, without limitation, rights of privacy, publicity, copyright (whether common law or statutory, throughout the universe), trademark, publication or performance rights, or rights in any other property, and any rights to consultation regarding the Material or any element thereof.

8.3 In addition to the foregoing, all representations and warranties and indemnities of the parties set forth in the Author's Certificate of Authorship pertaining to the Picture are incorporated in full in this Agreement by reference.

8.4 Author has full right and power to enter into this Agreement and perform all obligations hereunder, including, without limitation, all rights necessary to convey each and every right granted herein.

9. Indemnification. If any claim, action, suit, or proceeding is brought or threatened alleging facts that if true, would constitute a breach of Author's representations, warranties, and covenants under the Agreement or the Certificate of Authorship, Author shall immediately notify Company and Company's legal counsel thereof in writing. Company will have the sole right to control the legal defense against such claims or litigation, including the right to select counsel of its choice and to compromise or settle any such claim, demand, or litigation. Author shall indemnify and hold harmless Company, the members and corporations comprising Company, and its and their respective employees, officers, agents, assigns, and licensees from and against any and all liabilities, claims, costs, damages, and expenses (including reasonable attorneys' fees and court costs) arising out of or in connection with a breach or alleged breach of the foregoing covenants, warranties, and representations. Company agrees to immediately notify Author of any claims alleging facts that if true, would constitute a breach by Author of any representations, warranties, or covenants under the Agreement or the Certificate of Authorship and to indemnify and hold Author harmless from and against any and all liabilities, claims, costs, damages, and expenses (including reasonable attorney fees and court costs) arising out of any claim or legal action with respect to content added to the Material by Company and in connection with claims arising from the production, distribution, and exploitation of the Picture (except for matters covered by Author's representations and warranties under this Agreement or any other agreements relating to Author's grant of rights to, or rendition of services for, Company).

10. **Insurance Coverage.** Author will be covered as an additional insured under Company's policies of errors and omissions and general liability insurance, if Company procures these policies, subject to the policies' terms, conditions, and exclusions.

11. **Reimbursements.** Author shall be reimbursed for all reasonable advances or expenses incurred by him in his capacity as screenwriter pursuant to this Agreement with respect to the production of the Picture, such as for location travel, housing, and the like, provided such expenses have been approved by Company in advance and Author provides adequate documentation and receipts of the expense.

12. **Unique Services.** It is hereby agreed and understood that Author's services to be furnished hereunder are special, extraordinary, unique, and not replaceable, and that there is no adequate remedy at law for breach of this contract by Author.

    12.1 Company shall be entitled to both legal and equitable remedies as may be available, including both injunctive relief and damages. Company may elect not to submit arbitration for the purpose of seeking emergency, preliminary, or temporary injunctive relief.

    12.2 Author's services shall be in such time, place, and manner as Company may reasonably direct in accordance with customary motion picture industry practice. Such services shall be rendered in an artistic, conscientious, efficient, and punctual manner to the best of Author's ability to adhere to the budget and shooting schedule.

13. **Resolution of Disputes.**

    13.1 The MBA sets forth the grievance and arbitration procedures relating to all matters under the jurisdiction of the WGA.

13.2 Any disputes not subject to the MBA shall be resolved by arbitration in accordance with the then rules of the American Arbitration Association ("AAA"). Any party hereto electing to commence an action shall give written notice to the other party hereto.

13.3 The arbitrator or the referee shall diligently pursue determination of any Arbitration under consideration and shall render a decision within one hundred twenty (120) days after the arbitrator or referee is selected. The determination of the arbitrator on all matters referred to it hereunder shall be final and binding on the parties hereto; provided, however, that except as specified in Section 12, above, the arbitrator shall be bound by the terms of the Agreement and the Certificate of Authorship so that all awards shall be for monetary award exclusively and no injunctive relief or specific performance can be brought against the parties.

13.4 The award of such arbitrator may be confirmed or enforced in any court of competent jurisdiction. The referee, arbitrator, or its designee shall have full access to such records and physical facilities of the parties hereto as may be required. The costs and expenses of the referee or arbitrator, and the attorneys' fees and costs of each of the parties incurred in such, shall be apportioned between the parties by such arbitrator, as the case may be, based upon such arbitrator's determination of the merits of their respective positions.

14. **Confidentiality; Publicity.** Company shall have the exclusive right to issue and to license others to issue advertising, press information, and publicity with respect to the Picture, and Author shall not circulate, publish, or otherwise disseminate any such advertising or publicity without Company's prior written consent. Author shall treat and hold all budgeting, financial information, and nonpublic production information in confidence and shall not disclose such information to any third party without the prior written approval of Company.

15. **Assignment.** Author agrees that Company shall have the right to assign, license, delegate, lend, or otherwise transfer all or any part of its rights or duties under this Agreement at any time to any person. Author acknowledges that the personal services to be rendered by him hereunder are of the essence of this Agreement and agrees

that he shall not assign this Agreement, in whole or in part, to any person, and that any purported assignment or delegation of duties by Author shall be null and void and of no force and effect whatsoever. This Agreement shall inure to the benefit of Company's successors, assigns, licensees, grantees, and associated, affiliated, and subsidiary companies.

16. **No Obligation.** Company agrees to use all reasonable efforts to cause the Picture to be produced, however, the parties recognize that the production of an independent motion picture is an inherently difficult undertaking. Company is under no obligation to produce the Picture hereunder. In the event Company abandons production of the Picture hereunder, Author is entitled to such fixed compensation as had previously accrued and is not entitled to any additional compensation, damage, or loss as a result of such failure to undertake or complete the Picture.

17. **Assurances.** Each party shall execute all documents and certificates and perform all acts deemed appropriate by the Company or required by this Agreement in connection with this Agreement and the production of the Picture.

18. **Complete Agreement; Merger.** This Agreement together with the Certificate of Authorship constitutes the complete and exclusive statement of the agreement among the parties with respect to the matters discussed herein and therein and they supersede all prior written or oral statements among the parties, including any prior statement, warranty, or representation.

19. **Section Headings.** The section headings that appear throughout this Agreement are provided for convenience only and are not intended to define or limit the scope of this Agreement or the intent or subject matter of its provisions.

20. **Applicable Law.** Each party agrees that all disputes arising under or in connection with this Agreement and any transactions contemplated by this Agreement shall be governed by the internal law, and not the law of conflicts, of the State of _____.

21. **Amendments; Notices.** Any amendments, modifications, or alterations to this Agreement must be in writing and signed by all of the parties hereto. Any notice or other writing to be served upon either party in connection with this Agreement shall be in writing and shall be deemed completed when delivered to the address listed above.

22. **Severability.** Each provision of this Agreement is severable from the other provisions. If, for any reason, any provision of this Agreement is declared invalid or contrary to existing law, the inoperability of that provision shall have no effect on the remaining provisions of the Agreement and all remaining provisions shall continue in full force and effect.

23. **Counterparts.** This Agreement may be executed in counterparts, each of which shall be deemed an original and all of which shall, when taken together, constitute a single document.

IN WITNESS WHEREOF, the parties hereto have executed and delivered this agreement as of the date written below.

PRODUCTIONS, LLC   AUTHOR

_____ Date _____   _____ Date _____

By: Jane Doe, Manager   _____

      PRODUCTIONS, LLC   Print Name

2. Certificate of Authorship

I, _____, an individual, certify that, pursuant to an agreement ("Agreement") between Productions, LLC ("Company") and me in connection with a motion picture photoplay tentatively entitled "The Picture" ("Picture"), all literary material of whatever kind or nature, written or to be written, furnished or to be furnished, by me, and all of the results and proceeds of my services in connection with the Picture (all such literary material and all such results and proceeds being referred to collectively herein as the "Material") was or will be solely created by me as a "work made for hire" specially ordered or commissioned by Company for use as part of the Picture, with Company being deemed the sole author of the Material and the owner of all rights of every kind or nature, whether now known or hereafter devised (including, but not limited to, all copyrights and all extensions and renewals of copyrights) in and to the Material, with the right to make all uses of the Material throughout the universe and all changes in the Material as Company deems necessary or desirable. The Material will also include, without limitation, any and all ideas, characters, stories, trademarks, treatments, screenplays, and other material, of whatever kind or nature, in connection with or relating to the Picture, created or written by me at any time prior to the date of the Agreement (collectively, the "Preexisting Material") and I irrevocably grant, assign, and vest Company with all rights of every kind and nature, whether now known or hereafter devised (including, but not limited to, all copyrights and all extensions and renewals of copyrights) in and to the Material and the Preexisting Material, and the Preexisting Material will constitute part of the Material for all intents and purposes under this Certificate of Authorship.

Without limiting the foregoing, I irrevocably assign, license, and grant to Company, throughout the universe, in perpetuity, any and all of my rights to authorize, prohibit, or control the renting, lending, fixation, reproduction, or other exploitation of the Picture by any media and means now known or hereafter devised as may be conferred upon me under applicable laws, regulations, or directives, in any jurisdiction throughout the world, including, without limitation, any rental and lending rights pursuant to any European Union ("EU") directives or enabling or implementing legislation, laws, or regulations enacted by the member nations of the EU.

I waive all rights of "Droit Moral" or "Moral Rights of Authors" or any similar rights or principles of law that I may now or later have in the Material. It is agreed that my consideration for the Material is included in the compensation to be paid pursuant to the Agreement.

I warrant and represent that: (a) I have the right to execute this document; (b) except to the extent that it is based on material assigned to me by Company to be used as the basis therefor, the Material is or will be original with me; (c) the Material does not and will not defame or disparage any person or entity or infringe upon or violate the rights of privacy, publicity, or any other rights of any kind or nature whatsoever of any person or entity; (d) the Material is not the subject of any litigation or of any claim that might give rise to litigation; (e) I have not done, nor will I do, any act or thing that diminishes, impairs, or otherwise derogates from the full enjoyment by Company of all of Company's rights in and to the Material; and (f) I have not heretofore assigned, conveyed, encumbered, or otherwise disposed of or impaired any rights in and to the Material. If any claim, action, suit, or proceeding is brought or threatened alleging facts that if true, would constitute a breach by me of my representations, warranties, and covenants under the Agreement or this Certificate of Authorship, I will immediately notify Company and Company's legal counsel thereof in writing. I agree that Company will have the sole right to control the legal defense against such claims or litigation, including the right to select counsel of its choice and to compromise or settle any such claim, demand, or litigation. I will indemnify and hold harmless Company, the members and the corporations comprising Company, and its and their respective employees, officers, agents, assigns, and licensees from and against any and all liabilities, claims, costs, damages, and expenses (including reasonable attorneys' fees and court costs) arising out of or in connection with a breach or alleged breach of the foregoing covenants, warranties, and representations; and Company agrees to immediately notify me of any claims alleging facts that if true, would constitute a breach by me of my representations, warranties, or covenants under the Agreement or this Certificate of Authorship and to indemnify and hold me harmless from and against any and all liabilities, claims, costs, damages, and expenses (including reasonable attorney fees and court costs) arising out of any claim or legal action with respect to material added to the Material by Company and in connection with claims arising from the production, distribution, and exploitation of the Picture (except for matters covered by my representations and warranties under this Agreement or any other agreements relating to my grant of rights to, or rendition of services for, Company).

I agree to execute any documents and do any other acts as may be required by Company or its assignees or licensees to further evidence or effectuate Company's rights as set forth in this Certificate of Authorship or the Agreement. On my failure promptly to do so within five (5) business days following Company's request and delivery to me of the applicable documents or within five (5) business days following Company's request for such other acts, I hereby appoint Company as my attorney-in-fact for such purposes (it being acknowledged that such appointment is irrevocable and coupled with an interest) with full power of substitution and delegation.

I further acknowledge that: (a) in the event of any breach of the Agreement by Company, I will be limited to my remedy at law for damages, if any, and I will not have the right to terminate or rescind this Certificate or to restrain, enjoin, or otherwise impair the production, distribution, advertising, publicizing, or exploitation of the Picture or any rights in the Picture, and (b) nothing herein will obligate Company to use my services or the results or proceeds thereof in the Picture or to produce, advertise, or distribute the Picture.

I agree that Company's rights with respect to the Material or my services may be freely assigned and licensed, and in the event of an assignment or license, this Agreement will remain binding on me and inure to the benefit of any assignee or licensee; provided, however, that on an assignment by Company, Company will remain secondarily liable for its obligations under the Agreement unless such assignment is to: (a) a "major" or "mini-major" (as customarily understood in the motion picture industry) motion picture company or to a United States free or pay television network or other financially responsible party that assumes in writing all of Company's obligations under this Agreement; (b) an entity into which Company merges or is consolidated; (c) an entity that acquires all or substantially all of Company's business and assets; or (d) a person or entity that is controlled by, under common control with, or controls Company; in which event Company will be relieved of its obligations under Author's Agreement. I agree that except as provided in the Author's

Agreement, I will not have the right to assign this Certificate of Authorship or delegate the performance of my obligations to any person or entity and any purported assignment or delegation will be void.

I have caused this document to be executed as of _____ [date].

_____

_____, individual

Print Name

ACCEPTED AND AGREED TO: Productions, LLC

By: _____

Jane Doe, manager

3. Producer Agreement

This Agreement is made and entered into as of the date first ascribed below, by and between XYZ Film Company, LLC, 1234 Main Street, Hollywood, California 90210 ("Company") and John Doe, an individual, 5678 W. 46th St., New York, NY 10021 ("Producer"), with reference to the following facts:

Company is a wholly owned limited liability company owned by Jane Roe ("Writer/Director").

Company has or will acquire rights to a screenplay to be written and directed by Writer/Director and desires to make such screenplay into a motion picture (the "Picture"); and

Producer has extensive professional experiences as a line producer and producer of feature motion pictures.

Now Therefore, In consideration of the mutual covenants, conditions, and undertakings hereinafter set forth, the parties hereto agree as follows:

1. **Services Provided.** Company hereby employs the services of Producer, and Producer hereby accepts such employment, for the purpose of serving as producer and line producer of the Picture, for the period of [three (3)] weeks of preproduction, [five (5)] weeks of principal photography on an exclusive basis, and such postproduction as is reasonably necessary for completion of the Picture on a nonexclusive but first-priority basis. Each week shall include six working days. The Producer will provide such services as are generally performed by producers, including his service coordinating the creative, financial, technological, and administrative process throughout the term of this agreement, subject to the direction and control of Company and such other contracts as Company shall enter with other parties.

2. **Term.** The term of this Agreement shall commence on the date hereof and shall continue thereafter until Producer has fully completed all services required hereunder, unless sooner terminated in accordance with the provisions of this Agreement.

3. **Credit.** Provided Producer completes all services required hereunder and the Picture is completed by Company, then Producer shall

receive credit on the screen, in motion picture trailers, and in paid print advertising issued by Company and under Company's control which is at least 10 inches or larger. The credit shall be "Produced by John Doe." On the screen such credit shall be displayed above or before the title of the Picture in a size of type not less than *fifty percent* (50%) of the size of type used to display the title of the Picture. At its sole discretion, Company may assign "Produced by" credit to one or more additional persons in addition to Producer in the event Company determines such other person or persons provided substantial producer services in addition to Producer. No casual or inadvertent failure to comply with the provisions of this clause shall be deemed to be a breach of this Agreement by Company. Producer shall notify Company of any breach of this paragraph, after which Company shall take reasonable steps to correct all new prints, copies, and advertising on a prospective basis, but Company shall not be required to recall or alter any prints, copies, or advertisements in production or distribution. No monetary damages are available for breach of Company's duties under this paragraph.

4. **Consideration.** In consideration for Producer's services hereunder and provided Producer is not in default hereunder, Company shall pay Producer as follows:

   (a) Fixed Consideration. Producer shall receive a stipend of [$100.00] per day actually worked during preproduction and principal photography, not to exceed [Forty-Eight Hundred ($4,800.00)] Dollars. The payment shall be paid on a weekly basis.

   (b) Net Profits. If Company produces the Picture, Producer shall receive an amount equal to [ten percent (10%)] of one hundred percent (100%) of Net Profits in the Gross Receipts of the Company in the Picture or [One Hundred Thousand ($100,000)] Dollars, whichever is lower.

      (i) Gross Receipts means all income, if any, actually received by Company from the sale, exhibition, or distribution of the Picture in theaters, video/DVD or similar format, broadcast television, satellite, cable exhibition, or any other method of exhibition, display, or performance now known or hereafter created. Gross Receipts does not include income from any other source related to the Picture, including, without limitation, income derived from sale of sequel, prequel, or remake rights, publishing interests such as novelizations, comic books, etc., sales of the screenplay, "making of" or other related projects, or any other spin-offs or related Company projects or activities.

(ii) The term Net Profits shall mean the Gross Receipts, less the deductions of all Company expenses of every kind related to the Picture. Without limiting the foregoing, the deductions shall include all costs, charges, and expenses paid or incurred in connection with the preparation, production, completion, and delivery of the Picture, deferred compensation, charges for any services, union or trade obligations, interest expenses, obligations to any completion guarantor, legal and accounting charges, the cost of all material, services, facilities, labor, insurance, taxes (other than income, franchise, and like taxes), copyright royalties attributable to the Picture for music, artwork, script, or other, judgments, marketing and promotional expenses, distribution fees, recoveries, settlements, losses, costs, and expenses, including reasonable attorneys' fees, sustained or incurred by Company in connection with the Picture or anything used therein and in connection with the production thereof. Company shall pay Producer twice annually all amounts due hereunder for all monies accrued during the preceding six-month period, not later than forty-five (45) days following the end of each such period.

(c) Reimbursements. Producer shall be reimbursed for all reasonable advances or expenses incurred in the production of the Picture, such as for location scouting, equipment rental, and the like, provided such expenses have been approved by Company in advance and Producer provides adequate documentation and receipts of the expense.

5. **Authority.** Company shall coordinate with Producer throughout the production to the greatest extent practicable throughout production; provided, however, Company reserves final approval of all essential production elements including, without limitation, script, budget, casting, locations, and film editing. Subject to direction of Company, Producer shall comply with all contractual and union and guild obligations and Company requirements.

6. **Termination.**
(a) This Agreement may be terminated by Company at any time, with

or without cause. If Company elects to terminate this Agreement and Producer is not in default hereunder, Company shall pay Producer his accrued fixed compensation and a pro rata proportion of the contingent compensation. (By way of example, if Producer is terminated after 12 days, he will receive 12/48 of his contingent compensation, equal to 25% of 10%, meaning 2.5% of the Net Profits.) The costs of additional producer(s) shall be added to the cost of production. In the event Company determines Producer has materially breached his obligations hereunder, no contingent compensation shall be paid.

(b) This Agreement may be terminated by Producer upon seven days' advanced written notice. Unless otherwise agreed in writing by the parties, in the event Producer terminates this Agreement, he shall receive only his accrued fixed compensation, but shall not be eligible for any contingent compensation.

7. **Work Made for Hire.** Company shall own the copyright in the Picture without any claim by Producer. Producer is employed as on a work made for hire as a specially commissioned audiovisual or motion picture work and acknowledges that the copyright in the Picture shall vest exclusively in Company as author.

(a) The Picture shall be registered for copyright in Company's name both in the United States and elsewhere.

(b) To the extent Producer has created any copyrighted elements incorporated into the Picture and such work-made-for-hire provision is not recognized by the jurisdiction, Producer hereby assigns all rights or the maximum rights allowed under that jurisdiction's laws to Company, including, without limitation, Rental Lending Rights if recognized, rights to enforce any claim of attribution and integrity, or rights to exploit any interest in the Picture in any media now known or hereafter developed.

8. **Unique Services.** It is hereby agreed and understood that Producer's services to be furnished hereunder are special, extraordinary, unique, and not replaceable, and that there is no adequate remedy at law for breach of this contract by Producer.

(a) Company shall be entitled to both legal and equitable remedies as may be available, including both injunctive relief and damages. Company may elect not to submit to arbitration for the purpose of seeking emergency, preliminary, or temporary injunctive relief.

(b) Producer's services shall be in such time, place, and manner as Company may reasonably direct in accordance with customary motion picture industry practice. Such services shall be rendered in an artistic, conscientious, efficient, and punctual manner to the best of Producer's ability to adhere to the budget and shooting schedule.

(c) Producer grants to Company the perpetual nonexclusive right to use and license others to use Producer's name, biography, and reproductions of Producer's physical likeness and voice in connection with the production, exhibition, advertising, promotion, or other exploitation of the Picture and all subsidiary and ancillary rights therein and thereto; provided, however, Company shall not use or authorize the use of Producer's name or likeness as a direct endorsement of any product or service without Producer's prior consent.

9. **Resolution of Disputes.** ANY AND ALL DISPUTES HEREUNDER SHALL BE RESOLVED BY ARBITRATION OR REFERENCE. ANY PARTY HERETO ELECTING TO COMMENCE AN ACTION SHALL GIVE WRITTEN NOTICE TO THE OTHER PARTY HERETO. THEREUPON, IF ARBITRATION IS SELECTED BY THE PARTY COMMENCING THE ACTION, THE CLAIM ("ARBITRATION MATTER") SHALL BE SETTLED BY ARBITRATION IN ACCORDANCE WITH THE THEN RULES OF THE AMERICAN ARBITRATION ASSOCIATION ("AAA"). The arbitrator or the referee shall diligently pursue determination of any Arbitration under consideration and shall render a decision within one hundred twenty (120) days after the arbitrator or referee is selected. The determination of the arbitrator on all matters referred to it hereunder shall be final and binding on the parties hereto. The award of such arbitrator may be confirmed or enforced in any court of competent jurisdiction. The referee, arbitrator, or its designee shall have full access to such records and physical facilities of the parties hereto as may be required. The costs and expenses of the referee or arbitrator, and the attorneys' fees and costs of each of the parties incurred in such, may be apportioned between the parties by such arbitrator, as the case may be, based upon such arbitrator's determination of the merits of their respective positions.

10. **Confidentiality; Publicity.** Company shall have the exclusive right to issue and to license others to issue advertising and publicity with

respect to the Picture, and Producer shall not circulate, publish, or otherwise disseminate any such advertising or publicity without Company's prior written consent.

11. **Assignment.** Producer agrees that Company shall have the right to assign, license, delegate, lend, or otherwise transfer all or any part of its rights or duties under this Agreement at any time to any person. Producer acknowledges that the personal services to be rendered by Producer hereunder are of the essence of this Agreement and agrees that he shall not assign this Agreement, in whole or in part, to any person, and that any purported assignment or delegation of duties by Producer shall be null and void and of no force and effect whatsoever. This Agreement shall inure to the benefit of Company's successors, assigns, licensees, grantees, and associated, affiliated, and subsidiary companies.

12. **No Obligation.** Company agrees to uses all reasonable efforts to cause the Picture to be produced, however, the parties recognize that the production of an independent motion picture is an inherently difficult undertaking. Company is under no obligation to produce the Picture hereunder. In the event Company abandons production of the Picture hereunder, Producer is entitled to such fixed compensation as had previously accrued and is not entitled to any additional compensation, damage, or loss as a result of such failure to undertake or complete the Picture.

13. **Assurances.** Each party shall execute all documents and certificates and perform all acts deemed appropriate by the Company or required by this Agreement in connection with this Agreement and the production of the Picture.

14. **Complete Agreement.** This Agreement constitutes the complete and exclusive statement of the agreement among the parties with respect to the matters discussed herein and it supersedes all prior written or oral statements among the parties, including any prior statement, warranty, or representation.

15. **Section Headings.** The section headings that appear throughout this Agreement are provided for convenience only and are not intended to define or limit the scope of this Agreement or the intent or subject matter of its provisions.

16. **Attorneys' Fees.** In the event any action or arbitration proceeding be instituted by a party to enforce any of the terms or conditions

contained herein, the prevailing party in such action shall be entitled to such reasonable attorneys' fees, costs, and expenses as may be fixed by the court or arbitrator.

17. **Applicable Law.** Each party agrees that all disputes arising under or in connection with this Agreement and any transactions contemplated by this Agreement shall be governed by the internal law, and not the law of conflicts, of the State of _____.

18. **Notices.** Any notice or other writing to be served upon either party in connection with this Agreement shall be in writing and shall be deemed completed when delivered to the address listed above.

19. **Amendments.** Any amendments, modifications, or alterations to this Agreement must be in writing and signed by all of the parties hereto.

20. **Severability.** Each provision of this Agreement is severable from the other provisions. If, for any reason, any provision of this Agreement is declared invalid or contrary to existing law, the inoperability of that provision shall have no effect on the remaining provisions of the Agreement and all remaining provisions shall continue in full force and effect.

21. **Counterparts.** This Agreement may be executed in counterparts, each of which shall be deemed an original and all of which shall, when taken together, constitute a single document.

Dated _____

"Company"   "Producer"
XYZ Film Company, LLC   John Doe

By: _____   By: _____
Title: _____   John Doe

4. Actor Employment Agreement (for SAG Modified Low Budget Agreement)

When countersigned below, the following will constitute the terms and conditions of the agreement ("Agreement") between Productions, LLC ("Company"), and the artist identified below ("Artist") in respect to the motion picture tentatively known as "The Picture" ("Picture").

1. The Parties anticipate that the Picture shall be directed and produced as follows:

    DIRECTOR:
    COMPANY EXECUTIVE:
    PRODUCTION COMPANY:
    CASTING DIRECTOR:
    LOCATIONS:

2. The Artist's name and contact information is as follows:

    NAME OF ARTIST:
    NAME OF ARTIST FOR CREDIT (IF DIFFERENT):
    ROLE: ROLE #:
    ADDRESS:
    RESIDENCY/CITIZENSHIP:
    TELEPHONE:
    CELL OR PAGER:
    SOCIAL SEC#:
    CORP: FED ID#:
    GUILD MEMBERSHIP: STATION 12 CHECKED: _____
    [Station 12 is the SAG member eligibility clearance, a requirement for all SAG productions.]

    ARTIST'S AGENCY/AGENT:
    AGENT'S ADDRESS:
    AGENT PHONE / FAX:
    MANAGER:
    MANAGER ADDRESS:
    MANAGER PHONE / FAX: (p) / (f)

3. **Dressing Facilities.** One room in a double banger or equivalent space.

4. **Travel.** To be determined (coming from _____).

5. **Hotel.** First-class accommodations (otherwise known as Bed/Breakfast with private bath) in _____.

6. **Transportation.** Nonexclusive transportation with top-tier cast to and from set.

7. **Start Date.** The anticipated start date is on or about _____. Employment shall continue from and after the starting date for the period necessary to complete all continuous services required by Company from Artist, but for not less than said guaranteed period.

8. **Consideration.** In consideration for Artist's services hereunder and provided Artist is not in default hereunder, Company shall pay Artist as follows:

    (a) SAG Agreement. Company and Artist are each subject to the Screen Actors Guild Modified Low Budget Production Contract, (SAG Agreement), which terms are hereby incorporated into this Agreement by reference. Unless otherwise provided in the SAG Agreement, the fixed compensation shall be paid as follows:

    (i) Salary. As a portion of consideration for Artist's services hereunder, Artist shall receive a salary of $933.00 per five-day week (Salary).

    (ii) Guarantee. Once the Picture commences principal photography, the Artist will receive compensation for not less than one (1) weeks of production.

    (iii) Postproduction. Any postproduction compensation will be paid at the minimum SAG Agreement scale.

    (iv) Per Diem. Artist shall receive an additional $__.00 per day worked as a per diem to cover the costs associated with food, travel, and related out-of-pocket expenses.

    (b) All compensation payable hereunder on a weekly basis shall be payable not later than Thursday of each week for the period ending on the preceding Saturday. Payments for any period of less than a week shall be at a daily rate determined by prorating the weekly rate on the basis of the number of days in the five-day workweek at the time and place involved, subject to the SAG Agreement. No additional payments shall be required in respect of services rendered at night or on Sundays, Saturdays, or holidays or for meal delays, hazardous work, violation of rest periods, or otherwise, or for exhibitions of the Picture on television or in supplemental markets, except to the minimum extent, if any, specifically required by the SAG Agreement.

[For above-the-line talent only, include (c) and (d)]

(c) Payment Schedule. Company shall pay Artist four times annually all amounts due hereunder for all accrued Net Profits during the preceding period for the first three years following the theatrical release of the Picture and twice annually thereafter. Such payments shall be due sixty (60) days following the completion of the prior accrual period.

(d) Net Profits. If Company produces the Picture, Artist shall receive an amount equal to [two percent (2%)] of one hundred percent (100%) of Net Profits in the Gross Receipts of the Managers of the Company in the Picture. Gross Receipts means all income, if any, actually received by Company from the sale, exhibition, or distribution of the Picture in theaters, video/DVD or similar format, broadcast television, satellite, cable exhibition, or any other method of exhibition, display, or performance now known or hereafter created. Gross Receipts does not include income from any other source related to the Picture, including, without limitation, income derived from sale of sequel, prequel, or remake rights, publishing interests such as novelizations, comic books, etc., sales of the screenplay, "making of" or other related projects, or any other spin-offs or related Company projects or activities.

The term Net Profits shall mean the Gross Receipts to Managers of the Company, less the deductions of all Company expenses of every kind related to the Picture. Without limiting the foregoing, the deductions shall include all costs, charges, and expenses paid or incurred in connection with the preparation, production, completion, and delivery of the Picture, deferred compensation, charges for any services, union or trade obligations, interest expenses, obligations to any completion guarantor, legal and accounting charges, the cost of all material, services, facilities, labor, insurance, taxes (other than income, franchise, and like taxes), copyright royalties attributable to the Picture for music, artwork, script, or other, judgments, marketing and promotional expenses, distribution fees, recoveries, settlements, losses, costs, and expenses, including reasonable attorneys' fees, sustained or incurred by Company in connection with the Picture or anything used therein and in connection with the production thereof.

9. **Services Provided.** Artist will render services, whenever and wherever Company may require, in a competent, conscientious, and professional manner, having due regard for the production of the Picture within the budget, and as instructed by Company in all matters, including those involving artistic taste and judgment; but there shall be no obligation on Company to actually utilize Artist's services, or to include any of Artist's work in the Picture, or to produce, release, or continue the distribution of the Picture. If, after the expiration or termination hereof, Company should require further services of Artist in the making of retakes, added scenes, looping, post-synching, publicity interviews, personal appearances, stills, and similar matters, Artist shall render such services on a daily basis, subject to Artist's availability with compensation at the SAG Agreement minimum, except that no compensation shall be payable for looping or post-synching, or for publicity interviews, personal appearances, and stills, and if Artist completes all continuous services required by Company from Artist before the expiration of said guaranteed period, and is dismissed by Company, no compensation shall be payable for the number of days equivalent to the number of working days between such dismissal and the expiration of said guaranteed period.

10. **Premieres/Film Festivals.** Should Artist render all services required herein and appear substantially in the film, Producer shall use its best efforts to obtain invitations to premieres/film festivals, with such invitations extended on a favored nations basis with other cast members.

11. **Term.** The term of this Agreement shall commence on the date hereof and shall continue thereafter until Artist has fully completed all services required hereunder, unless sooner terminated in accordance with the provisions of this Agreement.

12. **Credit.** Provided Artist completes all services required herein and appears recognizably in the Picture as released, then Artist shall receive credit on the screen. The screen credit shall use the Name of Artist for Credit listed above. No casual or inadvertent failure to comply with the provisions of this clause shall be deemed to be a breach

of this Agreement by Company. Artist shall notify Company of any breach of this paragraph, after which Company shall take reasonable steps to correct all new prints, copies, and advertising on a prospective basis, but Company shall not be required to recall or alter any prints, copies, or advertisements in production or distribution. No monetary damages are available for breach of Company's duties under this paragraph. If Artist is to receive credit in paid advertisements, said obligations shall apply only to the billing portion (excluding artwork and advertising copy) of advertisements issued by Company or under its direct control relating primarily to the theatrical exhibition of the Picture and which are issued prior to the date five (5) years after the release of the Picture. Billing requirements shall not apply at any time to teasers, trailers, radio and television advertising, group, list, or special advertisements, commercial tie-ups or by-products, or any advertisements of eight column inches or less.

[For above-the-line talent only, include (a) and (b)]

(a) Screen Credit. Company shall give Artist an on-screen credit in the main title sequence of the motion picture on a single card and in all listings of cast.

(b) Paid Advertising. Should Artist render all services required herein and appear recognizably in the Picture as released, Company shall provide Artist credit in the billing block in paid print advertising issued by Company which is at least 10 inches or larger and where the billing block appears. Position in the paid ads will be the same as on the main title cast credits at the same size of type and prominence as other actors accorded credit in the billing block. Paid ads will also be accorded in the same manner on all posters and one-sheets when a billing block is included.

13. **Work Made for Hire and Transfer of Rights.** All results and proceeds of Artist's services hereunder (including, but not limited to (i) all acts, poses, plays, and appearances of Artist, (ii) all literary, dramatic, and musical material written, supplied, or improvised by Artist whether or not in writing, (iii) all designs and inventions of Artist hereunder, and (iv) all photographs, drawings, plans, specifications, and sound recordings containing all or any part of any of the foregoing) shall constitute works prepared by Artist as an Artist of Company within the scope of Artist's employment hereunder, and accordingly,

the parties agree that all of the foregoing are and shall be considered "works made for hire" for Company; and that Company is and shall be considered the author thereof for all purposes and the owner throughout the world of all of the rights comprised in the copyright thereof, and of any and all tents, trademarks, and other rights thereto. Artist will, upon request, execute, acknowledge, and deliver to Company such additional documents as Company may deem necessary to evidence and effectuate Company's rights hereunder, and hereby grants to Company the right as Artist's attorney-in-fact to execute, acknowledge, deliver, and record in the U.S. Copyright Office or elsewhere any and all such documents.

(a) To the extent any Rights are not transferred to Company as a work made for hire, Artist hereby exclusively and irrevocably transfers such Rights to Company.

(b) To the extent Artist has created any copyrighted elements incorporated into the Picture and such work-made-for-hire provision is not recognized by the jurisdiction, Artist hereby assigns all rights or the maximum rights allowed under that jurisdiction's laws to Company, including, without limitation, Rental Lending Rights if recognized, rights to enforce any claim of attribution and integrity, or rights to exploit any interest in the Picture in any media now known or hereafter developed.

14. **Additional Services of Artist.**

(a) Dubbing. Company shall have the right to use a double to represent Artist's physical appearance and to dub or simulate Artist's voice and other sound effects, in whole or in part, in English and all other languages; provided, however, that Company will not dub Artist's voice in the English language, except as follows: (i) when necessary to expeditiously meet the requirements of foreign exhibition; (ii) when necessary to expeditiously meet censorship requirements, both foreign and domestic; (iii) when Artist shall fail and refuse to render the required services, or when Artist is not readily available when and where Artist's services are required hereunder; and (iv) when, in Company's opinion, Artist's voice, accent, or other performance hereunder, including singing and rendition of instrumental music, does not meet Company's requirements in connection with the role.

(b) Soundtrack recordings. Company and its successors, assigns, and licensees shall have the right to use the name, voice, and likeness of Artist in connection with phonograph records, CDs, or any other media now known or hereafter created, produced, or reproduced from the soundtrack of the Picture or any part thereof without additional compensation to Artist.

(c) Related services. Artist shall (i) render services prior to the starting date without compensation in connection with wardrobe preparation, fittings, tests, auditions, rehearsals, prerecordings, consultations, publicity interviews, and similar matters, subject to Artist's availability; (ii) act, pose, sing, speak, play such musical instruments as Artist is capable of playing, and otherwise appear and perform in said role; and (iii) render services in connection with promotional films, trailers, and electrical transcriptions produced in connection with the advertising and exploitation of the Picture. Such services shall be rendered either during or after the term hereof, but if after the term hereof, subject to Artist's availability. Behind-the-scenes footage and clips from the Picture and (subject to clearance from the owners thereof) from other motion pictures in which Artist has appeared may be utilized in connection with such promotional films and trailers. No additional compensation for the services referred to in this subdivision (c) or for the use of such clips or such footage shall be payable.

15. **Wardrobe.** Artist shall provide such modern wardrobe for said role as Artist may possess and all other wardrobe and clothing which is not visible on the screen. Company shall provide all visible character and period wardrobe for said role, if any. Any wardrobe which Artist is required to furnish hereunder shall be suitable, in Company's opinion, for said role. All wardrobe furnished or paid for by Company shall be and remain its property and shall be returned promptly to Company. If any wardrobe furnished by Artist is damaged without Artist's fault while being used in connection with Artist's employment hereunder, Company will be responsible for such damage.

16. **Unique Services.** It is hereby agreed and understood that Artist's services to be furnished hereunder are special, extraordinary, unique, and not replaceable, and that there is no adequate remedy at law for breach of this contract by Artist.

(a) Company shall be entitled to both legal and equitable remedies as may be available, including both injunctive relief and damages. Company may elect to not to submit arbitration for the purpose of seeking emergency, preliminary, or temporary injunctive relief.

(b) Artist's services shall be in such time, place, and manner as Company may reasonably direct in accordance with customary motion picture industry practice. Such services shall be rendered in an artistic, conscientious, efficient, and punctual manner to the best of Artist's ability to adhere to the budget and shooting schedule.

(c) Artist grants to Company the perpetual nonexclusive right to use and license others to use Artist's name, biography, and reproductions of Artist's physical likeness and voice in connection with the production, exhibition, advertising, promotion, or other exploitation of the Picture and all subsidiary and ancillary rights therein and thereto; provided, however, Company shall not use or authorize the use of Artist's name or likeness as a direct endorsement of any product or service without Artist's prior consent.

17. Representations and Warranties.

(a) Company warrants and represents that it has the full right, power, and authority to enter into this Agreement and to grant all rights granted herein, that it is not under, nor will it be under, any disability, restriction, or prohibition with respect to its rights to fully perform in accordance with the terms and conditions of this Agreement, and that there shall be no liens, claims, or other interests which may interfere with, impair, or be in derogation of the rights granted herein.

(b) Artist warrants and represents that Artist is free to enter into this agreement and not subject to any conflicting obligations or any disability which will or might prevent Artist from or interfere with Artist's execution and performance of this agreement; that all literary, dramatic, and musical material, designs, and inventions of Artist hereunder will be original with Artist or in the public domain throughout the world, and shall not infringe upon or violate any copyright of, or the right of privacy or any other right of, any person, and that Artist is a member in good standing of such labor organization as may have jurisdiction, to the extent required by law and applicable collective bargaining agreements.

18. Indemnifications.

(a) Company hereby agrees to indemnify Artist from and against any damages, liabilities, costs, and expenses, including reasonable attorneys' fees actually incurred, arising out of or in any way connected with any claim, demand, or action inconsistent with the Picture, its obligations under this Agreement, or any warranty, representation, or agreement made by Artist herein.

(b) Artist hereby agrees to indemnify Company, Company's successors, licensees, distributors, subdistributors, and assigns, and the respective officers, directors, agents, and Artists of each of the foregoing, from and against any damages, liabilities, costs, and expenses, including reasonable attorneys' fees actually incurred, arising out of or in any way connected with any claim, demand, or action inconsistent with its obligations under this Agreement, the Rights, or any warranty, representation, or agreement made by Artist herein.

(c) The warranties and representations of this paragraph shall survive the termination of this Agreement.

19. Resolution of Disputes.
The provisions of the Screen Actors Guild Codified Basic Agreement for Independent Producers with respect to the arbitration of disputes shall be applicable to Artist's employment. Any dispute not subject to arbitration by the Screen Actors Guild shall be subject to arbitration by the American Arbitration Association.

20. Employment.
All payments made for services under this Agreement will be treated as wages for the purpose of all taxing authorities, including U.S. federal, state, and local income-related and employment-related taxes. Company will deduct all taxes as may be required by any lawful authority.

21. Confidentiality; Publicity.
Company shall have the exclusive right to issue and to license others to issue advertising and publicity with respect to the Picture, and Artist shall not circulate, publish, or otherwise disseminate any such advertising or publicity without Company's prior written consent. Artist hereby grants to Company the right to issue and authorize publicity concerning Artist, and to use Artist's name, voice, and likeness and biographical data in connection with the distribution, exhibition, advertising, and exploitation of the Picture. Without limiting the generality of the foregoing, Company may use Artist's name, voice, and likeness provided refer-

ence is made to the Picture or the literary property or screenplay upon which the Picture is based, or any part thereof, or to Artist's employment hereunder, and provided Artist is not represented as using or endorsing any product or service.

22. **Assignment.** Artist agrees that Company shall have the right to assign, license, delegate, lend, or otherwise transfer all or any part of its rights or duties under this Agreement at any time to any person including, without limitation, Artist's name, likeness, and biographical data, and all representations and warranties hereunder. Artist acknowledges that the personal services to be rendered by Artist hereunder are of the essence of this Agreement and agrees that he shall not assign this Agreement, in whole of in part, to any person, and that any purported assignment or delegation of duties by Artist shall be null and void and of no force and effect whatsoever. This Agreement shall inure to the benefit of Company's successors, assigns, licensees, grantees, and associated, affiliated, and subsidiary companies.

23. **No Obligation.** Company agrees to use all reasonable efforts to cause the Picture to be produced, however, the parties recognize that the production of an independent motion picture is an inherently difficult undertaking. Company is under no obligation to produce the Picture hereunder. In the event Company abandons production of the Picture hereunder, Artist is entitled to such fixed compensation as had previously accrued and is not entitled to any additional compensation, damage, or loss as a result of such failure to undertake or complete the Picture.

24. **Contingencies.**

(a) Artist's services and the accrual of compensation hereunder, and the running of any periods herein provided for, shall be suspended without notice during all periods (i) that Artist does not render services hereunder because of illness, incapacity, default, or similar matters beyond Company's control; (ii) that production of the Picture is prevented or interrupted because of force majeure events (i.e., any labor dispute, fire, war, governmental action, or any other unexpected or disruptive event sufficient to excuse performance of this agreement as a matter of law), or the death, illness, or incapacity of the director or a principal member of the cast. All dates herein set forth or provided for shall be postponed for a period equivalent to the period of such event. If any matter referred to in (i), other than default, shall exist for five business days or more, or if any matter referred to in (ii) shall exist for eight weeks or more, or in the event of any refusal to perform or other default on the part of Artist, Company may terminate Artist's engagement hereunder. Notwithstanding anything herein contained, if any suspension under (ii) shall continue for two weeks or more, Artist may render services for others during the continuance of such suspension, subject to immediate recall on the termination of such suspension.

(b) Company may secure life, health, accident, cast, or other insurance covering Artist, or Artist and others, and Artist shall have no right, title, or interest in or to such insurance. Artist will submit to usual and customary medical examinations for Company's insurance purposes (including self-insurance) and will sign such applications or other documents as may be reasonably required in the premises. Artist may have Artist's own physician present at any such examination at Artist's own expense. Company has the right to terminate this Agreement in the event that Artist fails to pass such medical examination or does not provide the necessary documentation to allow for an insurance policy to be written.

25. **Assurances.** Each party shall execute all documents and certificates and perform all acts deemed appropriate by the Company or required by this Agreement in connection with this Agreement and the production of the Picture.

26. **Complete Agreement.** This Agreement constitutes the complete and exclusive statement of the agreement among the parties with respect to the matters discussed herein and it supersedes all prior written or oral statements among the parties, including any prior statement, warranty, or representation. Except as herein expressly provided, this agreement cancels and supersedes all prior negotiations and understandings relating to the Picture and contains all of the terms, conditions, representations, and warranties of the parties hereto in the premises. Nothing herein contained shall be construed so as to require the commission of any act contrary to law and wherever there is any conflict between any provision of this agreement and any present or future statute, law, ordinance, or regulation, the latter shall prevail, but in such event the provision of this agreement

affected shall be curtailed and limited only to the extent necessary to bring it within legal requirements.

27. **Section Headings.** The section headings which appear throughout this Agreement are provided for convenience only and are not intended to define or limit the scope of this Agreement or the intent or subject matter of its provisions.

28. **Applicable Law.** Each party agrees that all disputes arising under or in connection with this Agreement and any transactions contemplated by this Agreement shall be governed by the internal law, and not the law of conflicts, of the State of _____.

29. **Notices.** Any notice or other writing to be served upon either party in connection with this Agreement shall be in writing and shall be deemed completed when delivered to the address listed above.

30. **Amendments.** Any amendments, modifications, or alterations to this Agreement must be in writing and signed by all of the parties hereto.

31. **Severability.** Each provision of this Agreement is severable from the other provisions. If, for any reason, any provision of this Agreement is declared invalid or contrary to existing law, the inoperability of that provision shall have no effect on the remaining provisions of the Agreement and all remaining provisions shall continue in full force and effect.

32. **Counterparts.** This Agreement may be executed in counterparts, each of which shall be deemed an original and all of which shall, when taken together, constitute a single document.

IN WITNESS WHEREOF, the parties hereto have executed and delivered this agreement as of the date written below.

PRODUCTIONS, LLC   ARTIST

_____   _____

By: Jane Doe, Manager
    PRODUCTIONS, LLC   _____
                                          Print Name

DATE: _____

5. Actor Nudity Rider

When countersigned below, the following will constitute the terms and conditions of the nudity rider agreement ("Rider Agreement") between Productions, LLC ("Company"), and the artist identified below ("Artist") in respect to the motion picture tentatively known as "The Picture" ("Picture").

The parties hereto acknowledge that the Picture has "nude scenes" that will require the Artist to render services in the nude. The Artist has read the screenplay for the Picture prior to receipt of this agreement and hereby consents to rendition of such services in the nude as may be required.

The Artist [shall/shall not] be in any scenes requiring below-the-belt frontal nudity.

Producer hereby agrees that during any phase of production involving nudity, the set shall be closed to all persons having no business purpose in connection with the production. Producer further agrees that there shall be no still photography of nudity and all provisions of the Screen Actors Guild Basic Agreement relating to the filming of nudity shall apply.

Except as provided herein, all terms related to the parties shall remain those set forth in the Actor Employment Agreement.

IN WITNESS WHEREOF, the parties hereto have executed and delivered this agreement as of the date written below.

PRODUCTIONS, LLC   ARTIST

_____   _____

By: Jane Doe, Manager
    PRODUCTIONS, LLC   _____

Print Name

DATE: _____

6. Talent and Appearance Release

This release is appropriate for extras and for individuals shown in background photographs.

For valuable consideration, receipt of which is hereby acknowledged, I hereby give Productions, LLC, including its assignees or licensees, or anyone associated with the Picture (collectively "Company") the absolute, irrevocable right and permission, forever and throughout the world, in connection with the motion picture tentatively entitled "The Picture" (the "Picture"), the following:

1. The perpetual and universal right to photograph and rephotograph me (still and moving) and to record and rerecord, double, and dub my voice and performances, by any methods or means, and to use and authorize others to use my name, voice, and likeness for and in connection with the Picture. Copyright for all such work shall vest exclusively in Company as a work made for hire of an audiovisual work. If such vesting of copyright is deemed invalid, then I hereby assign any copyright to Company.
2. I hereby approve the use of my name, voice, and image by Company in any manner related to the Picture and forever release and discharge Company from any and all claims, actions, and demands arising out of such use.
3. [This paragraph is the *Borat*-style long-form release, to be used when "any and all claims" in paragraph 2 is likely to be challenged.] I agree to waive any and all claims against the Company or against any of its assignees or licensees, or anyone associated with the Picture, that includes assertions of (a) infringement of rights of publicity or misappropriation (such as any allegedly improper or unauthorized use of my name or likeness or image) (b) intrusion (such as any allegedly offensive behavior or questioning or any invasion of privacy), (c) false light (such as any allegedly false or misleading portrayal of Participant), (d) infliction of emotional distress (whether allegedly intentional or negligent), (e) defamation (such as allegedly false statements made on the Picture), or (f) intellectual property rights (such as copyright, trademark, unfair competition, trade secrets, patents, Lanham Act, or other state or federally protected interests).
4. For purposes hereof, the Picture shall include audiovisual works of any kind now known or hereafter created (including, without limita-

tion, motion pictures, episodic productions, sequels, or prequels), soundtracks (including soundtrack albums), trailers, and documentary and/or "making of" pictures, advertising, and packaging for any or all such materials.

5. Company is under no obligation to produce the Picture hereunder. This Agreement shall inure to the benefit of Company's successors, assigns, licensees, grantees, and associated, affiliated, and subsidiary companies.

6. This Agreement shall constitute our full understanding unless amended to the contrary in writing and signed by both parties. I acknowledge and agree that in entering into this agreement I have not relied upon or been induced by any promise or representation (express or implied, oral or written) of Company or any person acting for Company, which is not contained in this Agreement. This Agreement shall be governed by and construed in accordance with the laws of the State of _____ applicable to contracts entered into and fully performed therein.

Date: _____   ACCEPTED AND AGREED

_____   _____
Print Name of Talent   Age

_____   _____
Signature   Productions, LLC

For Talent under 18 years of Age: I   By: _____
represent I am the parent or guardian   Print Name
of the above named Talent. For value
received I hereby consent to this
Agreement in his or her behalf.

_____
Print Name of Talent Parent/Guardian

_____
Signature of Parent or Guardian

7. Location Release Form

I hereby give Productions, LLC, its employees, agents, independent contractors, parents, subsidiaries, affiliates, licensees, successors, and assigns (collectively "Company") for good and valuable consideration, receipt of which is hereby acknowledged, permission to access, enter upon, and use the property identified below and the contents thereof and the appurtenances thereto (the "Property") for the purpose of photographing and recording images, audiovisual works, and sound recordings at this location (the "Material") in connection with a motion picture ("Picture") on or about the shooting date(s) listed below.

1. Company may place all necessary facilities and equipment on the Property and agrees to remove same after completion of work and leave the property in as good of condition as when received. Company will use reasonable care to prevent damage to said Property. Company shall provide me certificate of insurance naming the Property owner as additional insured.

2. I irrevocably grant to Company all rights of every kind in and to the Material including, without limitation, the right to exploit the Material throughout the world, in any and all languages, an unlimited number of times, in perpetuity in any and all media, now known or hereafter invented, in and in connection with the Picture, and for advertising and promotional purposes in connection therewith, and all rights, including copyright in the Material shall be and remain vested in Company. Copyright for all such work shall vest exclusively in Company as a work made for hire of an audiovisual work. If such vesting of copyright is deemed invalid, then I hereby assign any copyright I may have acquired in the Material to Company.

3. I release and discharge Company from any and all claims, actions, and demands arising out of or in connection with the Material, including, without limitation, any and all claims of infringement of copyright, libel and slander, and invasion of privacy. Company shall indemnify the Property owner against any third-party claims of copyright infringement, libel and slander, and invasion of privacy regarding the Material or Picture.

4. For purposes hereof, the Picture shall include audiovisual works of any kind now known or hereafter created (including, without limitation, motion pictures, episodic productions, sequels, or prequels),

soundtracks (including soundtrack albums), trailers, and documentary and/or "making of" pictures, advertising, and packaging for any or all such materials. Company is under no obligation to produce the Picture hereunder.

5. I represent that I own or control all rights to grant entry to this location and am authorized to negotiate this release and that I have read and fully understand the contents hereof.

The signature below shall provide the same permission whether permission was authorized before or after the actual filming of the Material.

Location Address/Description: _____

Shoot Dates: _____

Name: _____   Title: _____

Signature _____   Date: _____

WGA Writing Credit Definitions

Excerpted from Screen Credits Manual, *part III, "Guild Policy on Credits," www.wga.org/subpage_writersresources.aspx?id=167 (as of August 1, 2008).*

A. Definitions

1. Writer

The term "writer" is defined in the Minimum Basic Agreement. In general, the term "writer" means a person employed by a Company to write literary material or a person from whom a Company purchased literary material who at the time of purchase was a "professional writer," as defined in the Minimum Basic Agreement.

For purposes of credit, a team of writers, as defined in the Screen Credits Manual Section I.B., is considered as one writer.

If literary material covered under the Minimum Basic Agreement is written by one member of a team, separate and apart from the work of the team, such literary material shall be considered separate from the literary material by the team for purposes of assessing contributions to the final shooting script. Therefore, such individual is eligible to receive writing credit as an individual writer and/or as a member of a team.

2. Literary Material

Literary material is written material and shall include stories, adaptations, treatments, original treatments, scenarios, continuities, teleplays, screenplays, dialogue, scripts, sketches, plots, outlines, narrative synopses, routines, and narrations, and, for use in the production of television film, formats.

3. Source Material

Source material is all material, other than story as hereinafter defined, upon which the story and/or screenplay is based.

This means that source material is material assigned to the writer which was previously published or exploited and upon which the writer's work is to be based (e.g., a novel, a produced play or series of published articles), or any other material written outside of the Guild's jurisdiction (e.g., literary material purchased from a non-professional writer). Illustrative examples of source material credits are: "From a Play by", "From a Novel by", "Based upon a Story by", "From a series of articles by", "Based upon a Screenplay by" or other appropriate wording indicating the form in which such source material is acquired. Research material is not considered source material.

4. Story

The term "story" means all writing covered by the provisions of the Minimum Basic Agreement representing a contribution "distinct from screenplay and consisting of basic narrative, idea, theme or outline indicating character development and action."

It is appropriate to award a "Story by" credit when: 1) the story was written under employment under Guild jurisdiction; 2) the story was purchased by a signatory company from a professional writer, as defined in the Minimum Basic Agreement; or 3) when the screenplay is based upon a sequel story written under the Guild's jurisdiction. If the story is based upon source material of a story nature, see "screen story" below.

5. Screen Story

Credit for story authorship in the form "Screen Story by" is appropriate when the screenplay is based upon source material and a story, as those terms are defined above, and the story is substantially new or different from the source material.

6. Screenplay

A screenplay consists of individual scenes and full dialogue, together with such prior treatment, basic adaptation, continuity, scenario and dialogue as shall be used in, and represent substantial contributions to the final script.

A "Screenplay by" credit is appropriate when there is source material of a story nature (with or without a "Screen Story" credit) or when the writer(s) entitled to "Story by" credit is different than the writer(s) entitled to "Screenplay by" credit.

7. "Written by"

The term "Written by" is used when the writer(s) is entitled to both the "Story by" credit and the "Screenplay by" credit.

This credit shall not be granted where there is source material of a story nature. However, biographical, newspaper and other factual sources may not necessarily deprive the writer of such credit.

8. "Narration Written by"

"Narration Written by" credit is appropriate where the major writing contribution to a motion picture is in the form of narration. The term "narration" means material (typically off-camera) to explain or relate sequence or action (excluding promos or trailers).

9. "Based on Characters Created by"

"Based on Characters Created by" is a writing credit given to the writer(s) entitled to separated rights in a theatrical or television motion picture on each theatrical sequel to such theatrical or television motion picture.

Where there are no separated rights, "Based on Characters Created by" may be accorded to the author of source material upon which a sequel is based.

10. "Adaptation by"

This credit is appropriate in certain unusual cases where a writer shapes the direction of screenplay construction without qualifying for "Screenplay by" credit. In those special cases, and only as a result of arbitration, the "Adaptation by" credit may be used.

B. Rules for Determining Credit

In determining relative contribution, the relevant factors shall be what material was actually used, not the Arbitration Committee's personal preference of one script over another.

Screen credit for screenplay will not be shared by more than two writers, except that in unusual cases, and solely as the result of arbitration, the names of three writers or the names of writers constituting two writing teams may be used. The limitation on the number of writers applies to all feature length photoplays except episodic pictures and revues.

C. Production Executives

The term "production executives" includes individuals who receive credit as the director or in any producer capacity. The following rules govern writing credits of production executives who also perform writing services when there are other writers involved on the same project.

1. Automatic Arbitration Provisions

Schedule A of the Minimum Basic Agreement provides:

"Unless the story and/or screenplay writing is done entirely without any other writer, no designation of tentative story or screenplay credit to a production executive shall become final or effective unless approved by a credit arbitration as herein provided, in accordance with the Guild rules for determination of such credit."

2. Notice Requirements

If a production executive intends to claim credit as a team on any literary material with a writer(s) who is not a production executive, he/she must, at the time when such team writing begins, have signified such claim in writing to the Guild and to the writer(s) with whom he/she claims to have worked as a team. Failure to comply with the above will preclude such production executive from claiming co-authorship of the literary material in question, and such literary material shall be attributed to the other writer.

D. Remakes

In the case of remakes, any writer who has received writing credit under the Guild's jurisdiction in connection with a prior version of the motion picture is a participating writer on the remake. As such, those prior writers are entitled to participate in the credit determination process and are eligible to receive writing credit pursuant to the rules for determining writing credits. The final shooting script written by a prior writer(s) shall be considered literary material.

If under the "Rules for Determining Writing Credits" (Section III.B.) the Arbitration Committee determines that such prior writer(s) is not entitled to receive writing credit, the Arbitration Committee may, within its discretion, accord such prior writer(s) a credit in the nature of a source material credit, such as "Based on a Screenplay by. . . ."

However, the rules do not preclude a prior writer(s) from receiving both writing credit and a credit in the nature of a source material credit at the discretion of the Arbitration Committee.

Remakes shall be considered non-original screenplays under Section III.B.4.b.(2) of this Manual.

E. Withdrawal from Credit

Prior to the time a credit question has been submitted to arbitration, a writer may withdraw from screen writing credit for personal cause, such as violation of his/her principles or mutilation of material he/she has written. If the other writer-contributors do not agree, the question shall be referred to arbitration. The Arbitration Committee in such cases shall base its determination on whether there is such personal cause.

After screen credits have been determined by arbitration, a writer may not withdraw his/her name from screenplay credit. He/she may, however, by notification to the Guild, withdraw from any other form of credit.

Withdrawal from writing credit will result in loss of any and all rights accruing from receipt of writing credit. Use of a pseudonym rather than withdrawing from credit will not result in such a forfeiture.

Best Practice Guide for Fair Use in Documentaries

Documentary Filmmakers' Statement of Best Practices in Fair Use, November 18, 2005

By the Association of Independent Video and Filmmakers, Independent Feature Project, International Documentary Association, National Alliance for Media Arts and Culture, and Women in Film and Video (Washington, D.C., chapter), in consultation with the Center for Social Media in the School of Communication at American University and the Program on Intellectual Property and the Public Interest in the Washington College of Law at American University, and endorsed by Arts Engine, the Bay Area Video Coalition, CINE, Doculink, Electronic Arts Intermix, Grantmakers in Film and Electronic Media, Full Frame Documentary Festival, the Independent Television Service, National Video Resources, P.O.V./American Documentary, the University Film and Video Association, Video Association of Dallas, and Women Make Movies.

This Statement of Best Practices in Fair Use makes clear what documentary filmmakers currently regard as reasonable application of the copyright "fair use" doctrine. Fair use expresses the core value of free expression within copyright law. The statement clarifies this crucial legal doctrine, to help filmmakers use it with confidence. Fair use is shaped, in part, by the practice of the professional communities that employ it. The statement is informed both by experience and ethical principles. It also draws on analogy: documentary filmmakers should have the same kind of access to copy-

righted materials that is enjoyed by cultural and historical critics who work
in print media and by news broadcasters.

Preamble

This Statement of Best Practices in Fair Use is necessary because documentary filmmakers have found themselves, over the last decade, increasingly constrained by demands to clear rights for copyrighted material. Creators in other disciplines do not face such demands to the same extent, and documentarians in earlier eras experienced them less often and less intensely. Today, however, documentarians believe that their ability to communicate effectively is being restricted by an overly rigid approach to copyright compliance, and that the public suffers as a result. The knowledge and perspectives that documentarians can provide are compromised by their need to select only the material that copyright holders approve and make available at reasonable prices.

At the same time, documentarians are themselves copyright holders, whose businesses depend on the willingness of others to honor their claims as copyright owners. They do not countenance exploitative or abusive applications of fair use, which might impair their own businesses or betray their work.

Therefore, documentarians through their professional organizations, supported by an advisory board of copyright experts, now offer the statement that follows.

Background

"Fair use" is a key part of the social bargain at the heart of copyright law, in which as a society we concede certain limited individual property rights to ensure the benefits of creativity to a living culture. We have chosen to encourage creators by rewarding their efforts with copyright. To promote new cultural production, however, it also is important to give other creators opportunities to use copyrighted material when they are making something new that incorporates or depends on such material. Unless such uses are possible, the whole society may lose important expressions just because one person is arbitrary or greedy. So copyright law has features that permit quotations from copyrighted works to be made without permission, under certain conditions.

Fair use is the most important of these features. It has been an important part of copyright law for more than 150 years. Where it applies, fair use is a right, not a mere privilege. In fact, as the Supreme Court has pointed out, fair use helps reconcile copyright law with the First Amendment. As copyright protects more works for longer periods, it impinges more and more directly on creative practice. As a result, fair use is more important today than ever before.

Creators benefit from the fact that the copyright law does not exactly specify how to apply fair use. Creative needs and practices differ with the field, with technology, and with time. Instead, lawyers and judges decide whether an unlicensed use of copyrighted material is "fair" according to a "rule of reason." This means taking all the facts and circumstances into account to decide if an unlicensed use of copyright material generates social or cultural benefits that are greater than the costs it imposes on the copyright owner. Fair use is flexible; it is not uncertain or unreliable. In fact, for any particular field of critical or creative activity, such as documentary filmmaking, lawyers and judges consider professional expectations and practice in assessing what is "fair" within the field. In weighing the balance at the heart of fair use analysis, courts employ a four-part test, set out in the Copyright Act. In doing so, they return again and again to two key questions:

- Did the unlicensed use "transform" the material taken from the copyrighted work by using it for a different purpose than the original, or did it just repeat the work for the same intent and value as the original?
- Was the amount and nature of material taken appropriate in light of the nature of the copyrighted work and of the use?

Among other things, both questions address whether the use will cause excessive economic harm to the copyright owner.

If the answers to these two questions are affirmative, a court is likely to find a use fair. Because that is true, such a use is unlikely to be challenged in the first place. Documentary films usually satisfy the "transformativeness" standard easily, because copyrighted material is typically used in a context different from that in which it originally appeared. Likewise, documentarians typically quote only short and isolated portions of copyrighted works. Thus, judges generally have honored documentarians' claims of fair use in the rare instances where they have been challenged in court.

Another consideration underlies and influences the way in which these questions are analyzed: Whether the user acted reasonably and in good faith, in light of general practice in his or her particular field. In the future, filmmakers' ability to rely on fair use will be further enhanced by the Statement of Best Practices in Fair Use that follows. This statement serves as evidence of commonly held understandings in documentary practice and helps to demonstrate the reasonableness of uses that fall within its principles.

Documentarians find other creator groups' reliance on fair use heartening. For instance, historians regularly quote both other historians' writings and textual sources; artists reinterpret and critique existing images (rather than merely appropriating them); scholars illustrate cultural commentary with textual, visual, and musical examples. Equally important is the example of the news media: fair use is healthy and vigorous in daily broadcast television, where references to popular films, classic TV programs, archival images, and popular songs are constant and routinely unlicensed.

The statement that follows describes the actual practice of many documentarians, joined with the views of others about what would be appropriate if they were free to follow their own understanding of good practice. In making films for TV, cable, and theaters, documentarians who assert fair use often meet with resistance. All too frequently they are told (often by nonlawyers) that they must clear "everything" if they want their work to reach the public. Even so, some documentarians have not been intimidated. Unfortunately, until now the documentarians who depend on fair use generally have done so quietly, in order to avoid undesired attention. In this statement, documentarians are exercising their free speech rights—and their rights under copyright—in the open.

This statement does not address the problems that result from lack of access to archival material that is best quality or the only copy. The statement applies to situations where the filmmaker has ready access to the necessary material in some form.

The statement also does not directly address the problem of "orphan works"—works presumably copyrighted but whose owners cannot be located with reasonable effort. Generally, it should be possible to make fair use of orphan works on the same basis as clearly sourced ones. Sometimes, however, filmmakers also may wish to use orphan works in ways that exceed fair use. A more comprehensive solution for orphan works may soon be provided through an initiative spearheaded by the U.S. Copyright Office (for more information, see www.copyright.gov/orphan).

This statement finally does not concern "free use"—situations when documentarians never need to clear rights. Examples of types of free use are available in documents at www.centerforsocialmedia.org/fairuse.htm.

The Statement

This statement recognizes that documentary filmmakers must choose whether or not to rely on fair use when their projects involve the use of copyrighted material. It is organized around four classes of situations that they confront regularly in practice. (These four classes do *not* exhaust all the likely situations where fair use might apply; they reflect the most common kinds of situations that documentarians identified at this point.) In each case, a general principle about the applicability of fair use is asserted, followed by qualifications that may affect individual cases.

The four classes of situations, with their informing principles and limitations, follow.

One: Employing Copyrighted Material as the Object of Social, Political, or Cultural Critique

Description: This class of uses involves situations in which documentarians engage in media critique, whether of text, image, or sound works. In these cases, documentarians hold the specific copyrighted work up for critical analysis.

Principle: Such uses are generally permissible as an exercise of documentarians' fair use rights. This is analogous to the way that (for example) a newspaper might review a new book and quote from it by way of illustration. Indeed, this activity is at the very core of the fair use doctrine as a safeguard for freedom of expression. So long as the filmmaker analyzes or comments on the work itself, the means may vary. Both direct commentary and parody, for example, function as forms of critique. Where copyrighted material is used for a critical purpose, the fact that the critique itself may do economic damage to the market for the quoted work (as a negative book review could) is irrelevant. In order to qualify as fair use, the use may be as extensive as is necessary to make the point, permitting the viewer to fully grasp the criticism or analysis.

Limitations: There is one general qualification to the principle just stated. The use should not be so extensive or pervasive that it ceases to function as critique and becomes, instead, a way of satisfying the audience's taste for the thing (or the kind of thing) critiqued. In other words, the critical use should not become a market *substitute* for the work (or other works like it).

Two: Quoting Copyrighted Works of Popular Culture to Illustrate an Argument or Point

Description: Here the concern is with material (again of whatever kind) that is quoted not because it is, in itself, the object of critique but because it aptly illustrates some argument or point that a filmmaker is developing—as clips from fiction films might be used (for example) to demonstrate changing American attitudes toward race.

Principle: Once again, this sort of quotation should generally be considered as fair use. The possibility that the quotes might entertain and engage an audience as well as illustrate a filmmaker's argument takes nothing away from the fair use claim. Works of popular culture typically have illustrative power, and in analogous situations, writers in print media do not hesitate to use illustrative quotations (both words and images). In documentary filmmaking, such a privileged use will be both subordinate to the larger intellectual or artistic purpose of the documentary and important to its realization. The filmmaker is not presenting the quoted material for its original purpose but harnessing it for a new one. This is an attempt to add significant new value, not a form of "free riding"—the mere exploitation of existing value.

Limitations: Documentarians will be best positioned to assert fair use claims if they assure that:

- the material is properly attributed, either through an accompanying on-screen identification or a mention in the film's final credits;

- to the extent possible and appropriate, quotations are drawn from a range of different sources;
- each quotation (however many may be employed to create an overall pattern of illustrations) is no longer than is necessary to achieve the intended effect;
- the quoted material is not employed merely in order to avoid the cost or inconvenience of shooting equivalent footage.

Three: Capturing Copyrighted Media Content in the Process of Filming Something Else

Description: Documentarians often record copyrighted sounds and images when they are filming sequences in real-life settings. Common examples are the text of a poster on a wall, music playing on a radio, and television programming heard (perhaps seen) in the background. In the context of the documentary, the incidentally captured material is an integral part of the ordinary reality being documented. Only by altering and thus falsifying the reality they film—such as telling subjects to turn off the radio, take down a poster, or turn off the TV—could documentarians avoid this.

Principle: Fair use should protect documentary filmmakers from being forced to falsify reality. Where a sound or image has been captured incidentally and without prevision, as part of an unstaged scene, it should be permissible to use it, to a reasonable extent, as part of the final version of the film. Any other rule would be inconsistent with the documentary practice itself and with the values of the disciplines (such as criticism, historical analysis, and journalism) that inform reality-based filmmaking.

Limitations: Consistent with the rationale for treating such captured media uses as fair ones, documentarians should take care that:

- particular media content played or displayed in a scene being filmed was not requested or directed;
- incidentally captured media content included in the final version of the film is integral to the scene/action;
- the content is properly attributed;

- the scene has not been included primarily to exploit the incidentally captured content in its own right, and the captured content does not constitute the scene's primary focus of interest;
- in the case of music, the content does not function as a substitute for a synch track (as it might, for example, if the sequence containing the captured music were cut on its beat, or if the music were used after the filmmaker has cut away to another sequence).

Four: Using Copyrighted Material in a Historical Sequence

Description: In many cases the best (or even the only) effective way to tell a particular historical story or make a historical point is to make selective use of words that were spoken during the events in question, music that was associated with the events, or photographs and films that were taken at that time. In many cases, such material is available, on reasonable terms, under license. On occasion, however, the licensing system breaks down.

Principle: Given the social and educational importance of the documentary medium, fair use should apply in some instances of this kind. To conclude otherwise would be to deny the potential of filmmaking to represent history to new generations of citizens. Properly conditioned, this variety of fair use is critical to fulfilling the mission of copyright. But unless limited, the principle also can defeat the legitimate interests of copyright owners—including documentary filmmakers themselves.

Limitations: To support a claim that a use of this kind is fair, the documentarian should be able to show that:

- the film project was not specifically designed around the material in question;
- the material serves a critical illustrative function, and no suitable substitute exists (that is, a substitute with the same general characteristics);
- the material cannot be licensed, or the material can be licensed only on terms that are excessive relative to a reasonable budget for the film in question;

- the use is no more extensive than is necessary to make the point for which the material has been selected;
- the film project does not rely predominantly or disproportionately on any single source for illustrative clips;
- the copyright owner of the material used is properly identified.

Fair Use in Other Situations Faced by Documentarians

The four principles just stated do not exhaust the scope of fair use for documentary filmmakers. Inevitably, actual filmmaking practice will give rise to situations that are hybrids of those described above or that simply have not been anticipated. In considering such situations, however, filmmakers should be guided by the same basic values of fairness, proportionality, and reasonableness that inform this statement. Where they are confident that a contemplated quotation of copyrighted material falls within fair use, they should claim fair use.

Some Common Misunderstandings About Fair Use

As already indicated, two goals of the preceding statement are to encourage documentarians to rely on fair use where it is appropriate and to help persuade the people who insure, distribute, and program their work to accept and support documentarians in these choices. Some common errors about fair use and its applicability may stand in the way of accomplishing these goals. Briefly, then, here are some correctives to these misunderstandings:

- *Fair use need not be exclusively high minded or "educational" in nature.* Although nonprofit or academic uses often have good claims to be considered "fair," they are not the only ones. A new work can be "commercial"—even highly commercial—in intent and effect and still invoke fair use. Most of the cases in which courts have found unlicensed uses of copyrighted works to be fair have involved projects designed to make money, including some that actually have.
- *Fair use doesn't have to be boring.* A use is no less likely to qualify as a fair one because the film in which it occurs is effective in attracting and holding an audience. If a use otherwise satisfies the principles and limitations described

in the Statement of Best Practices in Fair Use, the fact that it is entertaining or emotionally engaging should be irrelevant to the analysis.

- *A documentarian's failed effort to clear rights doesn't inhibit his or her ability to claim fair use with respect to the use in question.*
Everyone likes to avoid conflict and reduce uncertainty. Often, there will be good reasons to seek permissions in situations where they may not literally be required. In general, then, it never hurts to try, and it actually can help demonstrate the filmmaker's good faith. And sometimes (as in connection with Principle Four) it can be critically important.

For more information consult www.centerforsocialmedia.org/fairuse

Legal Advisory Board

Professor Julie E. Cohen
Georgetown University Law Center
Washington, D.C.

Michael C. Donaldson, Esq.
Donaldson & Hart
Los Angeles, California

Professor Michael J. Madison
University of Pittsburgh School of Law
Pittsburgh, Pennsylvania

Gloria C. Phares, Esq.
Patterson Belknap Webb & Tyler
New York, New York

J. Stephen Sheppard, Esq.
Cowan, DeBaets, Abrahams & Sheppard
New York, New York

Authoring Organizations

Association of Independent Video and Filmmakers (AIVF)
Works to increase creative and professional opportunities for independent video and filmmakers and to enhance the growth of independent media by providing services, advocacy, and information.

Independent Feature Project (IFP)
Fosters a sustainable infrastructure that supports independent filmmaking and ensures that the public has the opportunity to see films that more accurately reflect the full diversity of the American culture.

International Documentary Association (IDA)
Promotes nonfiction film and video around the world by supporting and recognizing the efforts of documentary film and video makers, increasing public appreciation and demand for the documentary, and providing a forum for documentary makers, their supporters, and suppliers.

National Alliance for Media Arts and Culture (NAMAC)
Provides education, advocacy, and networking opportunities for the independent media field.

Women in Film and Video (WIFV), Washington, D.C., Chapter
Works to advance the professional development and achievement for women working in all areas of film, television, video, multimedia, and related disciplines.

Academic Consulting Organizations

Center for Social Media
Directed by Professor Pat Aufderheide, showcases and analyzes media for social justice, civil society, and democracy, and the public environment that nurtures them, in the School of Communication at American University in Washington, D.C.

Program on Intellectual Property and the Public Interest
Directed by Professor Peter Jaszi, sponsors events and activities designed to promote awareness of the social, economic, and cultural

implications of domestic and international intellectual property law, in the Washington College of Law at American University.

Initial Endorsers

Arts Engine
Supports, produces, and distributes independent media and promotes the use of independent media through educational programs and nationwide outreach.

Bay Area Video Coalition
One of the nation's leading noncommercial digital media post-production facilities and multigenerational training centers.

Independent Television Service (ITVS)
Funded by the American people through the Corporation for Public Broadcasting, creates and presents independently produced programs that engage creative risks, advance issues, and represent points of view not usually seen on public or commercial television.

P.O.V./American Documentary
Through the P.O.V. series on PBS and through its portfolio of online and community activities, American Documentary pioneers collaborative activities for socially relevant content on television, online, and in community and educational settings.

University Film and Video Association (UFVA)
Brings together film and video production and the history, theory, and criticism of the media, serving individual and institutional members at more than 100 programs in higher education.

Funders

The Rockefeller Foundation
The John D. and Catherine T. MacArthur Foundation
Additional support from:
Grantmakers in Film and Electronic Media

Resource Listings

Unions and Associations

Directors Guild of America
7920 Sunset Blvd.
Los Angeles, CA 90046
(800) 421-4173
(310) 289-2000
www.dga.org

**International Alliance of Theatri-
cal Stage Employees (IATSE)**
1430 Broadway, 20th Floor
New York, NY 10018
(212) 730-1770
www.iatse-intl.org

Producers Guild of America
8530 Wilshire Blvd, Suite 450
Beverly Hills, CA, 90211
(310) 358-9020
E-mail: membership@
    producersguild.org
www.producersguild.org

Screen Actors Guild
5757 Wilshire Blvd., 8th Floor
Los Angeles, CA 90036
Motion picture division:
  (323) 549-6828
www.sag.org

Writers Guild of America, West
7000 W. Third St.
Los Angeles, CA 90048
(800) 548-4532
(323) 951-4000
www.wga.org

Breakdown Services

Breakdown Services, Ltd.
1120 S. Robertson Blvd.
Los Angeles, CA 90035
Los Angeles: (310) 276-9166
New York: (212) 869-2003
Vancouver: (604) 943-7100
www.breakdownservices.com

Script Clearance Services

Act One Script Clearance
230 N. Maryland Ave., Suite 208
Glendale, CA 91206
(818) 240-2416
Fax: (818) 240-2418
E-mail: info@actonescript.com
www.actonescript.com

Clearance Domain
27023 McBean Pkwy., Suite 243
Valencia, CA 91355
(310) 898-1233
E-mail: info@clearancedomain.com
www.clearancedomain.com

IndieClear Script Clearance
6532 ½ La Mirada Ave.
Los Angeles, CA 90038
(323) 828-8280
Fax: (323) 871-9220
E-mail: 411@indieclear.com
www.indieclear.com

Music Clearance Resources

BZ Rights and Permissions
2350 Broadway, Suite 224
New York, NY 10024
(212) 924-3000
Fax: (212) 924-2525
info@bzrights.com

Greenlight
Corbis Holdings, Inc.
710 Second Ave., Suite 200
Seattle, WA 98104
(866) 884-5600
www.greenlightrights.com

**National Music Publishers'
    Association (NMPA)**
101 Constitution Ave. NW, Suite
    705 East
Washington DC, 20001
(202) 742-4375
Fax: (202) 742-4377
www.nmpa.org
The Harry Fox Agency:
601 W. 26th St.
New York, NY 10001
(212) 834-0100
Fax: (646) 487-6779
www.harryfox.com

Insurance Companies

Abacus Insurance Brokers
12300 Wilshire Blvd., Suite 100
Los Angeles, California, 90025-
1020
(310) 207-5432
Fax: 310-207-8526
E-mail: info@abacusins.com
www.abacusins.com

AIG MEMSA Insurance
Company
Dubai International Financial Center
The Gate, 11th Floor, West Wing
P.O. Box 117719, Dubai, UAE
+971 4 362 1700
Fax: +971 4 362 0841
E-mail: customerservicememsa@
aig.com
www.aigmemsa.com/aig/memsa/
products/pro_financial
_multimedia.jsp

Chubb Group of Insurance
Companies
15 Mountain View Rd.
Warren, NJ 07059
(908) 903-2000
Fax: (908) 903-2027
Telex: 299719
www.chubb.com/businesses/csi/
chubb833.html

First Media, a Division of
OneBeacon Professional
Partners
4350 Shawnee Mission Pkwy.,
Suite 350
Fairway, KS 66205
(800) 753-7545
(913) 384-4800
Fax (main): 913-384-4822
Fax (claims): 913-677-2893
www.firstmediainc.com

Media/Professional Insurance
2300 Main St., Suite 800
Kansas City, MS 64108-2404
(816) 471-6118
Fax: (816) 471-6119
www.mediaprof.com

Short Term Productions
www.shorttermproductions.com

Travelers Encore Entertainment
700 N. Central Ave., 8th Floor
Glendale, CA 91203
(818) 409-4300
Fax: (866) 308-3217
E-mail: kmtopper@travelers.com
www.travelers.com/business/
nationalprograms/entertainment/
index.aspx

Financial Services

**American Film Marketing
  Association**
10850 Wilshire Blvd., 9th Floor
Los Angeles, CA 90024-4321
(310) 446-1000
Fax: (310) 446-1600
E-mail: info@ifta-online.org
www.ifta-online.org

**Association for Independent
  Video and Filmmakers
  (Foundation for Independent
  Video and Film)**
304 Hudson St., 6th Floor
New York, NY 10013
(212) 807-1400
Fax: (212) 463-8519
www.aivf.org

**Comerica Entertainment
  Industries**
9920 S. La Cienega Blvd., Suite
  1010
Inglewood, CA 90301
(310) 417-5449
Fax: (310) 417-5644

**Horwitz Entertainment Finan-
  cial Services**
5320 Orrville Ave.
Woodland Hills, CA 91367
Phone/Fax: (818) 888-8203
Cell: (310) 985-1194
E-mail: magicbnkr@aol.com
www.hefsi.com

Completion Bond

**CineFinance, HCC Insurance
  Holdings**
1875 Century Park East, Suite
  1970
Los Angeles, CA 90067
(310) 226-6800
Fax: (310) 226-6810
fmilstein@cinefinance.net
www.hccsu.com/products/
  movieandtv/cinefinance/
  cfmain.htm

Fireman's Fund Insurance
777 San Marin Dr.
Novato, CA 94998
(800) 227-1700
Fax: (415) 899-3600

Sales Agents

Cinetic Media
555 West 25th St., 4th Floor
New York, NY 10001
(212) 204-7979
Fax: (212) 204-7980
www.cineticmedia.com

Creative Artists Agency
9830 Wilshire Blvd.
Beverly Hills, CA 90212
(310) 288-4545

The Film Sales Company
151 Lafayette St., 5th Floor
New York, NY 10013

(646) 274-0945
Fax: (212) 981-8195
www.filmsalescorp.com

Jeff Dowd & Associates
3200 Airport Ave., Suite 1
Santa Monica, CA 90405
(310) 572-1500
Fax: (310) 572-1501
www.jeffdowd.com

Submarine Entertainment
132 Crosby St.
New York, NY 10012
(212) 625-1410
Fax: (212) 625-9931
www.submarine.com

Summit Entertainment
1630 Stewart St., Suite 120
Santa Monica, CA 90404
(310) 309-8400
Fax: (310) 828-4132
www.summit-ent.com

William Morris Independent/ William Morris Agency
1 William Morris Place
15 El Camino Drive
Beverly Hills, CA 90212
(310) 859-4315
Fax: (310) 859-4138
www.wma.com

Film Commissions

California Film Commission
7080 Hollywood Blvd., Suite 900
Hollywood, CA 90028
(800) 858-4749
(323) 860-2960
Fax: (323) 860-2972
E-mail: filmca@film.ca.gov
www.film.ca.gov

FilmL.A.
1201 W. 5th St., Suite T-800
Los Angeles, CA 90017
(213) 977-8600
Fax (main): (213) 977-8610
Fax (permits): (213) 977-8601
www.eidc.com

Mayor's Office of Film, Theatre and Broadcasting
1697 Broadway, Suite 602
New York, NY 10019
(212) 489-6710
Fax: (212) 307-6237
www.ci.nyc.ny.us/html/filmcom/ home.html

Other Trade Associations

Theater and Film Bookstores

AIVF Guide to Int'l Film and Video Festivals
625 Broadway, 9th Floor
New York, NY 10012
(212) 473-3400

Drama Book Shop
250 W. 40th St.
New York, NY 10018
(212) 944-0595
www.dramabookshop.com

Larry Edmunds Bookshop
6644 Hollywood Blvd.
Hollywood, CA 90028
(323) 463-3273
www.larryedmunds.com

Motion Picture Association of America (MPAA)
15301 Ventura Blvd., Bldg. E
Sherman Oaks, CA 91403
(818) 995-6600
Fax: (818) 285-4403
www.mpaa.org

Samuel French Bookstore
11963 Ventura Blvd.
Studio City, CA 91604
(818) 762-0535
www.samuelfrench.com

Samuel French, Inc.
7623 Sunset Blvd.

Los Angeles, CA 90046
(323) 876-0570
www.samuelfrench.com

Motion Picture Distributors: The Majors

MGM/United Artists
10250 Constellation Blvd.
Los Angeles, CA 90067-6241
(310) 449-3000
www.mgm.com

Paramount Pictures Corporation
5555 Melrose Ave.
Los Angeles, CA 90038
(323) 956-5000
www.paramount.com/
paramount.php

Sony Pictures Entertainment
10202 W. Washington Blvd.
Culver City, CA 90232
(310) 244-6926
www.sonypictures.com

20th Century Fox Film Corp.
10201 W. Pico Blvd.
Los Angeles, CA 90064
(310) 369-1000
www.foxmovies.com

Universal Studios
10 Universal City Plaza, Suite 3200
Universal City, CA 91608
www.universalpictures.com

Walt Disney Company
500 S. Buena Vista St.
Burbank, CA 91521
http://disney.go.com

Warner Bros.
4000 Warner Blvd.
Burbank, CA 91522
www.movies.warnerbros.com

Significant Independent Producers

First Look Studios
2000 Avenue of the Stars, Suite 410
Century City, CA 90067
(424) 202-5000
www.firstlookmedia.com

Fox Searchlight Pictures
10201 W. Pico Blvd., Bldg. 38
Los Angeles, CA 90064
(310) 369-4402
Fax: (310) 369-2359
www.foxsearchlight.com

HBO Enterprises
1100 Avenue of the Americas
New York, NY 10036
(212) 512-1000

IFC Films
11 Penn Plaza
New York, NY 10001
www.ifcfilms.com

Image Entertainment
20525 Nordhoff St., Suite 200
Chatsworth, CA 91311
www.image-entertainment.com

Lionsgate Entertainment
2700 Colorado Ave.
Santa Monica, CA 90404
(310) 449-9200
www.lionsgate.com

Magnolia Pictures
49 West 27th St., 7th Floor
New York, NY 10001
(212) 924-6701
Fax: (212) 924-6742
www.magpictures.com

Media Asia Entertainment Group
24/F Causeway Bay Plaza II
463–483 Lockhart Rd.
Causeway Bay, Hong Kong
+852 2314 4288
Fax : +852 2314 4248
E-mail: wwdist@mediaasia.com
www.mediaasia.com

Newmarket Films
202 N. Canon Dr.
Beverly Hills, CA 90210
(310) 858-7472
Fax: 310-858-7473
www.newmarketfilms.com

Overture Films, a Starz company
9242 Beverly Blvd., Suite 200
Beverly Hills, CA 90210
(424) 204-4000
Fax: (424) 204-4010

New York Office:
521 5th Ave., Suite 1900
New York, NY 10175
(212) 905-4200
Fax: (212) 905-4287
www.overturefilms.net

Palm Pictures
76 Ninth Ave., Suite 1110
New York, NY 10011
(212) 320-3600
Fax: (212) 320-3639
www.palmpictures.com

Pathé International
Kent House, 14–17 Market Place
    Great Titchfield St.
London W1W 8AR United Kingdom
+44 (0)20 7323 5151
Fax: +44 (0)20 7631 3568
www.pathe.com

Samuel Goldwyn Films
9570 W. Pico Blvd., Suite 400
Los Angeles, CA 90035
(310) 860-3100
Fax: (310) 860-3198
www.samuelgoldwynfilms.com

Showtime Networks
1633 Broadway
New York, NY 10019
(212) 708-1600
Fax: (212) 708-1217
www.sho.com

Studio Canal/Canal Plus
1 place du spectacle

92863 Issy-les-Moulineaux,
    France
+33 1 7135 3535

Tartan Films USA
8322 Beverly Blvd., Suite 300
Los Angeles, CA 90048
(323) 655-9300
Fax: (323) 655-9301
www.tartanfilmsusa.com

Village Roadshow
3400 Riverside Dr., Suite 900
Burbank, CA 91505
(818) 260-6000
Fax: (818) 260-6001
E-mail: mlake@vrpe.com
www.village.com.au

**The Weinstein Company/
    Dimension Films**
345 Hudson St., 13th Floor
New York, NY 10014
(646) 862-3400
Fax: (917) 368-7000
www.weinsteinco.com

Wild Bunch
99 rue de la Verrerie
75004 Paris, France
+33 1 5301 5030
Fax: +33 1 5301 5049
London Office:
231 Portobello Rd.
London W11 1LT United Kingdom
+44 (0)20 7792 9791
Fax: +44 (0)20 7792 9871
www.wildbunch.biz

Selected Bibliography

↓

Contracts and Form Agreements

Baumgarten, Paul A., Donald C. Farber, and Mark Fleischer. *Producing, Financing, and Distributing Film: A Comprehensive Legal and Business Guide.* 2nd ed. New York: Limelight Editions, 2004.

Farber, Donald C., ed. *Entertainment Industry Contracts.* New York: Matthew Bender, 2001–. Looseleaf updates.

Garon, Jon M. *Entertainment Law and Practice.* Durham, NC: Carolina Academic Press, 2005, suppl. 2007.

———. *Own It: The Law and Business Guide to Launching a New Business Through Innovation, Exclusivity and Relevance.* Durham, NC: Carolina Academic Press, 2007.

Kohn, Al, and Bob Kohn, *Kohn on Music Licensing.* 3rd ed. Gaithersburg, MD: Aspen Publishers, 2002.

Litwak, Mark. *Contracts for the Film and Television Industry.* 2nd ed. Los Angeles: Silman-James Press, 1999.

Vogel, Harold L. *Entertainment Industry Economics: A Guide for Financial Analysis.* Boston, MA: Cambridge University Press, 2007.

Other Law-Related Books of Interest

Cones, John W. *Dictionary of Film Finance and Distribution: A Guide for Independent Filmmakers.* Spokane, WA: Marquette Books, 2007.

Donaldson, Michael. *Clearance and Copyright*. Los Angeles: Silman-James Press, 1996.

Erickson, Gunnar, Mark Halloran, and Harris Tulchin. *The Independent Film Producer's Survival Guide: A Business and Legal Sourcebook*. 2nd ed. New York: Schirmer Trade Books, 2005.

Goodell, Gregory. *Independent Feature Film Production*. Rev. ed. New York: St. Martin's Griffin, 1998.

Moore, Schuyler M. *The Biz: The Basic Business, Legal and Financial Aspects of the Film Industry*. Los Angeles: Silman-James Press, 2000.

Parks, Stacey. *The Insider's Guide to Independent Film Distribution*. Boston, MA: Focal Press, 2007.

Samuels, Edward. *The Illustrated Story of Copyright*. New York: St. Martin's Griffin, 2000.

Nonlegal Reference Books

Ascher, Steven, and Edward Pincus. *The Filmmaker's Handbook: A Comprehensive Guide for the Digital Age*. New York: Plume, 2007.

Collier, Maxie. *The iFilm Digital Video Filmmaker's Handbook*. Los Angeles: Lone Eagle Publishing, 2001.

Langer, Adam. *The Film Festival Guide*. Chicago, IL: Chicago Review Press, 2000.

Long, Ben, and Sonja Schenk. *The Digital Filmmaking Handbook*. Hingham, MA: Charles River Media, 2000.

Maier, Robert. *Location Scouting and Management Handbook*. Boston, MA: Focal Press, 1994.

Maschwitz, Stu. *The DV Rebel's Guide: An All-Digital Approach to Making Killer Action Movies on the Cheap*. Berkeley, CA: Peachpit Press, 2007.

Rabiger, Michael. *Directing the Documentary*. 4th ed. Boston, MA: Focal Press, 2004.

Rodriguez, Robert. *Rebel Without a Crew: Or How a 23-Year-Old Filmmaker With $7,000 Became a Hollywood Player*. New York: Plume, 1996.

Rosen, David. *Off Hollywood: The Making and Marketing of American Specialty Films*. New York: Independent Feature Project and Sundance Institute, 1987.

Sales, John. *Thinking in Pictures*. Boston, MA: Houghton Mifflin, 1987.

Trottier, David. *The Screenwriter's Bible: A Complete Guide to Writing, Formatting, and Selling Your Script*. Los Angeles: Silman-James Press, 1998.

Endnotes

↓

Part 1 Making a Film Company to Make a Movie

2. The Film Company

[1] "Classification of certain business entities," *Code of Federal Regulations* 26, § 301.7701-3 (2006).

[2] *Internal Revenue Code*, § 351 (2001).

3. Duties of the Film Company

[1] This story is related in the documentary *Hearts of Darkness: A Filmmaker's Apocalypse* (American Zoetrope, 1991), written by Fax Bahr and George Hickenlooper with documentary footage and direction by Eleanor Coppola. An extended version of Coppola's film, *Apocalypse Now Redux*, restores the extravagant "French plantation scene."

4. The Property of the Film Company: The Film Concept

[1] *Night on Earth* (JVC, 1991), written and directed by Jim Jarmusch.

[2] *U.S. Code* 17, § 101 et seq. (2006).

[3] *U.S. Code* 17, § 106. In the case of sound recordings, copyright holders also have the exclusive right to perform the work publicly by means of a digital audio transmission.

[4] *U.S. Code* 17, § 101.

⁵ *Stewart v. Abend*, 495 U.S. 207 (1990).

⁶ *Russell v. Price*, 612 F.2d 1123, 1128 (9th Cir. 1979).

⁷ *U.S. Code* 17, § 204.

⁸ *U.S. Code* 17, § 304(b). But note that works for which copyright expired before 1976 remain in the public domain. The rules for each piece of material may vary greatly, so it is vital that the copyright of an older work be reviewed before it is assumed that the work is in the public domain.

⁹ See *Russell v. Price*, 612 F.2d at 1124. Even here, however, the possibility exists that copyright protection still exists in some parts of Europe, because Germany provided a longer copyright term than other European nations. Under the rules of the European Union, the greatest protection in any EU country must be extended to the citizens of every other member. As a result, it may be that works that had been in the public domain in England now enjoy additional copyright protection.

¹⁰ *U.S. Code* 17, § 102. The law lists eight categories of works subject to copyright protection:

1. literary works;
2. musical works, including any accompanying words;
3. dramatic works, including accompanying music;
4. pantomimes and choreographic works;
5. pictorial, graphic, and sculptural works;
6. motion pictures and other audiovisual works;
7. sound recordings; and
8. architectural works.

¹¹ For works first published prior to January 1, 1978, the copyright symbol may have been required to secure copyright. The filmmaker must be careful, however, not to assume that an older work is in the public domain simply because the copyright symbol was omitted.

¹² *U.S. Code* 17, § 102(b) ("In no case does copyright protection for an original work of authorship extend to any idea, procedure, process, system, method of operation, concept, principle, or discovery, regardless of the form in which it is described, explained, illustrated, or embodied in such work").

¹³ *Hoehling v. Universal City Studios, Inc.*, 618 F.2d 972 (2d Cir. 1980), *cert. denied*, 449 U.S. 841 (1980).

¹⁴ See *Davies v. Krasna*, 54 Cal. Rptr. 37 (Ct. App. 1966), *superseded on other grounds*, 14 Cal.3d 502 (1975).

[15] *Restatement (Second) of Torts*, § 559 (1977). Under California law, "libel is a false and unprivileged publication by writing . . . which exposes any person to hatred, contempt, ridicule, or obloquy, or which causes him to be shunned or avoided, or which has a tendency to injure him in his occupation." *Cal. Civ. Code*, § 45 (West 1999).

[16] *New York Times Co. v. Sullivan*, 376 U.S. 254, 279–280 (1964).

[17] *James v. San Jose Mercury News, Inc.*, 17 Cal. App. 4th 1, 10 (App. 6th Dist. 1993), quoting *Mosesian v. McClatchy Newspapers*, 205 Cal. App. 3d 597, 608–609 (App. 5th Dist. 1988), *cert. denied*, 490 U.S. 1066 (1989).

[18] *Mosesian v. McClatchy Newspapers*.

[19] *Gertz v. Robert Welch, Inc.*, 418 U.S. 323, 344 (1974).

[20] *Davis v. Costa-Gavras*, 654 F. Supp. 653, 655 (S.D.N.Y. 1987).

[21] *Masson v. New Yorker Magazine*, 501 U.S. 496, 522 (1991).

[22] *Springer v. Viking Press*, 90 A.D.2d 315, 457 N.Y.S.2d 246 (1st Dept. 1982), *aff'd*, 60 N.Y.S.2d 916, 470 N.Y.S.2d 579 (1983).

[23] *Restatement (Second) of Torts*, § 652E.

[24] *Gertz v. Robert Welch, Inc.*

[25] William Lloyd Prosser, *Handbook of the Law of Torts*, 4th ed. (St. Paul: West Pub. Co., 1971), 802–804. "The right to withdraw from the public gaze at such times as a person may see fit, when his presence in public is not demanded by any rule of law is also embraced within the right of personal liberty." *Pavesich v. New England Life Ins. Co.*, 122 Ga. 190, 196, 50 S.E. 68, 70 (1905).

[26] *Restatement (Second) of Torts*, § 625B ("One who intentionally intrudes, physically or otherwise, upon the solitude or seclusion of another or his private affairs or concerns, is subject to liability to the other for invasion of his privacy, if the intrusion would be highly offensive to a reasonable person.").

[27] *Price v. Hal Roach Studios, Inc.*, 400 F. Supp. 836, 843 (S.D.N.Y. 1975).

[28] *Zacchini v. Scripps-Howard Broadcasting Co.*, 433 U.S. 562 (1977). In this case, Zacchini—a human cannonball—was taped doing his entire 15-second act at the local fair. He successfully sued the television company that broadcast his act without paying him.

[29] *Cal. Civ. Code*, § 3344(a) (West 1997). The statute also provides for $750 in statutory fees and injunctive relief.

[30] The popcorn manufacturer would also be unable to stop the newspaper from using the photograph of Spears eating its product.

[31] *KNB Enters. v. Matthews*, 78 Cal. App. 4th 362, 368, 92 Cal. Rptr. 2d 713, 718 (2d Dist. 2000) (holding use of models' photographs on subscription Web site constituted actionable violation of *Cal. Civ. Code* § 3344, not preempted by federal copyright laws).

[32] *KNB Enters. v. Matthews*.

[33] U.S. Copyright Office, *Dramatic Works: Scripts, Pantomimes and Choreography*, FL-119, revised June 2008, www.copyright.gov/fls/fl119.html (accessed September 11, 2008).

5. Contracts

[1] U.S. Copyright Office, *How to Investigate the Copyright Status of a Work*, circular 22, www.copyright.gov/circs/circ22.html (accessed September 11, 2008).

[2] The term generally used would be "exploit." *Exploit* has the correct connotation, because the filmmaker can do anything to the material the contract allows—and the contract should be drafted to allow him to do almost everything as well as nothing. Be careful not to treat an independent film as if it can be made in a "kinder and gentler" fashion. The film project may be sold prior to filming and the filmmaker should have enough control over the material to satisfy a studio if one decided to buy out the project.

[3] *Desny v. Wilder*, 299 P.2d 257, 265 (Cal. 1956); *Buchwald v. Paramount Pictures*, 1990 Cal. App. LEXIS 634, 13 U.S.P.Q.2d 1497 (Super. Ct. 1990).

6. Financing the Film Project

[1] One specific breakdown is as follows: 20 percent paid weekly during preproduction; 60 percent paid weekly during principal photography; 10 percent paid upon delivery of the rough cut; and 10 percent paid upon delivery of the completed picture. Paul A. Baumgarten, Donald C. Farber, and Mark Fleischer, *Producing, Financing, and Distributing Film*, 2nd ed. (New York: Limelight Editions, 1992).

[2] The *Independent* (formerly published by the Association of Independent Video and Filmmakers) provides an updated list of potential funding resources. It is available at www.independent-magazine.org/node/405 (accessed September 11, 2008).

[3] *Treasury Regulation* § 1.721-1(b)(1) (the income should be based on the value of the service at the time provided); *Revenue Procedure* 93-27, 1993-2 C.B. 343 (providing nontax treatment for profit participation or partnerships); Louis A. Mez-

zullo, "Qualified Plans, Professional Organizations, Health Care, and Welfare Benefits," *ALI-ABA Course of Study Materials*, vol. I (February 13–15, 1997).

[4] *Internal Revenue Code*, § 721(a) and 707(a)(2).

[5] *Code of Federal Regulations* 26, § 301.7701-3(a) (2006).

[6] Contrast this with a purchase-money home mortgage, which in some states may limit the buyers' liability to the current value of the property. If the loan is instead a second mortgage or a line of credit, these protections will not apply.

[7] This is not apocryphal—copyright lasts 70 years past the life of the author, so management of the work must include some planning for the period after the filmmaker has died.

[8] Proportional or *pro rata* payments would mean that each dollar earned is split by each person or group in proportion to the amount that each party is entitled to receive. In the example above, $40 in income would be paid $15 to the investor and $25 to the parties entitled to deferred compensation.

8. The Investors' Package

[1] *TSC Industries, Inc. v. Northway, Inc.,* 426 U.S. 438, 449 (1976); *Basic, Inc. v. Levinson,* 108 S. Ct. 978 (1988).

[2] *Securities Act of 1933*, § 4 (2), codified at *U.S. Code* 15, § 77d(2) (2006), available at United States Securities and Exchange Commission, *Q &A: Small Business and the SEC*, www.sec.gov/info/smallbus/qasbsec.htm#eod6 under "Private Offering Exemption" (accessed September 12, 2008).

[3] *Securities Act of 1933* § 3(a)(11), codified at *U.S. Code* 15, § 77c(a)(11), available at United States Securities and Exchange Commission, *Q &A: Small Business and the SEC*, www.sec.gov/info/smallbus/qasbsec.htm#eod6 under "Intrastate Offering Exemption" (accessed September 12, 2008).

[4] But § 10(b) of the Securities Exchange Act of 1934 would apply regarding any fraud or misrepresentation, as long as an instrument of interstate commerce was used—something like a telephone, e-mail, or U.S. post.

[5] Securities Act Regulation D, *Code of Federal Regulations* 17, §§ 230.501–508 (2008).

[6] Id.

Part 2 Filming the Movie: Preproduction and Production

9. Assembling the Production Team

[1] Writers Guild of America West, *Screen Credits Manual*, www.wga.org/subpage_writersresources.aspx?id=167 (accessed September 11, 2008).

10. The Key Members of the Independent Film Company

[1] Producers Guild of America, "Frequently Asked Questions," www.producersguild.org/pg/about_a/faq.asp (accessed September 12, 2008).

[2] One technique to preserve comic moments is to note where the cast laughed at the script during the first live reading. Often, working and reworking a scene can drain any humor out of the material, and reminders about where the humor once resonated may help to keep the material fresh.

[3] Directors Guild of America, *DGA Basic Agreement*, § 7-101, available at www.dga.org/contracts/agreements_ctr.php3 in both PDF and online formats (accessed September 12, 2008).

[4] *Encyclopedia Britannica Online*, s.v. "acting," www.britannica.com/EBchecked/topic/4329/acting (accessed September 12, 2008).

[5] Breakdown Services, Ltd., Web site, www.breakdownservices.com (accessed September 12, 2008).

[6] CastPages.com Web site, www.castpages.com/CastingDirectors (accessed September 12, 2008). Star Caster Network, a former competitor to both Breakdown Services, Ltd., and CastPages.com, has partnered with Breakdown Services, Ltd., and no longer operates independently.

13. Special Considerations for Documentaries and Films Based on True Life Stories

[1] *Diaz v. Oakland Tribune*, 139 Cal. App. 3d 118, 126 (1983).

[2] *Shulman v. Group W Prod., Inc.*, 18 Cal.4th 200, 214–242 (1998).

[3] *U.S. Code* 17, § 107 (2006).

[4] Id.

[5] Pat Aufderheide and Peter Jaszi, "Fair Use and Best Practices: Surprising Success," *Intellectual Property Today*, October 2007.

[6] Id.

[7] C-Span Video Library, "Licensing and Permission," www.c-spanarchives.org/library/index.php?main_page=specialuse (accessed September 12, 2008).

[8] Universal Newsreels, Internet Archive, www.archive.org/details/universal_newsreels (accessed September 12, 2008).

14. Music

[1] See *U.S. Code* 17, § 115 (2006). At present, the statutory rate for each recording manufactured is 9.1 cents or 1.75 cents per minute of playing time or fraction thereof, whichever is greater.

[2] For more information, see Al Kohn and Bob Kohn, *Kohn on Music Licensing*, 3rd ed. (Gaithersburg, MD: Aspen Publishers, 2002). For the non–music lawyer, this is perhaps the most comprehensive and clear single volume available. The forms in the book are explained fully and readily usable for film licensing, and they are included on an accompanying CD-ROM. In addition, the authors maintain a comprehensive Web site concerning legal issues surrounding the use of music: Kohn on Music Licensing, www.kohnmusic.com (accessed September 12, 2008).

16. Special Considerations for the No-Budget Production

[1] Jon M. Garon, *Own It: The Law and Business Guide to Launching a New Business Through Innovation, Exclusivity and Relevance* (Durham, NC: Carolina Academic Press, 2007), 87–88.

Part 3 Selling the Movie: Distribution and Marketing

18. Nontheatrical Commercial Distribution

[1] Academy of Motion Picture Arts and Sciences, *80th Academy Award Rules for Distinguished Achievements in 2007*, rule 2, www.oscars.org/80academyawards/rules/rule02.html (accessed September 12, 2008).

[2] Id. at rule 3, www.oscars.org/80academyawards/rules/rule03.html.

About the Author

↓

Jon M. Garon is a professor at Hamline University School of Law, where he served as dean from 2003 to 2008. He was also interim dean of the Hamline University Graduate School of Management from 2005 to 2006. A Minnesota native, he received his bachelor's degree from the University of Minnesota in 1985 and his juris doctor degree from Columbia University School of Law in 1988.

Professor Garon has taught a number of courses in intellectual property, including Entertainment Law; Music Licensing and Management; Law of Motion Pictures and the Performing Arts; Copyright; Multi-Media Licensing; and First Amendment Law. His business courses have included Agency & Partnership; Business Dispute Resolution; Charitable Institutions; Contracts; Contract Drafting; Corporations; Federal Income Tax; and Nonprofit Business Organizations.

Professor Garon is of counsel to the law firm of Gallagher, Callahan & Gartrell in New Hampshire and is admitted to practice law in California, New Hampshire, and Minnesota.

Among his publications on intellectual property, Professor Garon has written the following books:

- *Own It: The Law and Business Guide to Launching a New Business Through Innovation, Exclusivity and Relevance* (Carolina Academic Press, 2007)
- *Entertainment Law and Practice* (Carolina Academic Press, 2005, suppl. 2007)

- *Theater Law: Cases and Materials* (Carolina Academic Press, 2004) coauthor: chapter contributor on theatrical directors

His academic articles include:

- "Reintermediation" (*International Journal of Private Law*)
- "Playing in the Virtual Arena: Avatars and Identity Reconceptualized Through Virtual Worlds and Computer Games" (*Chapman Law Review*)
- "What if DRM Fails?: Seeking Patronage in the iWasteland and the Virtual O" (*Michigan State Law Review*)
- "Acquiring and Managing Identity Interests" (*Entertainment Law Review*, University of Florida)
- "Normative Copyright: A Conceptual Framework for Copyright Philosophy and Ethics" (*Cornell Law Review*)
- "Entertainment Law" (*Tulane Law Review*)
- "The Electronic Jungle: The Application of Intellectual Property Law to Distance Education" (*Vanderbilt Journal of Entertainment Law & Practice*)
- "Media and Monopoly in the Information Age: Slowing the Convergence at the Marketplace of Ideas" (*Cardozo Arts & Entertainment Law Journal*)
- "Star Wars: Film Permitting, Prior Restraint and the Government's Role in the Entertainment Industry" (*Loyola of Los Angeles Entertainment Law Journal*)

Professor Garon can be reached at Hamline University School of Law, 1536 Hewitt Ave., St. Paul, MN 55104, by telephone at (651) 523-2535, or via e-mail at jgaron@hamline.edu. Gallagher, Callahan & Gartrell may be reached at (800) 528-1181 or www.gcglaw.com. Professor Garon's books, blogs, and other materials may be found at www.lawbizbooks.com.